SCHOLASTIC HUMANISM AND THE UNIFICATION OF EUROPE

VOLUME I

In memory of
R. F. I. BUNN
1899 – 1991

schoolmaster

Scholastic Humanism
and the
Unification of Europe

VOLUME I

Foundations

R. W. SOUTHERN

Blackwell
Publishing

First published 1995
First published in paperback 1997
Transferred to digital print 2002

Blackwell Publishers Ltd
108 Cowley Road
Oxford OX4 1JF, UK

Blackwell Publishers Inc.
350 Main Street
Malden, Massachusetts 02148, USA

British Library Cataloguing in Publication Data
A CIP catalogue record for this book is available from the British Library

Library of Congress Cataloging in Publication Data
Southern, R. W. (Richard William), 1912–
Foundations / R. W. Southern
p.   cm. — (Scholastic humanism and the unification of Europe; v.I)
Includes bibliographical references and index.
ISBN 0–631–19111–9 (hbk. alk. paper) — ISBN 0–631–20527–6 (pbk)
1. Humanism — History. 2. Scholasticism — History.
I. Title. II. Series: Southern, R. W. (Richard William) 1912–
Scholastic humanism and the unification of Europe; v.I
B738.H8S68   1994   93–47307
189'.4—dc20   CIP

Copy-edited and typeset in 11 on 13 Sabon
Grahame & Grahame Editorial, Brighton
Printed in Great Britain By Marston Lindsay
Ross International Ltd, Oxford

Preface

The origins of this work go back at least thirty years, and parts of this and the following volumes have been written at different dates throughout the whole of this period. In my volume *Western Society and the Church in the Middle Ages* (1970) I dealt with the medieval Church as a social and political phenomenon, and in *Medieval Humanism* in the same year with various aspects of personal and intellectual history. It was in the course of writing these two books that the need to examine more carefully the links between the intellectual and organizational creations of the twelfth and thirteenth centuries, as a contribution towards understanding the foundations of European order, became increasingly clear. In particular, the ecclesiastical organization of these centuries cannot be understood without first understanding the programmes of the schools. In their totality, these scholastic programmes represented an attempt to make the created universe, and its relationship to the eternal being of God and the heavenly hierarchies, as fully intelligible as the limitations of fallen human nature allow. The methods used for achieving this understanding were also the methods which were thought necessary for, and capable of, achieving order in all human relationships whether ecclesiastical or secular.

The practical application of this intellectual programme produced a reorganization of medieval society along lines which were very generally operative until the eighteenth century. It was the abandonment of this programme, after it had been variously redefined and gradually abandoned from the sixteenth to the eighteenth centuries, which caused the great crisis of disbelief in the existence of any attainable body of knowledge about an eternal state of Being, to which many works of the nineteenth century give poignant expression.

This is the main background of the present work. A minor,

but still potent, influence in determining the direction of the studies which led to the writing of this book was an unexpected discovery which I made, or believed that I had made, with regard to the school of Chartres. Like everyone else, I had accepted as a fact the great importance of the school of Chartres in the formation of twelfth-century humanism, and I was surprised to find that I had not collected any body of evidence to illustrate its importance.

Supposing that this was attributable to my own carelessness, I set about trying to fill this discreditable gap in my knowledge. To my surprise, an increasingly detailed examination of the evidence forced me to the conclusion that the whole Chartrian structure was built on the flimsiest of foundations. In (I think) 1965, I read a paper in the presence of Professors Knowles and Jacob to set out the grounds for my disappointment. I have a vivid recollection of the disbelief with which it was received. I published the paper in the second of the two volumes mentioned above, and once more it was received with a good deal of scepticism. I have printed it again in this volume and I have answered the objections that have been raised against my interpretation of the evidence.

Although this 'discovery' (on which I leave the reader to pronounce judgement) plays only a modest part in understanding the humanism of the great schools of the twelfth and thirteenth centuries, I retain it here as a useful prelude to understanding the nature, methods and physical circumstances which made possible both the scholastic innovations of the twelfth century and their widespread practical implementation.

I was approaching, as I thought, the end of all that I could usefully say about this issue, when I had two new sources of inspiration. From 1969 to 1981, I had the good fortune of being in daily contact with the results of a remarkable attempt in the early seventeenth century by St John's College, Oxford, to restore to the shelves of its library the medieval learning that had been thrown out during the previous century. The chief instigator of this initiative was William Laud, Fellow and later President of the College, and finally Archbishop of Canterbury; and the results of the effort, in the vast editions that had come from Continental presses during the previous hundred years, still remain more or less undisturbed on the shelves which had been built to accommodate them. In making this effort, Laud and his like-minded friends had a more than collegiate aim: they wished to bring the university of Oxford, and ultimately the Church of England, back into contact with this earlier tradition of European learning, and restocking the College Library with the main works of medieval scholastic learning was a first step towards an end which – at that time – did not long survive the execution of their leader. In the present context, it is sufficient to say that the opportunity which I had to get to know the great bulk of medieval learning which Laud and his friends had added to the College library between about 1595 and 1640, gave a powerful and unexpected impetus to my inexpert efforts to understand the main drift of the scholastic studies of the twelfth and thirteenth centuries.

It was at this point that I received the further stimulus of an invitation from the university of Glasgow to give the Gifford Lectures in the academic year 1971–2. This provided the occasion for writing a first draft of the work of which this is the first volume, and I must express my gratitude to the Glasgow electors and apologize to them for the long delay in bringing these lectures to publication. The main reason for the delay, apart from the pressure of other work, has been the size and complication of the undertaking, and I could scarcely have persisted in the midst of problems of a quite different nature if the Laudian library had not daily been before my eyes and in my thoughts.

I mention these details, partly to explain the difficulties I have experienced (and doubtless by no means fully overcome) in organizing the results of researches undertaken over such a long period on subjects themselves so widely scattered in place and time, and partly to indicate the nature of the unity which binds them together and will – I hope – become clearer as the subject unfolds.

The only additional remarks that seem necessary at this point are, first, that anyone who reads this volume may reasonably think that I turn too often to England for my examples. The main reason for this no doubt is that the English sources are those which I know best. But also there are some subjects – mainly legal and administrative, but also to some extent intellectual –

on which the English evidence is better preserved than elsewhere; and there are other subjects on which English sources, owing to the semi-detached position of England in relation to the Continent, throws a brighter light than can easily be found elsewhere.

As for the substantial shortcomings of this work and the evident gaps in my knowledge, I can only say that they would have been much worse if I had not at various times had the help of many who have come to my assistance. At an early stage Richard Hunt and Beryl Smalley read various parts, and later Donald Matthew, Susan Hall, Martin Brett, Michael Clanchy and my wife have helped me over many obstacles. Most recently John Davey and Ginny Stroud-Lewis of Blackwell Publishers, and Anthony Grahame of Brighton, have helped to elicit such degree of order as the contents now have. To all of them, and to others who will (I hope) forgive my forgetfulness, I owe a very great debt for their help and encouragement.

I am also indebted to Professors Robert L. Benson and Giles Constable for permission to include in this volume an extensively revised version of my contribution to the Haskins commemoration conference in November 1977, which was published among the papers of that conference in the volume *Renaissance and Renewal in the Twelfth Century*.

This first volume is dedicated to the memory of a successor of the school masters at the centre of this work. It was R. F. I. Bunn at the Royal Grammar School, Newcastle upon Tyne, who first turned my mind to the study and love of the past. Like many of the students who appear in the following pages I have tried more than once to go forward or upward to other things – only to return to the past. So the dedication is a grateful tribute to the source of an illumination which has proved so irresistible.

Then finally, when this work reaches its final shape, I shall dedicate the third volume to that President of St John's College whose inspiring vision of the re-integration of the learning of the Middle Ages with that of his own time I have mentioned above. Just in case this final volume is never reached, let his name at least stand as the last word of this Preface: *laudemus Guillelmum Laud.*

Contents

CONTENTS

CONTENTS

Maps and Plates

Acknowledgement is gratefully made to the Bibliothèque Municipale, Valenciennes, for permission to publish Plates 3 (i) and (ii); to the British Library for Plate 4 (i); to the Bayerische Staatsbibliotek, Munich, for Plate 4 (ii); and to the administrator of the Ducal Palace, Sassuola, for Plate 5.

Abbreviations
and Short Titles

AHDL   *Archives d'histoire doctrinale et littéraire du Moyen Âge*.

Bartlett, 1982   Robert Bartlett, *Giraldus Cambrensis, 1146–1223*, Oxford.

BEC   *Bibliothèque de l'École des Chartes*, Paris, 1839–.

Benson and Constable, 1982   *Renaissance and Renewal in the Twelfth Century*, ed. Robert L. Benson and Giles Constable, Harvard.

BGP(T)MA   *Beiträge zur Geschichte der Philosophie (und Theologie, 1930–) des Mittelalters*, 1892–.

Bliemetzrieder, 1919   F. P. Bliemetzrieder (ed.), *Anselms von Laon Systematische Sentenzen, BGPMA*, vol. 18, ii–iii.

Brooke, 1931   Z. N. Brooke, *The English Church and the Papacy from the Conquest to the reign of John*, Cambridge.

Cahiers, Copenhagen   *Cahiers de l'Institut du Moyen Âge Grec et Latin*, Copenhagen, 1969–.

CC   *Corpus Christianorum*, Turnhout, 1953–.

Councils   *Decrees of the Ecumenical Councils*, ed. Norman P. Tanner, 2 vols, London and Washington, 1990 (gives texts, translations and notes on decrees of all General Councils from Nicaea I to Vatican II).

Councils and Synods   *Councils and Synods with other documents relating to the English Church*, i, 871–1204 (1981, ed. D. Whitelock, M. Brett and C. N. L. Brooke); ii, 1205–1313 (1964, ed. F. M. Powicke and C. Cheney).

C.U.Par.   *Chartularium Universitatis Parisiensis*, ed. H. Denifle and E. Chatelain, 4 vols with supplement, Paris, 1889–1907.

Dict. Sp.   *Dictionnaire de Spiritualité*, ed. M. Viller, Paris, 1937–.

Dronke, 1969   Peter Dronke, 'New Approaches to the School of Chartres', *Anuario de estudios medievales*, vol. 6, Barcelona, pp. 117–40.

Dronke, 1978 (ed.)   Bernardus Silvestris, *Cosmographia*, Leiden.

Dutton, 1991   P. E. Dutton, ed. 'Bernard of Chartres, *Glosae super Platonem*', Toronto.

EHR   English Historical Review, 1886–.

Fuhrmann, 1972–4   H. Fuhrmann, *Einfluss und Verbreitung der pseudo-Isidorischen Falschungen, MGH, Schriften*, xxiv, 3 vols.

Gibson, 1969   Margaret Gibson, 'The Study of the *Timaeus* in the 11th and 12th centuries', *Pensamiento*, xxv, 183–94.
   1978   *Lanfranc of Bec*, Oxford.
   1981 (ed.)   *Boethius: his life, thought and influence*, Oxford.

Giraldus Cambrensis   *Opera, RS*, 8 vols, 1861–91.

Grabmann   Martin Grabmann, *Geschichte der Scholastischen Methode*, 2 vols, 1909–11, Freiburg-i-B.

Gratian   *Decretum Magistri Gratiani*, vol. 1 of *Corpus iuris Canonici*, ed. Aemilius Friedberg, Leipzig, 1879.

Häring (sometimes Haring), N. M.
   1953i   'A hitherto unknown commentary on Boethius's *De Hebdomadibus, Mediaeval Studies*, Toronto, xv, 1953, 212–21.
   1953ii   'A Latin dialogue on the doctrine of Gilbert of Poitiers', *Mediaeval Studies*, Toronto, xv, pp. 243–89.
   1962   'The Porretans and the Greek Fathers', ibid., xxiv, pp. 181–209.
   1965   'Bischoff Gilbert II von Poitiers', *DA*, xxxi, 150–171.
   1966   'Two catalogues of medieval authors', *Franciscan Studies*, xxvi, 195–211.
   1970   'Epitaphs and Necrologies on Bishop Gilbert II of Poitiers', *AHDL*, 36, 57–87.
   1974   'Paris and Chartres revisited', *Essays in honour of A. C. Pegis*, ed. J. R. O'Connell, Toronto, 1974, 268–329.

Haskins, 1927   C. H. Haskins, *Studies in the History of Medieval Science*, 2nd edn, Harvard.

Holtzmann, *Papsturkunden*.   Walther Holtzmann, *Papsturkunden in England*, in *Abhandlungen der Gesellschaft der Wissenschaften zu Göttingen, phil.-hist. Klasse*, 3 vols, 1930, 1935, 1952.

Jaffé, *Bibl.*   Philip Jaffé (ed.), *Biblioteca rerum Germanicarum*, vols 1–6, Berlin, 1864–73.

Jeauneau, 1973   Edouard Jeauneau, *Lectio Philosophorum: Recherches sur l'école de Chartres*, Amsterdam.

JL   P. Jaffé and S. Loewenfeld, *Regesta Pontificum Romanorum ad annum 1198*, 2 vols, 1885–1888, Leipzig.

John of Salisbury *Historia Pontificalis*, ed. R. L. Poole, Oxford, 1927; ed. and transl. M. Chibnall, Oxford, 1956.

Metalogicon, ed. C. C. I. Webb, Oxford, 1929; ed. J. B. Hall and K. S. B. Keats-Rohan, Turnhout, 1991.

Policraticus, ed. C. C. I. Webb, Oxford, 2 vols, 1909; (also, ed. K. S. B. Keats-Rohan, *Corpus Christianorum*, vol. 1, 1993).

Klibansky, 1961 R. Klibansky, 'The school of Chartres', in Marshall Clagett, *Twelfth Century Europe and the Foundations of modern Society*, Madison, pp. 3–14.

Kuttner, 1937 Stephan Kuttner, *Repertorium der Kanonistik, 1140–1234, Studi e Testi*, lxxi, Vatican.

Libelli de Lite Libelli de Lite Imperatorum et Ponticum saeculis XI et XII conscripti, 3 vols, MGH, 1891–97.

Lottin, 1959 O. Lottin, *Psychologie et Morale aux XIIe et XIIIe siècles*, vol. 5: *Problèmes d'histoire Littéraire*, Gembloux.

Manitius, 1931 Max Manitius, *Geschichte der Lateinischen Literatur des Mittelalters*, vol. 3, Munich.

MARS Medieval and Renaissance Studies, ed. R. Klibansky and R. W. Hunt, London, 6 vols, 1941–68.

Mat. Becket Materials for the History of Thomas Becket, ed. J. C. Robertson, *RS*, 7 vols, 1875–85.

Mediaeval Studies Mediaeval Studies, published by the Pontifical Institute of Mediaeval Studies, Toronto, Canada, 1938–.

MGH Monumenta Germaniae Historica (see under individual titles).

M. Paris Matthew Paris, *Chronica Maiora*, ed. H. R. Luard, *RS*, 7 vols, 1872–83.

Nielsen, Lauge N. *Theology and Philosophy in the 12th Century: a study of Gilbert de la Porrée's Thinking . . . during the period 1130–1180*, Leiden, 1982.

Ordericus Vitalis *Historia Ecclesiastica*, ed. A. Le Prévost, 5 vols, Paris, 1838–55; ed. Marjorie Chibnall, 6 vols, Oxford, 1968–90.

Ott, 1937 L. Ott, *Untersuchungen zur theologischen Briefliteratur der Frühscholastik*, BGPTMA, 34.

Overmann, 1895 A. Overmann, *Gräfin Mathilde von Tuscien, ihr Besitzungen, Geschichte ihres Gutes*, 1115–1230, Innsbruck, 1895.

Paris, 1887* *Cartulaire Générale de Paris*, ed. R. de Lasterie.

Paris, 1909* L. Halphen, *Paris sous les premiers Capétiens*.

Paris, 1951* A. Friedmann, *Paris: ses rues et ses paroisses du Moyen Age à la Révolution*.

Paris, 1969* A. L. Gabriel, *Garlandia*.

Paris, 1976* A. Lombard-Jourdain, *Paris: Genèse de la ville*.
* Paris is the place of publication of all these works.

PL *Patrologia Latina*, ed. J. P. Migne, 221 vols, Paris, 1844–71.

Peter Lombard, *Sentences* *Magistri Petri Lombardi, Sententiae in IV Libris Distinctae*, ed. Coll. S. Bonaventurae ad Claras Aquas, Rome, 3rd edn, 4 vols, 1971.

Pollock and Maitland F. Pollock and F. W. Maitland, *The History of English Law before the time of Edward I*, 2nd edn 1898 (to which I refer); revised edn by S. C. F. Milsom, Cambridge, 1968.

pseudo-Isidore *Decretales pseudo-Isidorianae*, ed. P. Hinschius, Leipzig, 1863.

RS *Rolls Series: Chronicles and Memorials of Great Britain and Ireland during the Middle Ages*, 1858–96.

RTAM *Recherches de théologie ancienne et médiévale*.

Southern, R. W.
   1953 *The Making of the Middle Ages*, London.
   1970i *Medieval Humanism and other studies*, Oxford.
   1970ii *Western Society and the Church in the Middle Ages*, Penguin History of the Church, vol. 2.
   1982 'The Schools of Paris and the School of Chartres', in *Renaissance and Renewal in the Twelfth Century*, ed. Robert L. Benson and Giles Constable, Cambridge, Mass.
   1984 'From schools to University', in *The History of the University of Oxford*, vol. 1, ed. J. Catto, Oxford, pp. 1–36.
   1992 *Robert Grosseteste: the Growth of an English Mind in Medieval Europe*, 2nd edn with 'A last review', pp. xvii–lxvi.

Schmitt, i–vi F. S. Schmitt, ed. *S. Anselmi, Opera omnia*, 6 vols, Edinburgh, 1938–61.

Wetherbee, 1972 Winthrop Wetherbee, *Platonism and Poetry in the Twelfth Century: the literary influence of the school of Chartres*, Princeton.

Weisweiler, 1936 Heinrich Weisweiler, *Das Schrifttum der Schule Anselms von Laon und Willelms von Champeaux in deutschen Bibliotheken*, BGPTMA, vol. 33, parts 1–2, Münster.

Wortkoncordance *Wortkoncordance zum Decretum Gratiani*, ed. Timothy Reuter and Gabriel Silagi, MGH Hilfsmittel, no. 10, 5 vols, 1990.

ZRG *Zeitschrift der Savigny – Stiftung für Rechtsgeschichte:*
      kan. Abt.: Kanonistische Abteilung
      Rom. Abt.: Romanistische Abteilung.

Two Preliminary Maps

The two maps which follow provide the geographical background of the scholastic developments which are the subject of this volume. The map of the cathedral towns of northern France from about 980 to 1140 shows the main geographical area of work of the progenitors of the scholars who elaborated the body of systematic doctrine about the nature of God and of the universe, with mankind holding a middle place between the hierarchies of eternal beings above, and of creatures ruled only by instinct beneath.

The main steps in the systematic articulation of this body of doctrine were taken in the cathedral schools of northern France, and the programme was brought to its fullest development in the schools of Paris, which alone could make provision for a continuing association of many scholars with a steady stream of pupils over a long period of time. This combination of the liberal arts and theology was the main achievement of the medieval schools. But, in the decades after 1140 there took place an equally important amalgamation of Roman and canon law in Bologna, which provided the legal counterpart to the amalgamation of the liberal arts and theology in the schools of northern France.

The cathedral schools of northern France[1]

Although the essential function of cathedral schools was diocesan education, these schools also – though only intermittently throughout the late tenth and eleventh centuries – had masters who briefly achieved a widespread fame and attracted students from distant parts of Europe. As early as 972 Gerbert of Aurillac, after a local education in his home town, had gone to Reims for further study, and here he soon became a master who attracted students from all parts of Europe. Gerbert's students included another Italian, Fulbert, who (during the years from about 990 until his death in 1028) was master of the cathedral school, and then bishop, of Chartres. He too attracted students from many parts of Europe.[2] After his death, one of his pupils, Berengar, drew a similar flow of students to the schools of Angers and then Tours. Among Berengar's students was Lanfranc, who on becoming a monk at Bec relieved the poverty of the monastery by setting up a school of biblical exposition, logic and grammar, and he too attracted pupils from all parts of Europe. Then, after Lanfranc had given up teaching in 1063, Master Anselm at the cathedral school at Laon attracted the most powerful international body of students in the same range of studies from the 1070s until his death in 1117. And, during these same years, Master Bernard at Chartres had a similar, but smaller, succession of students, mainly in grammar, until his death in 1124.

These were all spasmodic efforts of outstanding masters who opened up the subjects of the future. But they were unable to provide the long continued effort by a succession of many masters and pupils, which was necessary for systematic progress. The conditions which made this possible were found ultimately and only in Paris, and by the time of the deaths of Master Anselm at Laon and Master Bernard at Chartres, Paris was already on the threshold of the long scholastic development, which will be elaborated later in this work.

The map shows archiepiscopal (CAPS) and episcopal (small type) cities of northern France. In all these cities there was a school attached to the cathedral with the general responsibility of providing an education for the clergy of the diocese. Circled numbers indicate places where two or more masters were active simultaneously before 1140, generally in schools only loosely attached to the cathedral.

---

[1] Although a school was an ancient part of a cathedral's equipment in the service of the diocese of which it was the centre, the obligation for every cathedral to have a school seems first to have been expressed in general legislative form by Gregory VII in 1078 – *Das Register Gregors VII*, ed. E. Caspar, *MGH, Epistolae selectae*, 1920, p. 402.)

[2] The best documented of all groups of students before those in Paris in the period after 1120 is found in a poem eulogizing the students of Fulbert, from which J. Havet in 1884 made a brilliant reconstruction of his band of pupils: see Southern, 1953, pp. 198–9, for a summary.

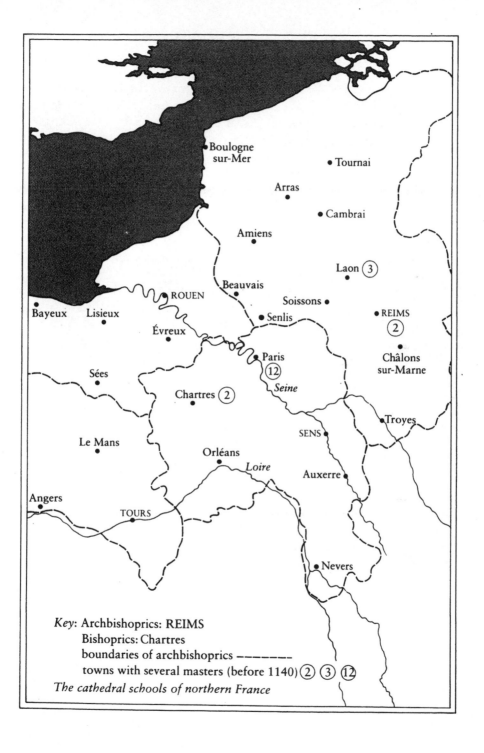

Key: Archbishoprics: REIMS
Bishoprics: Chartres
boundaries of archbishoprics --------
towns with several masters (before 1140) ② ③ ⑫

The cathedral schools of northern France

Bologna as the European centre for legal studies[3]

This map shows the position of Bologna as the most southerly of the great towns of the north Italian plain. It lay on the route which would have been followed by the majority of litigants and pilgrims from northern Europe to Rome, who paused in Bologna to prepare themselves to cross the Apennines on the last stage of their journey. The map illustrates those features in the situation of Bologna which contributed towards its becoming the greatest, and (during the years between about 1140 and 1170) the only, centre of the combined study of canon and Roman law. This combination soon became the counterpart of the study of arts and theology in that system of knowledge and practical enforcement with which we are here concerned.

In barest outline, Bologna's advantage in promoting the joint study of Roman and canon law was its long tradition of legal activity. This, however, was an advantage shared by several north Italian cities. More decisive were the following features of Bologna's position, for they gave it a particularly close association with the papacy which was the source of nearly all developments in canon law. First, it formed part of the lands bequeathed to the papacy by the Donation of Constantine. Second, it was contiguous to the new papal lands bequeathed by the Countess Matilda. Third, from the last years of the eleventh century, its bishops were appointed by the pope. And, finally, the very serious attempt of the Emperor Henry V in 1116 to win the support in the city by granting extensive remission of tolls, was a complete failure.

To add to these advantages, Bologna gained an early start over all possible rivals by being the scene of the labours of Gratian in making the definitive textbook of canon law. Consequently it alone was ready to meet the widespread demand for the teaching of canon law in conjunction with Roman law, which grew rapidly all over western Europe in the decades after 1140.

The shaded area encompassing Ferrara, Bologna and Ravenna shows the extent of the land given to the papacy in the Donation of Constantine. The striped area to the west, including Reggio and Modena, shows the main concentration of towns, castles and fiefs of the Countess Matilda, believed to have been bequeathed to the papacy by the Countess Matilda on her death in 1115.

---

[3] This map is a simplified version of the map in Overmann, 1895.

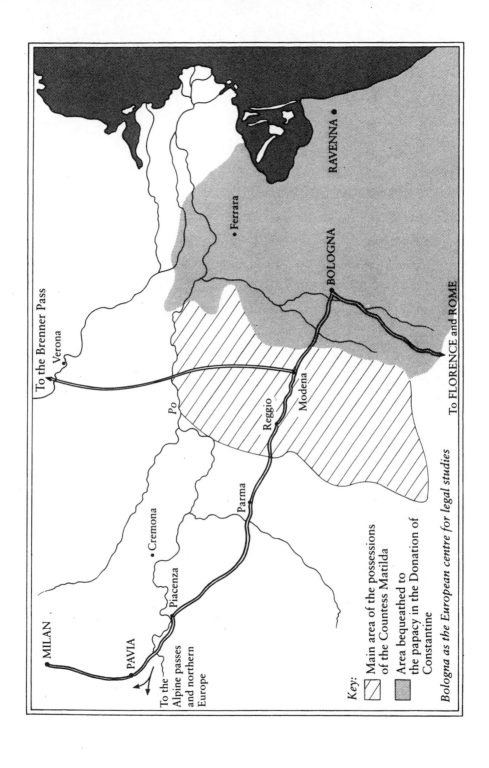

To the Brenner Pass

MILAN

PAVIA

To the Alpine passes and northern Europe

Piacenza

• Cremona

Verona

Parma

Po

Reggio

Modena

• Ferrara

RAVENNA •

BOLOGNA

To FLORENCE and ROME

Key:

Main area of the possessions of the Countess Matilda

Area bequeathed to the papacy in the Donation of Constantine

Bologna as the European centre for legal studies

Introduction

Theology, Law, and the liberal Arts were the three props on which European order and civilization were built during the twelfth and thirteenth centuries – that is to say, during the period of Europe's most rapid expansion in population, wealth and world-wide aspirations before the nineteenth century. All three of these props owed their coherence, and their power to influence the world, to the development of schools of European-wide importance. To these schools, masters and pupils came from all parts of Europe and took back to their places of origin, and sometimes much further afield, the sciences which they had learnt, and from which they proposed to make their livelihood by applying them to the practical issues of life and death, and to the advancement of their own general well-being.

The purpose of this work in its various parts is to examine the local and European environments of the scholastic studies of western Europe in the twelfth and thirteenth centuries, the aims and methods of these studies, and their influence on the lives and behaviour of European people. As everybody knows, these efforts of the medieval schools increasingly fell into widespread contempt from the fourteenth century onwards. But it should also be recognized that, despite the contempt of intellectuals, a large part of the teaching of the medieval schools continued to influence the thoughts and conduct of the majority of people in western Europe on both sides of the great divide between Roman Catholic and Protestant until the twentieth century, when the long-lasting tincture of scholastic principles which had survived among the great mass of the population of western Europe began to disappear altogether. As a counterblast to this apparently final dispersal, however, a remarkable revival took place. This owed its initial impetus to a growing appreciation of medieval civilization in all its aspects throughout the nineteenth century, but the rediscovery of the huge body of work produced in the schools was largely stimulated by Pope Leo XIII's encyclical *Aeterni Patris* of 1879, which created a scholarly activity of unparalleled force in the history of medieval studies. Although the aims of this work gradually diverged very markedly from that of the great encyclical, without the aid of the vast scholarly works produced under its impulse, almost none of the chapters of this present work could have been written.

But, to go back to the beginning: it was during the years from about 1100 to 1160 that the main lines of scholastic thought were laid down, and this is the period that will be dealt with most fully in this and the following volume with a view to understanding the new outlook on the world of nature and of organized Christian society for which the schools were largely responsible. Of course the greatest bulk of scholastic work, and by far the greatest impact of this work on European society, belong to the two centuries *after* 1160, when scholastic thought was the major directing influence on the formation of the outlook, institutions and individual lives of the greater part of the European population. But the moments of discovery in the years before 1160 are in many ways the moments which illuminate the whole scene. Thereafter, for nearly two centuries the initial programme was enlarged and diversified, and then chiefly concentrated either on elaborating minutiae or on piling up mountains of accumulated knowledge. When this happened the original programme became fragmented – deepened in some respects, but increasingly irrelevant as a directing influence on organized life. This 'irrelevance', which finally made the scholastic achievement an object of almost unrelieved derision among the most articulate writers from the seventeenth to the nineteenth centuries, was partly a result of inherent weaknesses in the scholastic method, especially in its treatment of the natural and historical sciences, and partly the result of the appearance of new social and political forces and new forms of sensibility, to which the doctrines of the schools were antipathetic. But it should not be forgotten that the influence of the doctrines of the medieval schools continued to be felt at every level of society, whereas the contempt was largely confined to an intellectual and social élite until it faded into pure ignorance.

INTRODUCTION

The originators of the phase of intellectual and practical innovation and systematization which we are to investigate in this and the following volume are to be found, on the one hand, in the schools of northern France, and pre-eminently in Paris, where a succession of masters transformed the universal map of knowledge; and, on the other hand, in the papal Curia and in the schools of Bologna, where a succession of innovators elaborated a legal system governing a large part of the personal life and organization of the whole of western Christendom.

The system of thought which the masters, and especially those of Paris and Bologna, were the first to elaborate was a corporate and European-wide achievement bringing a large-scale unity of life and ideals. Nevertheless it created many more problems than it solved, and under a formidable appearance of cohesion and universality there were many gaps and contradictions. Indeed, the schools would have lost their driving force if gaps and contradictions had not continued to keep the masters and their pupils active. But equally they would have stifled the whole enterprise if there had not been a continuing hope that the gaps could be filled and the contradictions eliminated. The ground of this hope was that the whole system, in its assumptions, its sources, its methods and aims, expressed a coherent view of Creation, of the Fall and Redemption of mankind, and of the sacraments whereby the redeeming process could be extended to individuals.

There were several reasons for this coherence, and it will suffice here to mention only a few. In the first place, the men who created the system all worked within a similar institutional framework. They all knew and used the same techniques for elucidating an ever-growing body of textbooks, and they all had the same idea of what constituted satisfactory answers to fundamental questions. They were familiar with similar routines of lectures, debates, and academic exercises, and – at least in their professional work – they all shared a belief that Christianity was capable of a systematic and authoritative presentation which could rightly demand the assent and obedience of all members of western Europe, apart from the one dissident group in its midst, officially tolerated, though increasingly harassed – the Jews.

Although the creators of the scholastic system often quarrelled about their conclusions, they took pride in their profession as masters. Like all teachers, they were strongly attached to the textbooks which they knew, and to the intellectual procedures with which they were familiar, and they defended their methods and conclusions by handing them on from one generation to the next, and by resisting the introduction of texts and methods which did not fit into the system.

This resistance, however, did not long delay the introduction into the scholastic curriculum of recently – mainly in the twelfth century – discovered ancient scientific texts; and, naturally, these texts once admitted could only be subjected to the same processes of analysis and debate that had been successful in producing a coherent body of doctrine from all other, earlier known, authoritative texts. Herein lay a danger to which we shall come in due course. For the moment it will suffice to emphasize the continuing importance of the place in society achieved, if not by the masters who inaugurated this great effort, at least by their successors who maintained and developed the methods which had brought to the schools their earliest successes in the first half of the twelfth century.

The full development of these benefits lay in the future. But, from a scholarly point of view, it was the twelfth-century innovators who first introduced systematic order into the mass of intellectual material which they had inherited in a largely uncoordinated form from the ancient world. The general aim of their work was to produce a complete and systematic body of knowledge, clarified by the refinements of criticism, and presented as the consensus of competent judges. Doctrinally the method for achieving this consensus was a progression from commentary to questioning, and from questioning to systematization. And the practical aim of the whole procedure was to stabilize, make accessible and defend an orthodox Christian view of the world against the attacks of heretics within, and unbelievers – or misbelievers – outside the area of organized Christendom.

In principle, they aimed at restoring to fallen mankind, so far as was possible, that perfect system of knowledge which had been in the possession or within the reach of mankind at the moment of Creation. It was generally agreed that this body of knowledge, after collapsing completely in the centuries from the Fall to the Flood, had thereafter been slowly restored by divinely-inspired prophets among the chosen people, and by the efforts of a succession of ancient scholars in the Greco-Roman world. The achievements of these great ancient restorers of the knowledge lost at the Fall had once more been corrupted, and partly lost, as a result of the waves of barbarian invasion which had overwhelmed Christendom in the fifth century and continued intermittently to threaten its existence until the eleventh. But, although the tradition of learning had been threatened by these disasters, the great texts of ancient learning had survived, and it was the work of the new succession of scholars from about 1050 onwards, in vastly more favourable conditions than those of their immediate predecessors, to take up once more the ancient task of restoring the knowledge that had been lost at the Fall.

In order to do this, it was necessary to bring together all surviving records of ancient learning, to clarify them where they were obscure, to correct errors caused either by the corruption of texts or by the only partial understanding of their ancient authors, and finally to systematize the results, and make them generally accessible throughout western Christendom. The *complete* knowledge of the first parents before the Fall had gone beyond recall, and there was a profound sense in which – once the intuitive knowledge of the first parents of the human race had been lost – to seek to know *everything* was to fall into the sin of curiosity. But what could legitimately be sought was that degree of knowledge necessary for providing a just view of God, of nature and of human conduct, which would promote the cause of mankind's salvation. To reach this state it was necessary to free the records of ancient learning from corruptions and ambiguities, to elaborate them where necessary for understanding the divine purpose for mankind, and to give the truths thus clarified practical application by deducing from them appropriate rules of conduct.

The whole programme, thus conceived, looked forward to a time not far distant, when a two-pronged programme of world-wide return to the essential endowment of the first parents of the human race would have been achieved so far as was possible for fallen mankind. Not everything knowable would be known, but at least all reasonably obedient and well-disposed members of Christendom would have access to a body of knowledge sufficient for achieving order in this world and blessedness in the world to come. Instruction would indeed still need to be crowned by individual faith, hope and charity; but the outline of everything that knowledge could contribute to human well-being would have been made available for all, and would have been communicated to the whole world by a combination of preaching and teaching, by the reconquest of the lost lands of Christendom, and by extending this regained body of knowledge to the ends of the earth.

This was the end towards which western Christendom seemed to be moving by the end of the twelfth century. The divisions of opinion among scholars, violent though they sometimes were, were insignificant in comparison with their unity of method and aim, which had brought into existence a system of theoretical and practical knowledge capable of giving satisfaction in this life and contributing towards salvation in the next.

We are here concerned mainly with the doctrinal, not with the disciplinary, part of this programme. And here it was generally agreed that the scope for new discoveries where the giants of the past had harvested was limited, but that the scope for refinement, systematization and (above all) practical application was immense. The immediate need of mankind was for the clarification and practical application of that body of knowledge which had already been recovered by the efforts of ancient prophets and scholars, and it was important that this end should be achieved without delay. By far the greater part of the world's history, and of the possible rediscovery of that knowledge which had been lost at the Fall, lay in the past. The world would probably come to an end within decades or at most a few centuries, almost certainly before another millennium had passed. At all events, it would end when the perfect, but to us unknown, number of the redeemed had been accomplished, and the aim of the schools, as of the Church in general, was to prepare the world for this event, and to hasten it.

This constricted time-scale and concentration on putting

together the broken pieces of the work of earlier scholars may seem at first sight to introduce an element of gloom and of limited horizons into the aims and achievements of twelfth and thirteenth century scholars. But in practice the result was quite the opposite: in the early twelfth century there was a widespread sense of relief from the threats and limitations of the immediately preceding centuries, and this sense of enlargement lasted for nearly two centuries. During this period, scholars expressed their kinship, on the one hand, with their ancient predecessors who had prepared the way for the supreme revelation of God in the life of Jesus Christ and had brought into existence the books of the New Testament and the Church Fathers, and, on the other hand, with the great scholars of antiquity outside the Covenant, who had explored the world of human behaviour and natural phenomena, which could both now be combined within a single system of assured knowledge. The twelfth- and thirteenth-century scholars rejoiced to be the heirs of the abundance of the past.

It was a wonderful time for academically qualified men, and their services were in great demand. Of course there were dangers, as the great *causes célèbres* of the time, in which masters of the highest repute were charged with purveying heretical opinions, testify. These trials happened when a master of unusual power had excited the hostility of a section among his fellow scholars, who collaborated with important elements of opinion outside the schools to obtain the condemnation of opinions of which they disapproved. When this happened, scholars were in danger of being silenced. But, apart from this rare possibility, the twelfth century was a great age of scholastic freedom. As a body, the masters of the schools were the arbiters of orthodoxy under the protection of popes who showed a great reluctance to condemn the opinions of notable masters.

In addition to defining doctrines and the conduct compatible with these doctrines, and enforcing in law courts the conduct compatible with the doctrines that had been clarified in the schools, the masters had the further task of conveying through sermons, manuals for teachers and confessors, and handbooks of general interest, those parts of the intellectual system which impinged on faith and practice.

Every known science made its contribution to the total result.

INTRODUCTION

For organized life at an elementary level, the arts of the trivium (grammar, rhetoric and logic) aided by those of the quadrivium (especially arithmetic for accounting and elementary astronomy for the church calendar) provided the necessary material. At a higher level of sophistication, the sciences of systematic theology and law, which were equally essential for the government of both ecclesiastical and secular society, had been fully articulated by the mid-thirteenth century. In addition, to give practical effect to theological conclusions, there was a continuing flow of treatises on letter-writing and sermon-making, manuals laying down practical codes of behaviour, instructions for communicants and penitents, guides for priests, confessors, and rulers both secular and ecclesiastical. In all these fields, the schools of the twelfth and thirteenth centuries succeeded in providing a body of knowledge sufficient for most situations in life, and in bringing the results of the schools into the lives of ordinary people in parochial churches.

Nearly everyone deferred to theology in principle, but the greatest career-makers and money-spinners were always law and medicine, and the greatest sources of talented activity were the liberal Arts of grammar and rhetoric, which produced a literature of entertainment as well as a foundation for the higher forms of theological and legal learning.

The predominance of Arts students was partly a reflection of the claims of local life, which needed many literate men in parishes and in the lower offices of administration. Of those who reached the highest positions on grounds of merit rather than of birth, the great majority had studied either Roman and Canon Law or Theology, and these were studies of formidable complexity. It is often impossible, without knowing the context of a question discussed in the schools, to decide whether a particular discussion belongs to a work on physics, metaphysics or theology, and whether it is taking place in the lecture room of a master of Arts or of Theology. This was not, as is sometimes thought, because medieval science was dominated by theology. If anything, it was for the opposite reason, that science made increasing inroads into theology. Consequently, the leading scientists and the leading theologians were often the same men, and the union, or confusion, of science and theology arose from the familiarity of theologians with all the basic forms of secular learning.

The steps by which this state of affairs came into existence must be left to be surveyed, so far as is practicable, in later volumes. Here it will suffice to say that the body of knowledge which the masters had created by their exegetical method of investigation was based on a uniform routine of asking questions about the meaning of statements in authoritative texts. And since these texts covered every area of human knowledge, the final aim of the schools – namely the systematization of all knowledge – appeared to be well served by this method of investigation.

Further, since the methods of investigation which were used to elucidate doctrinal statements about the Christian religion were equally applicable for elucidating statements on every other subject, anyone who had mastered the method could move from one subject to another without any essential change. It was mainly a matter of mastering the relevant ancient sources. This was not easy, but it was no more difficult than it is now for a historian to move from economic to political, or from ecclesiastical to social history. However different the angle of vision of these various branches of study may be, the same documentary disciplines, the same criteria of probability, the same forms of presentation, are applicable to all. So it was with all branches of scholastic thought: however different the subject matter, the method of investigation was the same, and there was a prospect of final systematization which would cover all areas of knowledge.

Moreover, since the number of basic texts in all subjects taken together was very small indeed by the standards of any area of modern academic study, it seemed no very unattainable aim to bring all knowledge under a similar scrutiny. Probably, at the moment of widest expansion, three or four hundred volumes of moderate size would have contained all the basic texts on all subjects capable of exact and systematic study. Of course, small in bulk though they might be, the labour of exact scrutiny of even this limited body of material was very great, and the authoritative texts within each main area of study had by the fourteenth century produced a literature many times the size of

9

the original texts, and containing many conflicting conclusions. We shall later notice some examples of these conflicts, and seek the reasons why apparently insoluble conflicts, at first rather rare, gradually came to invade every subject and to undermine all hope of agreement. Nevertheless, the theory of knowledge which represented the task of learning as a laborious reconquest of that which the human mind had once held without effort, encouraged the view that the minute study of the reconquered territory of the mind would in the end bring about that restoration of the knowledge of mankind to a state as nearly approaching its first state of innocence as was consistent with mankind's fallen state. This was the goal of all scholastic effort.

The hope of a final synthesis in the not too distant future gradually faded in the early fourteenth century. By then, the literature based on the foundations of scholastic debate had become many times more bulky than the texts on which the whole body of knowledge was based. This literature represented the co-operative labours of hundreds of masters and thousands of pupils working in the schools during the preceding two hundred years, and their commentaries had themselves become objects of frequently acrimonious study. Consequently the final goal of authoritative agreement receded in proportion as the journey progressed. This was certainly a matter of great concern, but there appeared to be no way in which the scholastic effort could be stopped, or essentially changed, either in method, materials or aim.

The universities, which had developed as corporations of masters and students dedicated to this task, had made one great contribution to systematic thought by providing the continuity of method and stability of life for an endless flow of masters, pupils and questions. But they also exhibited in full measure the vices as well as the virtues of permanent corporations, as failure to advance towards an agreed system of universal knowledge turned into bitter and unending dissension from which there seemed to be no means of escape.

The process whereby this state of affairs came into existence will be gradually elucidated in the course of the succeeding chapters, so far as lies in my power. But one general cause of the vast and apparently unbridgeable cleavages which developed in all fields of knowledge may immediately be mentioned.

The scholastic method of analysis of words and meanings, of general concepts and individual instances, and of forms of argument, was appropriate for studying ancient texts on many different subjects. When the Arts subjects of grammar and logic had been mastered, their rules and conventions were applicable to problems in theology or canon law, for the simple reason that all these areas of knowledge demanded in the first place a careful study of authoritative texts. Consequently the first requirement for all of them was a knowledge of the meanings of words and of grammatical and logical constructions, followed by correlating the general doctrines of authoritative texts with an accumulation of exemplary details. Thus all subjects required a broadly similar progression from texts to individual problems to general systematic knowledge. So whoever made the transition from the Arts of grammar and logic to theology could make the comparable transition to law. They were all essentially concerned with the study of texts which presented similar problems of elucidation. Hence a complete system of knowledge could reasonably be expected to emerge from these interlinked fields of study.

Moreover, the theory of knowledge on which the scholastic system was based – that is to say, the idea that all knowledge was a reconquest of that which had been freely available to mankind in the pre-lapsarian state – encouraged the expectation of a slowly enlarging body of authoritative doctrine growing from century to century, and needing in this last age of the world only to be harvested and organized. If this was a true account of the function of the schools, it would be equally applicable to the natural sciences as to the sciences of theology, law, logic and grammar. They all exemplified the slow recovery of that intuitive knowledge of all things with which the human race had been endowed at the Creation, and which – despite the ravages of sin – it was slowly reconquering by recovering and combining in a single system the knowledge lost by Adam and Eve.

Nothing, therefore, seemed more reasonable than to apply to ancient books on the natural sciences the methods of careful study and analysis that had been so successfully applied to all the traditional areas of scholastic knowledge. It took a long time to realize that – even if the theory of the gradual reconstruction of lost human knowledge through the centuries was workable for the traditional scholastic subjects – it by no means followed that the scientific knowledge which would have been available in the unfallen state of mankind, could be recovered by the same methods of textual analysis and logical refinement.

This was in the end to prove the greatest stumbling-block in the whole field of scholastic knowledge, and we shall observe the effects of this problem at a later stage in our enquiry. Meanwhile it will suffice to say that the greatest virtue of the medieval scholastic system was that it stabilized and systematized knowledge of theology and law, which were the subjects of greatest importance for the creation of a fairly orderly and basically hopeful society, and which had been immensely successful in producing works of the highest genius in Christian doctrine, devotion, imagery and order. The role of the schools was fundamental to this whole effort since they produced the systematic body of doctrine on which a way of life and a body of works of piety and devotion, and of imaginative force, were created which can never lose their power to attract, however much they may lose their power to convince.

From a date which we shall later find grounds for locating fairly precisely in the fifty years from 1270 to 1320, the hope of achieving a harmony of thought and practice, of schools and ecclesiastical authority, and of lay and ecclesiastical society, began to recede, as did also the hope of achieving an ideal completeness of the knowledge accessible to human enquiry.

The period of disintegration was necessarily very prolonged, if only because, from the beginning, contradictions had played a necessary role in the scholastic process of truth-finding, and without a supply of contradictions awaiting resolution the whole system would have become moribund. Consequently, in its most flourishing period, scholastic thought represented a vast three-storeyed edifice of problems resolved, and problems awaiting a solution, and problems judged to be insoluble – a kind of scholastic heaven, purgatory and hell. It had always been known that there were some *insolubilia*, but they were thought to be fairly few, confined to extreme cases, and amusing rather than dangerous. Yet slowly the problems beyond resolution became more numerous, and the conceptual hell of the scholastic method came to occupy a growing and finally an engulfing position on the map of scholastic knowledge. When this happened, it brought the end of scholasticism as the dominant method of intellectual enquiry, offering not only a system of unalterable truth, but also a system which could bring peace and the hope of salvation to the whole body of Christendom.

It was in the course of the fourteenth century that the stage of scholastic development was reached in which the increase of insoluble problems was accompanied by an increasing prolixity in developing the knowable, and scholastic thought began to sink under the growing weight both of the knowable and of the unknowable. When this happened the scholastic method of discovering truth by patient analysis and compilation was gradually superseded by different methods of investigation, whether descriptive, intuitive, visionary, or systematically experimental. Nevertheless, even in this state of decline, the rules of behaviour which gave practical effect to the results of scholastic thought continued to influence the social life of Europe until the twentieth century. Despite the religious divisions of western Christendom, the requirement that conduct should be based on theological principles continued to be generally accepted as a necessary basis for peace and prosperity. So long as this state of affairs prevailed, the results of scholastic thought still had a continuing influence in European affairs.

It was only as a result of the vast secularization of the twentieth century that the principles laid down for the communities of western Christendom in the twelfth and thirteenth centuries ceased to provide rules of conduct for their descendants. But then, just as scholastic thought had emerged in the first place from the threatened breakdown of order in the tenth and eleventh centuries, so the detailed *study* of scholasticism emerged as a model of order at a time of increasing disorder on a worldwide scale in the late nineteenth and twentieth centuries. With what results time alone will show.

Part One

Aims, Methods and Environment

1

Scholastic Humanism

I Contrasting Types of Humanism

The use of the word 'humanism' at once introduces a problem: the word has two distinct meanings, and historians have used it sometimes in one sense, sometimes in the other, and sometimes in a mixture of the two. The most general meaning of the word – and I follow here the *Oxford English Dictionary* – is 'any system of thought or action which is concerned with merely human interests, or with those of the human race in general'. It is in this sense that the word is now in popular use, emphasizing the centrality of the effort to extend human knowledge and activity, and consequently to limit, or more often abolish, the intrusion of the supernatural in human affairs. The main instrument of such humanism is scientific knowledge, which (it is hoped) will lead ultimately to a single coherent view of nature, including the nature of mankind.

Most of those who now practise this type of humanism look on the scholastic works of the medieval period with their emphasis on the supernatural end of man, with their assumption of the primacy of theology among the sciences, with their source in a predominantly clerical culture and hierarchical organization under a universal papal authority, as an embodiment of all that they oppose.

Yet nothing could be further from the truth. The great intellectual achievement of the schools and the works which they produced in the two centuries after 1100, was vastly to extend the area of rational investigation into every branch of human life and cosmic being. The scholastic programme did not indeed seek to exclude the supernatural. Quite the opposite: it *required* the supernatural as a necessary completion of the natural world. But this extension did not diminish the area of rational investigation: it simply added a further dimension to the complexity and richness of the scene of human life. Modern secular humanists, therefore, even though they differ from their medieval predecessors in excluding the supernatural from their area of enquiry, can still find in the schools of the twelfth and thirteenth centuries their direct ancestors.

But alongside this view of humanism as the embodiment of an urgent and consistent effort to enlarge the field of natural reason, there is another view of humanism which goes back to the Renaissance, and which gives a central humanistic role to the study of ancient Latin and Greek literature. The essential aim of this study was not to extract systematic doctrine from ancient literature, but to develop sensibility and linguistic skill. From the sixteenth century onwards, the study of ancient literature in order to cultivate refinement of speech and sentiment was regarded as pre-eminently humane in contrast to the formal, systematic and supposedly 'desiccated' studies of logic, theology and canon law, which remained as the supposedly moribund monuments of the medieval schools.

Post-medieval 'literary' humanists looked on the medieval schools as the enemies of their kind of humanism – quite rightly, for the products of the medieval schools are certainly not models of literary elegance, and are not much concerned with human sensitivity or feelings. But the humanistic critics of the medieval schools also commonly claimed that the medieval scholastic concern with minute metaphysical and logical distinctions demonstrated an indifference to matters of practical human importance.[1] This criticism has indeed some truth when applied to the schools of the fourteenth and fifteenth centuries, but it was

---

[1] Milton was especially severe on this aspect of scholastic studies, for example, *On Education*: 'I deem it an old error of universities not yet well recovered from the Scholastick grossness of the barbarous ages that . . . they present their novices at first coming up with the most intellective abstractions of logic and metaphysics.' But he was only reiterating in the 1620s a view that had been popularized thirty years earlier by Pierre Charron in his book *De la Sagesse* (1595), which had already been translated into English and several other languages, in which he equated the scholastic method with pedantry and obfuscation.

wildly mistaken so far as the scholastic thought of the twelfth and thirteenth centuries was concerned.

Historians during the last hundred years have often protested against these criticisms, and have brought to light medieval lovers of classical literature and writers of elegant Latin prose and poetry, especially in the early twelfth century. But these modern defenders of medieval humanism have themselves too often erred in the claims they have made for twelfth-century scholars, because they supposed that twelfth-century scholars were interested in the literary works of the ancient world for reasons similar to their own. On closer inspection, however, the twelfth-century scholars who have been praised as lovers of ancient literature, and therefore as precursors of a Renaissance type of humanism, can be seen to have been interested in this literature chiefly for the doctrines which were the subject of scholastic enquiry. Hence one of the commonest results of their labours was the compilation of collections of passages (under the title of *Florilegia*) likely to be useful in scholastic enquiries.

For example, John of Salisbury is often credited with a Renaissance-type literary humanism because of his very extensive knowledge of classical texts. But as we observe him striding through the classics, heaping his pages with schematically-arranged quotations from a dozen authors, with a total concentration on their use as illustrations of the doctrine he is discussing, and with a sovereign indifference to the aims of the authors themselves or the differences of personality depicted in their creations, we must ask what kind of sensitivity to ancient literature this great man possessed. Like every other scholastically-trained writer, John of Salisbury was motivated by a strong desire to get from all the ancient texts at his disposal their maximum contribution to doctrine, quite regardless of the literary aims of the works in which these choice fragments of general truth were embedded.

'Doctrine' was his goal. Even at the beginning of his course of studies in Paris, when he fled from the contentious logic-chopping of Abelard's pupils and sought out William of Conches as the great master of ancient literature, he was concerned, not with literary appreciation, but with building up that stock of knowledge which he turned into the political philosophizing of his *Policraticus* and into a discussion of the place of logic in human knowledge in his *Metalogicon*, and finally into his later advocacy of Thomas Becket's ecclesiastical policy. The aim of all his studies was to build up systematic knowledge as a basis for right action. That was the humanism of the schools: the humanism of systematic thought and action, not the humanism of refined sensibility.[2]

A similar remark can be made about the only surviving twelfth-century commentary on the *Aeneid*.[3] It is a work of very great interest in giving a scholastic view of the greatest Latin literary work of the ancient world. But it concentrates exclusively on the allegory of the various world-historical stages which the poem allegedly displays. It is a guide, therefore, to world history, and the commentary shows not the slightest interest in the stylistic perfections, nor in the characters, personal traits or sufferings of any of the people in the poem; not a thought for the *lacrimae rerum*. If we compare the twelfth-century interpreter's appreciation of the fourth book of the *Aeneid* with Christopher Marlowe's portrayal of the character of *Dido* on this occasion, the contrast between the scholastic humanism of the twelfth century and the humanism of the Renaissance is at once revealed.[4] Of course it may be objected that these works were intended for very different audiences, the one professional, the other popular; but that is part of the difference between them, and helps to explain why the twelfth-century interpreters of this as of other ancient texts were almost exclusively concerned with them as sources of doctrine. As further examples of the doctrinal emphasis of twelfth-century humanism, it may be remarked that, when Wibald of Korvey assiduously collected the works of Cicero, or when William of Malmesbury collected

2   John of Salisbury's *Metalogicon* is an important document in urging that true knowledge requires both a complete familiarity with all aspects of Aristotelian logic and an avoidance of logic-chopping. On this subject, see especially *Metalogicon*, ii, cc. 1, 7, 9–15. For further discussion of ii, c. 10, see below, pp. 215–21.
3   For a recent edition, see *The Commentary on the first six Books of the* Aeneid *of Vergil commonly* (but improbably) *attributed to Bernardus Silvestris*, ed. Julian Ward Jones and E. F. Jones, Lincoln, Nebraska, 1977.
4   *The tragedie of Dido Queene of Carthage*, in *The Works of Christopher Marlowe*, ed. C. F. Tucker Brooke, Oxford, pp. 393–439, especially the death scene with its final words, 'Live false Aeneas, truest Dido dyes' – a sentiment wholly alien to twelfth-century doctrine.

extracts from all available sources for his *Polihistory*, they too were showing their interest in classical literature as a mine of information from which systematic knowledge of history or of human nature could be drawn.[5] They are exhibiting the common twelfth-century scholastic thirst for organized knowledge. They are not humanists in the sense of the later Renaissance founders of the study of *literae humaniores*.

The confusions which have arisen from a failure to distinguish between these two main types of humanism could be discussed without end. So, instead of pursuing these themes any further, let me state quite simply why, and in what sense, I believe that the scholastic development of the period from about 1050 to the end of the thirteenth century represents the first great age of a humanism which is scientific rather than literary in character and aim.

If the distinction I draw is correct, then – far from disappearing after about 1150 to re-emerge in Petrarch two centuries later – the scholarly humanism of the early twelfth century should be regarded, not as the first short-lived expression of Renaissance-type humanism, but as the first expression of a scientific humanism which went on developing for two hundred years until it was submerged in a sea of doubts and contradictions in the schools of the early fourteenth century, to reappear with very different pre-suppositions in the scientific developments of the nineteenth and twentieth centuries. When scholars from Petrarch to Milton derided the aridity of scholastic aims, they did so because they knew the medieval schools only in their period of doctrinal disintegration – very different from the period from Hugh of St-Victor and Abelard to Duns Scotus and Dante, whose works all display great systematic boldness and desire to

---

[5] For William of Malmesbury's works, see R. M. Thomson, *William of Malmesbury*, Boydell, Woodbridge, 1987. As for Wibald, he is the epitome of the twelfth-century scholar administrator, and his collection of Cicero's speeches is more complete than that of any known earlier collector. For a brief account of the range of his interests, see a few admirable pages in Max Manitius, *Geschichte der lateinischer Literatur des Mittelalters*, Munich, 1931, vol. 3, pp. 289–92, and L. D. Reynolds and N. G. Wilson, *Scribes and Scholars: a guide to the transmission of Greek and Latin Literature*, Oxford, 1991, 3rd edn, p. 114. Wibald surely saw himself standing like Otto of Freising (on whom see below, pp. 208–12) at the beginning of a new age of scholastic revival in the service of imperial government.

extend human powers to their utmost. It is this which makes it the precursor of modern scientific humanism – but with this great difference: in its medieval form, scientific humanism did not reject the supernatural but looked on it as the final, however imperfectly knowable, end and goal of all intellectual enquiry.

II CHARACTERISTIC FEATURES OF SCHOLASTIC HUMANISM

1 The dignity of human nature

The first fundamental characteristic of the products of the schools is a strong sense of the dignity of human nature. Without this there can be no humanism of any description, and it is a conspicuous force in the schools of the twelfth and thirteenth centuries. That Man is a fallen creature, who has lost that immediate knowledge of God which was the central feature of human nature before the Fall; that human instincts are now deeply disturbed and are often in conflict with reason; that human beings are now radically disorganized and disorientated – all this is common ground to all Christian thinkers at all times. We must not expect a denial of this condition in the Middle Ages, or in the Renaissance for that matter, or at any time which is not blinded by excessive optimism about human capacities. But what we may reasonably claim for the twelfth-century schools is that they were the first institutions in Europe to make it their main purpose to set about systematically restoring to the fullest possible extent the knowledge that had been forfeited at the Fall. The method employed for effecting this restoration was to study the works of the ancient scholars who had begun the slow process of repairing the ravages of sin in destroying mankind's knowledge of both the natural and supernatural worlds, and to elucidate and complete this process – so far as is possible in this world – by systematizing and elaborating the truths regained by ancient scholars or revealed to Old Testament prophets, and more fully available to later Christian Fathers and students. The expectation was that, when all had been gathered in, a very great part of the knowledge lost at the Fall would once more be available for the guidance and instruction of human beings.

This was the first aim of the twelfth-century schools. But then there was a further aim closely connected with the first. Just as human nature has an inherent dignity which, though ruined by the Fall, has not been altogether lost, so too the whole natural order is in a similar situation. The continuing human power to recognize the grandeur and splendour of the universe, to understand the principles of the organization of nature, and to order human life in accordance with nature, is symptomatic of the survival of human dignity, in however depleted a form, after the Fall. But it is also symptomatic of the continuing dignity of the natural world itself that it is intelligible. Consequently, when human beings understand the laws of nature, they not only achieve their true dignity as nature's keystone, holding the whole created order together in an intelligible union, but they also recognize the rationality of nature itself. Further, this position gives human minds access to the divine purpose in the Creation, and therefore, in some degree, access through reason, as well as through Revelation, to the divine nature itself.

Can humanism go further than this? Only by rejecting the whole idea of a divinely created universe within which mankind was created to be the keystone. Within the bounds set by mankind's post-lapsarian propensity to sin with all its consequences in diminishing the human power of understanding, the programme of the medieval schools may be judged an expression of the highest degree of 'scientific' humanism ever incorporated in an institutional form, for it promised not only an understanding of the plan of divine Redemption, but also a capacity to understand the natural universe, and, at least in outline, the nature of God and the supernatural orders of being with which mankind is linked.

These various levels of knowledge, which we may broadly distinguish as redemptive, natural and supernatural, drawn from the textbooks in which the learned advances of the past were recorded, formed the basic subjects of all scholastic sciences.

Very few scholars could successfully undertake a course of study in more than one of these subjects, and most had to be content with mastering the elementary Arts of language and argument which were necessary for performing the humblest offices in the Church. To go further and study the works of Priscian, Cicero, and Aristotle on grammar, rhetoric and logic, was to reach a platform which would equip any man for a career of some distinction. To go further still and study the laws of organized society in the *Corpus Iuris Civilis* of Justinian, and the rules of organized Christian life in the decrees of Councils, the letters of Popes and the works of the Fathers, was not only to open up a vast prospect of systematic knowledge but also to possess the tools for the very highest offices in either secular or ecclesiastical government. To go further still and study the whole body of doctrine about God and God's purpose in the Creation and Redemption of the world was to reach the ultimate goal of human nature. To diverge from these well-explored avenues in order to study the movements of the planets or the physical organization of human and other living bodies in the ancient texts which dealt with these subjects, was to diverge considerably from the common run of scholastic studies, but this extension too – for aims which were largely either medicinal or political – became fairly common by the end of the twelfth century.

The main features of all these studies were, first, that they aimed at systematic knowledge of the whole area of the knowable; and, second, that they sought to achieve this aim by studying the whole deposit of knowledge which had been acquired during the centuries before the destructive barbarian invasions of the Roman Empire. In addition, some scholars – as we shall see – sought new knowledge through individual observations; but by far the greater part of the knowable was to be found in the authoritative works of ancient scholars. Although this dependence on ancient authorities came to be much derided by later critics, it followed naturally from the general conception of the slow rebuilding of knowledge after the Fall which was the foundation of the whole scholastic enquiry.

In seeking to understand the main features of this scholastic programme, we may begin by noting one point of contrast between the twelfth and the immediately preceding centuries. The conception of the inherent dignity – that is to say, the intelligibility and rational plan – of nature, whether human or cosmic, had scarcely existed in the period of stress from which western Europe was just emerging in the second half of the eleventh century. Everything that was great or dignified in human life had been associated with miracles and supernatural forces, with symbolism and ritual; and human life had been organized mainly with a view to making the greatest possible use of these aids. Consequently the rituals of corporate life had been very elaborate and impressive, and they had provided a framework of order in strong contrast to the apparently ineradicable chaos in both the human and natural worlds.

Even in the darkest centuries of invasion and pillage the study of ancient texts for the knowledge which they contained had never been abandoned. But on the whole such enlargement of life as could be found in pre-scholastic Europe had come from prayer and penance, from the miraculous aid of the saints, and from the observance of ancient rituals. It was only in wearing symbolic garments and performing sacramental acts, in touching the earthly remains of those who already belonged to the world of eternity, that any great enlargement for humanity could be hoped for.

It may indeed well turn out that this awe-struck sacramental view of man's place and powerlessness in the universe ultimately gives a more satisfactory account of the human situation than the elaborate structures of knowledge and disciplined behaviour of the succeeding centuries. And it must always be understood that these structures, even at their most elaborate, never reversed the final impotence of man with regard to sin. Consequently they never diminished the need for supernatural aid in resisting sin with its final consequence of damnation.

But within this final limitation, which can never be overcome so long as the universe is conceived as a divine creation marred by sin and intermittently subject to supernatural intervention in the form of miracles and signs, the sharp change of emphasis after 1100 in bringing hope of human enlargement, both in understanding and in practical life, through natural means is very evident.

2 *Introspection as an instrument of enquiry*

Part of the new emphasis on the value of human effort in acquiring a systematic view of the universe can be connected with an increasingly serious search for knowledge of the human mind itself; and this draws attention to another important feature of twelfth-century scholastic thought. Although it was a product of schools situated in towns and greatly influenced by the active municipal and secular life to which they owed their strength and continuity, all scholastic learning drew much of its inspiration from developments that had taken place in monastic life during the eleventh century. Any attempt, therefore, to understand the scholastic procedures of the twelfth and thirteenth centuries must begin within the monasteries, for it was in these communities that an extensive view of a coherent universe was first developed. A monastically based world-view is necessarily supernatural in its orientation. But within this orientation, in the late eleventh century there are the first signs of a change that had a profound effect on the rational structures of Europe. Briefly, the change took the form of an increasing concentration on the resources within the human mind in progressing towards a knowledge of God. The significance of this for the future lay in its making the exploration of the human mind, and of human nature generally, an integral part of the growth in knowledge.

The search for God within the soul became one of the chief innovations of the monastic leaders of this period. One of the earliest and most significant moments in this search was in 1079, when Anselm at Bec 'entered into the chamber of his mind', excluded everything but the word *God*, and found that suddenly the word articulated itself into a demonstration of God's necessary existence, which he believed to be both new and true. It was certainly new. Whether or not it was true is a question that has been discussed from that day to this. But whether true or not, the idea of finding something that was both new and important was itself new to a generation which believed itself to be committed mainly to the task of preserving, and then very slowly building upon, the deposit of the past. Suddenly to find new things so close at hand, and so central to human aspirations, was a revelation of the powers that lay within the human mind.[6]

Anselm himself did not see his discovery in this light. So far as he was concerned, he had discovered by an intense effort, and by God's grace, something that would have been self-evident to a mind not clouded by sin. God had momentarily removed the cloud, and he saw. From Anselm's point of view, the most important lesson of his discovery was the extent of human frailty, and it encouraged a great pessimism about the efficacy of human effort. But in this reaction Anselm was going against the current. Already by the 1130s, St Bernard, who would have thought himself an enemy of humanism, was basing his whole programme of spiritual growth on the ancient maxim, 'Know thyself'. In pursuit of this programme, Bernard found a positive value in self-love, and his programme for growing in the knowledge and love of God was based on the gradual refinement of self-love until it developed into love of one's neighbour, and by further refinement, love of God.[7]

Here then, in an unexpected source, we find an appreciation of the self at the root of a new programme of spiritual growth, beginning with human nature in its most unpromising aspect of self-love, and ending in the most refined forms of love of others and ultimately of God. This progression from the natural to the supernatural, which is the guiding principle of the twelfth-century schools, is therefore also the guiding principle of the new monasticism of the Cistercians and also of the Augustinian canons. Among the latter we find St Bernard's younger and more scholastically-centred contemporary, Richard of St-Victor, writing:

[6] See Anselm, *Proslogion*, cc. 1–3, ed. F. S. Schmitt, vol. 1, pp. 97–103. For a translation, see Jasper Hopkins and Herbert W. Richardson, *Anselm of Canterbury*, London and Toronto, 1974, vol. 1, pp. 91–5. The intense effort of introspection which led to his (as he believed) single conclusive proof of the reality of God's existence is vividly described in the account which he gave his biographer as reported in Eadmer's *Life of St Anselm*, ed. and transl. by R. W. Southern, Oxford, 1962, pp. 29–31.

[7] For St Bernard's four stages of love, starting with the lowest form of carnal love whereby a man loves himself above all others for his own sake, and rises by stages to the spiritual love whereby he loves nothing, not even himself, except for God's sake, see his *Tractatus de diligendo Deo*, cc. 8–10, PL, 182, 987–90.

A man, who has not yet succeeded in seeing himself, raises his eyes in vain to see God. Let a man first understand the invisible things of himself before he presumes to stretch out to the invisible things of God . . . for unless you can understand yourself, how can you try to understand those things which are above yourself?[8]

This search for God by understanding the nature of the self was at first a monastic programme, but it fitted easily into the scholastic programme of progressing from the study of nature to the study of the supernatural world. It is also associated with another important development, which was mainly monastic in origin but later widely studied in the schools: the doctrine of friendship in both its cosmic and human setting.

3 The cultivation of friendship, human and divine

If self-knowledge is the first step in the rehabilitation of man-kind, friendship – which is the sharing of this knowledge with someone else – is an important auxiliary, for through sharing, self-knowledge is more than doubled. Here again, it was St Anselm who first in his generation found words to express the intensity of his sense of union with his friends in his search for God. As so often with Anselm, there is a mystery in this intensity, in that it did not lead him to be interested in the personalities of his friends. Rather the opposite, he was concerned only with their common supernatural purpose, and with looking through their personalities to the view which opened out beyond them.[9]

From this beginning, however, and in other hands, friendship came to have a new place in the relationship between God and human beings. Although this theme was first and most fully elaborated in Aelred of Rievaulx's treatise On Friendship, writ-ten in the Cistercian monastery of Rievaulx in about 1160, it made its way also into the schools. Aelred's work must be dealt with later in another context. For the present it must suffice to

8 Benjamin minor, c. lxxi, PL, 196, 51.
9 For a discussion of this point, see Southern, 1990, pp. 143–53.

say that he enunciated a principle which also had its application in scholastic thought: 'Nature prompts human beings to desire friendship; experience fortifies this urge; reason regulates it; and the religious life perfects it.'[10]

This association of nature and humanity with reason and religion is central in all twelfth-century intellectual development, and it had a peculiar development in arguments on the subject of friendship. To mention only one: of all the forms of friendship explored in the twelfth century, there was none more eagerly sought than the friendship between God and man. This may seem a commonplace theme, and one which has been debased by countless sentimentalities and trivialities. But it was once fresh, and it lifted a great weight from human lives. In the early Middle Ages God had appeared as Creator, Judge, Saviour, but not as a friend. By great labour and exertion, by crippling penances and gifts to the Church, by turning from the world to the monastic life, God's anger might be averted; but God was very difficult to approach, except through the mediation of the saints; more difficult still to appease, except through an endless burden of penances. Then quite suddenly the humanity of the Redeemer began to appear not simply as a divine stratagem to outwit the Devil, but as an expression of God's fellowship with mankind. In the light of this discovery, the terror faded, the sun shone, and prayers, poems, devotions of all kinds, mingling scholastic with monastic themes, began to pour forth to express the humanity of God.

This theme was capable of infinite elaboration to cover all the situations of life. For example, a short fragment from a thirteenth-century treatise on the uses of adversity will show how the theme of the common humanity which God himself shared could sweeten every scene of sin, misery and impotence:

> Tribulations illuminate the heart of man with self-knowledge, and this is the perfection of the human condition. Just as lovers send letters to each other to refresh their memories of one another, so Christ sends tribulations to refresh our memories of him and his sufferings. By denying us earthly satisfactions God forces us to seek

[10] *De Spirituali Amicitia*, PL, 195, 669–72. This work will be more fully discussed in Volume II.

those which are heavenly, just as an earthly lord who wants to sell his own wine orders the public houses to close until his stock is sold out.[11]

These religious developments, despite the sentimentality from which they were rarely wholly free, were the greatest triumph that religious humanism could ever achieve, for they not only brought the universe within the reach of human understanding, but also disclosed God as so much the friend of mankind that His actions could be interpreted in terms almost indistinguishable from those of ordinary human relationships. Consequently the scholastic discussions, as well as the hymns and meditations, in which these themes were developed from the mid-twelfth century onwards, provide some of the most convincing evidence of a growing sense of the proximity of God and Man.

4 Systematic intelligibility

The dignity of human and cosmic nature is the foundation of scholastic humanism; the intelligibility of nature is its symptom; and the friendship between God and Man is an expression of this theme on the very boundary between reason and sentiment. And since God is the creator and upholder of both human and cosmic nature, a similar intelligibility and sentiment must (so far as human limitations permit understanding) characterize the nature of God and His relationship with the Creation. The elaboration of this intelligibility was central to the whole programme of the schools. As the most famous master of the school at Tours in the 1140s, Bernard Silvestris, wrote:

> The animals express their brute creation
> By head hung low and downward looking eyes;
> But man holds high his head in contemplation

[11] Quoted from an anonymous *Tractatus de duodecim utilitatibus tribulationum*, mistakenly attributed to Peter of Blois and printed among his works in *PL*, 207, 989–1006. For a new edition with a discussion of its true context in the mid-thirteenth century, see A. Auer, *Leidenstheologie im Spätmittelalter*, 1952.

To show his natural kinship with the skies.
He sees the stars obey God's legislation:
They teach the laws by which mankind can rise.[12]

The images in these lines were largely borrowed from Ovid, but in Ovid they were a poetic fiction. For twelfth-century scholars they were scientific facts, and they provided a basis for thinking that rational investigation could find an answer to all the problems of nature. Of course knowledge could not atone for sin: participation in Christ's atoning sacrifice alone could do this. But one of the effects of sin, in hiding from human eyes the truth about God and nature, could be repaired by the knowledge that comes from the use of reason.

It may seem strange that scholars who had so recently emerged from an extremely pessimistic view of human capacities, and who still believed that man's faculties had been grievously impaired by sin, should now rush to the other extreme and believe that almost everything short of the direct vision of God could once more be known by patient study of the great works of the past. But all revolutions, not least those of the intellect, hold out exaggerated hopes, and they do so for the same reason: since some truths which had seemed lost beyond recovery have turned out to be discoverable by the careful use of new methods, there is a tendency to think that all problems will be equally easily solved. So at first all seems easy; it is only the task of filling in the details that takes a long time and comes up against increasingly intractable, dispiriting and ultimately insoluble difficulties. That is the history of all revolutions, and intellectual revolutions, including that initiated by the twelfth-century schools, are no exception.

Besides, there was for the scholastic revolution a further initial reason for optimism. In the early twelfth century, scholars discovered that there existed a scientific basis for hoping that the process of restoring the lost knowledge of mankind would largely succeed. This optimistic hope was grounded in the scientific fact – as it was taken to be – that mankind, alone of all created creatures, is composed of *all* the elements that make up

---

[12] This is a rough translation of Bernardus Silvestris, *Cosmographia* (otherwise known as *De Mundi Universitate*), *Lib.* 2, x, lines 27–32, ed. with notes and introduction by Peter Dronke, Leiden, 1978, p. 141.

the universe. From this it was concluded that mankind, being the epitome of the universe, is so constructed as to be able to understand everything about the composition of the universe. Despite the ravages of sin, this total congruity between the elements of human nature and those of the whole natural order had survived. Consequently mankind had an in-built capacity for understanding the whole order of nature.

A further link between mankind and nature was that the sin of mankind had communicated itself also to the natural order, and this had led to a general infection of nature making it 'red in tooth and claw'. So the restoration of mankind was also associated with the restoration of man's knowledge of nature, and by a further extension with the restoration of nature itself to its primitive excellence. At the furthest stretch of human vision it could dimly be seen that there would come a time when the lion would lie down with the lamb, and this union would express the restoration of nature to its primitive perfection.

This distant vision lay in the future. But already in the early twelfth century secular masters, with comprehensive enthusiasm, began to let fall such *dicta* as these: 'The dignity of our mind is its capacity to know all things'; 'We who have been endowed by nature with genius must seek through philosophy the stature of our primeval nature'; 'In the solitude of this life the chief solace of our minds is the study of wisdom'; 'We have joined together science and letters, that from this marriage there may come forth a free nation of philosophers'.[13]

These insights into the relationship between human nature and the capacity to know the truth about the whole framework of nature were also expressed in verses which had a wide circulation:

Nobilitas hominis – naturae iura tenere;
Nobilitas hominis – nisi turpia nulla timere;

[13] These phrases are taken from the revised version of William of Conches's *Philosophia Mundi*, ed. C. Ottaviano, pp. 19–20 and from Thierry of Chartres, *Prologus in Eptatheucon*, ed. E. Jeauneau in *Medieval Studies*, 1954, xvi, 171–5. For the way in which the four elements are combined in the cells of the brain to make every kind of knowledge possible, see William of Conches, *Philosophia Mundi*, iv, 24, *De cerebro* (PL, 172, col. 95) and for the combined powers of *sensus, imaginatio, ratio, intellectus* by which man knows, see William of Conches's glosses on the *Timaeus*, ed. E. Jeauneau, 1965, pp. 100–2.

Nobilitas hominis – virtutum clara propago;
Nobilitas hominis – mens et deitatis imago.[14]

The nobility of Man shows itself in keeping the laws of nature,
in fearing nothing but disgrace,
in giving birth to glorious virtues,
and in having the mind and image of God.

These lines, in one form or another, became very popular in medieval collections of verse, but in their earliest setting they are closely related to the programme of the schools in eliciting the excellences of human nature by the study of the learning of the past.

It was a dazzling prospect, and for the first time ever we find scholars confident that nature could be fully understood, and thus in part redeemed from the curse that had afflicted the whole of nature as a result of Man's Fall. Although mankind at present still knew little, everything *could* be known, and already, as it seemed to those optimistic masters, more was known than had ever been known before. In a famous phrase of Bernard of Chartres, the one great master of Chartres in the first quarter of the twelfth century, they 'stood on the shoulders of the giants, and could see further than their great predecessors'; or, as Master Thierry's panegyrist wrote of him:

> His eagle eye could clearly see
> through each perplexed obscurity
> of all the seven liberal arts.
> He knew them well in all their parts,
> and made quite clear to everyone
> truths that for Plato dimly shone.[15]

It was surely a very bold idea that an early twelfth-century master of the schools could see further and more clearly than Plato, but there was nothing miraculous about it: it was the result of a greater mastery of the works of a longer past than Plato could have had. Consequently by 1150 Thierry was only

[14] For lists of the numerous MSS in which these verses are found, see Alfons Hilka and Otto Schumann, *Carmina Burana*, Heidelberg, 1930, vol. 1, i, p. 9; and Hans Walther, *Carmina Medii Aevi posterioris latini*, Göttingen, 1969, vol. 1, p. 608.

[15] A. Vernet, 'Une épitaphe inédite de Thierry de Chartres', *Recueil de travaux offert à C. Brunel*, 1955, ii, 660–70 – an extract which gives only a dim impression of perhaps the finest eulogy on any twelfth-century scholar.

one of several masters who either made this claim or had it made for them.

Of course in plain truth, the claim was fanciful, partly because twelfth-century scholars possessed much less of the learning of the ancient world than they imagined, and partly because even the whole of ancient knowledge itself was only a fragment of the knowable. Nevertheless the incentive to know more was there: twelfth-century masters could reasonably believe that they only had to continue to study the works of the past in greater detail and with meticulous attention to the meanings of words, the construction of sentences and arguments, and the relationship between these arguments and the nature of the universe and the divine plan for the universe, in order to reach a more complete understanding of the physical and spiritual universe than had ever been attained since the Fall. Never has an intellectual revolution set out with higher hopes. Indeed, when all imperfections have been taken into account, these masters can be seen to have initiated an intellectual revolution certainly as ambitious, and probably as productive, as any in European history.

Like most intellectual revolutions, that of the twelfth-century schools was based on developing and integrating methods of enquiry which had hitherto been applied only timidly or incompletely. The new masters applied themselves to the grammatical and logical analysis of the works of the ancient world as the foundation for understanding all statements in authoritative texts, for distinguishing between true and false interpretations, and for building up a systematic body of knowledge in all subjects. In pursuing this aim, they made a meticulously careful study of the Bible a normal part of the programme of the secular schools. By amalgamating the results of this programme, they developed a body of systematic theology, which covered the whole field of Christian doctrine and practice, and they associated with this body of doctrine a legal system which aimed at securing a consistency of behaviour, as well as of belief, throughout the whole of western Christendom.[16]

---

[16] See below, Part Two, chapters 7, 8, and 9 for an account of the stages by which, and influences under which, this was accomplished.

We must later ask whether there was not a fallacy at the root of this intensive study of fundamental texts in all subjects; but at the very least it provided a uniquely integrated view of the divinely created and rationally sustained universe, and associated with this intellectual effort the creation of an orderly routine of life for the Christian population of western Europe.

None of these features had been present in a more than fragmentary way in either the learning or practice of the period before 1100, and no comparable intellectual development took place in the neighbouring civilization of contemporary Islam, where, after a period of prodigious intellectual activity, the secular and sacred sciences split apart. This indeed was ultimately to happen in western Europe also. But in the period of the greatest success of the schools from the early twelfth until the early fourteenth century, the scholastic programme, with the hope it expressed of achieving a large-scale reversal of the debilitating intellectual consequences of the Fall, was responsible for the most deeply interesting scholastic works of the Middle Ages – comparable, as has often been pointed out, in the beauty, power and sublime logic of interlocking forces, to the great Gothic cathedrals of the same period.

III The Problem of the Natural Sciences

Of all the new features which the twelfth-century schools introduced into the total view of mankind's place in the universe, the most important was a greatly enhanced estimate of the dignity of human nature and of the whole natural order in the divine plan of Creation. At first sight it might seem that, in any plan of knowledge based on this principle, the natural sciences would play an important, and perhaps even a leading, role. But this is not necessarily the case. Although the primacy and intelligibility of nature was an essential foundation of the scholastic curriculum, the study of nature first began with the natural products of the human mind, and the natural sciences – at least as we know them – had at first no role in the scholastic programme and it was extraordinarily difficult to find a place for them.

There were two reasons for this. In the first place, a theoretical acknowledgement of the primacy of nature in human behaviour and understanding requires no detailed study of the natural sciences. Indeed, it is more easily entertained in the absence of detailed knowledge. What is important in fitting mankind into a universal scheme of Nature is the recognition that mankind was created as the link between the natural and supernatural orders, living in the natural order, but with the ability to understand also the divine plan of Creation and ultimately to enter the universe of eternal being. For this purpose, a detailed knowledge of botany, physiology, astronomy and physics was quite unnecessary – indeed detailed knowledge did more than anything else to destroy the beautiful vision of mankind's connecting role in the universe of being. In following the development of scientific studies of the medieval schools, therefore, it is important to understand their ambiguous position.

It is also important to recognize a further obstacle to the integration of the natural sciences with the other areas of knowledge in the scholastic programme. The Latin West in its most flourishing classical days from the first to the fourth centuries AD had never absorbed that part of the Greek tradition of learning which dealt in detail with the natural sciences. The Greek literary tradition had very early been assimilated: it had been the great boast of Horace that he had domesticated Greek metres in Latin verse; and it was Virgil's greatest claim to fame that he had given the Latin language an epic worthy to stand beside the *Iliad*. But the ancient Latin West was resistant to the scientific and even philosophical achievement of Greece. It was not until the late fourth century that Martianus Capella and Macrobius in their own works, and Calcidius in his partial translation and commentary on Plato's *Timaeus*, made the outline of Plato's cosmology accessible in Latin. But by then Ambrose, Augustine and Jerome were producing masterpieces of Christian theology, and thereafter it seemed to most Christian scholars that, with the Latin Bible of Jerome, the Grammar of Donatus, the linguistic teaching of Cicero, and the smattering of Platonic science available in Latin, the West had enough learning from the past for all essential purposes.

There was indeed still one conspicuous gap in the intellectual armoury of the West, which Boethius in the early sixth century was alert enough to recognize and attempt to fill: the logical works of Aristotle had not been made available in Latin. Boethius set about filling this gap, and by the time of his martyrdom in 524 he had succeeded in providing Latin versions of, and commentaries on, the elementary Aristotelian logical works. These translations and commentaries long lay neglected and relatively unknown, but they were brought to light in the Latin West by the labours of scholars in the late tenth and eleventh centuries. So, by the mid-eleventh century, the main linguistic, grammatical, logical and rhetorical parts of the Greco-Roman inheritance together with the greater part of Plato's *Timaeus* were available in Latin and ready for use in the schools when western Europe began its rise to political and economic prosperity.

One great gap, however, still remained: that part of the Greek inheritance which dealt with the natural sciences of biology, medicine, geometry, and astronomical observation with its attendant science of astrology, had never found a place in Latin literature, and it might have seemed that this part of ancient scholarship was lost for ever.

But by a strange split in the transmission of Greek thought, the scientific learning which the Latin West had failed to assimilate was transmitted in another direction to the Muslim invaders of the eastern and southern areas of the Greco-Latin world.[17] Consequently, by the eleventh century, in areas as far separated as Persia and Muslim Spain, the scientific part of the ancient legacy which the Latin West had never assimilated had been eagerly studied in Islam during the centuries when western Europe was in a state of turmoil. But then came the moment when, in the years from about 1075 to 1125, western Christendom began to reoccupy Spain, Sicily, southern Italy and the area of western Crusading activity in the eastern Mediterranean, and western scholars quickly found in these former Islamic areas the scientific works of Greek learning which had never been known in the West. They found also scholars capable of interpreting them. In this way a large part of the scientific thought of the Greeks, not

[17] For a masterly outline of the split in the transmission of Greek learning to the Latin and Muslim areas of the Mediterranean world, see R. Walzer, 'L'éveil de la philosophie islamique', *Revue des études islamiques*, Paris, vol. xxxviii, i–ii, 1970.

all at once, but piecemeal and haphazardly, became widely known in western Europe as itinerant scholars discovered, translated and brought this new material to the notice of western scholars.

On the surface it might seem that, with the emphasis on *nature* in scholastic thought, the new texts on the natural sciences would at once have taken a foremost place in the scholastic scheme of human knowledge. But there were several reasons why this did not happen. In the first place, before these new works had penetrated into the West in any bulk, the scholastic programme with its emphasis on texts on grammar, logic, rhetoric and theology, rather than on those areas of knowledge concerned with the physical universe, had become well established, and could not easily or profitably be adapted to admit the new material.

The reason for this difficulty is quite simple. The established texts all required – and only required – the meticulous study of their words and the systemization of their doctrines to make them fully intelligible, and lecture rooms were the ideal place for studying them. But, in the physical sciences, a commentary and elucidation of the texts had to be sought by observing afresh such phenomena as the movements of the stars.

None of this work could be done inside the class-room. The texts were guides, but the measurements and observations which they recorded required to be checked and supplemented, step by step, by direct observation of the natural events that they described. Consequently the elaboration of the texts on the natural sciences of medicine, astronomy, astrology, physiology, and optics – all subjects on which important new texts were becoming increasingly available during the century after about 1120 – was best carried on by scholars working alone on the fringes of royal or aristocratic courts, or in monasteries or parsonages where individual scholars had freedom for observations and were not required to teach.

The consequence of this state of affairs was that, whereas the greatest concentrations of schools produced the best results in grammar and logic, and in theological and legal studies, lonely scholars were best able to make use of new material in the physical sciences. Indeed, several of the discoverers, translators, and elaborators of the new texts are known to have deliberately turned their backs on the schools in order to go in search of new knowledge, and – instead of returning to the schools with their new materials – they turned rather to the courts of magnates, if their studies were medical or astronomical and astrological, or to monasteries if their studies were calendarial.

The experts on these subjects were not interested in integrating their new material with the learning of the schools; and, even if they had wished, the difficulties of integrating the new knowledge with the old were very great indeed. So throughout the twelfth century the growth of knowledge of the natural sciences went on among individual explorers, translators, astrologers, experts on the calendar, and physicians, on the frontiers of western Europe, and in courts, monasteries, and towns with mixed populations, quite independent of the growth in systematic scholastic knowledge. The two groups of scholars lived in different worlds and served different purposes. When the masters of the schools left their schools to go into the world, they became immersed in the work of law courts, in lay and ecclesiastical administration, in organized government, in instructing people from the pulpit. By contrast, the natural scientists sought employers for whom they could cast horoscopes, prophesy future events, provide medicines, and perhaps employ new methods of arithmetical calculation. The great schools were simply not the right place for these operations.[18]

How and whether the two groups of scholars – those in the schools and those on the frontiers of knowledge and of Christendom – could ever be amalgamated was a problem which the twelfth century left unsolved. Very great efforts were made in the thirteenth century to amalgamate the two great branches of knowledge and this effort will require more detailed study in the next volume of this work. But it may be said at once that the most conspicuous result of the amalgamation was to add to the growing burden of unresolved problems.

[18] I have discussed more fully the reasons for, and consequences of, this split between the natural and scholastic sciences in the twelfth century in Southern, 1992, where bibliographical references will be found.

IV Summits of Success

To return to the schools: their programme was based on two convictions: first, that the human intellect was created capable of understanding both the purpose of God in the Creation and the structure of the whole created order; and, second, that – even after the Fall – by the special revelation of God and by the efforts of inspired and able scholars, the main outlines of the structure and development of the universe had become accessible to human minds. By a further extension of this general intelligibility, it was also believed that the means that God had used to redeem mankind by the Incarnation and sacrifice of Christ on the Cross were also capable of being understood.

St Anselm had been the first, in his *Cur Deus Homo*, to raise explicitly, as a problem capable of a strictly rational solution, the question implied in the title of this great work. But, though in some ways this work may be thought of as announcing the new age of scholastic enquiry, both its intention and its method are very different from those of later scholastic enquiry. In the first place the title does not ask a question; it simply introduces a discussion demonstrating the absolute powerlessness of mankind to contribute to human redemption, and it portrays God throwing His last reserve in the Person of His Son into a struggle against evil: a struggle that would otherwise have been lost, with the eternal frustration of the whole divine plan for the universe. Then also, there is nothing in the work at all suggestive of the value of *human* resources, except in its clarity and beauty of exposition.

Anselm argued that the Incarnation was strictly and logically necessary because man had sinned beyond the possibility of redemption by any other means than by a new divine intervention in human affairs, comparable to a new act of Creation. In Anselm's view, God became Man not because there was anything in human nature itself intrinsically worth saving, but because the total ruin of mankind would have frustrated the divine aim in the Creation. God's intervention in history by the birth of the Son of God was, therefore, by no means illustrative of the innate dignity of Man. It was a new initiative undertaken as the only possible way of carrying the divine plan

40

of Creation to its pre-ordained end after human nature in the persons of its first parents had shown itself inadequate to the task assigned to it. To resolve this enigma God was in a sense reduced to a subterfuge: since justice required that the price for the forgiveness of human sin should be paid by Man, and since mankind could not, and only God could, produce the price which was required, it was necessary for God to become Man and to provide the resources which were lacking. That is the Anselmian solution.

But, if we go on to about 1230, we find Robert Grosseteste writing on the Creation. He was a fairly recent recruit to theology having spent the greater part of his adult life in scientific studies, and he viewed the theological scene in the light of the new twelfth-century assessment of the splendour of nature. He was engaged on the congenial task of writing about the Six Days of Creation, and he ventured to give a new turn to the doctrine of the Incarnation in the light of God's creative purpose as seen by a scholar with an extensive view of natural phenomena. He had studied Anselm's work with care, and in the light of God's creative purpose he saw a new way through the whole problem. In his view, God had from the beginning envisaged the Incarnation as the coping stone of Nature, expressing in its ultimate form the dignity of the created universe. This could only be fully expressed by God Himself assuming the highest nature in the created universe, and thus providing an indissoluble link between the Creator and the created orders of being.[19]

For Grosseteste, therefore, the Incarnation would have happened even if mankind had preserved the original innocence that properly belonged to the human race. But it would have happened earlier. In its essential role it was the final act of Creation,

[19]   For Grosseteste's doctrine of the Incarnation, see its first outline in his *Hexaemeron*, ed. Richard C. Dales, London, 1982, p. 276, summed up in the sentence, *Et ita in Christo, Deo et Homine, sunt omnia recollecta et commodata ad unitatem; nec esset ista consummatio in rerum naturis nisi Deus esset homo.* ('And so in Christ, who is both God and Man, all things are brought together in unity; nor would this consummation of the natural order have been achieved unless God had become man.') This theme is elaborated at much greater length in Grosseteste's *De Cessatione Legalium*, ed. Richard C. Dales and Edward B. King, London, 1986, pp. 118–55 – pages which have some claim to contain the most original single theological argument of their time. For a discussion of the argument, see D. J. Ungar, in *Franciscan Studies*, 16, 1956, 1–36.

making both Mankind and Nature complete, and binding the whole created universe together in union with God.

Whether Anselm's or Grosseteste's account is the better theology I do not know. But Anselm's is pre-scholastic in its depreciation of human powers. Grosseteste's – incipiently at least – is post-scholastic in going beyond the agreed harmony of the schools. Grosseteste's view is certainly inspired by the vision of the beauty and dignity of the natural order which the schools had developed over the previous hundred years, and which had been given a new substance by the discovery and study of new scientific texts outside the schools. There is a sense in which Grosseteste's account of the Incarnation was the climax of the persistent tendency of the scholastic centuries to make man appear more rational, the divine ordering of the universe more open to human inspection, and the whole complex of Man, nature and God more fully intelligible, than the bitter experience of either the earlier or later centuries of the Middle Ages made at all likely.

If we look on the process of scholastic development between the late eleventh and mid-thirteenth centuries simply as an effort to comprehend rationally the structure of the universe to the furthest possible extent, and (in the striking image of William of Conches) to demonstrate the dignity of the human mind by showing that it can know all things, we can see Grosseteste's theory as the culmination of two centuries of scholastic effort and as one of the most ambitious affirmations of the scope of human knowledge and potentiality ever made.

At a more systematic level, in covering the whole ground of knowledge soberly and with calm assurance, the two *Summae* of Thomas Aquinas mark the highest point of scholastic humanism. A sympathetic reader of either of these works may be tempted to say: 'Of course there are things man cannot yet understand, and all men but Christ are sinners, but how wonderfully the ravages of sin have been restored by the combination of reason and Revelation, and how natural, how rational are the steps to salvation.' The natural faculties are no longer in ruins. In collaboration with God's redemptive activity, reason and nature have come into their own.

The work of Thomas Aquinas is full of illustrations of the benign congruity between reason, nature and faith. His judgements give human nature its full due. He reversed the ancient opinion that the body is the ruined habitation of the soul, and held with Aristotle that it is the embodiment in this life of the soul's being. Man indeed, as he now is, needs supernatural grace, but his final Redemption can be seen as the completion of the perfection which was his by nature at the Creation. The dignity of human nature is not simply a poetic vision as it had been in the work of Bernard Silvestris, quoted above: it has become a central truth of both philosophy and theology.

Thomas Aquinas and Dante are the two greatest interpreters of the scholastic tradition in which human beings are given a fully intelligible place in a universe in which order has been extracted from disorder. But, of course, neither they nor any other scholastic thinker intended to dispense with the need for supernatural grace. Even Grosseteste's argument, which envisages the incarnation of the second Person of the Trinity as the coping stone of the whole natural universe, retains the essential distinction between the *eternal* essences of the heavens and the *everlasting* existence of perfected human souls, and of course he says nothing to diminish mankind's need for Redemption through the offering of Christ on the Cross. And, on the other hand, the more sober system of Thomas Aquinas envisages that, even in the fallen world as it now is, the supernatural can be understood at least in its essential outline by human reasoning.

This interpenetration of natural and supernatural was the culmination of scholastic humanism. Its noblest expression can be found in the concluding pages of Dante's *De Monarchia*:

Man is a mean between the corruptible and the incorruptible. Just as every mean partakes of both extremes, so Man has a dual nature. And since every nature is ordained for a definite end, it follows that Man has two ends: on the one hand the happiness of this life, and on the other, the happiness of eternal life. The former consists in the exercise of Man's human power and is symbolized by the terrestrial paradise which we attain through the teachings of philosophy and the practice of the moral and intellectual virtues. The latter consists in

43

the enjoyment of the vision of God, to which Man cannot attain except by God's help.[20]

This statement allows the fullest expansion within their own spheres to both the supernatural and the natural orders. In the natural order, reason rules and makes the universe intelligible; and reason also certifies the human need to seek eternal satisfaction in the realm beyond reason. Reason, therefore, testifies both to the autonomy of nature and to the necessity for that which is above nature. This is the humanism of the medieval schools. It is as far removed from the élitism of Renaissance humanism as it is from the godlessness of modern secular humanism; but whether we consider its inherent grandeur or its influence on the future, it has a good claim to be considered the most important kind of humanism Europe has ever produced.

This was the essential contribution of scholastic thought to the future: it depicted the role of mankind in a large and systematic way as the uniquely endowed, conscious and co-operating link between the created universe in space and time, and the divine intelligence in eternity. The ground of this role for mankind in the realm of the divine Creation lay in Man's ability to understand the nature and purposes of God, to live in conscious obedience to the will of God, and thus to achieve, despite the impediment of Original Sin, a state of understanding approximating to the full nobility of which the natural order is capable.

In achieving this understanding, human beings were regaining their primordial role of bringing all parts of the created universe into harmony with the divine will. This role was to be accomplished at three levels: first, in understanding the created universe through the study of the liberal arts; second, in elaborating and clarifying the doctrinal system of the Church and developing a corresponding system of individual behaviour; and third, in regulating the social life of the Christian community in conformity with ecclesiastical doctrine and natural law. Much will be said

---

[20] Dante, *De Monarchia*, iii, c. 16. A convenient edition of the original text is in *Le opere di Dante*, ed. E. Moore and P. Toynbee, 5th edn, Oxford, 1963. My paraphrase reproduces only the main outline of Dante's argument.

in what follows about the scholastic efforts in achieving the first two of these aims. But the third proved to be beyond the range of successful enquiry, and a few words may suffice to show the very limited extent to which scholastic thought could succeed in this area.

V THE REGULATION OF SOCIAL LIFE

One great obstacle to progress in the practical sciences was that authoritative statements about them inherited from earlier centuries were very defective. Early Christian writers had dealt with social and economic areas of activity in a very summary and dismissive way: their counsel had been mainly to renounce the aims of the world or to contract them to the very minimum necessary for survival. This solution, notionally at least, had been acceptable in the embattled condition of life in Europe in the early Middle Ages. But it was scarcely compatible with the expanding energies of the twelfth and thirteenth centuries and the new acceptance of the world of nature and human effort. From this acceptance there arose the problem of devising rules of behaviour which would satisfy the requirements of religion without excluding the burgeoning life of the time.

This was a task of immense difficulty and it was never undertaken with the same completeness or systematic oversight that characterized the elaboration of strictly theological questions. One reason for this is that practical life and the formation of new social entities are the result of uncontrollable and largely unseen developments which can only imperfectly be comprehended. It must therefore suffice here simply to indicate the direction in which thought about these subjects moved during the twelfth and thirteenth centuries, and to outline the difficulties of finding satisfactory answers on a few important issues: private property, trade and war.

1 Property

Up to the twelfth century there was a very meagre theory of

ownership derived from the Bible and the Fathers. The theory of ideal communism was set out in the earliest organization of resources among believers: 'No one said that anything he possessed was his own, but they had all things in common.' From this, early biblical commentators concluded that all private property had the nature of sin, and that private property would not exist in a perfect state. When St Benedict included in his monastic Rule the provision that all things were to be held in common, he was expressing not just a rule for a religious society, but an ideal for all society, and this was still the ideal in Gratian's compilation of canon law in about 1140.[21]

But at this point the lawyers got to work on Gratian's texts, and they began to make distinctions. They discovered that common *use* did not exclude private *ownership*; indeed, that common use was not a law of nature, but only a last resort in an emergency; consequently, in ordinary circumstances private ownership, despite its dangers of possessive pride, had the social virtue of ensuring stability and orderly administration. These distinctions of course are not in the biblical text, but they were not contradicted by it, and they could be seen as legitimate explanations of primitive doctrine in a world which was becoming increasingly complicated and commercial. Consequently, the biblical precepts which discouraged private ownership began to wear very thin indeed.[22]

All that was needed to complete the process of demolishing the early ideal of Christian communism was the arrival in the West, in the mid-thirteenth century, of Aristotle's *Ethics* and *Politics*. These two works cleared private property in principle of the taint of sin, however deplorable the motives of individuals might be. Consequently the Aristotelian view of property began to prevail over the primitive communism of the early Church, which came to appear as the exceptional state, while private property, far from being naturally bad and therefore

21 *Acts*, 2.44; 4.32; *Regula S. Benedicti*, c. 33. For Gratian's selection of texts on private property, all stressing the original state of common possession, see his *Decretum*, Dist. 1, c. 7; Dist. 8, c. 1; Dist. 47, c. 8; C. 12, q. 1, c. 2; and for their general setting, see below, chapter 9.
22 The fullest statement of Thomas Aquinas in favour of private property is in *Summa Theologiae*, 2, 2, q. 66, art. 1, 2. In general Aquinas here follows Aristotle, *Politics*, ii, 5, 8.

permissible only within very narrow limits, came to be seen as naturally good, generally necessary for the good life, and only to be condemned in special cases when the possession of private property came into conflict with religious vows.

Gathering all these strands together, Thomas Aquinas produced a comprehensive defence of private property. He elaborated its natural necessity and virtues, defined the legitimate motives for seeking temporal gain, and drew the boundaries of legitimate appropriation. The ancient ideal of Christian communism was reduced to a counsel, literally, of despair; 'he who suffers from extreme need can take what he needs from another's goods if no one will give to him'.[23]

This development is an example of a general tendency to give priority to nature, and to explain the custom of the early Church, not as an ideal which had been gradually worn away by the avarice of later centuries, but as a temporary expedient adopted in exceptional circumstances. In the new system, as it was progressively defined in the schools from the early twelfth century onwards, nature formed the base, reason provided the system, and the Bible reported an exceptional deviation (having all things in common) which was now obligatory only for those members of religious orders who had adopted it with ecclesiastical sanction.

The more nature was studied, the more extensive the claims of the natural order became, for they were capable of endless elaboration. There were those who fought this worldly trend and continued to preach the stark ideal of a property-less perfection. But they were swimming against the tide. The last defenders of this social conservatism were found in the Franciscan Order, and they were condemned in 1323 by Pope John XXII, who declared that the doctrine of the complete poverty of Christ and his disciples was heretical – a conclusion which would have seemed incomprehensible two hundred years earlier.[24]

[23] Thomas Aquinas, *Summa Theologiae*, 2, 2, q. 66, art. 7, where (after quoting Gratian's quotation from St Ambrose in Dist. 47, c. 8) he goes on to declare that he who suffers from extreme need can lawfully take what he needs for sustaining his own life or that of another.

[24] For John XXII's *Cum inter nonnullos* of 12 Nov. 1323, with an account of the controversy that led to it, see John Moorman, *A History of the Franciscan Order from its Origins to 1517*, Oxford, 1968, pp. 307–17.

This was the end of the long road from the austerities of the persecuted primitive Church to the acceptance of the natural man with his urge for ownership. Henceforward it was not ownership which needed to be justified, but restrictions on ownership. This was a matter for the law courts rather than the schools, and thereafter it is in their records rather than in those of the schools that debates about restrictions on the use of property are to be found.

2 Trade

A similar process can be observed with regard to trade. Lawyers of the mid-twelfth century were still quoting the old biblical texts and interpretations to the effect that trade is no fit occupation for a Christian, that it is wrong to buy an article hoping to sell it unchanged at a higher price, that it is wrong to vary the price according to the demand, and that profit from such practices is sinful.[25]

Once again the lawyers got to work. They moved more slowly here than in the case of property, partly because merchants were socially unpopular, and partly because Aristotle agreed with the biblical commentators in thinking trade inconsistent with virtue.[26] But even here the lawyers moved in the end. They set about determining the elements of a just price, and in so doing they – quite unwittingly – laid the foundations of the science of economics. They examined the motive of profit, and determined the extent to which it was morally justified. They analysed interest, and distinguished sinful usury from risk-bearing investment. They discussed the place of merchants in

---

[25] For the early doctrine that he who buys not for his own use but to sell more dearly is guilty of *turpe lucrum*, see Charlemagne's capitulary of 806 (*MGH*, LL, i, 123). This position is maintained in the collections of Burchard and Ivo. Gratian's main section on Trade (Dist. lxxxviii) is concerned only with the prohibition of trading by clergy, but the ignobility of trading is emphasized in several of his authorities and in Gratian C. xiv, q. 4, c. 9, and it still had a very long history ahead of it. Indeed as late as 1930 no Oxford graduate went willingly 'into trade' except in pursuit of a political objective or to inherit a grand old firm.

[26] Aristotle, *Politics*, vi, 4 (1319A; 1328B) arguing that there is no room for moral excellence in traders; therefore, trade is by its nature ignoble and inimicable to virtue.

society, and gave them a grudging, but still distinct, recognition as necessary instruments of social well-being.[27]

Here as elsewhere Aristotle was at once a stimulus and a barrier. He was a stimulus in encouraging the formulation of a much more elaborate general theory of social classes than the old classification of *aratores, oratores, bellatores* of earlier centuries. But he was a barrier in the support which he gave to the anti-commercial prejudices of an aristocratic and agrarian society. In theory, the concept of the legitimacy of that which is natural brought a new freedom into social life; but in practice it was a freedom which favoured those in possession, and especially those who possessed land. Just as no thief escaped the gallows by pleading the apostolic privilege of the common purse, so the 'just price' was more effective in keeping the price of

---

[27] The beginnings of greater refinement in legislation on the subject may be observed in Alexander III's rule that, if something can be shown to have been sold for less than half of its value, the buyer must either make up the difference or renounce his purchase. Similarly Innocent III, in 1203, ordered a buyer to restore houses and olive groves to the heir of the seller (now dead), and repeated the principle of Pope Alexander III. For these texts, see Gregory IX, *Decretales*, III, *Titulus* xvii, *De Emptione et Venditione* (a title taken from Roman Law *Instit.*, iii, 24.)

See also Thomas Aquinas, *Summa Theologiae*, 2, 2, q. 77, art. 1, 2, 3 for discussion of the question of whether it is legitimate to sell something for more than it is worth. The conclusion is: the seller may add something to the price in respect of special damage he receives in selling; but he may not add anything for the special benefit the buyer receives in buying. (That is to say: the value of an object offered for sale is properly to be determined only by the value to the seller, and not by the need of the buyer.) This would have been an important principle, especially in times of famine, but of course it was then wholly inoperative. The only concession permitted by Aquinas in this regard was that the *buyer* may properly take into account the special value to the *seller* and *voluntarily* add something to the price. As a further refinement, Article 2 of Aquinas's discussion enquires whether a defect in the goods renders the sale illicit. The answer is, Yes, if the defect was known to the seller and concealed; but No, if unknown to seller, who should nevertheless pay compensation. Slightly later Duns Scotus *In IV Sent.*, dist 15, q. 2 (vol. ix, pp. 185–6), discusses the scope for variations in prices in various circumstances.

On these points, see R. de Roover, 'The concept of the just price', *J. of Econ. Hist.*, xviii, 1958. It will be noticed that, in most of these cases and discussions, the emphasis is on attempting to assess value on the basis of work done and privations suffered by the seller. As we might expect, the discussions are extremely careful, but for their enforcement the conclusions would all have required agents with adequate power, and this would have required a vast increase in the already oppressive number of officials. Indeed there is a case for saying that the whole scholastic ideal of government broke down because of the growing cost of administration as western Europe moved into a situation of generally declining wealth.

labour down after the Plague than in restricting the rising price of corn after a drought. This was part of the price of humanism: like nature, it works best for those who are healthy and strong.

3 War

A similar development took place in thinking about war. The Bible was indeed a somewhat ambiguous guide on this subject, but there could be no doubt about the direction in which it pointed: 'he who takes the sword shall perish by the sword', 'thou shalt not kill'. The thought of the early Middle Ages sought to follow these pointers. The only war which was thoroughly approved was the holy war against invading pagans. To this just cause of war it was permissible to add bloodshed in defence of the church, of widows and orphans, or of one's own life. Legitimate violence long continued to be narrowly drawn within these limits. On the eve of the scholastic age, even in a cause so well authenticated by papal approval as the Norman Conquest of England, the bishops of the Norman conquerors themselves – not those of the conquered English – laid down a severe code of penances for the victors to atone for the blood which had been shed in the great battle of Hastings, and these penances scarcely differed from those imposed for acts of plain murder.[28]

We do not find such startling severity at any later date, but the change to an easy admission of justifiable war between Christian rulers was not rapid. Seventy years after the battle of Hastings, Gratian, the father of medieval canon law, still showed a strong inclination to restrict legitimate warfare within very narrow limits: the only war that he explicitly approved was war against heretics, waged by episcopal authority under papal direction.[29]

Gratian's collection of texts said nothing about the wars of

[28] For the detailed penances imposed on the Norman fighters at the Battle of Hastings, see *Councils and Synods with other documents relating to the English Church*, ed. C. R. Cheney, Dorothy Whitelock and Martin Brett, vol. I, pt. 2, 1066–1204, Oxford, 1981, pp. 581–4.
[29] Despite its limited range, the long series of questions on War in Gratian's *Decretum*, C. xxiii, cols. 889–965, provides the first detailed attempt to deal with the legal aspects of War in medieval literature.

secular rulers in defence of what they believed to be their legitimate rights. Yet we can see a hint of the distinctions which were to transform the discussion of all social questions in Gratian's personal *dictum* in which he stated that such biblical precepts as that about turning the other cheek were to be fulfilled in the heart, and not necessarily in the body.[30] Once this distinction was drawn, the way was open for further distinctions, such as that of Thomas Aquinas, who said that a subject who takes the sword at the command of his prince does not himself *take* the sword: he only *uses* the sword which has been committed to him by his prince. And even the prince does not *take* the sword, for it has been committed to him by God. Therefore neither the prince nor the subject acting at his command is guilty of 'taking' the sword, and neither will be subject to the threat of perishing by the sword as a result having 'taken' it.[31]

It is easy to see how such an argument virtually eliminated the practical application of the biblical text. Consequently, although Aquinas's doctrine of the just war was very carefully defined, it left decisions of war or peace wide open to the judgement of secular rulers, unless they directly impinged on the properties or rights of the Church.

In all three of these areas, therefore, the new definitions allowed much more liberty for the exercise of human judgement in defence of worldly possessions than had been allowed in pre-scholastic religious thought. And since the main driving force in the exercise of this freedom was likely to be the self-interest of the strong, it is clear that the increased scope for human judgement was unlikely to make the world a better place for the weak.

VI The Loss of Hope

Anyone who compares the state of human understanding of man,

---

[30] Gratian's *Dictum*, C. xiv, q. 1, c. 1, sums up his position: *Illud vero evangelii, 'Si quis abstulerit tibi tunicam etc.', non precipientis est sed exhortantis.* And he later adds: *'Sic et cetera accipies'.*

[31] See *Summa Theologiae*, 2, 2, q. 40, art. 1; supplemented by 2, 2, q. 64, art. 3.

nature and God in western Europe in the early eleventh century with these aspects of human knowledge and experience three hundred years later must conclude that – however limited in its social doctrines – the systematic understanding of the nature of a divinely created and divinely directed universe, as well as of the natural processes of the universe, had been immensely enlarged in the intervening period. Why then did the intellectual procedures which had been developed during these centuries, and which were largely responsible for the results I have briefly outlined, come to seem in retrospect so hostile to humanistic values?

This is a question of great complexity, but there is one external cause of scholastic disintegration, which can be mentioned without further ado. Just as scholastic development was associated with the rapid increase in the wealth and population of western Europe from the late eleventh to the late thirteenth centuries, so the disintegration of scholastic thought, which began to be evident in the early years of the fourteenth century, was associated with a long continuing series of disasters – years of drought succeeded by recurrent outbursts of plague, catastrophic decline in rural population and prosperity, devastating wars, and a renewal of external threats after two centuries of expansion. One after another, beginning with years of scarcity and declining population, calamities piled up throughout the fourteenth century. By 1320 Europe had entered a period in which the growth which had buoyed up the scholastic efforts of the previous two centuries was abruptly reversed. The forward movement in settlement and expansion, which had done much both to bring to light the sources of ancient scientific and political thought and to enlarge the uses of scholastic thought in the work of government, came to an end. The disorder, depopulation and agrarian decline in all parts of western Europe spread a general sense of malignancy in the universe inconsistent with the whole impetus of scholastic thought.

Until these symptoms of the breakdown of orderly development began to appear, a general expectation of growing prosperity and order had prevailed. It had seemed reasonable to believe that the increasing knowledge about the universe, both in its supernatural and natural aspects, could be fitted into one

grand universal plan, that the papal system of universal authority would in time bring universal peace to Christendom, that
the Greek church would come into line with the Latin, that
the tide of Islam would definitively be rolled back, that the
pagan world beyond the furthest limits of Islam would be as
accessible to Christianity as the Germanic peoples had been in
the fifth and sixth centuries. Then, further, the long period of
European growth from the eleventh to the fourteenth centuries
had encouraged the view that God's nature and plan for the
world, as elaborated and systematized in the schools, would
prove to be acceptable, not only for those for whom it had
primarily been elaborated, but also for the whole world. As late
as 1270, all these expectations seemed well within the bounds
of the possible. Then quite suddenly the whole scene changed.
Western Christian expansion into Asia received a sharp setback,
from which it never recovered. In practical terms, this was signalized by the loss of Acre, the main western stronghold in
the Holy Land, in 1291. Meanwhile, intellectually, the systematic results already achieved were coming under attack from
within. Consequently political contraction and increasing intellectual fragmentation set in, and gradually it seemed that not
only western Europe, but the universe itself, might prove to be
increasingly chaotic.

It does not need an overall disaster to change the intellectual
outlook of a civilized society. The combined effects of the end of
European expansion – the drying up of new sources of ancient
systematic learning, a persistent series of setbacks, the depressing
sense that nothing was going well – brought an end to the
conditions which had inspired the humanistic programme of the
schools.

Scholastic humanism had been inspired by the vision of systematic knowledge accompanied by the perfecting and extension of an organized Christian society. For its continuance there
had to be a prospect of on-going prosperity. When this prospect disappeared there emerged a new kind of humanism which
was concerned, not with exploring an ever-growing area of systematic intelligibility and of general well-being, but with the
perfecting of individual sensibility among a social élite. Petrarch,
who above all stood for this new kind of humanism in the

mid-fourteenth century, looked back with disillusionment at the achievements of the last two centuries. The kind of intellectual and practical order at which theologians, lawyers and administrators had aimed, and that had seemed only fifty years earlier to be within reach, suddenly appeared quite unattainable:

> Turn where you will, there is no place without its tyrant; and where there is no tyrant, the people themselves supply the deficiency. When you escape the One, you fall into the hands of the Many. If you can show me a place ruled by a just and mild king, I will take myself there with all my baggage ... I will go to India or Persia or the furthest limits of the Garamantes to find such a place and such a king. But it is useless to search for what cannot be found. Thanks to our age, which has levelled all things, the labour is unnecessary.[32]

The hopes of the past had to be buried. But such hopes are never buried with simple quiet resignation: they have to be buried with scorn and derision, and a certain sense of betrayal. Hence the change of mood which set in during the middle years of the fourteenth century gradually hardened during the next two centuries into a fixed belief that the clerical schools of what came contemptuously to be envisaged as a trough between two periods of civilization – and therefore dismissively called the Middle Ages – with their formalized procedures and legalistic distinctions, were not simply the agents of a great failure, but the promoters of a great deception.

All systems of thought have some pervasive weakness built into their structure, and the weakness is all the more ineradicable when it forms in some sense the strength of the system. The characteristic strength of medieval scholastic thought was its elaboration of the authoritative statements of the past. These were the bricks from which the system was formed; they provided the material for argument and the foundations for the most daring conclusions. But they also defined limits beyond which the system could not develop.

This is not a phenomenon peculiar to medieval thought, nor

[32] Petrarch, *Invectiva contra quendam magni status hominem sed nullius scientie vel virtutis*, ed. P. G. Ricci, 1949, p. 15.

to scholastic processes of argument. It is a universal phenom-enon in the development of every system. But the scholastic system came to appear peculiarly deceptive when the ancient sources of learning, which had seemed so reliable that they could be accepted as statements of unvarying truth, were discovered to be defective in large areas of the knowledge – especially in geography, cosmology, politics, even systematic theology – to which they had seemed to provide the key.

The disillusionment was particularly severe when it was also discovered that the qualities which were coming to be seen as the real virtues of ancient literature – not its information but its literary beauties and its understanding of human nature – had been neglected by the pedants (as they came to appear) of the schools. With this discovery there also came the recognition that the products of the twelfth and thirteenth-century schools were not beautiful, but were in fact repulsive to the eye as well as to the understanding. Unlike some 'outworn' systems which have left monuments of such beauty that even their critics are reluctant to raise a hand against them, the products of the medieval schools were certainly not pleasing either to the eye or to the ear. No books have ever been written whose outward appearance gives less invitation to study than the manuscripts of the medieval schools; their illegible script, crabbed abbrevia-tions, and margins filled with comments even less intelligible than the text, repel curiosity. When the details were so repellent, it was difficult to think that the ends which they served could be anything but barbarous and inhuman. And closer inspection revealed no beauty of style or vivacity of wit to encourage inves-tigation. The beauty of scholastic thought lies entirely in the grandeur of the whole enterprise and in the careful elaboration of details to form a systematic body of doctrine.

When the leaders of opinion lost confidence in the power of the scholastic system of thought to achieve the promised ends, which had sustained the concentrated efforts of successive generations of scholars throughout the period from about 1070 to about 1320, the whole effort began to seem increasingly repellent and wasteful, and it has required a hundred years of dedicated scholarship from the late nineteenth to the late twen-tieth century to dispel (even now without general agreement) the almost universal condemnation of scholasticism which prevailed from the seventeenth to the late nineteenth centuries.

Hence, when the hope of universal order faded in the early fourteenth century, the way was open for the cultivation of sensibility and personal virtue, and the nostalgic vision of an ancient Utopia revealed in classical literature. Instead of the confident and progressive scholastic humanism of the central Middle Ages, the new humanism retreated into the individual, and consequently into the aristocracy of privileged individuals and the constellation of scholars and artists whom they supported. The aristocracy replaced the clergy as the guardians of culture; and literature and observation replaced systematic theology and science. The refinement of a cultivated few rather than the order of a universal system, sensibility rather than the restoration of the primeval God-given gift of universal knowledge, came to be regarded as the marks of humanism. When this happened, the systematic thought of the schools of the twelfth and thirteenth centuries came to be regarded as symptomatic of a barbarous and nit-picking turning away from the real world.

Nothing could be further from the truth than this misconception, but the error was difficult to unmask because the works of the medieval schools required a training in methods of argument which by the end of the seventeenth century had almost everywhere been abandoned. As for the manuscripts themselves with all their abbreviations and forgotten technicalities, they too required a familiarity with long forgotten procedures, and their appearance alone might seem sufficient to prove that they were the works of grovelling pedants. It is only during the last hundred years that the devoted labours of scholars – very largely members of religious orders – have brought to light, edited and made accessible to all medieval historians a substantial fragment of the scholastic products of the twelfth and thirteenth centuries. The chapters which follow will scarcely do more than skim the surface of this learned literature in attempting, not so much to expound the scholastic thoughts of the great period of the medieval schools, as to understand the circumstances and opportunities which provoked this system of thought, and the aims and attitudes which it expressed.

But, before setting out, it will help to define the issues if I re-elaborate some *invidiosi veri* about a concept of twelfth-century humanism which, despite its allurements, points in quite the wrong direction for those who wish to understand the nature and results of the humanism of the schools of the twelfth and thirteenth centuries.

2

Chartrian Humanism: a Romantic Misconception

I INTRODUCTION

The scholastic programme which emerged from the efforts of the masters of the first half of the twelfth century was an attempt to create a single complete and unified field of knowledge extending from the sciences of the mind (grammar, logic and rhetoric), through the sciences of the external natural world (arithmetic, astronomy, geometry and music), to the new sciences of systematic theology and canon law. In its totality, therefore, this programme covered the whole area of the natural world and its relationship with the supernatural universe, and defined the laws of the Christian community of western Europe in the light of this relationship.

Of course it was not possible, and it would be absurd to suppose, that all students studied all these subjects, or that they studied them with the same aims. But increasingly, from the mid-twelfth century onwards, scholars of superior genius, though they necessarily started with the sciences of the mind as codified in the doctrines of grammar and logic, found themselves drawn either to the natural sciences – especially medicine, astronomy and astrology – or to the divinely inspired sciences of theology or canon law in one form or another.

No doubt, within this general framework of scholastic intellectual endeavour we must expect to find many variants, but broadly speaking (as we shall see in chapters 6 and 9) there were compelling reasons why the Parisian schools should have come to dominate the combined area of the Arts subjects and of Theology only a few years before the schools of Bologna took up a leading position in the combination of Arts with Roman and Canon Law. The developments in these areas of knowledge are the great achievements of medieval scholastic learning, and by about 1160, the groups of schools situated in Paris and Bologna had succeeded, far more than all others put together, in laying the foundations of a transformation in the intellectual structure and in the organized practical life of western Europe. They depended for their success in this enterprise on the convergence of three distinct processes: first, on the continuing growth in prosperity and population of western Europe; second, on the continuing trust in the reliability of the knowledge amassed by ancient scholars; and finally on the possibility of assembling this whole body of knowledge in an intellectually coherent and practically effective form.

In the face of this grand alliance of temporal and eternal knowledge, it may seem extremely pettifogging to insist on distinctions between one place and another in producing this quite overwhelmingly important result. But these things happened in particular places because some places provided the conditions in which they could happen, and others did not. Moreover, the places where such developments did not occur offered opportunities and incitements to the building up of other branches of knowledge which finally presented a challenge to the far more coherent and practically important bodies of knowledge of the great schools. These centrifugal forces will require examination in later volumes. But there is one place and one school – the place itself of wonderful attractiveness, and its alleged intellectual contribution likewise of appealing beauty – which will not make any later appearance. So it is necessary to explain the reason for this omission at once.

The place is Chartres, for which a special position of influence and originality of outlook has been claimed and very generally recognized in nearly all writings on the schools of the twelfth century during the last hundred years, and it seems desirable that the grounds of its omission from the pages which follow should be clarified.

59

I set out in a volume published in 1970 the main reasons which persuaded me that the great reputation which the school of Chartres had achieved during the last hundred years was based on a mistaken interpretation of the evidence. My argument has met with severe and very determined criticism in some quarters, and with only partial agreement in others. So it seems fairest to all parties to reprint my argument in its original form, and then to answer briefly the criticisms which have been levelled against it before going any further.

I ought to begin by mentioning – as the pages which follow make clear – that I do not argue that the school of Chartres played no part at all in the scholastic development of the twelfth century. I argue that it had a level of importance similar to that of several other cathedral schools in northern France during this period, but that the idea of a large-scale or a distinctive contribution by the school of Chartres is based on a combination of errors, and must be abandoned.

Indeed, if the only issue were the degree of importance to be attached to the school associated with one of the most splendid of all the cathedrals of northern France, the issue might be left to rest in peace. But there is more to it than this. What has been claimed for the teaching and learning of the school of Chartres is a very particular kind of humanism, standing in strong contrast to the supposedly anti-humanistic tendencies of the more successful schools of Paris and of the whole programme designated by the words 'scholastic' and 'scholasticism', and this I believe to be wholly mistaken and to limit our understanding of the development of scholastic thought. So, although the article printed below is chiefly concerned with the question of the *amount* of scholastic activity that can reasonably be ascribed to the school of Chartres, it is also aimed at those numerous scholars who have drawn an unwarranted contrast between the aims of the scholars allegedly attached to Chartres and those who were active in Paris. The distinction, I believe, is unfounded and has partly been responsible for a misunderstanding of the nature of the whole scholastic enterprise. The problem therefore is more important than a mere question of environment; it concerns the general unity and aim of the whole scholastic enterprise. The other chapters in this volume and the one which will

60

follow are concerned with the nature and practical application of the scholastic programme in detail. But, first, it is important to clear away the hypothesis of a contrasting programme and achievement which have been portrayed as a highly promising enterprise untimely nipped in the bud. Hence this reprint of my article of 1970 with a reply to those critics who have resisted this clearing of the ground as an act of vandalism.

II Humanism and the School of Chartres[1]

I

There are few institutions which have been praised more consistently than the school of Chartres. It has won everybody's sympathy and admiration: their sympathy because it has been seen standing for a humanistic ideal soon to be overwhelmed in a rising tide of law and theology, which most men in their hearts do not much like, and their admiration because it has been seen as the chief medieval exponent of a general literary culture in a world of growing specialization. It went out, it is alleged, in a blaze of glory. There was no slow decline from height to lesser height, but after standing on a pinnacle for fifty years, it suddenly sank into obscurity, and was never heard of again except by diggers for curious facts.

It has been praised for many things: as an almost solitary advocate of Platonism before Aristotle quenched all the poetry in philosophy; as a mother of art, eloquence and style before the study of the ancient authors was crowded out of the academic curriculum; for its touch of paganism in a world becoming ever more closely regimented in the paths of orthodoxy. Finally, if we feel no enthusiasm for paganism, there has been in recent years the pleasure of discovering that the apparent paganism was after all orthodox Christianity. So everyone has been pleased, and

---

[1] The text which follows is (with only minor corrections) that published in *Medieval Humanism and other studies*, 1970, pp. 29–60, but I have made some additions to the footnotes giving references relevant to the wider issues discussed in later chapters of this volume and its successor.

the reputation of Chartres stands higher now than it has ever done.

This whole triumphal march of reputation has been accomplished in a little over a hundred years, and it epitomizes the rise of medieval studies in general over this period. The authors of the volume of the *Histoire littéraire de France* which appeared in 1814 knew nothing, or almost nothing, of the school of Chartres. They still lived in an atmosphere in which almost everything scholastic was centred on Paris, and they bluntly assigned to Paris the teaching activities of the two brothers, Bernard and Thierry, who were soon to be acclaimed as the chief luminaries of the school of Chartres. Even in 1850 the young Barthélemy Hauréau, in his prize-winning essay on medieval scholasticism, had time for only a passing glance at Chartres. But the tide was turning. In 1855, another young man, L. Merlet, who was to make a notable contribution to Chartrian studies, published a collection of letters which demonstrated for the first time (as he claimed) the prosperity of the school of Chartres in the early twelfth century.[2]

Then in 1862 the same line of thought received an important extension from the argument of C. Schaarschmidt that the schools of Chartres were sufficiently important in 1138 for John of Salisbury to leave Paris in order to spend two years there, listening to William of Conches.[3] Thus two of the greatest names of twelfth-century scholarship were added to the Chartres roll of honour. Bernard (surnamed Silvestris) and Thierry of Chartres were joined by William of Conches and John of Salisbury, and the four names became the cornerstones of the school of Chartres.

These articles and suggestions belong to the prehistory of the school of Chartres. Its modern history begins with the appearance of R. L. Poole's *Illustrations of the History of Medieval Thought and Learning* in 1884. This brilliant work of a young scholar contained a chapter entitled 'The School of Chartres' in which the phrase was first used in the modern sense to describe

---

2 L. Merlet, 'Lettres d'Ives de Chartres et d'autres personnages de son temps'. *BEC*, 1855, 4th ser., i, 443–71.

3 C. Schaarschmidt, *Johannes Saresberiensis*, 1862, pp. 14–23.

something that was at once an institution and a way of thought. This chapter did more than anything else to give a character and outline to the history of the school. Despite many errors, which Poole himself was foremost in correcting, his general characterization has never been seriously questioned. The main drift of the story may be summarized in his own words. After describing the eminence of the school under Bishop Fulbert who died in 1028, he says that shortly before 1115

> the school emerges again into notice under the rule, first, it should seem, of Theodoric and then of his brother Bernard, and thence forward, down to near the middle of the twelfth century, it enjoyed a peculiar distinction, continually growing until it attained an almost unapproached pre-eminence among the schools of Gaul.

This pre-eminence Poole ascribed to the combined efforts of Theodoric 'who boldly pushed the principles of realism to their furthest issues', and Bernard Silvester his brother and successor as chancellor, 'a devout Platonist', 'a humanist' and a scholar who 'with frank vigour' 'portrayed the cosmogony according to a scheme compatible only with some form of pantheism'. Under these men, using the methods 'rather of a university than a school', Chartres attracted perhaps not so many pupils as some other schools, but a 'distinctly higher class of students than Melun or Ste-Geneviève or the Petit-Pont at Paris'. As evidence of this he adduced John of Salisbury's willingness to quit Paris 'after two years under famous dialecticians at Paris' to spend three more years under the masters at Chartres. These masters included such men as William of Conches, 'Platonist, cosmologist and grammarian, whose writings are a good example of the freedom of thought that issued from the classic calm of Chartres', Richard Bishop, 'whose virtues as a man and a scholar are celebrated in no ordinary terms', and Gilbert de la Porrée.

If Poole provided the eloquence and the vision, it was left to the Abbé Clerval to fill in the details eleven years later. His book, *Les Écoles de Chartres au Moyen-Âge*, which appeared in 1895, is one of the most influential books of local history ever written.

Clerval, besides being professor of ecclesiastical history in the local seminary, was librarian of the town, and he was the first to use the manuscripts of Chartres to illustrate the history of the school. Their use made it possible to give the school a substantial existence and an atmosphere which only a local historian could have created. The study of the manuscripts, and the contemporary studies of the art and architecture of the cathedral, made Chartres a symbol of the intellectual life of the twelfth century. Clerval wrote of the masters and pupils, the studies and organization of the schools, as if the whole scene were present to his eyes. He developed the theme which Poole had first announced. The schools of Chartres from the eleventh century onwards 'constituaient une véritable académie; leur organisation persévère et se développe. La valeur de leurs chanceliers et de leurs écolâtres, dont la suite se continue avec une gloire ininterrompue, l'importance et l'éclat de leurs doctrines théologiques ou philosophiques, en font des écoles à part, ayant leur cachet et leur individualité particulière.' After 1150 the glory was suddenly eclipsed by the rivalry of Paris, which 'malheureusement ne tardera pas à exercer sur les écoliers chartrains une irrésistible attraction'. But for half a century Chartres had stood on a pinnacle of fame and influence, and Clerval was able to describe the life of the schools during this period of greatness in much detail. The account he gave may be summarized thus.

Under Ivo (d. 1115) the bishop himself taught, but his successors, being too occupied with external duties, were brilliantly replaced in this task by chancellors and masters, whom they appointed. Teaching in the schools was the chief duty of the chancellors and masters, whom the chancellor chose in concert with the bishop. These masters of the schools were men of great weight and dignity, the advisers of the bishop in theological matters, and aspirants to the chancellorship at Chartres and bishoprics elsewhere. The best of these masters rose to be chancellors at Chartres. At the beginning of the century the chancellor Wulgrin had Bernard as his assistant master. When Bernard became chancellor he was assisted by Gilbert and Thierry, who in their turn also became successive chancellors. Masters so famous as these 'ne pouvaient manquer d'élèves'. Those of Bernard indeed formed 'une véritable colonie', but almost equally plentiful were the pupils of his successors. They were bound together by an 'esprit de solidarité' which gave the school a unity and cohesion both in its institutional life and in the literary and philosophical principles which guided its teaching.[4]

Such was the picture drawn by Clerval, and in its main outline it has won universal acceptance. It gained the scholarly approval of R. L. Poole, who had been the first to give the school of Chartres a noble accolade in his *Illustrations of Medieval Thought and Learning* in 1884, and who completed and corrected some of the details in a masterly article which appeared in 1920.[5] This article has all Poole's usual lucidity and sobriety, and its caution strengthened rather than weakened the general outline given by Clerval.

Until this point everything had developed very smoothly, but nothing had been done to add to the intellectual content of the school's activity. Indeed, in the intellectual sphere the school had suffered a substantial loss, for which Clerval deserves the credit. The early reputation of the school, that is to say its reputation from about 1850 to 1890, had been built on the supposition that Bernard the Chancellor of Chartres was the same man as Bernard Silvestris who wrote the considerable work of Platonic cosmology called *De Mundi Universitate*. So long as this identification stood, one could believe many things about the Platonic tradition at Chartres. But Clerval showed that Bernard Silvestris was a master of Tours, and had nothing to do with Chartres, and later work has entirely borne out this conclusion.[6]

It is strange that this loss did not much affect the now triumphant reputation of the school of Chartres, though it was not until 1938 that any substantial attempt was made to fill the gap. In this year J. M. Parent produced a book which initiated a new age in Chartrian studies – the age of the systematic publication

[4] The names and details quoted above will be found on pp. 143–79 of A. Clerval, *Les Écoles de Chartres au Moyen-Âge du X au XVI siècle*, Paris, 1895.
[5] 'The Masters of the Schools at Paris and Chartres in John of Salisbury's time', *EHR*, 1920, xxxv; reprinted in R. L. Poole, *Studies in Chronology and History*, 1934, 223–47.
[6] *Les Écoles de Chartres au Moyen Âge*, pp. 158–62. R. L. Poole sums up the evidence in *Studies in Chronology and History*, pp. 228–35.

of the lecture notes of the masters in whom we are interested.[7] Until this time almost nothing that came from their class-rooms had been printed. Since 1938, with the exception of the war years, there has been a steady stream of studies and editions which have brought the work of the masters to life. For the first time we begin to be able to see them at work in their lecture rooms. Yet it is remarkable how little the earlier picture of the school of Chartres and its masters has so far been altered by these revelations. The role of Bernard Silvestris has been quietly filled by Thierry and William of Conches, but the accents remain unchanged. Recent accounts of the programme and ideas of the school of Chartres, and of the special character of its attempt to reconcile Platonism and Christianity, simply give a new documentation to the judgement formed by R. L. Poole as a result of studying the work of Bernard Silvestris; they do not substantially change it. The same may be said of the flow of publications since the war, which have brought to light a new range of texts and a new generation of scholars to carry on the work of Clerval and Poole.[8]

II

The picture of the school of Chartres, both as an institution and as the source of a scholastic programme which has emerged from all these labours, is certainly very impressive and quite unusually coherent. This is largely the result of the confidence with which later scholars have been able to use the work of their predecessors. Recent workers concentrating on the scholastic programme have taken the institutional framework built up by earlier scholars more or less for granted. In working on the large connections of thought and outlook represented by the masters associated with Chartres, they have been able to assume that the base is firm. Chartres with its schools is, so to

[7] J. M. Parent, *La doctrine de la Création dans l'école de Chartres*, 1938.
[8] Some of the most notable of these publications are mentioned below, pp. 81–5, in discussing the work of the masters chiefly claimed for the school of Chartres.

speak, the launching pad from which the philosophical missiles are projected into outer space. The routine is well established: the labours of earlier scholars have made the preparatory stages almost accident-proof, and after a brief count-down – Bernard, Thierry, Gilbert, William – we are off into a state of weightlessness among the Platonic ideas. But before we lose sight of the earth we may ask, how secure is the foundation from which we have been launched on this journey? In other words, what do we know about the school of Chartres?

The answer to this is, remarkably little: much less than is generally supposed. Let us ask first about the organization of the school, then about the masters who taught there, and finally about the pupils who studied there.

First, the organization. It is certain that there was a school of some kind at Chartres: but this in itself tells us little. Schools existed in cathedral cities and other important centres all over northern France and England at this time, and the letters published by Merlet in 1855, which first drew attention to the school at Chartres, tell us as much about the schools at Laon, Le Mans, Orleans and Châteaudun as about the school at Chartres. They tell us, that is to say, that there was a master with pupils at each one of these places; but about the level of instruction or size of the enterprise in any of them they tell us nothing at all. Secondly, we may be sure that the chancellor of the cathedral had a general responsibility for the school – that is to say, he probably appointed a schoolmaster. But we cannot assume, as Clerval did, that the supervision of the school was the main part of his duties, or that he himself taught in the school. He may have done so, but the existence of a famous man as chancellor of the cathedral cannot be accepted as proof that this famous man was himself teaching in the school – any more than the appearance of a famous master among the witnesses to the bishops' charters can be accepted as proof that this master was teaching in the school. There are many cases where it is clear that this deduction cannot be drawn: consequently each case must be examined in the light of the available evidence. The chancellor had many duties besides making provision for a school. He had to conduct the correspondence of the chapter, look after the library and archives, administer the property attached to his prebend, and live as befitted a dignitary of the church. His own learning cannot be taken as an index of the learning of the school: many cathedrals had learned chancellors without having famous schools, and vice versa.

It would be unwise to attempt to settle the question on negative evidence. We may simply note that on the only occasion when we have positive evidence of a chancellor of Chartres teaching in a school in the first half of the twelfth century, he was teaching not at Chartres but at Paris.[9] This was Gilbert de la Porrée, whom John of Salisbury heard lecturing at Paris on Mont-Ste-Geneviève in 1141.[10] He had been chancellor of Chartres since 1126, and it is generally assumed that he had given up his chancellorship in order to lecture in Paris. There is no evidence to support this supposition. But in any case, the fact that Gilbert went to teach in Paris suggests that he did not find sufficient scope for his teaching in Chartres. Whether he went to Paris while he was still chancellor of Chartres, or resigned his chancellorship in order to teach in Paris, it is hard to reconcile his appearance in Paris with the generally accepted account of his presiding over a great and famous school at Chartres.

But after all, it may be said what counts in a school is not the head but the masters, and the quality of the teaching, and the pupils. What do we know about these?

Clerval has provided us with a long list of masters who taught at Chartres during the first half of the twelfth century: Bernard, Gilbert de la Porrée and Thierry, before they became successive chancellors; and, during their chancellorships, Guy, Hugh, Ivo, Belotin, Garin, Odo, Robert le Petit, William de Modalibus and Rainald. To this list most scholars would be prepared to add William of Conches.

Faced with this impressive list, it is important to begin by stating that the only evidence for some of these names is their

---

[9] I was wrong here in saying that Paris is the *only* place for which there is positive evidence of Gilbert's teaching. See below, p. 227, for the evidence, and judge whether it weakens the argument of this paper. Notice also the twelfth-century list of masters from Anselm of Laon to Peter Lombard, in which Gilbert appears as *primum scholasticus Parisiensis, deinde episcopus Pictaviensis* (Häring, 1966, p. 209).

[10] *Metalogicon*, ii, 10, ed. C. C. J. Webb, 1929, p. 82.

appearance with the title *Magister* in lists of witnesses of the bishops' charters. This is quite unsatisfactory. So far as I can discover the only man on the list for whom there is quite convincing evidence of a teaching career at Chartres is the first one, Bernard. Bernard appears in a list of canons at Chartres of 1119–24 as *magister scolae*, and he is evidently the master referred to as 'Master B' in the letters printed by Merlet.[11] John of Salisbury has left a magnificent account of Bernard's teaching, which he must have had from men who were Bernard's pupils. The evidence which connects Bernard with the school of Chartres in his day is very solid, and it makes the contrast with the period after Bernard all the more striking. There must have been a master, and there must have been pupils at Chartres. But this is something that can be said about many cathedral schools. We need more evidence than this for the special distinction of the school of Chartres, and evidence is, to say the least, hard to find – much harder than it is at Paris or Laon.

To test this assertion, we may leave aside for the moment the minor characters mentioned by Clerval, and concentrate on the three men who have done most, after Bernard, to make Chartres famous. They are Thierry, Gilbert de la Porrée and William of Conches – undoubtedly three of the most important writers of the period. What is their common connection with Chartres?

First of all Thierry. Clerval established the now traditional account of his career: he was the brother of Bernard of Chartres; while his brother was chancellor he taught at Chartres; on his brother's death about 1126 he went to Paris, but he returned

---

[11] The most important document for Bernard's career as a teacher at Chartres is printed in R. Merlet and A. Clerval, *Un manuscrit chartrain du XIe siècle*, 1893, pp. 195–6: it is an oath taken by the canons of Chartres, including *Bernardus scolae magister*, at some time between 4 November 1119 and 1124, and probably nearer the earlier of these two dates. In 1124 he appears as chancellor in an agreement between the monks of St Peter of Chartres and those of Nogent (*Cartulaire de St Denis de Nogent-le-Rotrou*, ed. Ch. Métais, 1895, pp. 240–3). For the attribution to him of a commentary on the *Timaeus*, see below p. 81, n. 29. Two years later, in a charter of 27 November 1126, Gilbert (de la Porrée) appears as chancellor, though in another charter of the same day he is called simply *canonicus* (*Cartulaire de l'abbaye de S. Père de Chartres*, ed. M. Guérard, 1840, pp. 263, 267). For Gilbert's later appearances in charters, see below, p. 91; and pp. 221–3, 227, 232, for Paris as Gilbert's normal place of teaching. See also Plate 3.

to teach at Chartres as chancellor from 1141 till his death in 1151.

It is rather tedious to analyse these bare and apparently harmless statements. But so much has been built on them, and so much scholastic history depends on similar chains of reasoning, that criticism has a wider importance than might seem likely. The reputation of Chartres has been kept afloat by a disinclination to niggle, but niggle we must. To begin with, was Thierry the brother of Bernard of Chartres? Apart from this relationship, he would scarcely have begun to have a place in the early history of the school. The only evidence comes from Otto of Freising, who tells us *apropos* of Breton cleverness that there have been three very clever Bretons in his day: Abelard, and the brothers Thierry and Bernard.[12] It is certain that the Thierry referred to here was the later chancellor of Chartres, but it is pure hypothesis to say that his brother Bernard whom Otto mentions was Bernard of Chartres. Otto does not tell us this; nor does John of Salisbury, though he has plenty to say about both Bernard of Chartres and Thierry;[13] nor does Abelard, who is our only other source of information about Thierry's brother. Abelard's evidence indeed points in a quite different direction. He describes Thierry's brother as a very incompetent theologian with an absurd view of the efficacy of the words of consecration in the Mass.[14] It is possible of course that this theologian whom Abelard thought so incompetent was Bernard of Chartres, the great teacher of the liberal Arts whom John of Salisbury admired so extravagantly, but we need some evidence before we are persuaded. Besides, there are minor incongruities in the theory which could be insisted on: the fact that John of Salisbury mentions Bernard of Chartres and Thierry in the same sentence without hinting that they were brothers; the fact that Bernard of Chartres died nearly thirty years before Thierry. But why insist on these things? The point is quite unimportant, except that it provided an initial link between Thierry and Chartres, which made Clerval think that he

[12] *Gesta Frederici Imperatoris*, i, 49, ed. G. Waitz, *Scriptores in usum scholarum*, 1912, p. 68.
[13] *Metalogicon*, ed. Webb, pp. 17, 29, 53–81, 93, 94, 124, 136, 205–6 (on Bernard); pp. 16, 80, 191 (on Thierry).
[14] *Theologia Christiana*, PL, 178, 1286.

had seen Thierry's name as a master of the school of Chartres in some charters of the time of Bernard the Chancellor.[15] If any such charter exists, I have been unable to find it. Failing this, there is not the slightest evidence of a connection between Thierry and Chartres until he became chancellor in 1142. Nor is there any evidence that he taught at Chartres while he was chancellor. The only place where he is known to have taught is Paris, and it was certainly there that he spent the main part of his teaching life.

It would be quite wrong to blame Clerval for misleading us. Every historian interprets evidence under the influence of his vision. For Clerval, the most solid thing in the twelfth century was Chartres, and Chartres was given the benefit of every doubt. When he wrote, the scholastic world was thinly populated, and he did not know, as we now know, how many people with the same name and similar occupations were apt to be around at the same time. He therefore allowed Chartres to draw every suitable unattached name into its orbit.

He approached Bernard's successor as chancellor, Gilbert de la Porrée, with the same preconceptions.[16] Just as every Master B. was available as Bernard of Chartres, so every Master G. might be Gilbert de la Porrée. This tendency was already

[15] *Les écoles de Chartres*, p. 160, Clerval quotes two charters of 1119–1124, which Bernard witnesses as chancellor, 'tandis que son frère Thierry, dans les mêmes pièces, s'attribue le titre de *'magister scolae'*. Thierry's name however does not appear in the charters to which Clerval refers. Further, Clerval says (p. 170) that a reference by Abelard (*Hist. calamitatum*, PL, 178, 150) to Thierry as *quidam scolarum magister* is shown by the context to refer to Chartres. But so far as I can see the context shows nothing of the kind. I should now add however that, although all Thierry's teaching seems to have been in Paris, there is evidence that, while he was teaching in Paris, he was archdeacon of Dreux in the diocese of Chartres in the 1130s, and therefore must have been a canon of Chartres. So both he and Gilbert de la Porrée taught in Paris while holding an office in the chapter at Chartres. (The main reason for identifying Master Thierry with the Thierry who witnesses charters as archdeacon of Dreux is that the necrology of Chartres gives him the titles 'cancellarius et archidiaconus'. For the evidence, see Häring, 1974, p. 272.)

[16] After quoting charters witnessed by Gilbert as canon and chancellor of Chartres, Clerval proceeds: 'C'est alors (1124–1137) qu'il enseigna avec la collaboration sans doute de Thierry, et qu'il eut pour disciples; Rotrou, Jordan Fantosme, Jean Beleth et Nicolas d'Amiens' (*Écoles de Chartres*, pp. 164–5). The evidence for this statement is the picture reproduced in Plate 3. It certainly reflects Gilbert's fame as a teacher, but the pupils are associated with Paris.

at work in 1855. Among the letters published in this year by Merlet there is one to Master B. from his disciple G. The disciple expresses the wildest enthusiasm for his master: he owes everything to him and can scarcely endure to be separated from him; he has become a schoolmaster in Aquitaine, but he continues to sigh for his old master, and so on. Well, it is very likely that Master B. is Bernard of Chartres. But who is the disciple? Certainly Gilbert de la Porrée, said Merlet. Poole agreed: 'there can be absolutely no doubt about its attribution'. Naturally Clerval did not dissent.[17]

It seems harmless enough, especially since Gilbert de la Porrée probably was anyhow a pupil of Bernard of Chartres. But even here the habit of easy attribution paved the way for exaggerations and false conclusions. This attribution helped to suggest that the school of Chartres had a central place in Gilbert's scholastic life. But on a cool view the identification of Gilbert de la Porrée with this raving young admirer of Master B. is quite unlikely.

Our picture of Gilbert's connection with Chartres must be based on quite different evidence, and the small amount of evidence that exists suggests that Gilbert studied grammar under Bernard of Chartres, and then went on to Laon to study theology. It was at Laon that he wrote his first great work which made him famous. The man to whom he submitted it for criticism and approval was not Bernard of Chartres, but Anselm the great master of Laon.[18] It is true that Gilbert became a canon of Chartres by 1124 and chancellor in 1126 and he *may* have taught there, but there is a striking absence of pupils who can be shown to have studied under him at Chartres during those years. His teaching career still needs to be elucidated, but for the moment the only certainty attaches to his teaching in Paris in 1141, and there is some evidence that his influence radiated from this centre.

---

[17] Merlet, *BEC*, 1855, pp. 461–2; Poole, *Illustrations of Medieval Thought and Learning*, p. 134n; Clerval, p. 164.
[18] *Explicit Glosatura magistri Giliberti Porretani super Psalterium quam ipse recitavit coram suo magistro Anselmo causa emendationis.* Balliol College, Oxford, MS 36, f. 145v. For a description, see R. A. B. Mynors, *Catalogue of the Manuscripts of Balliol College, Oxford*, 1963, p. 26.

We turn now to William of Conches. Here again there is a quite strong presumption that he was a pupil of Bernard of Chartres. No contemporary or near contemporary source actually tells us this, but John of Salisbury twice associates the two names, first when he says that William followed the same method of teaching as Bernard, and secondly when he calls William the richest and most fertile grammarian of his day after Bernard of Chartres.[19] Certainly this is not proof, but in the web of hypotheses from which the school of Chartres has been created, it is as near proof as we can get. Much more important, however, is the question whether William of Conches himself taught at Chartres. If this could be established we should have a perfect case of the continuity of the Chartrian tradition over a period of perhaps thirty years from 1110 to 1140.

We have now reached the point of central importance for the history of the school of Chartres. The suggestion which has been accepted almost without dispute for the last hundred years, is that William of Conches studied at Chartres, and then taught at Chartres, and that the great John of Salisbury was his pupil at Chartres. The evidence is John of Salisbury's own account of his student days. He tells us that he left England in 1136 and studied logic on Mont-Ste-Geneviève in the suburbs of Paris from 1136 to 1138. Then he left the Mount and followed the lectures of William of Conches and others for three years from 1138 to 1141. Finally in 1141 he returned and studied logic and theology under Gilbert de la Porrée.[20] The great question for us is, where did John of Salisbury spend the years from 1138 to 1141, and in particular where did he hear the lectures of William of Conches?

Until 1848 scholars took it for granted that everything described in John of Salisbury's account of his student days took place in Paris. Then Petersen, the editor of John of Salisbury's *Entheticus* pointed out that if he *returned* in 1141, he must previously have *left*. This seemed reasonable, and it started a search for the place where he had gone. Petersen thought that he had returned to England. But then Schaarschmidt hit on the idea

---

[19] *Metalogicon*, i, 5; i, 24; ed. C. C. J. Webb, pp. 16–17, 57.
[20] Ibid., ii, 10; pp. 77–82. See also below, pp. 217, 220–2.

that he had gone to Chartres.[21] His main argument was that he could only have written the very full account of the teaching of Bernard of Chartres, which he gives in the *Metalogicon*, if he had been an eyewitness. We know now that the argument is certainly false, because Bernard had died long before John came to France, and he must have got his information from Bernard's pupils, whom he could meet anywhere. By the time this was known, however, the reputation of the school of Chartres was showing its power of surviving the demolition of the evidence on which it was built. Schaarschmidt's other arguments amount to nothing. Nevertheless he succeeded in making it an established doctrine that John of Salisbury went to Chartres in 1138 and studied for three years under William of Conches. It is an attractive hypothesis, but is it true?

If it is true, it is certainly odd that John of Salisbury should not have mentioned the place where he spent three important years, and we may ask whether Petersen did not pose an unreal problem in insisting that John must have left Paris. He certainly left Mont-Ste-Geneviève; but we must remember that the Mount was a suburb of Paris outside the city walls. The sense of John's account of his life would be amply met if he left the Mount to go down into Paris, to the schools by the river, and returned to the Mount after three years. This would fit very well into the other details he gives. For instance, he tells us something, though in a rather confused way, about the other masters with whom he apparently studied during the three years from 1138 to 1141: one of them was Adam de Petit-Pont, who certainly taught in the city; another was Thierry, who was certainly teaching in Paris at this time; a third was the Parisian master Petrus Helias. Altogether it is hard to avoid the conclusion that Petersen started a false trail by forgetting that a man could leave Mont-Ste-Geneviève to go, not away from, but into, Paris. Schaarschmidt then hit on a popular, but wholly unproved, answer to Petersen's question, and his successors have been only too willing to make the pilgrimage to Chartres.

If my analysis of the evidence is correct, William of Conches

21   See C. Schaarschmidt, *Johannes Saresberiensis*, 1862, pp. 14–22, where the earlier views are discussed and the new solution to the problem of John of Salisbury's whereabouts between 1138 and 1141 is proposed.

must join Thierry and Gilbert de la Porrée among the masters who can be found teaching at Paris, but – apart from the single piece of evidence relating to Gilbert discussed below – not at Chartres; and John of Salisbury also must join the many students who studied at Paris but not, so far as we know, at Chartres.[22] And if they go, who is left? It is very difficult to say.

III

Apart from the details, there are, it seems to me, three general sources of misunderstanding in the traditional account of the school of Chartres. Of these, the first and least important is the tendency to exaggerate the importance of Chartres as a teaching centre, and to draw into the orbit of Chartres any works which exhibit certain 'humanistic' characteristics and have no other obvious local attachment. The second is the widely-accepted conception of a 'humanism' which came into existence, flourished briefly, and was suddenly extinguished in the first half of the twelfth century, especially in the scholastic environment of Chartres. The third is the conception of an 'anti-humanistic' tendency, especially associated with the studies of logic, systematic theology and law at Paris and Bologna, which (wrongly as I believe) have been seen as being in competition with the humanism of Chartres and as a main cause of the decline of Chartres and of Chartrian humanism.

To speak briefly of each of these misconceptions in turn:

1 Chartres was only one of many cathedral schools in northern France whose continuous existence can be observed from the eleventh century onwards. Several of these schools had at some moment in their history one master of more than local significance who drew pupils from a large area. For a time these masters gave their school a wide fame. But we must be careful to distinguish between this short-lived fame, which depended on one man, and the lasting fame of the later universities, which depended on a tradition of scholastic success and a large variety of teachers and students. The cathedral schools existed to serve

---

[22] See below, pp. 217–21, for a fuller discussion of John of Salisbury's whereabouts during his student years.

a limited and local need: their main purpose was to equip the higher ranks of the diocesan clergy with useful learning. Unless an outstanding master created quite exceptional conditions, these schools did not normally draw pupils from far afield. Their resources did not allow for the coexistence of many masters: their main purpose was to provide fairly elementary instruction at a diocesan level. Accidents of personality apart, they had not the resources of teachers or students to make possible or desirable a permanently higher level of instruction than that of a grammar school.

Yet by the early twelfth century there was a substantial and growing demand for something more than this. Ambitious young men who wished to reach the highest places in government, whether ecclesiastical or secular, needed to be equipped with an advanced knowledge of systematic theology and canon law: they needed to operate easily in the intricacies of highly technical argument. It was quite beyond the resources of a cathedral organization to meet this need, except in the lifetime of an outstanding master with talents superior to the function for which he was employed. In the period from about 1090 to 1120, by far the most successful of the cathedral masters in meeting the new demand were the brothers Anselm and Ralph at Laon; but even they could not found a school capable of surviving for long at the level to which they had raised it.

Almost within the lifetime of these two brothers, it was becoming clear that the only two places in Europe with the special qualities necessary for perpetuating higher studies were Paris and Bologna. They both provided – for reasons which are discussed below[23] – opportunities for many masters to teach, and for many students to come and go as they wished. From a period quite early in the twelfth century, the number of masters and the wide choice open to students gave Paris a position quite different from that of any other city in northern Europe. In the years between 1136 and 1148, when John of Salisbury was a student, he was able to hear the lectures of ten or twelve masters, of whom six or seven were men of the first importance in their

---

[23] For a clarification of the 'reasons' for the scholastic supremacy of Paris and Bologna, see below, pp. 200–2, and 313–16.

subject.[24] This fact gave Paris an overwhelming advantage over every other centre of study in the North. At the same time Bologna, where the schools were fostered as a political and economic asset, and had no connection with the cathedral, was laying the foundation for a similar lead in southern Europe.[25] Both these cities had freed themselves from the restrictions of ordinary cathedral schools; Oxford, which became a competitor for international fame in the arts, theology and law sixty years later, had no cathedral at all.

The framework of a cathedral organization was quite inadequate for the development of permanent institutions of advanced teaching. This fact does not detract from the achievement of those early cathedral masters who won a general fame in their own day. Quite the opposite. It merely explains why they did not found schools of permanent importance. Chartres is unique among cathedral schools in having *two* masters of international standing, separated by a century: Fulbert in the early eleventh century and Bernard in the early twelfth.

Both Fulbert and Bernard are examples of something very rare in the history of scholarship: they were men of the highest intelligence who made teaching their first concern. They were not original thinkers, but they commanded the learning of their day, and they had the power and impulse to make it accessible to others. There is indeed much more evidence for the number and diversity of Fulbert's pupils than for Bernard's a century later. This may be partly due to chance, for we are exceptionally well informed about the names and occupations of Fulbert's pupils; but I think it is also likely that Fulbert was better equipped to provide what his age required. By contrast, Bernard in his time was somewhat old-fashioned. His type of learning no longer held the imagination or satisfied the ambition of younger men. They were turning elsewhere: to Laon for theology, to Spain for science, to Paris for the multiplicity of masters and the wide range of opportunity. Even when Bernard was at the height of his powers, Laon was vastly more attractive to the ambitious young man than Chartres, and Paris already enjoyed a

---

24 For a list of Parisian masters in the 1140s, see below, pp. 232–3.
25 For this later, as I now think, development, see below, chapters 8 and 9.

freedom of scholastic movement that Chartres could never hope to emulate.

Chartres was, and long continued to be, a sweet and pleasant place. The genial liberality of its counts, the lack of tension in its political relations, the freedom of its ecclesiastical society, the wealth and numbers of its cathedral canons, all helped to provide an atmosphere of well-being and learning in the church. In the course of the century it had many learned and distinguished men as bishops, chancellors and canons; even in a century of great cathedrals, the cathedral of Chartres must be reckoned one of the finest monuments of the age. All these factors must give Chartres a special place in our mental image of the twelfth century, but when we transfer this image to the *school* of Chartres we must beware. As an institution the school attached to the cathedral suffered from the limitation of most cathedral schools. It existed to serve a local need, and when Bernard died or retired in 1124, it reverted to this, its proper function.

2 The second misconception concerns the 'humanism' of Chartres. 'Humanism' is a word that it is sometimes necessary to use, and there is nothing wrong with it except that it stands for many different things. Any study of the seven liberal arts, which were the foundation of all education from the Carolingian age, implies a certain degree of humanism. That is to say, in studying the Arts you are studying both the human mind and the external world: the human mind in its forms of expression in grammar, rhetoric and logic; and the external world in the arts of arithmetic, geometry, music and astronomy. The subjects may be extremely circumscribed, but they depended on the exercise of human powers and not on knowledge drawn from Revelation. They are therefore genuine humanistic studies, and every cathedral school of the period from the tenth to the twelfth centuries was in its general tendency humanistic. To this range of humanism the school of Chartres certainly contributed.

But was there a special type and intensity of humanism peculiar to the school of Chartres? I think not. There is, to say the least, no evidence that the works of William of Conches and Thierry represented the teaching of Chartres rather than that of Paris, or for that matter of Tours or Orleans. Their works represent a phase in European studies rather than a narrowly localized form of humanism. They are the product of that moment when ancient materials handed down in the West for centuries had been thoroughly assimilated, and masters could write about them with ease and confidence. They are among the last expressions of western scholarship before the deluge of new materials which destroyed literary ease in academic exercises for a long time to come. The problems that then arose were too difficult and complicated for easy reading.

Both William of Conches and Thierry were keen seekers for new materials, but they had no idea how plentiful the new materials would soon become. They are the last representatives of the generation which had derived its knowledge of the world of men and nature mainly from the tradition of the Latin world – from Ovid and Virgil, from Macrobius and Martianus Capella, from Boethius and Cassiodorus, and from that part of Plato's *Timaeus* which was available to the Latin world in the translation and commentary of Chalcidius. However eager they might be for new texts, their range of competence scarcely extended beyond the sources that had long been familiar, and two stout volumes could hold all the natural knowledge that Thierry considered really essential from the past.[26] This humanism was not shallow, but it was very limited in its range, and this range was available to contemporaries everywhere in northern Europe.

3   The third misconception at the root of the traditional account of the school of Chartres concerns the end of the humanism represented by William of Conches and Thierry. What 'came to an end' in fact was not humanism, but the limitations on humanism imposed by the paucity of ancient sources and the conservation of ancient methods of instruction. William of Conches and Thierry, and all the men of their generation who worked on the same sources, had reached the end of the road because they had come to the end of the available information. Plato's *Timaeus* may be a marvellous book, but if you read it as a scientific textbook, in isolation from Plato's other works,

[26]   The contents of this collection of texts were first analysed by Clerval, *École de Chartres*, pp. 220–48. The Prologue is printed by E. Jeauneau in *Medieval Studies*, 1954, xvi, 171–5. For an analysis of the contents and status of the volume, see G. R. Evans, 'The uncompleted *Heptateuch* of Thierry of Chartres', in *History of Universities*, 3, 1983, 1–13.

and in total ignorance of the scope of Greek scientific learning, it cannot take you very far: for any further advance, new material and new methods of systematic analysis were essential. These two things were brought into the schools in the late twelfth century, and their exploitation was essentially the work of the new conglomerations of schools which coalesced as universities as distinct from the cathedral schools.

IV[27]

It may not be out of place at this point to review the works of the masters who have been generally taken to represent the Chartrian tradition in the more general context which I have sketched. In this context the works of William of Conches and Thierry appear not as the products of a brilliant but short-lived tradition of a single school, but as the representatives of a phase in the continuous development of Western studies and of medieval humanism. Even Bernard of Chartres, the one great and indisputable Chartrian master of the twelfth century, must be seen not as a landmark in the history of a school, but as the last great schoolmaster in the late Carolingian tradition. It is with him that our survey must begin.

1 Bernard of Chartres

Nearly everything that we know about Bernard and his teaching comes from John of Salisbury. What John of Salisbury tells us is that he was a wonderful teacher who developed a method of teaching his pupils Latin which ensured that even a pupil of moderate ability could learn to speak and write Latin correctly within a year. The basis of his method seems to have been a thorough grounding in grammar and composition, enforced by a system of daily exercises which impressed the rules on his pupils'

[27] I retain this section of the paper as published in 1970 because, although much more needs to be said about these scholars (and some more will be said later in this and the next volume), these few pages at least outline the case against there being anything peculiarly 'Chartrian' in the message of these scholars.

minds. What John of Salisbury describes sounds very like the upper forms of a good English public school on the classical side – the formation of character and godliness going hand in hand with a careful attention to the niceties of the Latin language. We must remember that John was writing in the 1150s about a master of the previous generation, and he described his method in detail mainly because it was no longer followed. Even John's own Latin masters, William of Conches and Richard Bishop, who had followed the same method as Bernard of Chartres in earlier days, had given up because their pupils had insisted on getting on more quickly.[28]

The picture which emerges is of a great teacher, sober, methodical, conservative in his tastes and in his philosophy. His teaching, so far as we can reconstruct it, kept strictly within the framework of the Arts as they had been known in Europe since the tenth century. Yet with this conservatism of outlook and aim, Bernard had a power of crystallizing points in rough but memorable verses and pithy sayings by which a schoolmaster is remembered. In an unobtrusive way, Bernard was the main hero of John of Salisbury's survey of the learning of his day: he stood for the literary and moral virtues which John most admired.[29] Perhaps John himself would have liked to be a master such as

[28] See below, p. 216.
[29] The most recent suggested addition to our knowledge of Master Bernard is from P. E. Dutton, in his volume, 'Bernard of Chartres: *Glosae super Platonem*', Pontifical Institute, Toronto, 1991, where he has edited and attributed to Bernard of Chartres a hitherto unpublished Gloss on the *Timaeus*. Naturally it is a volume of very great interest in providing new evidence of the detailed interest in this text in the early twelfth century. But, so far as the attribution to Bernard of Chartres is concerned, it must be observed that the commentary published by Dutton has no attribution of authorship, and – if the attribution to Bernard is correct – it is strange that William of Conches, the greatest of Bernard's disciples, did not use it when he wrote his own commentary on the *Timaeus*. Moreover, with regard to the suggestion that the author of this commentary was an innovator, there is evidence that the revival of interest in the *Timaeus* in the eleventh-century schools had already led to the production of glosses by Master Manegoldus, who was active as a master in Paris in the period from about 1060 to 1090. These glosses (though now lost) were preserved in the fourteenth century in a manuscript at Peterborough. (Manitius, iii, p. 179, and G. Becker, *Catalogi Bibliothecarum Antiqui*, Bonn, 1885, p. 291.) In brief, whatever the truth about the attribution of these glosses to Master Bernard may be, there was nothing particularly Chartrian about an interest in this text, nor can Master Bernard be claimed as an initiator. For more details on these points, see Southern, 1979, pp. 8–15.

he imagined Bernard to have been, but by his day the prospects for an exponent of his kind of learning were not good, and John had to content himself with being an administrator.

2 William of Conches[30]

The first thing to be noticed about William of Conches is that his scholarly career falls into two fairly distinct parts. He was one of those men who do their best and most original work when they are young. He lived till about 1150, but already by 1125 he had produced his one work of first-class importance, which he never substantially added to or improved. This was his *Philosophia Mundi*.

It was the first attempt in the West to give a systematic account of the whole of nature on the basis of a few simple scientific ideas. I am not here forgetting the work of John Scotus Erigena two and a half centuries earlier, nor that of William's contemporary Honorius Augustodunensis. Nor am I forgetting the illustrated English scientific manuscripts contemporary with the *Philosophia Mundi*, which describe the world in a basically similar way.[31] But Erigena's work is primarily a work of mystical theology, the scientific survey of Honorius Augustodunensis is an encyclopaedia pure and simple, and the English scientific manuscripts, beautiful though they are, are too jejune for serious intellectual study. Only William's is a work of systematic science, that is to say a work in which the details are subordinated to a general scientific plan, and it deserves high praise on that account.

[30] For present purposes, it may suffice to mention the following publications as giving an idea of the range of William of Conches's interests: glosses on the *Timaeus*, ed. E. Jeauneau, 1965; glosses on Boethius's *De Consolatione Philosophiae*, ed. J. M. Parent, in *La doctrine de la Création dans l'école de Chartres*, 1937, 124–36; glosses on Priscian, ed. E. Jeauneau, in *RTAM*, 1960, xxvii, 212–47, and I. Rosier, *Cahiers*, Copenhagen, 1993, lxiii, pp. 115–44; glosses on Macrobius, E. Jeauneau, 'Glosses de Guillaume de Conches sur Macrobe': note sur les manuscrits', *AHDL*, 1960, xxvii, 17–28. See also pp. 215–20 below.
[31] See, for these, Southern, 1970i, pp. ix–x, and Plates IV–VIII, with scientific drawings from the monasteries of Thorney, Peterborough, and Worcester, of the period c. 1100–1130.

The scientific ideas of William of Conches were not his own. They came partly from the *Timaeus*, with elaborations drawn from Macrobius and Martianus Capella, and partly from Galen through the recent translations of Constantine the African. What William of Conches provided was organizing power and lucidity. It has been said that he read the *Timaeus* through the eyes of Macrobius, but this (I think) is to put the cart before the horse. Many men had lost themselves in the intricacies of Macrobius.

What William had the power to perceive was that these intricacies could be reduced to order if seen through the eyes of Plato, and that the same simplifying process could be extended through the whole field of human biology with the help of the great Arab physicians whose work had only recently become available in Latin. He went back to the fountain-head. Until the scientific works of Aristotle were translated into Latin, a strong interest in natural science led back to Plato's *Timaeus* because it was the source, directly or indirectly, of all universal scientific ideas. William of Conches wrote before Aristotle was known as a scientific teacher, but he illustrates very well the reasons for Aristotle's later scientific supremacy and Plato's decline: Plato provided very few facts, and William of Conches was already stretching out for more. He did not know the potential abundance of Aristotle; but he seems to have been the first to recognize that medical works newly translated from Arabic could help to complete Plato's picture of the universe. In this way he provides an early example of the restless search for new materials which would soon transform the scientific outlook of the West.

William of Conches was not alone in his interest in the workings of nature. His *Philosophia Mundi* has many indications of the existence of widespread discussion, and the rapid diffusion of his work confirms this impression. It was being read in Constantinople in 1165. By this date, apart from the version by the author himself, there were two other versions almost certainly made by others. In one form or another there are a hundred and forty manuscripts of the work now in existence. They mostly come from the twelfth and thirteenth centuries, and they demonstrate William's success in summing up the science of the pre-Aristotelian age.[32] The *Philosophia Mundi* was the best expression of the scientific interests of a whole generation seeking for an orderly description of the universe. The long effort to build up the school of Chartres has accustomed us to suppose that Chartres must somehow lie behind the interests displayed by William of Conches, but this is far too narrow a view. William of Conches was not the representative of a school, but of a generation. He is a bridge between the meagre scientific resources of the early Middle Ages and the massive influx of new material which began almost as soon as he had written his great work.

3 Thierry

Thierry was the complete teacher of the liberal Arts of his day. He has left nothing that is not a record of his lectures – on Boethius's *De Trinitate*, on Cicero's *De Inventione* and on Genesis chap. 1.[33] We must not be misled by the theological appearance of some of the titles: Thierry was not a theologian, though he illustrates the tendency for teachers of the Arts at this time to be drawn into theological controversies. He was essentially a teacher of the arts. His collection of texts on the seven liberal Arts, the *Heptateuchon*, is the best monument we have of the complete Arts course before it was drowned in the flood of new material and new interests in the late twelfth century. His preface to this collection is a noble statement of the aims of an old-fashioned master of the liberal Arts.[35] He wished, he said, to join together the trivium and quadrivium so that the marriage might

---

[32] These statistics are based on A. Vernet, 'Un remaniement de la *Philosophia* de Guillaume de Conches', *Scriptorium*, 1947, i, 252–9. The evidence for the work having reached Constantinople by 1165 is to be found in the *Liber thesauri occulti* of Paschalis Romanus, ed. S. Collin-Roset, *AHDL*, 1963, xxx, 111–98.

[33] Thierry's commentaries, lectures and glosses on Genesis and Boethius's *De Trinitate* have been printed by N. Häring in *AHDL*, 1955, xxii, 137–216; 1956, xxiii, 257–325; 1958, xxv, 113–226; 1960, xxvii, 65–136. Some of the glosses on Cicero's *De Inventione*, including an interesting preface, are printed in W. H. D. Suringer, *Hist. critica scholasticorum latinorum*, 1834, i, 213–53, and there are further extracts in M. Dickey, 'Some commentaries on the *De Inventione*', *MARS*, 1968, vi, 1–41.

[35] See V. Cousin, *Ouvrages inédits d'Abelard*, p. 471. R. L. Poole discusses the story, *Illustrations of Medieval Thought and Learning*, p. 363; see also Clerval, p. 192.

bring forth a free race of philosophers. He attached special im-importance to scientific subjects, or, as he would say, to the subjects of the quadrivium. One of Abelard's biographers tells us that Abelard heard him lecture on the quadrivium, and went to him for private instruction in mathematics, but he soon found the subject too difficult.[35] Whether or not this is true, Thierry's lectures on Genesis and Boethius are full of scientific interest. The view of the universe which they present is very similar to that of William of Conches's *Philosophia Mundi*. They used the same sources, and approached the study of the world and its constituent parts in a similar way.

Thierry was certainly a great teacher. Men dedicated their books to him and were glad to say that they had been his pupils.[36] He was sharp-tongued, independent, careless of popularity, and he attracted men who spoke of him with that exaggerated admiration which is the supreme reward of the teacher. Like William of Conches he had mastered the past, and he thought he saw further than the greatest scholars of antiquity, not because he had anything new to contribute, but because he could survey the whole field. Yet he too felt the need for new texts, and his *Heptateuchon* shows that he was touching the fringe of the great new discoveries of ancient writings.

At the moment when the old learning was assimilated, the old boundaries were beginning to break down. Every master of note at this time shows a tendency to break out in one direction or another – into theology, law, or natural science, and into specialized fields of independent study like logic or grammar. Some masters broke out more reluctantly than others, but they all did so to some extent. They had to, if they were to survive. It must often, then as now, have been difficult for a master to reconcile his private interests with those of his pupils,

---

[35] See V. Cousin, *Ouvrages inédits d'Abelard*, p. 471. R. L. Poole discusses the story, *Illustrations of Medieval Thought and Learning*, p. 363; see also Clerval, p. 192.
[36] For the dedication to Thierry of Bernard Silvestris, *De Mundi Universitate*, see now the edition of Peter Dronke (with the title, *Cosmographia*), 1978, p. 96; and for Hermann of Carinthia's dedication to Thierry of his translation of Ptolemy's *Planisphere*, see Clerval, *Enseignement des arts libéraux à Paris et à Chartres ... d'après l'Eptateuchon de Thierry*, 1889.

and the latter in the end always prevailed. William of Conches had to adapt his teaching to his pupils' demands, and Thierry's works also illustrate the strength of the pressure from below which drove the masters on. Just as we have three versions of William of Conches's *Philosophia Mundi*, so also we have three versions of Thierry's commentary on Boethius's *De Trinitate*, and I think it is very likely that two of them are the work of pupils who developed their master's teaching in different ways. These are just a few of the signs that the whole field of learning was in a state of upheaval, largely caused by the multiplication of students who would pay only if they got what they wanted.

The three masters of whom I have spoken all had sufficient power to leave the stamp of individuality on their works. But we must not exaggerate either their isolation from the general current of thought or the importance of their achievement. All their thoughts were old thoughts. They had the strength to make old thoughts live again, but they could not add to them. They had the strength to form this exiguous material into an intelligible whole, but they could not break far out of an ancient framework of knowledge.

To gather new material, to systematize the new material as they had systematized the old, to reach out to new patterns of thought, and to fill the vast empty spaces of ignorance, were tasks that belonged to the future. These tasks were beginning to be undertaken in the times of William of Conches and Thierry, and it was out of them that the complex system of studies of the medieval universities grew.

These later studies were not a reaction against humanism, Chartrian or otherwise; they were the necessary and inevitable development of what William of Conches and Thierry were trying to do. This development required the labours of many men, and the places where many masters and students could assemble had advantages which grew more conspicuous from year to year. In intellectual productivity, as in any complex process, numbers are important because they make specialization, competition and the growth of new techniques both possible and easy. In these respects, Chartres, even in the first half of the twelfth century, could not compete with Paris. Hence Thierry, Gilbert de la Porrée, and (as I think likely)[37] William of Conches all gravitated to Paris, and in so far as they represent a school at all, they represent the schools of Paris rather than the school of Chartres.

V

We may however finally ask why, if the foundations of what I may call the legend of Chartres were as insecure as I have suggested, they have seemed so firm to such excellent scholars as Clerval and Poole, and to all those who have accepted their conclusions.

I think there are several reasons, both personal and general. Of the two great founders of the legend, R. L. Poole had formed his views about the school of Chartres when he believed that Bernard Silvestris was the same man as Bernard of Chartres. This provided the school with a very solid foundation. Poole had also noticed the general coherence between the work of Bernard Silvestris and Thierry of Chartres, whom he wrongly believed to be his brother, and between Bernard Silvestris and William of Conches, whom he wrongly believed to be his pupil. He also believed that it had been demonstrated that William of Conches taught John of Salisbury at Chartres. The chain of evidence connecting these men and their habits of thought with Chartres seemed unbreakable. Yet not one of these links is firm, and most of them are demonstrably false. In part Poole recognized this, when he returned to the subject nearly forty years after writing his first book. But he was unwilling (as we all are) to alter his views more than was strictly necessary, and though he saw the weakness of some of Clerval's new arguments, he was willing to accept the support which Clerval provided for the main conclusions of his early work without thinking them out afresh.

As for Clerval, we must remember his circumstances. He was Professor of History at the Seminary of Chartres, and deeply concerned in building up the new centre of clerical learning,

[37] For further evidence on this point, see below, pp. 217–20, 232.

of which the pupils were still such a conspicuous feature in the cathedral close sixty years ago. It was very easy for him to think of the twelfth-century schools as a prototype of what he saw about him. He was encouraged to do this by the manuscripts of the library, which he was the first to use to reconstruct the history of Chartres. He saw Thierry's *Heptateuchon*, and he reconstructed from this and from other volumes of that impressive library a course of studies which he characterized as Chartrian. It was easy for him to forget that the *Heptateuchon* was probably a monument of Thierry's teaching at Paris. It was also easy to forget that the texts of the *Heptateuchon* were in the main the texts of a whole generation of masters, and not of Thierry alone.

The imaginative impact of these books on Clerval was very great. It was fatally easy for him to see everything as centred on Chartres, to make easy identifications of Masters B. and G. with Bernard and Gilbert (or if necessary William), and gradually to build a system held together by a logic of its own. Sometimes he was demonstrably wrong; more often he erred simply by giving Chartres the benefit of every doubt. The cumulative effect of building multiple benefits of this kind into a system is very great, and the system stood because, in the nature of the case, it could not conflict with many know facts.

I think the time has come to see these pieces of evidence, fragmentary though they are, as forming part of a much greater enterprise than anything envisaged by Clerval and Poole and those who have followed in their footsteps.

III REPLIES TO CRITICS

The criticisms levelled against the argument of the preceding paper can be divided into three main classes.

On the one hand, there are those who judged that my criticisms were wholly misguided, and that with one or two minor changes the cathedral school at Chartres can still be regarded as the outstanding school of the first half of the twelfth century in the quality of its masters, the innovating force of their teaching, and in the clarity and peculiar beauty of their doctrinal innovations.

On the other hand, there are those who, while accepting that the cathedral school at Chartres as a physical and institutional entity must henceforward be seen as only one among several cathedral schools of northern France with relatively few pupils and perhaps only a single master, go on to argue that the designation 'school of Chartres' may – quite apart from the precise place of origin – properly continue to be attached to a body of thought possessing a special style, poetical quality, Platonic philosophy and force of its own. Those who urge this view would add that, although this body of thought existed in only loose association with Chartres itself, it is quite distinct in aim and style from the main line of scholastic doctrine chiefly emanating from Paris.

Then, between these two, there is a single critic, Peter Dronke, who while agreeing with several of the arguments and facts in the paper reprinted above argues that there was a real division between the learning and learned attitudes represented by the school of, and at, Chartres and those of other schools, and that (despite, or because of, many ambiguities) the general Clerval–Poole hypothesis should broadly be maintained.

I shall reply to the advocates of each of these positions in turn.

1 The outright defenders of the Clerval–Poole hypothesis

The first of these positions, claiming that things still stand very much as they were, can, I think, be disposed of quite quickly. By far the most important protagonist of this view was the late Fr. Nicholas Häring, and, before coming to the substance of his criticism, I must mention two important matters. First, every student of twelfth-century thought owes him an immense debt for his prodigious labours in editing unprinted or ill-edited scholastic texts of the twelfth century, and nothing I shall say about his views on the school of Chartres in the least diminishes the importance of his great contribution to the study of twelfth-century scholastic thought. And second, the warm friendship which grew up between us out of our difference, and continued without either of us yielding one inch to the other's view in this matter, provided a striking confirmation of some indefinable humanism in the Chartrian atmosphere which I gladly recognize.

Fr. Häring's answer is stated at considerable length in his article 'Paris and Chartres revisited'.[38] It contains a mass of information about masters and schools, and especially about masters witnessing charters in various cathedral towns during the first half of the twelfth century, which cannot be found elsewhere. Nevertheless, I believe that none of the evidence quoted in the article, immensely valuable though it is for the history of various schools and their masters, has any bearing on the points at issue between us because Fr. Häring's interpretation of the facts he produces suffers from one of the most fatal faults in the whole case for the school of Chartres as built up by Clerval and Poole and adopted by their successors: they accepted that the appearance of a master as a witness of charters connected with Chartres could be used as evidence that they were teaching in the cathedral school.

This assumption first made it possible for Clerval to build up an army of masters in the school of Chartres, and it is wholly misleading. The real importance of the quite sudden increase in the number of masters in the witness lists of charters, at Chartres as elsewhere, is that they provide evidence of the speed with which scholars who followed the new scholastic courses were found to be indispensable for the work of government at every level and in every part of western Europe. But, in the absence of some qualifying word such as *Magister scolae*, the mere title *magister* no more tells us that the witness was teaching in the school of the cathedral at which the charter was issued, or in any other school for that matter, than the title 'MA Oxon.' would tell us that the witness to a modern document was teaching in the university of Oxford. So far as concerns the teaching resources of the school of Chartres, therefore, the whole line of argument based on evidence of this kind is

---

[38] See Häring, 1974, pp. 268–329.

worthless, and this invalidates the greater part of the evidence collected by Fr. Häring.

On one point in my paper, Fr. Häring did indeed correct an error. He showed that I was wrong in saying that there is no evidence that Gilbert de la Porrée taught at Chartres while he was chancellor of the cathedral from about 1125 to 1142. On this point he was certainly right and I was wrong: there *is* evidence that Gilbert taught both in Paris and in Chartres while he was chancellor of Chartres, and I shall have more to say about this later. But what may be said at once is that the evidence for Gilbert's teaching in Chartres also testifies to the fact that far greater audiences could be found in Paris.[39] Indeed Fr. Häring believed that Gilbert actually resigned the chancellorship of Chartres in order to teach in Paris. If this were true it would provide the clearest possible evidence of the superiority of Paris as a scholastic centre. But I do not think there was any reason – nor is there any evidence – for Gilbert's resignation of his chancellorship at Chartres in order to teach at Paris: this position, like similar positions in other cathedrals, did not demand constant residence.

Gilbert seems simply to have had a nephew who deputized for him as chancellor during his lengthy absences in Paris. The evidence for this consists of a number of charters of the cathedral of Chartres witnessed by a certain Guido variously described in cartulary copies of the charters as *Guido nepos cancellarii*, or *Guido cancellarii*, or once as *Guido cancellarius*.[40] Fr. Häring surmises that the last of these descriptions is correct, and concludes that Gilbert resigned the chancellorship in about 1138 and that Guido held the position of chancellor until 1142 when Thierry succeeded him. But by far the most likely explanation is that the last of these descriptions is simply one of a multitude of scribal errors, and that Guido acted as Gilbert's deputy during his absences from Chartres. There was certainly no incompatibility between Gilbert's holding the chancellorship of Chartres while lecturing in Paris, any more than there was

---

[39] See below, p. 227.
[40] The Cartularies containing charters witnessed by Guido are listed in Häring, 1974, p. 74, without however mentioning the various corruptions in the forms in which Guido's position is described.

between Thierry's being archdeacon of Dreux in the diocese of Chartres while also lecturing in Paris.[41]

The chancellorship did not carry any obligation to teach in the school over which the chancellor had jurisdiction. He appointed a master for this purpose. Further, as we shall see, it seems likely that Thierry, Gilbert's successor as chancellor, looked on his new position as an opportunity for retiring from teaching in Paris to collect his materials and to prepare for his withdrawal to a monastic life. Certainly there is not the slightest evidence that Thierry used his position as chancellor to enhance the scholastic activity of the school of Chartres, as Raymond Klibansky supposed when he wrote:

> Under him (Thierry), Chartres became the centre of the liberal Arts to which students came from all over Europe. In search of new knowledge his pupils crossed the Pyrenees and the Alps. They brought back new material and astronomical works in translation from Arabic, and new texts of Aristotle in versions made from the Greek. From Chartres this new learning was handed on to the Latin world.[42]

This is splendid rhetoric, but it is pure imagination. No doubt Thierry would have been a notable figure wherever he was, but there is not a scrap of evidence that he attracted pupils to Chartres from Spain and Italy, or that Greek and Arabic learning was disseminated from Chartres.[43] As for his teaching while he was chancellor, it is a strange feature of this whole discussion that modern scholars, who often complain about the burden of teaching and their desire to have time for thought or research, have a conviction that medieval scholars were always thirsting to teach. But the likelihood is that, like their modern successors, they taught only when their office required them to teach, or when they were glad to have their pupils' fees, or when they had a special message for which they sought an audience.

---

[41] For the evidence, see above, p. 71, n. 15.

[42] R. Klibansky, 1961, p. 9.

[43] I have analysed the early impulses and circumstances governing the introduction of Greco-Arabic science into the West in Southern, 1992, pp. xxvi–liv. The only Chartrian connection is the letter of Hermann of Carinthia, sending his translation of Ptolemy's *Planisphere* to Thierry when he was chancellor of Chartres. For the significance of this, see above, p. 85 and n. 36.

All these reasons for or against teaching were as powerful in the twelfth century as in the twentieth; and, for those who wished to teach, Paris simply offered much better opportunities for getting an audience than any other town.

2 *The advocates of a new Chartrian hypothesis*

I do not think there is more that can usefully be said about the out-and-out defenders of the influence and importance of the school geographically sited in Chartres during the first half of the twelfth century. So we may turn to the second class of critics. They accept that the cathedral school at Chartres played only a minor part among the schools of northern France in the first half of the twelfth century, but they claim that the phrase 'the school of Chartres' can still properly be used to describe, not primarily or even at all a geographical fact, but rather a mode of thought substantially different from anything displayed in the main stream of scholastic thought flowing from Paris.

According to the advocates of this view, the characteristics of 'Chartrian' thought – wherever it was found – were, first, a powerful advocacy of Platonism; and, second, arising from this, a type of humanism which is more imaginative, more poetical, more inclined to see the whole universe as exhibiting the genial features of rationality combined with beauty, than is to be found in the starker systematic rationality characteristic of the Parisian schools. This school of critics would be quite content to see most of the claims that have been made for the school *at* Chartres thrown overboard, provided that they can continue to attach the name of Chartres to this more poetical and imaginative kind of humanism.

The first protagonist of this de-localized view of the school of Chartres was Professor Wetherbee, who wrote:[44]

> It must be understood that the Chartrian label is largely a matter of convenience, and refers to a body of ideas and scholars and poets

[44] Wetherbee, 1972, p. xii.

who developed them, as well as to an institution precisely located in time and space.

It must also (I may add) be understood that this formula, with the words 'ideas . . . as well as . . . time and place' is phrased to make the best of both worlds: if the 'precisely located' school of Chartres proves to be seaworthy, well and good; but, if not, then there is the more general resource available for keeping the doctrinal furniture, which is claimed for Chartres by its advocates, afloat in different vessels under a Chartrian flag.

At first sight, this may seem a happy solution since it dispenses with topographical facts and concentrates on ideas. But before we fall too readily into this new embrace, we must ask precisely what we are doing: in the first place, what is the body of ideas we are looking for? Wetherbee answers this question thus:[45]

> Chartrian thought begins and ends in a kind of poetry: poetic intuition is finally the only means of linking philosophy and theology, pagan *auctores* and Christian doctrine, *sapientia* and *eloquentia*.

This is all very well, but linking philosophy and theology (or pagan *auctores* and Christian doctrine) is what all the masters of Paris, or for that matter, Reims or Laon, were doing. But, as for linking these mighty opposites by means of 'poetic intuition', this is certainly *not* what Thierry of Chartres, or any other master, thought he was doing. Thierry will require more careful study later, but it may at once be said that he *thought* he was explaining quite precisely, with the help of Plato's *Timaeus*, what the first chapter of Genesis means. And, like every other notable master of the early twelfth century, he thought that other pagan *auctores* could similarly be used to provide a fuller understanding of many Christian doctrines of all kinds.

There is nothing specially 'Chartrian' in this: the use of pagan authors to define the precise meaning of biblical and patristic texts was an essential part of the method of all scholastic theology. This method was of course not especially Parisian either, but it was in Paris that the greatest number of masters operated

[45] Ibid., p. 4, with much else in similar vein, pp. 18–19, 24, 29.

in a single area, and by their interactions and combinations gave the most powerful impetus and fullest development to this mode of interpreting authoritative theological texts. Except in so far as any systematic combination of precise statements gives aesthetic satisfaction, there is nothing especially poetic in this method.

At this point we may look at some further words of Klibansky, which are particularly apposite because they are used (and have been adopted by others) to describe the work of Thierry of Chartres, who as I have mentioned above is a central figure both in the old localized view of the school of Chartres and in the more idealistic version that is now presented to us. Even if it is agreed that Thierry's teaching career down to 1142 was centred on Paris, it is still true that he was chancellor of Chartres from 1142 to 1150; and even if he regarded his position as chancellor as an opportunity for retiring from teaching rather than for teaching at the centre of Chartrian humanism, he would have been an important man wherever he was. All this may be granted, but it still does not make the cathedral school at Chartres an important source of scholastic thought, nor does it provide the slightest reason for thinking that 'Chartrian humanism' is anything but an invention of nineteenth-century romanticism. This romanticism is well exemplified once more in Klibansky's words describing what he takes to be Thierry's aim in using the *Timaeus* as a source of information about the Creation:

> Naive as his account (of the Creation) may now seem to the modern scholar and scientist, this first systematic attempt to withdraw cosmology from the realm of the miraculous and win for physical theory a relative independence from theology, gives Thierry an outstanding place among philosophers.[46]

Professor Dronke in his turn has, with some hesitation, accepted these words as a 'brief but perceptive comment' which, with minor reservations, he proceeded to confirm and elaborate.[47]

And finally Professor Wetherbee has generalized the theme:

[46] Klibansky, 1961, p. 7.
[47] Dronke, 1969, p. 117.

The great originality of the Chartrians consisted in their emphasis on the rational and scientific as against traditional authority.[48]

So here we have the Chartrian theme renewed and put in a brilliant light as a model of thought about the world, which can be described either as more poetic, or more rational, or more independent of authoritative restraints and theological preconceptions; and when we add to this that Chartrian humanism is now not encumbered with geographical restraints, we are indeed in a wide world.

So what is to be said about this revised defence of the 'school of Chartres'? I think the first and main thing to be said is that, far from trying to give a scientific account of Creation divorced from theology or from Revelation, Thierry like other contemporary scholars was using the doctrines of ancient pagan writers to elucidate, not to by-pass, the revealed truths of the Bible. If I am right in thinking that, already in the 1120s and in Paris, Thierry was using the *Timaeus* to interpret the first chapter of Genesis, he was using – and certainly continued to use – a well-established method of drawing on secular texts to elucidate biblical and other authoritative Christian texts.[49] Thierry accepted the 'restraints' of dogmatic truth, as did every other scholastic writer, because dogmas were seen not as restraints, but as reliable statements of truths which gained, not more certainty, but more substance and wider ramification by the support of rational argument, scientific observation, and the learning of the past. Thierry is certainly remarkable for the fullness and originality of some of his observations; but he always wrote within the framework of earlier authorities, and his discoveries came from subjecting authoritative texts – whether authoritative because of their divine origin or because of the reputation and antiquity of their authors – to the methods of verbal analysis and systematic combination.

This was the method that was developed in many contemporary schools, but above all in Paris, and it led to the major intellectual achievements of the twelfth century. When we add that the only place at which Thierry is known to have taught

48   Wetherbee, 1972, p. 4.
49   See below, p. 210, for this aspect of biblical studies.

is Paris, it must be said that the claim that he represents in any intelligible sense a distinctive Chartrian mode of thought, rather than a more broadly scholastic one, seems singularly unsubstantial. Generalizations which set Thierry against the scholastic programme of his time break down under examination. Whatever can truly be said about Thierry's use of secular learning as an instrument of theological clarification can equally be said of all the known Parisian masters of the period. Rational and scientific enquiries were not undertaken in opposition to, or independently of, Revelation or authority. No master of any school thought that orthodoxy was a limitation on reason, and their main disagreements were all about details in harmonizing and defining the relationship between revealed and natural sources of truth. Whether in Paris, Laon, Reims or Chartres, the method of comparison and analysis of authoritative texts, both natural and revealed, was the road to all truth, and Paris was the place where all roads met.

Further, Klibansky's use of the word 'miraculous' in this context is simply emotive: the correct word is 'supernatural' and the aim of all the great masters of the period was to give, so far as possible, rational explanations of the ways in which the supernatural plan of Creation, Redemption, and divine Governance was elaborated in all its manifold details. This is what Thierry, following in the earlier footsteps of Adelard of Bath and William of Conches, was attempting to do. And this is what the whole scholastic programme was all about. Moreover, twelfth-century scholastic masters were continuing a long tradition of commentators on Macrobius and Martianus Capella, themselves dependent on Plato's *Timaeus*, who had filled out the exiguous knowledge contained in the first chapter of Genesis by using the doctrines of these texts.

In the field of cosmology, as cultivated by Thierry and by other masters of the period, the two texts that called most urgently for reconciliation were the first chapter of Genesis and that part of Plato's *Timaeus* which had long ago been translated into Latin. The combination of these two texts, the one based on Revelation, the other on reason, offered one of the greatest opportunities for progress in knowledge because, though several ancient texts reflected the doctrines of the *Timaeus*, Plato's work was, until the discovery of Aristotle's *Physics*, the sole known independent account of Creation outside the Bible. The greater part of the *Timaeus* had indeed long been translated into Latin, but it had scarcely been studied before 1050. After this date glosses and commentaries grew in number and detail, and were made by several scholars in places which for the most part cannot now be identified.[50]

It has often been alleged that the disappearance after about 1150 of the *Timaeus* from the list of ancient texts frequently commented on was a symptom of the decline of Chartrian humanism, and of 'Platonism' generally. But there were other and better reasons. First, the *Timaeus* began to be superseded by texts that provided more and clearer information about the universe and its elements; and, second, some of the doctrines of the *Timaeus* – in particular the *anima mundi* – proved to be irreconcilable with Christian doctrine, and therefore unusable and probably wrong. These were two deadly limitations to the usefulness of any text. So the *Timaeus* dropped out of circulation until new interests and outlooks revived an interest in Plato's works in the fourteenth and fifteenth centuries.

Seen in this light, it is obvious that the detailed study of the *Timaeus* from about 1050 to 1150 was neither a Chartrian symptom or innovation, nor was it an alternative to scholastic thought, nor an indication of a broader interest in Plato's philosophy: it was just the only available text which gave any hope of adding new substance to the account of Creation in Genesis. It was for this reason that scholars read and annotated the *Timaeus* from 1050 to 1150; and their interest declined after this date, not because scholars became less 'humanistic', but simply because at least one of the doctrines of the *Timaeus* (the *anima mundi*) proved to be incompatible with Christan doctrine, and the *Meno* and *Phaedo*, which were also translated into Latin about the middle of the twelfth century – contained still more

---

50   I have summarized the evidence for the role of the *Timaeus* in the schools from about 1050 to 1150 in Southern, 1979, pp. 8–15. To the evidence collected there may be added the gloss on the *Timaeus* which P. E. Dutton, 1991, has attributed to Bernard of Chartres. For this, see above, p. 81, n. 29. For a survey of the surviving manuscripts, see Margaret Gibson, 'The Study of the *Timaeus* in the eleventh and twelfth centuries', *Pensamiento*, 25, 1969, pp. 183–94.

unacceptable doctrine. Hence they found almost no readers, and led to no further translations of Plato for use in the schools, whereas all the works of Aristotle had been completely discovered, translated and made available for school use by about the middle of the thirteenth century.

It was only in the fifteenth century, when systematic doctrine came to seem less important than the refinement of sensibility, and when aristocratic courts rather than schools became centres of innovation, that Plato and Platonism began to flourish for the first time as a self-conscious movement away from the developments of the twelfth and thirteenth centuries.

In view of the general needs and principles which provided the impetus for the growth of the schools and formed the boundaries of scholastic thought, we may ask what distinctive quality is left, once the geographical link has been dropped, that can reasonably be associated, however vaguely, with Chartres rather than with Paris, or indeed any other place where scholastic principles of enquiry were operative. To call the principal driving force of this great intellectual effort either Platonist or Chartrian or, for that matter, Parisian, except in the sense that Paris had all the resources that most other towns lacked, is fundamentally misleading.

The driving force in the development of scholastic thought came from a growing demand for a full and detailed body of doctrine about the natural and supernatural worlds, which could be used for the instruction and building up of the organized life of the whole of western Christendom. As this demand grew in volume and in the increasing capacity to finance its realization, a unique combination of favourable circumstances brought about the concentration of one part of this programme in northern France, and pre-eminently in Paris, and of the other half of the programme in northern Italy, and pre-eminently in Bologna. The main features of this great movement of thought and action will be traced in later chapters of this work; but, as for the Platonist or Chartrian labels, they are best consigned to a place among that large body of hypotheses which have served their turn in stimulating interest in neglected areas of the achievements of the past, but are now best given an honourable burial, for, if they are kept alive, they can only generate further misconceptions.

But before leaving the question, I must briefly comment on the contribution of the most interesting and learned of the critics of the essay reprinted above, Peter Dronke.[51]

3 The 'Dronke' hypothesis

Dronke urges that, although the Clerval–Poole view can be challenged on many points of detail, there is still sufficient evidence to make it permissible to describe the four major scholars, Thierry, Gilbert de la Porrée, William of Conches, and John of Salisbury, as representatives of 'the school of Chartres'. My view is that the connection of all of them with Paris is much more fully attested than any known connection with the school of Chartres and that their work can best be understood in the context of the Parisian schools. In the end the issue must be judged by the extent to which their work is illuminated by, or throws light on, the work and thought of other scholars of the first half of the twelfth century. So the question is: which context, that of the schools of Paris or of the school of Chartres, gives us the fullest and most enlightening view of the aims and content of their work in the context of other scholars of the period? As I believe, and shall try to show more fully in later chapters of this work, the presence and teaching in Paris of the so-called 'Chartrian masters' is not only better documented than their presence in Chartres, but also the Parisian context is more enlightening for understanding the scholarship of the period in general. In the end everything must depend on this capacity to enlighten, for it is the only test of any significance. Is the learned work of Gilbert de la Porrée, Thierry, William of Conches and John of Salisbury better understood in association with the work of such contemporary Parisian masters as Abelard, Hugh of St-Victor, and Peter Lombard, and their immediate forerunners Anselm of Laon and William of Champeaux, and with the aims of such contemporary Parisian students as Otto of of Freising, William of Tyre, author of *Metamorphosis Goliae* and the enigmatic Everard of Ypres; or is it better understood in

---

51 See P. Dronke, 'New Approaches to the School of Chartres', *Anuario de estudios medievales*, 6, Barcelona, 1969, 117–40.

the context of Chartres – and, if so, on what evidence and in what connection?

Clearly all scholars, wherever they are teaching, have their own individual characteristics and emphases, even if they are handling the same material along broadly similar lines. But all the scholars and students with whom we are concerned in this discussion have the same idea of what constitutes an assured body of knowledge, and broadly speaking they all aimed at increasing and organizing the same body of knowledge by use of the same techniques of analysis and systematization. Dronke brings a welcome enrichment to the scholarship of the period, as also do the publications of Edouard Jeauneau, the most prolific contributor to the understanding of the works of Thierry and William of Conches.[52] But I do not think that the contributions of either of them alter the conclusions to which my paper pointed, and which will be strengthened when we turn to a more detailed study of these masters and their Parisian contemporaries.

---

[52] The majority of Jeauneau's contributions are collected in a volume with the title, *Lectio philosophorum: recherches sur l'école de Chartres*, Amsterdam, 1973, and – despite their author's continuing use of the Chartrian label – their great value lies in their contribution to scholastic development generally.

3

The Sovereign Textbook of the Schools: the Bible

I THE QUALITIES OF THE BIBLE IN SCHOLASTIC THOUGHT

The fundamental teaching method of the medieval schools, which they handed on to the universities that grew out of them, was the exposition of authoritative texts. And of all the texts expounded in the schools there was none that could claim anything like the degree of authority and range of influence possessed by the Bible. It is necessary to begin by saying this, because one of the most widely held and longest lasting misconceptions about scholastic thought, which has lasted from the sixteenth century – and even earlier – almost to the present day, has been that it diminished the role of the Bible in the totality of Christian thought. Indeed the diminishment would seem to be obvious. We shall later examine the huge increase in the number of quotations from secular sources in the *Summa Theologiae* of Thomas Aquinas as compared with the *Sentences* of Peter Lombard a century earlier.[1] Similar comparisons between the number of biblical quotations are more difficult to make because the language of the Bible is so widely diffused as to make comparisons almost meaningless. Nevertheless, the idea that the Bible was somehow losing ground as the main foundation of all discussion about Christian doctrine was fairly widespread even in the thirteenth century, and it had become a major bone of contention by the sixteenth century.

---

[1] To be examined in Volume III. Meanwhile see Southern, 1987.

One of the earliest and most outspoken expressions of this fear of biblical diminishment came from Robert Grosseteste, and it is worth examining his words if we are to understand how much and what kind of substance there is in his complaint. In about 1240, shortly after he had become bishop of Lincoln, an office which carried with it responsibility for the teaching in the University of Oxford, he wrote to the theological masters of the university warning them against a recent innovation whereby their morning lectures, which had traditionally been on the Bible, were being replaced by lectures on Peter Lombard's *Sentences*, the main textbook of systematic – as contrasted with biblical – theology. Grosseteste declared that this was inadmissible because the books of the Bible were the foundation stones on which all theological teaching was based, and that the best hours of the day should therefore be devoted to them.[2]

This may seem a somewhat pettifogging complaint, but anyone who has taken part in academic discussions about lecture timetables will know that these changes do indeed mirror deeper changes in the credit enjoyed by different parts of a university curriculum, and it is very likely that the change which was the source of Grosseteste's complaint marked a significant shift of emphasis in the weight attached to different parts of the curriculum. The teaching of systematic doctrine had long been growing in prestige as compared with the exposition of the biblical text. And for practical purposes, whether with a view to teaching doctrine even at a parochial level, or for the more advanced teaching in religious communities, it is easy to see that systematic teaching was more obviously useful than biblical exegesis.

So Grosseteste's reproof to the Oxford theologians raises two distinct questions: first, what role the Bible had in theology and in other scholastic subjects; and, second, in what ways this role could be held to have been diminishing. To put his complaint in its widest context, it must be remembered that scholastic thought was not a system of ideas, but a method, or rather a combination of methods, for eliciting a stable body of knowledge from authoritative texts, and the Bible formed only a small part

---

[2] *Roberti Grosseteste Epistolae*, ed. H. R. Luard, RS, 1861, pp. 346–7.

of the mass of authoritative material to be examined. Neverthe-less, consistency with the Bible was a fundamental requirement of all knowledge. There was even a sense in which all knowledge could be said to be contained in or implied in the Bible. This did not mean that the Bible stood over all knowledge like an usher with a birch, checking the biblical credentials of every item of knowledge; but it did mean that the Bible contained facts about human society and the physical world, and about principles of argument or conduct which were important for all areas of study, and that no conclusion in any subject could stand if it contradicted the Bible when correctly understood.

There are of course many apparently contradictory state-ments in the Bible itself, as there are in all authoritative texts. The scholastic answer to this situation was to elaborate methods for harmonizing them; and since texts of one kind or another provided the outlines of nearly all knowledge on all subjects, the methods of harmonization laid the foundations for the whole body of systematic knowledge.

In outline, these methods were, first to detect apparent contradictions either within or between authoritative texts, and then to analyse the words and constructions in which they occurred with a view to clarifying their meaning. These pro-cedures produced a number of refinements of meaning which allowed most apparently contradictory statements in the texts to be understood in such a way that they could be seen to be complementary. One such case will be examined presently, and it will be seen that this process of refinement produced a finer tissue of systematic truth than could have been arrived at without the apparent 'contradictions'. The only difference in the application of this method of refinement to the Bible as compared with other texts, was that all other texts would sometimes be convicted of error, but *never* the Bible. This stamped the Bible with a uniqueness that belonged to no other text however authoritative: errors in other authoritative texts were rare but possible; but, in the Bible, they were impossible except in cases of textual corruption.

With regard to the procedures for refining the meaning of texts to bring them into agreement with themselves and with other texts, the scholastic method of investigation employed various techniques, such as drawing attention to the distinction between literal and metaphorical statements, and between statements of general applicability and statements applicable only to certain categories of people or situations. Conceptual refinements would eliminate many apparent contradictions, and if any proved to be too stubborn to be removed, the area of discord could be left for further refinement at a later date. These procedures were applicable to all the authoritative texts on which scholastic doctrine in every area of knowledge was based. But the statements of the Bible were more important than those in any other source, partly because the Bible made some contribution to nearly every subject, and partly because the inerrancy of the Bible, in contrast to all other texts, was thought to be absolute.

In the light of this inerrancy, we may begin by asking what kind of information could be extracted from the Bible, what methods of extraction and of harmonization were used, and what results were achieved. In asking these questions, it must first be noticed that although there was no conscious desire to impose a set of ideas on the Bible, there were several assumptions, largely unspoken, which influenced and in some degree determined the results of all enquiries.

The first and least articulated of these assumptions was that the precepts of the Bible would not contradict the normal operations of society as they had developed in western Europe over the centuries. There was, therefore, a built-in requirement that the hierarchy of social classes should be maintained, that trade and capital accumulation, though carefully limited and regulated, should not be made impossible, and that the prohibition of killing should be interpreted in a way that would allow rulers a wide latitude in making war in defence of their rights and in imposing the death penalty for many offences including heterodox religious opinions.

These minimizing procedures imposed far-reaching restraints on the interpretation of such biblical passages as 'thou shalt not kill', 'he who takes the sword shall perish by the sword', 'thou shalt not lend on usury to thy brother', and 'swear not at all', 'give to him that asketh', and so on. Clearly social usages and changing techniques of commerce and doctrines of social order shaped the interpretation of these and many other biblical passages, but what contemporaries saw was not – as may appear to us – a watering down of biblical texts, but an increasingly refined understanding of their essential meaning.

Another guiding principle of biblical interpretation was the requirement that interpretations should conform to the discipline and usages of the western Church, and this limitation too was accepted without any general sense either of watering down or of conforming with the evils of the time, though this was often alleged by dissident minorities.[3] The existence of married priests in the New Testament, the community of goods among the early disciples, the absence of any requirement of the practice of confession in the biblical texts, were all thought to be capable of being harmonized with current practice by considerations which brought the texts into agreement with the authoritative statements and usages of the Church. In brief, although it may seem that harmonizing discordant texts with current practice did some violence to ordinary language, this was not how the matter presented itself to the masters who interpreted these texts in the schools.

It is important also to recognize that, although the Bible alone among texts was credited with complete inerrancy, all authoritative texts in all subjects were thought to have this quality in a high degree. This was the reason for their acceptance as textbooks, and this expectation of inerrancy arose from a static view of the nature of knowledge: whatever had once been

---

[3] For evidence of such 'watering down' see, for instance, B. Tierney, 'The decretalists and the deserving poor', *Comparative Studies in Society and History*, i, 1959, 360–73. The first steps in this direction were already being taken in the late eleventh century in the school of Laon: see, for example, O. Lottin, *Psychologie et morale aux XIIe et XIIIe siècles*, 1959, vol. 5, p. 65, for Anselm of Laon's account of loving one's neighbour as oneself 'in the same manner as' but not 'as much as' oneself, and the effect of this on the obligation to give bread etc. to whomsoever asks. A century later, Peter the Chanter, one of the great masters of Paris at the end of the twelfth century, still recalled with approval Master Anselm's words of caution to the seneschal of France who wanted to give Master Anselm's own nephews more than was good for them. See Peter the Chanter, *Verbum abbreviatum*, PL, 205, col. 151. The seriousness of the problem may be judged from the great variety of testimonies: the lawyers are not always the least generous – see, for example, Gratian (on whom more below, pp. 283–318) on hospitality: *Decretum*, Dist. xlii.

known – whether about logic, physics, the movements of the heavenly bodies, the virtues of stones or plants, the inadmissibility of usury, or whatever else – was thought to be forever true. Nevertheless, knowledge was not static. There was a strong sense, especially in the twelfth century, of the reconquest of lost knowledge, and of the need to refine the knowledge of the past. But of an essential instability of knowledge, there was no sense at all; and this was the case with all knowledge, not just with theological doctrines.

All the basic texts in use in the schools were authoritative because they could be depended on to be exceptionally free from error and to express truths which were true in all circumstances and for all time. The main difference between secular truths and the truths of the Bible, including the definitions of the Church which were drawn ultimately from the Bible, was that the Bible, except for such errors as had crept into the text through faulty transmission, was exempt from error in principle. And the reason for this was that, in the words of Thomas Aquinas, 'The author of Holy Scripture is God.'[4]

Various consequences followed from this fundamental statement. First, there followed the total inerrancy of the Bible, except for errors which had crept in through the carelessness or ignorance of scribes copying the sacred text. Second – as Thomas Aquinas was particularly concerned to emphasize in the passage in which he expressly stated God's authorship – there followed the unique power of God to use *events* and *objects*, as well as *words*, to express His meaning. And, third, unlike all other textbooks, which were authoritative only in their own field of knowledge, the inerrancy of the Bible extended to every area of knowledge.

These unique attributes of the Bible set it apart from all other authoritative textbooks of the schools, and suffice to explain why its position was not essentially changed by the great increase in the number of texts on special parts of the curriculum during the twelfth and thirteenth centuries. We cannot

---

[4]   Thomas Aquinas, *Summa Theologiae*, I, q. 1, art. 10: *Respondeo dicendum quod auctor Sacrae Scripturae est Deus, in cuius potestate est ut non solum voces ad significandum accommodet (quod etiam homo potest facere) sed etiam res ipsas.*

understand the structure of scholastic thought, unless we understand the ramifications of biblical inerrancy and universality. So a brief account of the way in which these characteristics manifested themselves in practice is desirable at this point.

1 The inerrancy of the Bible

In the task of establishing a firm foundation for the doctrinal and disciplinary role of the Church in medieval society, the schools had two main functions: first, to teach the formal rules for distinguishing truth from error; and second, to apply these rules to clarify the body of knowledge contained in authoritative texts. Without this body of assured knowledge it would have been impossible to construct a system of sufficient breadth for the task of organizing western Christendom, and the Bible contained the largest stock of irrefutable knowledge about the nature and purpose of the universe, the destiny of mankind, and the divine plan of creation.

There were indeed several intermediate sources of equally, or almost equally, unshakeable truth: papal decisions, decrees of Councils, the writings of the Fathers. But in the last resort, the foundations of all these sources of knowledge could be found in biblical texts. Consequently every certain truth known on earth could ultimately be derived either from clear and incontrovertible chains of reasoning based on self-evident facts, or from the revealed truths contained in or exemplified in the Bible, and given legislative force by persons authorized in biblical texts to do this. Just as God created the fruits of the earth without husbandmen or seeds, so he put into the hearts and minds of prophets, apostles and evangelists truths which were either expressed or foreshadowed in the Bible and committed for further clarification to the successors of the apostles to whom authority had been given in biblical texts.

This was the bedrock of certainty. But the scholastic readiness to accept the absolute truth of biblical statements was also supported by a general belief in the absolute once-for-all nature of all truth whatever its source. All that was known, whether through irrefragable reasoning or through divine revelation, was held to possess a finality which is seldom expected in any modern knowledge. There was no conception of a universe in which knowledge consists largely or wholly of fluctuating approximations shaped by historical circumstances and temporary hypotheses.

There existed indeed the idea of development in human knowledge: but the development came from the refinement of concepts, from a widening knowledge of the learning of the past, and from bringing together dispersed bodies of knowledge to form interrelated systems; never by an unsteady movement from one viewpoint to another. The great masters of the past were believed to have made discoveries which were forever true, but which needed to be cleared of later corruptions, refined by sharpening their definitions, and finally systematized and brought into harmony with other areas of knowledge. The carrying out of these processes was the aim of the schools of the twelfth and thirteenth centuries. All their achievements were built on discovering and clarifying the learning of the past in the assurance that to get back to what had been known in the past was to get back to the truth.

The certainties derived from the Bible were therefore not different in kind from the certainty of all knowledge, but they were guaranteed by the immediate stamp of divine inspiration, and they contributed to the study of more subjects than any other source of knowledge.

This brings us to the next characteristic of the Bible as a textbook of the schools: its universal range.

2 *The universality of the Bible*

The importance of the inerrancy of the Bible in helping to build up a complete system of knowledge in the medieval schools was immensely increased by the very wide area of knowledge which the contents of the Bible were thought to embrace. Nothing separates the medieval view of the Bible more abruptly from any generally accepted modern view than the area of assured information which it was believed to cover. Indeed, there were thought to be no limits to the range of knowledge potentially derivable from the Bible: a detailed account of the nature of God, of the Creation, of the divine plan for human Redemption, of the beginning, progress and end of human history; many details about the natures of plants, animals and terrestrial and celestial beings; a complete outline of the stages of universal history from beginning to end – all were explicitly or figuratively contained in the Bible. The primacy of the Bible on all these subjects was expressed with provocative sharpness by Nicholas of Lyre, whose glosses on the Bible in the early fourteenth century summed up the work of the previous two centuries:

> Sciences may be graded according to the nobility of their subject-matter and the certainty of their method. Holy Scripture may itself properly be called 'Theology' because it is the only textbook in the science which excels all other sciences because it has God, the summit of all nobility, as its subject-matter, and because it proceeds from divine revelation, which is more certain than any other source. Other sciences proceed by rational investigation which – even though there be no error in their first principles which are self evident (as Aristotle, *Metaphysics*, ii, makes clear) – can fall into error in drawing false conclusions from these first principles, especially if the chain of deduction is lengthy. False conclusions can of course be drawn from the Bible also, but – just as in philosophy whatever is unmistakably concluded from first principles is true – so whatever is manifestly concluded from Holy Scripture is also true.[5]

Further, to continue Nicholas of Lyre's statement:

> Whatever is repugnant to Holy Scripture is false. So Holy Scripture is not only Wisdom itself; it is also the understanding of this Wisdom.

Probably, when he wrote these words, Nicholas of Lyre was making a statement which was in some degree provocative in its disparagement of human sciences, and perhaps also in its disparagement of papal prerogative. But in the passage I have quoted, he was simply elaborating the substance of what Thomas Aquinas had said in the passage quoted earlier, and what any

---

5 Nicholas of Lyre (*c.* 1270–1340) in his *Prologus Primus* to his Postills on the Bible, in *Biblia Sacra cum glossa ordinaria et Postilla Nicolai Lyrani*, Lyon, 1590.

scholastic theologian would have approved: the conclusions to be drawn from the Bible covered the whole area of theology, made important contributions to all other subjects, and were in detail and in outline wholly free from error.

Every fact about Creation and every phase of universal history, and every rule of conduct, could in the last resort be found in embryo in the Bible, which was the fundamental source of information on the initial elements of the universe, the early history of man, the pattern of history through its seven ages, the end of the world, the origin of good and evil, and their ultimate rewards and punishments. Also, on many other subjects such as natural history, the principles of politics and economics, even of grammar, rhetoric and logic, if the Bible did not contain the truth systematically or fully set out, it contained an abundance of illustrations of truths which were otherwise only painfully discoverable by reason.

I do not think that anyone in the twelfth or thirteenth centuries would have gone as far as Cassiodorus in the sixth, in asserting that the learning of Greece was borrowed directly or indirectly from the learning of Moses and the prophets.[6] But in the medieval perspective of history, Abraham, Moses, David and Solomon were not just the equals of Aristotle and Plato in the secular sciences: they were their forerunners and in some degree the source of their knowledge. So, as well as being instruments of God's plan for human redemption, Abraham, Moses, David, Solomon and the Prophets had also been more important instruments of mankind's intellectual recovery after the Fall than the greatest scholars of Greece.

Overall, therefore, although the great theme of the Bible was human Redemption, various parts of the Bible were primary sources for several different branches of knowledge. In the Old Testament, the early chapters of Genesis and the books attributed to Solomon (Proverbs, Canticles, Ecclesiastes and Wisdom)

---

[6] Cassiodorus, *Institutiones*, ed. R. A. B. Mynors, Oxford, 1937, bk. 1, p. 6: *Quicquid autem in Scripturis divinis de talibus rebus (i.e. about the natural sciences) ... inventum fuerit ... postea doctores saecularium litterarum ad suas regulas prudentissime transtulerunt; quod apto loco in expositione Psalterii fortasse probavimus.* On similar lines, cf. Abelard *Dialectica*, ed. L. M. de Rijk, vol. 1, 1956, 333, ll. 22–25.

were unique storehouses of knowledge about cosmology and natural history, ethics, and the skills of human life. And, in the New Testament, the Gospels and Epistles besides containing outlines of Christian doctrine and the basic forms of ecclesiastical organization, also contained the rules of Christian conduct and gave an authoritative account of the future shape of world history and the Last Judgement.

Taken altogether, therefore, the Bible contained material for instruction in every branch of knowledge. The body of detailed knowledge which it contained could indeed be very extensively supplemented from the learning of ancient pagan authors. But, even if these aids had not existed, the close and continuing study of the Bible over the centuries would have brought to light an outline of the knowledge accessible to mankind in every field.

Further, just as the elaboration of human knowledge based on the learning of ancient Greece and Rome had in the past required, and would still require in the future, the continuing labours of scholars to bring it to perfection, so also the study of the manifold truths contained in the Bible had required and would require in the future a continuing labour of interpretation, arrangement and application to practical life. And just as ancient knowledge about the natural world could be completed and systematized only by those who searched the works of ancient scholars diligently, using the right methods and employing the appropriate instruments for resolving apparent contradictions, so a full understanding of the Bible demanded similar long labours, elaborate tools and intense study.

The methods for resolving apparent contradictions in all authoritative ancient sources were important tools in the scholastic treatment of texts on all subjects. For instance, all texts, whether biblical or not, which recorded historical events were liable to contain apparent contradictions arising from the different points of view from which the events had been observed. But the Bible also presented some varieties of apparent contradiction which were to be found in no other scholastic texts and which required special methods for resolving them. There were contradictions between the Law of the Old Testament and the teaching and practice of the New Testament; between the surface or historical meaning of words or events and their underlying and permanent meaning; between the apparent sense of prophecies and the manner of their fulfilment. There were also apparent contradictions in biblical accounts of the same incident. Many of these contradictions had been noted early in the history of the Church, and ways of reconciling them had been developed long before the twelfth century; there was no need to invent new methods, but only to apply old ones more rigorously and more systematically than earlier interpreters had done.

Of the three methods of reconciling apparent contradictions and drawing out the full meaning of the biblical text, two were common to all authoritative texts, and one was appropriate for biblical texts alone. The two methods common to all texts were, first, distinguishing the viewpoints of the differing reports; and, second, clearing up ambiguities and apparent contradictions by verbal and logical analysis. The method which was appropriate for the Bible alone was distinguishing between events as historical facts and these same events considered as symbols of permanent truths. A study of these methods, therefore, besides contributing to our understanding of the methods of biblical interpretation, will also provide an introduction to the general techniques of scholastic thought, and to the results that were achieved by their use. We may begin with the method which was appropriate for the Bible alone, and then go on to the two methods which were appropriate for all authoritative texts.

II Methods of Investigation

1 The divine language of symbols

I have already quoted Thomas Aquinas's statement that God was the author of Holy Scripture. To this statement he added a further and most important consequence:

> The author of Holy Scripture is God who has the power of signifying His meaning in words, as human beings also do; but has the further unique power of giving meaning to things themselves. Therefore,

although in all other areas of knowledge words are the signifiers of meaning, in the Bible alone *things* also act as signifiers.[7]

It follows from this, that God as the Creator of all things has the power to make things which are both objective realities and also have the power to convey messages. Consequently, when the inspired biblical writers of God's word describe events or objects, the student may look through these events and objects for the messages which they convey. Of course it may be objected that human authors also have the power of writing allegorically and thus of making things stand for words or ideas. But human authors writing allegories either make things stand for the characteristics displayed by existing things – as for instance a fox may stand for the creature's alleged characteristic of cunning – or they invent human stories which have a meaning that could equally well be conveyed in general propositions. In these cases we know that the story is 'make-believe', but the message is real. By contrast, God is the Creator of things and events as well as the source of their meaning. Consequently what God has created, including the historical events which flow from Creation, have (besides their factual truth) a universal meaning that is indestructably part of their reality. Events, therefore, are part of the language of God embodied primarily in the events of biblical history.

This capacity of the Bible, which is itself the work of God, to convey objective truths not only through words like other books, but also – unlike any other book – through the historical objects and events which the Bible describes, separates the Bible from all other writings. This characteristic played an important part in the earliest of all controversies within the Christian Church – namely the confrontation between Jewish and non-Jewish members of the early Church about keeping the Jewish law as laid down in the Old Testament Law and observed by the earliest followers of Christ. This law claimed to be everlasting: 'Cursed be he who does not keep all things which are written in the Law' (Deut. 27:26). How then could it lawfully be abandoned?

The Christian answer to this question was that the objects

---

7 *Summa Theologiae*, I, q. 1, art. 10. See above, p. 107, n. 4, for the context.

with which the Old Law was concerned were symbols for truths which would only be revealed in their full, and (at the time when they happened) incomprehensible, meaning – notably in predicting the Incarnation of God himself – when the time was ripe for their being revealed to the world. When this time came, such rules as the prohibition of the eating of pork, and such events as the crossing of the Red Sea, would be capable of being understood in their full reality. Then the symbol would no longer be needed, and Christian apologists could write:

> Truly the word of the Lord does not alter. It is never annulled, never changed. For example, the prohibition of the use of pork was given to the Jews in order to symbolize the deeper command to reject impurity and voluptuousness, which are represented by that animal. This symbolic instruction was no longer necessary after Christ, who is the Truth and who declares the Truth, had come into the world. Thereafter the symbol was no longer needed. Thus the symbol passes, and Truth remains.[8]

The argument with the Jews was entering a new stage in the late eleventh century when Jewish communities were becoming more widespread and increasingly important for the growing commerce and financial complexity of western Europe, and much might be said about the circumstances which, while provoking the development of scholastic thought, provoked also the growing anti-Jewish violence of the twelfth century. But, leaving aside the practical changes in the relationship between the Jewish and Christian communities, the basis of the argument on both sides remained what it had always been: the Jewish protagonists continued to argue that 'forever' meant what it said, while the Christian protagonists argued that 'forever' was to be understood in the light of the full meaning having become accessible in the life and words of God Himself in history.

The recognition of God's power to express truths through *things* as well as through words was an important tool for understanding the full message of the divinely inspired Scriptures.

---

[8] I here summarize the reply of *Christianus* to the criticism of *Judaeus* in Gilbert Crispin's *Disputatio Judaei et Christiani* written during the years 1090–1095. See *The Works of Gilbert Crispin, abbot of Westminster*, ed. A. S. Abulafia and G. R. Evans, London, 1986, pp. 17–23.

Once this divine power was recognized, it led to interpretations of many events in the Old Testament at every level of importance, from the grandeur of the passage through the Red Sea to the trivial detail of the axe-head of Elisha's servant floating on the water.[9] The real importance of both these events, widely disparate though they were in their external appearance and obvious importance, was that they conveyed to those who were capable of understanding them a message about the Incarnation which could only be recognized after the event.

When the full consequences of this truth about the Old Testament had been grasped, it had led to a vast reappraisal by Christian scholars of the whole body of biblical texts, and by the twelfth century there was scarcely a chapter of the Old Testament without its heavy load of symbolic interpretation. The twelfth-century schools did not greatly extend the bulk. What the schoolmen did was to collect and reorganize the vast body of earlier interpretations and make them available for preachers.

If it be asked why God should thus speak to mankind in symbols rather than in plain language, the answer is that verbal languages change, but the language of events remains forever: it is God's universal language. Human beings create words which act as symbols in communicating with each other, but their symbols vanish with their languages. God, who created all things, has a language at His command which has no linguistic barriers and will not perish so long as the universe exists.

Once this has been accepted, it is possible to study the grammar and syntax of this language of symbols, and to discover the common quality in classes of things and events which makes them appropriate vehicles of truth. For example, the seven Days of Creation are obviously an appropriate symbol for a statement about the seven Ages of history. Similarly, too, the phases in the history of the Chosen People characterize the Ages of universal history. When this principle is accepted, there is no end to the possibilities of elaboration. Consequently, by the twelfth century, the whole of the Old Testament had become a vast

9   For the symbolic meaning of the floating of the axe-heads in 4 Kings (or 2 Kings in the English version), c. 6, verse 5, see *Glossa Ordinaria*, Paris, 1590, vol. 2, cols. 889–890.

palimpsest capable of revealing the thread of universal history beneath the surface of biblical events.

Like any other palimpsest, the Old Testament needed careful searching to bring to light its vast store of underlying messages: the sacrifice of Isaac makes a statement about the crucifixion of Christ; the log thrown into the bitter waters of Marah to make them sweet signifies the Cross which purifies man's sinful state; and so on *ad infinitum*. In a similar way, God's commands to the Jews about circumcision, or about abstaining from eating pork, make statements about the moral law which are valid for ever, even though the practices themselves were abrogated by the coming of the truth in Christ.

If this divine use of things and events to serve as a language seems fanciful, it should be remembered that the message to be communicated is so far above human capacity of understanding that the idea of God's using every possible channel of communication is not one which can be lightly dismissed. To understand the thought of the Middle Ages, or for that matter Christian thought at all times, it is necessary to take seriously the divine method of conveying through symbolic events truths beyond any possibility of being understood by the impaired faculties of mankind after the Fall. The fundamental instrument of enlightenment is the Bible; and, in the Bible, the Psalms and Epistles are the two collections of texts with the greatest concentration of instruction about the divine plan. Peter Lombard, who summed up the results of the theological enquiries of the first two generations of scholastic theologians in his *Four Books of Sentences*, had prepared himself for his task by writing detailed commentaries on the two parts of the Bible, the Psalms and Epistles, which contained an outline of the whole range of biblical truth. He could not have prepared himself more carefully or deliberately for his great task, as his preface on the Psalms made clear:[10]

> David, the greatest of the Prophets, and the trumpet of the Holy Spirit, has said in a more excellent way all that the Prophets wrote by the revelation of the Holy Spirit. For all that the other Prophets wrote came to them under the influence of dreams and visions, and

[10] I have abbreviated and simplified Peter Lombard's words in his Preface to his commentary on the Psalms. For the whole text, see *PL*, 191, cols. 55–57.

wrapt in a cloak of images and words. But David's prophecies came to him from the Holy Spirit without any intermediate aid. Moreover, they cover the whole field of Time and Eternity, as you will see foreshadowed in the fact that there are a hundred and fifty Psalms: that is to say, eighty plus seventy, which numbers refer respectively to the eternity of Resurrection and the seven ages of Mankind in this world. In other words, the Psalms sum up the whole doctrine both of the Old and New Testaments, which is the whole body of doctrine.

In explanation of this account of David's power of explaining the past and foreseeing future events, it may be added that, like other prophets, he could describe the future only in symbolic terms because his understanding of the divine purpose in the future did not extend to factual knowledge. It was left to St Paul, who had experienced the historical reality which David could only foresee, to describe the foretold event.

It could therefore be said that the Psalms and the Pauline Epistles contain a compendium of the whole divine plan: what the Psalmist foresaw and expressed symbolically, Paul interpreted and declared as historical events. That was why these two parts of the Bible received more attention in the schools than all other books of the Bible put together. And of course this also is why Peter Lombard prepared himself for his main task of constructing a complete outline of doctrine by commenting first on these two parts of the Bible.

It was not the function of the schools to add new symbolic interpretations to the vast quantity that had come into existence in the course of the previous millennium. The function of the schools was to collect, clarify and arrange the biblical interpretations of the past, just as it was their function to collect, clarify and arrange the whole body of Christian doctrine and elucidate its consequences for human behaviour. The schools were not, and by the nature of their aims and methods could not be, the source of a new creative symbolism, such as we find in the early Middle Ages among scholars, and in the later Middle Ages among visionaries in hermitages, monasteries and friaries, and among groups of poor and persecuted people from the fourteenth to the seventeenth centuries.

The combination of circumstances which encouraged a widespread interest in the application of biblical symbolism to current events has been found only twice in the history of Europe: first, in the early Middle Ages, when the whole of life was permeated with symbolic actions and symbolic interpretations of common events, and when large parts of Christendom were being overrun by pagan or Muslim invaders; and, second, in the period from the fourteenth to the seventeenth centuries, when disappointed and frustrated groups found consolation in the perception that biblical texts symbolically expressed their sufferings and foretold the destruction of their enemies and a triumphant reversal of their own oppression.

In both of these two periods, symbolic interpretations of the Bible expressed the deepest experiences of life: in the earlier period, symbolism gave the oppressed a consolation and hope amidst the disasters of everyday events; and in the later period symbolic interpretations of events brought the assurance of victory to those whom the world despised. But in the twelfth century, when scholastic thought developed most rapidly and consistently, and when symbolic actions were losing their importance in ordinary life and in government, visionaries were isolated individuals whose influence lay in the future.[11] The central ground was occupied by the masters of the schools, whose role was not to experience great stirrings of symbolic insight, but to collect, arrange and make available for general use the symbols of the past. Arising from this activity, masters of the schools produced handbooks in which biblical symbols were arranged alphabetically or by subject matter, or, as a final step, in very large collections of alternative interpretations. This was the kind of work for which masters of the schools were peculiarly fitted, and for which there was a growing demand. Manuals of biblical symbolism were especially useful to preachers, who knew that an audience which would have been sent to sleep by elaborate distinctions of meaning might be awakened by colourful imagery.

It is of the greatest importance in judging the influence of the schools that the many channels through which scholastic

[11]   For a brief survey, see M. R. Reeves, 'Some popular prophecies from the fourteenth to the seventeenth century', in *Popular Belief and Practice: Studies in Church History*, vol. 8, ed. G. J. Cumming and D. Baker, 1972, pp. 107–34.

influence permeated western society should be appreciated. By far the most obvious route was through the scholastically-trained scholars who became popes and bishops. But the influence of the schools was also, and perhaps even more lastingly, communicated through parochial clergy and preachers, who – even if they had not themselves studied in any of the great schools – nevertheless had textbooks on preaching and summaries of law and theology which brought the fruits of scholastic studies to the world.

We can see biblical imagery being used to popularize doctrine very clearly in the work of the three theologians who dominated the schools of Paris in the late twelfth century: Peter Comestor, Peter the Chanter, and Stephen Langton. They had no major disputes on their hands, so they turned their minds to the production of works which would be useful in popular teaching.

From the point of view of biblical studies, Master Peter Comestor, who taught theology in Paris in the 1160s, is especially interesting. In his *Historia Scholastica*, the greatest and most influential of his works, he gave a concise, critical and informative account of Old Testament history drawn from all available sources. The single limitation which he imposed on his work was that he abandoned symbolism almost entirely and concentrated on historical facts. This was the work to which he owed his later fame. But, like all other masters in theology, he was also a preacher, and in his sermons, he – like other preachers – made much use of the symbolic interpretations of the Old Testament which he had excluded from his *Historia Scholastica*.

To take only one example: in one of his sermons to students in the 1170s, he took as his text Canticles 3:11: 'Go forth, ye daughters of Zion.' The 'daughters of Zion' (he explained) were the theological students listening to his sermon. Implausible? Not at all. Literally, Zion is the tower within the city of Jerusalem manned by the defenders of the city. But Jerusalem is the capital city of Judea and its daughters represent its future. Symbolically, therefore, Jerusalem is Christendom; the schools are its watch-tower; the daughters of Zion are the scholars in the schools, and the townsfolk are the people in the world. The preacher elaborated this image thus:

The words of my text are principally addressed to us, the men of the schools. We are in the watch-tower, the learned men to whom 'it is given to know the mysteries of the Kingdom of heaven', while to others it is not given to know them 'except in parables' . . . Hence we are symbolically called 'the daughters of *Zion*', the 'watchers'. By contrast, the 'daughters of *Jerusalem*' are the laity who live in the city and who are protected by the city's walls and by the signals they receive from those in the watch-tower. All of us are members of the Church, but we clergy, the 'daughters of *Zion*', have the duty of protecting and instructing those in the city.[12]

Here in a single passage we have the whole function of the schools expressed in a biblical image which makes use of the long tradition of the allegorical interpretation of the Bible. So here Peter Comestor, academically the great expounder of the literal meaning of the Bible, when he is in the pulpit turns to the symbolical interpretation which has been largely replaced in the schools by exact analysis and systematic exposition. In short, the scholastic method of analysis had diminished the exegetical role of symbolism in the schools; but, as doctrines became more elaborate and difficult to convey in common language, the need for symbols, images and anecdotes (*exempla* as they came to be called) as channels of communication with the unlettered world increased. This had the further consequence that dissident, and generally unlettered, groups in society increasingly found in symbols new ammunition for their attacks on the whole established order. The role of symbolism, therefore, which had diminished in the schools, was kept alive by preachers and came into its own as an instrument of popular instruction, and later as the expression of rebellion or resentment.

2 *Historical conflation*

The second method of reconciling apparent contradictions and displaying the fullness of biblical truth was historical conflation.

---

[12] For Peter Comestor's sermon on *Egregimini filiae Sion*, (on *Cant.* iii, 11), see *PL*, 198, 1772–5, and especially col. 1772: *per 'filias Jerusalem' laicos tanquam minus peritos et custodii egentes intelligimus; per 'filias Sion', litteratos, tum propter scientiae eminentiam, tum propter aliorum custodiam et instructionem, tum quia Sion 'speculatio' interpretatur.*

This now seems the least persuasive of all scholastic methods because the principle on which it was based has fallen into disrepute as a historical method. But the conflation of apparently contrasting evidence was an extremely common practice in historical work at least until the middle of the nineteenth century, for it offered historians a method of reconciling contradictions in their sources with the greatest possible use of all the material. How it did this can best be explained by examining one among many possible examples. It concerns –

St Peter's denials of Christ

All the Evangelists record Christ's prophecy of St Peter's three denials and the fulfilment of the prophecy; but two of them, Luke and John, place the prophecy *during* the Last Supper, and the other two, Matthew and Mark, place it on the Mount of Olives *after* supper. Then, with regard to the denials themselves, Matthew, Luke and John place all three denials before the first cock-crow, but Mark places only the first denial *before*, and the second and third, *after*, the first cock-crow. We might say that these differences are so unimportant that they do not deserve further analysis, and medieval critics were quite aware of this. But they rightly saw that, if small mistakes can be detected, they open up the possibility that much greater mistakes may pass without comment because they are less open to examination. Consequently, over several centuries of Christian exegesis, an immense amount of learning and ingenuity was lavished on this minute problem. In examining the problem and its various solutions, therefore, we are touching the fringe of a central theme of biblical exegesis: if a single error can be detected, the whole fabric of biblical inerrancy on which so much was built collapses. Hence the need to reconcile even trifling inconsistencies.

With regard to St Peter's denials and their relationship with the cock-crows, we may begin by setting out schematically the relationship between the versions given in the four Evangelists:[13]

---

[13]   For the predictions in the biblical texts, see Matth., xxvi, 33; Mark, xiv, 18; Luke, xxii, 34; John, xiii, 38; and, for Peter's denials, Matth., xxvi, 69–73; Mark, xiv, 66–72; Luke, xxvii, 56–62; John, xviii, 17, and 25–7.

SOURCE	PREDICTION	REALIZATION (D = denial; C = cock-crow)				
Matthew	after supper	D	D	D	C	
Mark	after supper	D	C	D	D	C
Luke	at supper	D	D	D	C	
John	at supper	D	D	C		

It might seem clear from this chart that not more than one Evangelist can be right about both the prediction and its realization. At least three must, therefore, in some degree be wrong, and if they can be wrong on a small matter, who can rely on their being right on important points? As the great biblical commentator of the fifteenth century, Denys the Carthusian, wrote:[14]

> If it be granted that the Apostles, Evangelists and Prophets have erred at any point, by the same token they may have erred elsewhere, and it would follow from this that the canonical Scriptures are not inspired by the Holy Spirit.

Given, therefore, the inerrancy of the Bible, these apparent contradictions must be reconcilable, and for over a thousand years scholars set themselves the task of showing how they could be reconciled. The groundwork for a solution was laid by Augustine. He pointed out that the integrity of the different accounts of Christ's prophecy could be preserved by making two suppositions: first, that Christ had repeated his prophecy at the Last Supper; and, second, that each of the Evangelists had given only a partial account both of the predictions and of their fulfilment.[15] In other words, the appearance of contradiction arises simply from varying modes of selection.

The few pages in which Augustine set out this view of the problem dominated all later discussion till the sixteenth century. The strength of his solution was that he solved the whole problem with masterly comprehensiveness. Its weakness was that his solution was quite implausible. For one thing, in order to accommodate Mark's version, Jesus had twice to make

[14] *Dionysii Carthusiani in quatuor Evangelistas Enarrationes*, Cologne, 1532, f. 89v. on Matth. xxvi, 17.
[15] Augustine, *De Consensu Evangelistarum*, iii, 2; iii, 6: PL, 34, 1159–63, 1168–73.

his prophecy and the twice-repeated words, 'The cock will not crow until you have thrice denied that you know me,' had to be taken to mean, 'The cock will not crow until you have begun the process of thrice denying me.'

There is no need to pursue the ramifications of this unhappy struggle to preserve the historical inerrancy of the Bible, except to note the importance attached to the principle which all interpretations sought to uphold, and which none could uphold without resorting to some strange uses of words. Nevertheless, the struggle for consistency occasionally produced flashes which are worth noting. For example, in about 1250, Albertus Magnus, using the new scientific learning which he was largely responsible for introducing into the scholastic programme, suggested a new refinement to account for the divergence between Mark and the other Evangelists:

> Animals have a keen sense of the changes in the atmosphere, brought about by the changing angles of the sun. The cock is especially gifted in this respect, and it crows at three important moments: when the celestial horizon of the sun changes from west to east at midnight; then, at first light before the sun rises over the horizon; and then again at sunrise. The first cock-crow, at midnight, is not generally noticed, and that is why it was mentioned by Mark alone. The second, at dawn – but still before sunrise – is more generally noticed, and that is why it was mentioned by all the Evangelists.[16]

Then, about two hundred years later, a new observation was introduced by Calvin, who pointed out that the dawn cock-crow does not consist of a single cry, but of many, and that all the cries are known collectively as the *gallicinium*. So he concluded:

> I have no doubt that Christ was aware of this fact when He said

16 Albertus Magnus was a keen observer of nature, and he had evidently given much thought both to the complicated phenomenon of the cock-crow and to its explanation, which he discussed on several occasions and in different contexts: for example, in his *Notulae super Matheum*, xxvi, 34; in his *Postills on Mark*, xiv, 30; his *Postills on Luke*, xxii, 34; and his *De Animalibus*, xxiii, 24. For these texts, see his *Opera Omnia*, ed. A. Borgnet, Paris, 1890–99, vols xii, 488; xiv, 30; xxi, 170, 706, 721–2; xxiii, 686, 700; xxiv, 523–4. It is hard to know which aspect of the problem interested him more: the proof of the inerrancy of Scripture, or the proof of the extreme fineness of texture of the natural world. But there is no doubt that both were of fundamental importance in his total world-view, and this raised problems to which we shall return in Volume II.

'before the cock crows', and equally when Matthew, Luke and John wrote 'Before the cock crows', they meant 'before the end of the *gallicinium*'; but only Mark particularized. If we found a similar distinction in a secular historian we would not say they contradicted one another, nor ought we to say that the Evangelists do so.[17]

Here then, over a period of a thousand years, we see increasing refinements introduced to support the doctrine of biblical inerrancy, and we may judge the importance of the principle by the lengths to which scholars were prepared to go in defending it. Biblical inerrancy was quite simply essential for the stability of the system of thought which had its fullest and finest elaboration in the medieval schools, and it could not be dropped without abandoning the doctrine of the divine authorship of the Bible and opening the floodgates of uncertainty.

When the principle of biblical inerrancy was breached – as it was bit by bit from the fourteenth century onwards, and irretrievably in the course of the eighteenth century – the whole system suffered a blow from which it never recovered.

To complete this outline of the methods of stabilizing the whole system of scholastic thought, we must finally turn to the method which was the peculiar strength of the medieval schools and shows them in their most characteristic posture:

3 The method and results of verbal and logical analysis

Symbolic interpretation of the Bible opened up large areas of universal history. The method of historical conflation defended the Bible from the suspicion of factual error. But the essential scholastic method of reconciling and elaborating the doctrines of authoritative texts was verbal and logical analysis, which not only dissipated contradictions and cleared up ambiguities in the sources, but also enlarged the area of truth. The main problems that analysis could solve were doctrinal in the widest sense of the word. Within this broad category, some of the problems which were first seriously tackled in the twelfth-century schools

[17] John Calvin, *Harmonia ex Evangelistis tribus composita*, Geneva, 1595, pp. 338–9.

were political or social, others were related to the discipline of personal life; but the most important were related to the central doctrines of Christianity.

The central doctrines, so far as they can be dealt with at all within the scope of this survey, must be left until we come to the succession of theologians, logicians and grammarians, who initiated the scholastic phase of European history. For our present purpose, a small example of the application of verbal and logical analysis to a problem of the relationship between God and individual believers will suffice to show that quite large results could be achieved with a modest intellectual outlay.

The example I have selected concerns the problem of Fear. It has the great merit that, small though the subject may seem among the great array of theological problems, everyone must in varying degrees of intensity have experienced fear in several forms, and it certainly has a place in all religious experience. So there was a pastoral as well as purely theoretical aspect to the problem, and it occupied the attention of nearly every major twelfth-century scholastic theologian at some stage in his career.

The problem of fear

We may start with the apparently contradictory biblical texts on the subject of fear. On the one hand we have:

1a 'The fear of the Lord is the beginning of wisdom.' (Proverbs 1:7)

1b 'The fear of the Lord endures for ever.' (Psalm xix (xviii):10)

And on the other hand:

2a 'Perfect love casts out fear.' (1 John 4:18)

2b 'He that fears is not perfect in love.' (1 John 4:18)

The formal problem raised by these texts is obvious: in the first pair, fear is represented as a permanent and desirable element in the relationship of Man with God; but in the second it is presented as a temporary, even undesirable, feature which disappears when love is perfect. Moreover, these states of mind

126

are to be expected not only in a few, but in all believers. It is impossible to believe (or even not to believe) without at some stage being subject to some kind of fear. So these texts raise a question that everyone must ask: does, or does not, this fear that I now experience represent a state of grace or of condemnation? Or, more generally, is fear a desirable and permanent, or an undesirable and finally unacceptable feature of religious life?

So here we have a scholastic debate at its most individual and its most general, and the procedure adopted for solving the problem is the most basic of all scholastic procedures: verbal analysis.

The first step was to analyse the different meanings of 'fear'; then to determine the character of the various forms of experience associated with these different meanings; and finally to mark out a progression of experience leading from one form to another.

This combination of analysis of words, relating these words to actual experiences, and arranging a progression from one state to another, provided a perfect scholastic exercise: it required the analysis of concepts, the identification of the experience associated with these concepts, and the tracing of a movement from one to another. When all these aspects of the problem had been closely analysed and integrated into a single system, the scholastic task was completed, and the texts were ready for use in a pastoral context.

The initial step towards a complete formulation of the problem was taken very early in the twelfth century, or even a little earlier. Master Anselm of Laon in his gloss on the Psalter picked out two passages in Augustine and Cassiodorus in which a distinction was made between the fear of losing worldly possessions, and the fear of offending a loved one.[18] The first of these states is clearly incompatible with happiness at a quite

[18] For the discussions on Fear in the school of Anselm of Laon, see O. Lottin, *Psychologie et Morale aux XIIe et XIIIe Siècles*, vol. 5, 1959, pp. 220–1, 293–5. For much new material illustrating the very widespread interest in the problem of fear among twelfth-century theologians, see R. Quinto, *Die Quaestiones des Stephan Langton über die Gottesfurcht* in *Cahiers de l'Institut du Moyen-Âge Grec et Latin*, Copenhagen, vol. 62, 1992, pp. 77–165. For an outline of discussions on Fear, see A. Landgraf, *Dogmengeschichte der Frühscholastik*, Regensburg, 1953–6, iv, 276–371. (I owe this reference to Miss E. Revell.)

primitive level, and it is certainly incompatible with eternal happiness. So Master Anselm called this first most primitive state of fear, of losing possessions, 'servile fear'.

As for the second kind of fear – the fear of offending a loved one – that's quite another matter. It is a necessary concomitant of even the highest possible relationship between God and a human being. It is therefore destined to 'last for ever'. So Master Anselm gave it the appropriate name of 'filial fear'.

Already, therefore, by the first decade of the twelfth century, the first step in the detailed analysis of the problem had been taken in establishing the two *termini* at either end of a chain of intermediate states.

The next step was to arrange the different kinds of fear in a graduated scale. Clearly 'servile fear' inspired by a fear of losing worldly possessions must be at the very bottom of any scale in which the individual is related to the Creator. But a distinction must be made: if the worldly possessions were ill-gotten, the fear of losing them is especially damnable; but if they were legitimately acquired and necessary for well-being in this life, then the fear of losing them may be judged to be perhaps self-centred and incompatible with final blessedness – but certainly natural. So, on analysis, 'servile' fear can be divided into two parts: first, the truly *servile* which is incompatible with spiritual growth; and, second, the *natural* which is capable of improvement.

To turn now from the bottom to the top of the scale of human progress towards God, to 'filial fear'. This also on analysis is found to have two different modes: it may be inspired by dread of God's anger arising from consciousness of guilt; or it may arise from that mingling of fear with joy, which no created being can be without even in a state of blessedness. So here too, approaching the summit of the ascent to God, there is a distinction to be drawn between a fear which is not compatible with eternal blessedness, and one which is not only compatible with, but inseparable from, such eternal blessedness as is consistent with humanity. In this last sense – and only in this sense – we can truly say with the Psalmist that fear 'endures for ever'.

So, by analysing this single concept, a whole sequence of different forms of fear has been established, stretching from a kind of fear which accompanies damnation, through intermediate states to a fear which is necessarily present in any creaturely enjoyment of God's presence.

The first step in this analysis was taken very early in the twelfth century or even earlier, by Anselm of Laon; the last, about fifty years later by Peter Lombard. Indeed, small though this example of scholastic reasoning is, we can trace it in remarkable detail. We find, for example that Peter Lombard, the great integrator of all theological discussion of the first half of the twelfth century, dealt with the problem of fear on two occasions; first when he glossed the Psalter in about 1140, and next, when he produced the final version of his *Sentences* in about 1159. In his glosses on the Psalter he repeated the analysis in which the two varieties of 'servile' fear were still undifferentiated; but in his *Sentences* he had made the distinction which settled the main outline of the subject definitively. So we may say that, so far as the formal development of the analysis was concerned, a succession of theologians between about 1100 and 1160 had completely analysed the types of fear referred to in the various biblical texts.

Looked at in isolation, this achievement may seem a small reward for all the labour spent upon it. But this step-by-step progress is characteristic of the scholastic mode of advancing by stages of ever greater clarification of terms and refinements in understanding towards a full understanding of the biblical texts and their relationship to the ascent of any individual towards God.

If we now think of similar results spread over the whole area of biblical interpretation and theological analysis, we can gain some idea of the way in which the process of detailed clarification led to an entire transformation of the intellectual map of western Christendom in the course of two or three generations. The steady advance is most conspicuous in the first sixty years of the twelfth century because the first stages were relatively simple. Thereafter the process became increasingly complicated as a result of the arrival of new texts in need of analysis, but the small area examined here displays one essential feature of the whole scholastic development: the obscurities and apparent contradictions in authoritative texts provided the opportunities for bringing into existence a system of clear and mutually compatible doctrines, capable of satisfying the most subtle enquirers and of giving practical guidance to people at every level of sophistication. It was by small advances over the whole field of exegesis, by the analysis of texts, by debate and systematization, that the schools developed a systematic body of knowledge about both theoretical problems and practical life. This was how the great results of the schools were achieved – not by grandiose speculations, but by minute refinements of meaning.

In the case which has been examined, we may observe that – without touching a single issue of major importance – refinements in the interpretation of a few texts provided a scheme of spiritual development open to anyone. *This* was the greatest achievement of the schools: for the first time for several centuries work in the world, and not flight from the world, could seriously be considered to offer salvation open to all believers. If we extend the small process of clarification we have just followed to the whole field of theology, we can get some idea of the central achievement of the scholastic method as practised in the schools of the twelfth and early thirteenth centuries.

Then, to take the subject one stage further, although the theological classification of the various types of fear had been completed by the time of Peter Lombard, there was still much to be done in exploring the natural features of fear, especially its physical symptoms and its place among the emotions. This extension of the enquiry was characteristic of the early thirteenth century, when the scientific works, first of Avicenna and then of Aristotle, began to circulate among scientifically interested scholars, first outside the schools, and then penetrating into the central core of the scholastic curriculum.

This part of our study must be reserved for a later volume, but the general sense of the development may be noted. The study of these scientific works drew attention to many physical features which could in fact be found in the Bible but had not been the subject of academic discussion. The recently discovered scientific works drew attention to passages in the Bible referring to physical features of fear which had not previously aroused interest: perturbation (Esther 15:18), immobilization (Tobit 2:14), trembling (Tobit 13:6), paleness (Esther 15:10), and confusion of thought (Wisdom 17:11). Albertus Magnus seems to have been the first scholastically-trained theologian to become interested in these natural symptoms. After he had left Paris and had become head of the Dominican school in Mainz in about 1245, he began his serious study of the scientific works of Aristotle, and it is a striking fact that Thomas Aquinas, who was certainly less attracted by scientific works than his master Albert, also found room in his *Summa Theologiae* to discuss these physical details and their implications. Nevertheless, Albertus went much further along the road than Aquinas in discussing those natural elements in fear which are contrary to honour and civic virtue.[19] With these distinctions we enter a new period of detailed interest among theologians in the natural order, and in human conduct in the context of the natural order. But, even before this happened, scholastic doctrine had penetrated into every corner of human life, and into the understanding of the universe as an intelligibly organized whole. In the emotive words of Cardinal Newman, scholastic doctrine had extended itself 'from the internal mysteries of the Divine Essence down to our own sensations and consciousness, from the most solemn appointments of the Lord of all down to what may be called the accidents of the hour, from the most glorious seraph down to the vilest and most noxious of reptiles'.[20]

III Bringing the Message of the Schools to the World

All the activities of the schools in analysing texts and systematizing the knowledge derived from them had some influence on

---

[19] For Thomas Aquinas, see his *Summa Theologiae*, 1, 2, qq. 41–45. For Albertus, see especially his commentary on Aristotle's *Ethics* (vol. 14 of his *Opera Omnia*, in two parts, 1968, 1987, pp. 127, 191, 299–301) where – having mentioned the theological distinctions discussed above – he draws a contrast between this view of the subject and the civil or political view in which fear leads to a flight from danger contrary to honour.

[20] J. H. Newman, *The idea of a University defined and illustrated*, 3rd edition, 1873, p. 45.

the world outside the schools, and biblical learning had most influence of all. What the world received was not the bare text of the Bible but the text as interpreted in the schools, and it is very remarkable how quickly the results of scholastic discussion were made available for a wider public outside the schools, and translated into rules of life for the whole population of western Europe. Sermons and the legislation of ecclesiastical councils were the most influential channels through which the doctrines of the schools were conveyed to the outside world. Less noticeably, students returning home with their notes can be found circulating them in several different ways: sometimes among members of a monastic community, sometimes in princely courts, sometimes in law courts, and soon in handbooks and collections of exemplary stories which became widely available. The very wide distribution of scholastically-trained masters in positions of pastoral and administrative authority, at every level of importance from parochial vicarages and rectories up to the very highest positions in the Church, all brought the secular world into touch with the results of scholastic teaching in everyday life.

A small example of the penetration of scholastic teaching into the secular world will suffice for the moment to illustrate this process.

Peter of Blois – about whom more later – had been a theology student in Paris in the early 1160s very soon after the completion of Peter Lombard's *Sentences*. He then had a long struggle to find a permanent job, and it was not until about 1175 that he was firmly situated as chancellor of the archbishop of Canterbury and a frequent visitor to the royal court of Henry II. The king in his youth – long before there had been much chance of his ever becoming king – had had William of Conches as his private tutor. William had written for his pupil a popularized version of his great work on cosmology, and there is evidence that Henry's interest in natural history persisted. When he became king he liked to have learned men around him, and he encouraged them to send him summarized versions of the learning of the day. Peter of Blois was one of the first who did this. The king evidently liked talking with him, and Peter wrote several works of edification for the king. One of them was an expression of sympathy and instruction at a time when the king was just recovering from the worst evil that could befall any medieval ruler – the rebellion of all his sons. Appropriately, Peter's work was a brief series of reflections on the trials and final prosperity of Job.[21]

In this work Peter encouraged the king to believe that all might yet be well if he followed in the footsteps of that man of many misfortunes. In the first place, he urged the king to seek strength to overcome his adversities 'in simplicity, in justice, and in *fear*,' and he elaborates the last of these requirements, distinguishing carefully the various kinds of fear: in particular he distinguishes the servile fear of punishment from the loving fear of grace, and encourages the king to cultivate the latter. He elaborates this point a little, and we recognize at once that he is giving a sketch of the nature of Fear as set out in Peter Lombard's *Sentences*,[22] which had been completed only a few years before Peter of Blois – who had begun by studying letter-writing in Tours and then Law in Bologna – moved to Paris where he studied Theology in the early 1160s.

So here we have an early instance of the theological learning of the schools being given practical application at a very high level in the lives of the laity. It is indeed a mere crumb from the theological table, but it serves to show that even the most recondite scholastic discussions could find a rapid circulation in the world and a permanent place in one of the more widely-read popularizations of scholastic learning in the twelfth century. We stand here at the beginning of the intimate influence of the schools, not only on the processes and aims of government, but more fundamentally on the formation of the personal lives of the whole population from top to bottom.

---

[21] *PL*, 207, 795–826, and esp. 798.
[22] *Sententiae*, ii, xxxiv, cc. 3–9.

4

The Social and Political Roots
of Scholastic Thought

I Pre-scholastic and Scholastic Europe

What relationship was there between the social and political development of western Europe in the twelfth and thirteenth centuries and the contemporary development of scholastic thought? Clearly it is not a simple case of cause and effect, for some of the elaborations of Christian doctrine would have taken place as a result of changing habits of thought and devotion in religious communities even if there had been no contemporary social changes outside these communities. Nevertheless, social changes, particularly the growth in population, trade, wealth, urban life, and very extensive changes in the relationship of western Europe with the Byzantine and Muslim worlds, provoked new definitions in all relationships, including that of mankind with God.

Social and economic changes also produced the means of supporting a continuing stream of students and a demand for masters to teach them, without which the elaborate intellectual systems of the twelfth and thirteenth centuries could not have been created. Moreover, since orthodox Christian belief and practice had long been, and were now more than ever, looked on as essential requirements for possessing any social rights at any level of society, means had to be found to make doctrines, and the practices which doctrine required, known and acceptable to those who were required to propagate and enforce them, as well as to those who were required to believe and practise what they were taught. Without economic growth and the consequent formation of relatively well-organized instruments of government, a very large part of the scholastic activity of the twelfth and thirteenth centuries would have been impossible, and the development of western Christendom would have run along quite different lines.

Of course, long before the twelfth century, uniformity of belief and behaviour had been thought to be necessary for the well-being of the whole community, and from the late eighth century onwards Councils had exhorted kings and bishops to make their households into *scholae* for the training of *strenuos milites Christi* and (as proof of their diligence) to bring *scholasticos* with them to Councils.[1] But, in two important respects, the legislation which expressed these aspirations in the eighth and ninth centuries differed profoundly from the conciliar legislation of the twelfth and thirteenth centuries with which we are chiefly concerned. First, in the earlier period, the legislation was the joint product of lay and ecclesiastical authorities; and, second, the main emphasis of the earlier legislation was on the elaboration and refinement of corporate worship. It was only from the mid-eleventh century onwards that the aim of elaborating and enforcing uniformity of belief and practice in great detail and permanance gained an effective impetus.

This came from two sources. First, the growing wealth, productivity and complexity of western society brought the resources for a more thorough organization of thought and practice than had ever previously been possible. And, second, the new and specialized governmental role of the clerical order within society, of which the causes will be discussed presently, led to the clergy becoming more fully organized, more distinctly aware of their rights and privileges, and better equipped for providing and enforcing a fuller and more coherent body of doctrine and code of behaviour to go with it, than had ever been possible at any earlier date.

---

[1]   Among many exhortations to scholastic activity, see *Concilium Rispacense*, 798, (every bishop to have a *scola* in his cathedral town); *Paris*, 829 (bishops to educate *strenuos milites Christi* and to bring *scholasticos* with them to councils); c. 858: appeal by bishops of the provinces of Reims and Rouen to Louis, King of Germany, to turn his household into a *scola*. (For these and other comparable efforts, see *MGH, Legum sectio III: Concilia*, vol. 2, 1906, pp. 199, 271, 632, 829.)

So far as a distinct starting point for the emergence of a more detailed and doctrinally more systematic organization of western European society can be found, the decree of the Roman council of 1059 which made clerical celibacy mandatory for all clergy from the rank of deacon upwards may be selected as providing one important element in the special role of the clerical order in society.[2] There had indeed been many earlier directives of a similar kind, and it took a hundred years or more for the 1059 decree to become fully operative, but 1059 marked the beginning of a continuing and broadly successful effort of enforcement. After this date there could no longer be any doubt that the children of clergy had no rights of secular inheritance nor any possibility of a clerical career without a special act of papal legitimatization.

The rule of clerical celibacy – and more especially the con- sequence that clerical children were excluded from all rights of succession to property – was successful because it was widely acceptable to the lay aristocracy in limiting the number of claimants to the inheritance of secular estates. By eliminating clerical descendants from the competition, the problem of preserving the integrity of a family's property – a major aim of all dynastic planning – was greatly simplified. And equally the exclusion of the children of clergy from high positions in the Church without a special papal dispensation also safeguarded the claims and opportunities of the legitimate children of great families in this area of advancement also. Indeed, the unmarried clergy who were excluded from succession to family or ecclesiastical estates became some of the most enthusiastic promoters of the fortunes of their families, and no members of the ecclesiastical hierarchy were more fully imbued with this spirit of family aggrandizement than the popes.

It is necessary to insist on these temporal advantages because,

---

2 There is a useful survey (one among many) of this complicated subject in the *Dictionnaire de Spiritualité*, Paris, vol. 2, 1953, 385–92. For the texts which are central to its detailed enforcement in western Europe with all its consequences for the descent of family estates, see (for 1059) *PL*, 143, 1314–16, and later, cc. 7 and 21 of the Council of 1123, c. 7 of the Council of 1139 (*Councils*, vol. 1, pp. 191, 194, 198), and the great collection of documents in Gratian's *Decretum*, *Dist.* xxvii, c. 8, xxviii and xxxi–xxxiv.

without them, clerical celibacy would have been very much more difficult to enforce, and without clerical celibacy the enhanced role of the clergy as instruments for propagating new rules of doctrine and behaviour would have been subject to much greater pressure from the laity. Of course these were not considerations which motivated the main advocates of clerical celibacy, but at a time when the preservation and increase of hereditary family wealth was the main aim of all possessors of political power, clerical celibacy was a welcome aid in pursuing this policy. Consequently, there was little determined lay opposition either to clerical celibacy or to the ensuing growth centralization of ecclesiastical government and control of the highest ecclesiastical appointments by the pope. The main opponents of the second of these developments were kings and emperors who saw their own jurisdictional functions and profits thereby diminished. But the lay aristocracy as a whole were indifferent or hostile to royal or imperial power. So in general they supported, or at least raised no strong objection to either the enforcement of clerical celibacy or to the enlargement of the clerical role in government.

I mention these familiar developments of the late eleventh century because – quite apart from the theoretical grounds which could be urged in their favour – they were symptomatic of a rapidly expanding society which required a much greater degree of organization and a more highly articulated definition of rights and doctrines than had ever been necessary or possible at any earlier time.

The schools, which (with very few exceptions) were wholly clerical both in composition and in the careers which they opened up, were the main instruments in providing both the doctrines and the literate officials needed for reorganizing western Europe in response to its growing wealth, population and power. This triangular linkage between the growing wealth and complexity of western society, the need for new organizational procedures in law and administration, and for more clearly defined doctrines governing the faith and practice of the whole population, gave the schools and their clerical population of teachers and learners a quite new and immensely powerful position in western European society from the late eleventh century onwards.

But, it may be objected, the population of western Europe

had accepted the Christian faith long before the eleventh century, and the need for instruction in doctrine and in the practical results of Christian doctrine had long existed. So what was new in the situation of western Christendom in the eleventh century that provoked new approaches to the problems of religious teaching and organization?

To answer this question it is necessary to remember that, in the main, Christianity seems to have been received by barbarian Europe without much debate. And the reason for this was that the new religion was perceived as possessing an insuperable force in overcoming evil spirits, in bringing success in war, in effecting miraculous cures, and in providing symbols and ceremonies which made rulers feel more secure, and gave them a new sense of grandeur. Largely as a result of the perception of these benefits, pagan Europe had been converted to Christianity by the conversion of rulers, who brought the communities under their jurisdiction into the Church with almost no need for prolonged argument.

Even when the rulers' expectations of supernatural aid faded, the work of carrying into the lives of ordinary people the experience of the supernatural was continued by the dispersal throughout barbarian Europe of the relics of ancient saints exported from the homelands of Christian origins, and by their far-famed miracles at the sites of their new 'resting places'. To these sites were also added a growing number of relics of local saints of a more recent date.

Associated with this dispersal of miracle-working saintly remains, there was a rapid growth in the number of monasteries which brought to all parts of the barbarian West visible evidences of heavenly splendour, partly miraculous, partly simply awe-inspiring, but always providing evidence of unearthly forces at work.

Moreover, at a more mundane level, the growing number of monasteries at which these saintly relics were preserved also solved the problem of making provision for the sons and daughters of the rulers of Europe for whom no suitable marriages and consequently no long-term family careers were available. To these offspring for whom there was no sufficient inheritance or well-endowed spouse in prospect, monastic life gave dignity in this world, and hopes of salvation in the next. And, in addition, the families who endowed the monasteries were provided with places of burial, commemoration and expiation. From the eighth century to the eleventh, the monasteries made the greatest contribution to the faith and rituals of everyday life and death, and the support which they gave in all the emergencies of life brought Europe through the worst days of invasion, famine and destruction.

But by the later years of the eleventh century, these rituals and miraculous experiences, which had sufficed to give hope to a much harassed population for four hundred years, were becoming increasingly incapable of meeting the needs of a growing population, or of providing answers to the problems of organized society or indeed to the problems raised by ordinary believers. The declining role in the corporate and religious life of western Europe of the territorially well-endowed Benedictine monasteries of the earlier centuries was partly offset by the creation of new religious orders. But nothing could bring back the old immediate contact with supernatural glory which the older monasteries had provided. Faith therefore needed new aids, and these had to be found in explanations of the contents and basis of faith and in more particularized rules of life, which brought assurance of salvation to those who observed the rules.

Expectation of miraculous interventions indeed continued to play a very important role in ordinary life, but the huge area of the supernatural in everyday events, which had been a conspicuous feature of the early Middle Ages, was diminishing. What gradually took its place was an expectation that the miraculous would be largely confined to individual cures, and that the promise of eternal life would be available to all who observed highly elaborated, but not impossible, rules of faith and conduct.

The multiple ills and temptations of life required, not more relics of the saints (though indeed they never lost their potency), but more rules, fuller explanations of the faith, the aid of preachers and confessors, as well as courts and lawyers for the regulation of behaviour in accordance with the rules laid down by the Church. Unlike the provision of relics and miracles which had been so abundantly supplied in the past and which gradually diminished (despite the appearance of new miracle-working saints like St Thomas Becket), the new aids to religious life and death came from increasingly refined doctrines and rules of life, and these had generally been elaborated in the schools before being incorporated in legislation. The general result of this change was a slow, reluctant, but in the end irreversible, movement away from supernatural interventions and towards doctrinal and disciplinary sources of help. It was this movement that gave the schools a vastly greater role in the management of life than they had ever had in earlier centuries.

One uncovenanted consequence of this new phase in the organization of society was that the Latin language and the whole corpus of ancient learning in Latin was given a new lease of life. From about 750 to 1050, there had been a considerable flow of translations of ancient texts into the vernacular languages. But – strange as it may at first sight seem – this flow diminished as the needs of a wider audience grew. The reason for this was that Latin was the only available language with a sufficiently stable and conceptually well-developed vocabulary for the discussion of complicated technical problems. Consequently, one of the first results of the growing complexity of society was to slow down the progress that had been made in translating ancient learning into the vernacular languages and to intensify the demand for Latin as the language of government and of all serious thought.

Latin took on new life as the necessary tool for precise thought and for European government for another five hundred years. Meanwhile the vernacular languages, apart from the needs of daily life, developed mainly as vehicles of entertainment, private prayer, and elementary religious instruction, especially for women, who were excluded from the schools and in general, even in religious communities, from the whole area of advanced instruction.

It was in these circumstances that the schools rapidly gained a new position in western Europe as the institutions which produced the experts with the learning and argumentative skills necessary for governing a society of increasing complexity, which had quite suddenly exchanged a seemingly endless succession of disasters for an experience of unprecedented internal growth and external expansion. It was not, therefore, an accident that this change took place at the moment when the ecclesiastical hierarchy was becoming more clearly distinct from secular society than ever before, and when the schools as the articulate source of doctrine were becoming more active than they had ever previously been.

Indeed all these developments are intertwined: a large and continuing growth in population and wealth, the cessation of attacks on the heartland of Europe, the new opportunities for large-scale organized government and for meeting the intellectual challenges within Christendom, and the growth of Latin-based and clerically-populated schools which produced an integrated system of thought that – despite the contempt of later critics – was one of the most formidable and coherent intellectual and governmental structures that has ever been produced.

Although the detailed causes of this great change in European history can only very partially be understood, there can be no doubt that in its outcome it brought about the greatest intellectual and governmental expansion before the industrial age. These results could not have followed if the schools had not succeeded in creating a body of organized knowledge, together with rules for the guidance of corporate and individual behaviour, which remained widely current until the seventeenth century, and of which many isolated effects remained until the twentieth century.

II The New Symbiosis of Schools and Government

Up to and including the eleventh century, rulers discharged their governmental duties through personal appearances throughout their territories, through rituals which made the supernatural source of their authority visually apparent, and of course through displays of armed force, whether actually used or simply exhibited. Emperors and kings had been consecrated in religious ceremonies, and in their public appearances they had worn hieratic robes, displayed relics, invoked divine aid in giving judgement, and at the highest level had issued decisions as 'Vicars of Christ'.[3] The functions, therefore, of what would later be regarded as secular government were heavily encased in supernatural aids.

This manner of performing the functions of government necessarily changed when new techniques of financial and legal administration were required to deal with complicated situations. Nowhere were these techniques more in demand than in recently conquered areas such as Norman Sicily or England, where a new aristocracy, ignorant even of the language of the countryside, had seized huge areas of a foreign country of whose forms of government they knew little. In both these areas, the usurping conquerors were foremost in creating new financial and administrative aids to government which required the services of scholastically-trained officials, and of course the use of Latin as the main means of official communication. It is not surprising therefore that some of the earliest students in the European schools, who expected to make their fortunes in government, came from post-Conquest England.[4]

The other area of government in which the change from a predominantly ritualistic to a predominantly administrative form of government was especially rapid was in the administration of the Church. It was a change dictated not by choice, but by the growing complications of life, and it could not have taken place without a rapid growth in the number of agents and instruments of government at every level of society. These officials all needed some degree of scholastic training, beginning with an adequate Latinity, which was required even in the lowest levels of government, and ending at the higher levels with a need for a whole range of scholastically-acquired sciences culminating in theology and law. These demands could only be met by a rapid

---

[3] On the significance of this title, see M. Maccarrone, *Vicarius Christi: storia del titolo papale (Lateranum, nova series*, xviii, 1952). I have discussed the importance of the change of usage whereby the title 'Vicar of Christ', which had been available for kings and emperors, became the exclusive property of the pope, in Southern, 1970, pp. 94–105. For its ecclesiastical consequence, note that already in about 1125 Honorius Augustodunensis in his *Gemma Animae*, i, 189 (PL, 172, 602) drew the further conclusion that, since the pope is the Vicar of Christ, the bishops are vicars of the Apostles: a downgrading therefore for the bishops as well as the secular rulers.

[4] For some examples, see below, pp. 167–8.

growth in the number and quality of schools available for a floating and ever-growing number of pupils from all parts of Europe, all of them clergy and all therefore under ecclesiastical jurisdiction, but all available for the work of secular as well as ecclesiastical government, and all of them payable – for this was the secular aristocracy's *quid pro quo* for the independence of the ecclesiastical hierarchy – with ecclesiastical revenues in the form of tithes.

The necessary support for this growing number of students came partly from remittances from their families, partly from teaching, and partly (especially among the more senior students of theology or canon law) from benefices which produced tithes from which they could support themselves in the schools and pay a deputy to discharge their local duties. In making this source of income available to them, it was important that recent ecclesiastical legislation had declared that tithes were available only to men in holy orders.[5] Thus local landowners were excluded from the receipt of tithes. But, since they could pay their officials by giving them ecclesiastical positions (most commonly parochial vicarages), the lay aristocracy was indirectly reimbursed for its renunciation of ecclesiastical revenues. In a roundabout way, therefore, the tithes with which rulers of earlier centuries had endowed the Church were now reclaimed for governmental work. The circle was complete: the problems of organized government demanded more elaborate and costly procedures than those which had sufficed in the past; the new wealth of a rapidly-expanding population stimulated the growth of the schools which could provide solutions to these problems; the most easily disposable part of this new wealth consisted

[5] The first definitive statement on this point was by Gregory VII in the decrees of his Council in November 1078 (E. Casper, *Registrum Gregorii VII*, p. 404: *Decimas quas in usum pietatis concessa esse canonica auctoritas demonstrat, a laicis possideri apostolica auctoritate prohibemus.*) It will be noticed that it was not presented as a conciliar decision but as a purely papal declaration at the Council. It does not seem to have been repeated by Gregory's successors, and only slowly found its way into collections of canon law texts – notably that of Deusdedit and in the last recension of Ivo of Chartres's *Panormia* (whatever may be true of the *Panormia* as a whole, this at least was certainly added after Ivo's death), lib. 8, c. 145, *PL*, 161, col. 1342. It was first given general circulation by the Lateran Council of 1139 (see *Councils*, vol. 1, p. 199), and in Gratian's *Decretum*, c. 1, c. 16 q. 7, for which see below, pp. 294–6.

of the tithes of a growing agricultural population; and this source of revenue helped to support both those who were teaching or studying in the schools and those who had left the schools to engage in the work of government.

All governments, whether secular or ecclesiastical, needed the services of experts instructed in theology and canon law as well as in the elaborate rules for the composition of letters and formal documents. It was the social function of the schools to provide these skills, and it was the practical duty, and also the interest, of all ambitious rulers to support schools with privileges and monopolies. As for the scholars who made themselves available for the work of government after they left the schools, the numerous benefices in the gift of rulers were available to reward them. It was this combination of practical need, and the availability of ecclesiastical resources for rewarding the clerical servants of both lay and ecclesiastical rulers, which ensured the steady development of universities and of scholastic thought closely associated with the work of government.

Further, it was not enough simply to lay down the law and set up procedures and rewards for administering it: it was also necessary that the rules of faith and behaviour, which the whole population – apart from the increasingly harassed Jewish communities – was required to observe, should be widely known and generally acceptable. This meant that the rules had to be supported by arguments which in the end most people would accept. This need for general acceptability is an aspect of law brutally clear to modern legislators; but – though less clearly expressed – general acceptability is an essential ingredient of law at all times, and the need for it was well understood in the Middle Ages.

In the twelfth and thirteenth centuries, general acceptability was the product of protracted arguments in the schools. Scholastic arguments, remote though they were in their terminology from everyday language, performed many of the functions of arguments in political assemblies today: they brought the issues of faith and behaviour before a continuing stream of men, many of whom would one day have to administer what today they discussed. Western society was not naturally conformist: the population was divided into too many semi-autonomous groups, and the inclination to oppose authority was too strong to be lightly disregarded. The arguments in the schools served the purpose of bringing to light the objections which would be raised outside the schools, so a congruity of outlook between schools and the outside world was an essential basis of practical success. Far more than the meetings of the royal council which came to be called 'parlements', the schools were the parliaments of medieval Europe.

But this role has two sides to it: it ensured a wide area of agreement to the definitive decisions taken by popes and councils, but also ensured that rival solutions, so long as they had scholastic support, were not forgotten. Just as the existence of a parliament ensures that there will always be an opposition, so the dialectical methods of the schools ensured that forbidden doctrines would not easily disappear. For example, by 1160 the celibacy of all clergy above sub-deacon had been confirmed on many occasions. But when Gerald of Wales went to Paris in about 1170, he heard Peter Comestor, one of the most respected theological masters of the day, say, in the hearing of his whole school, that the devil had never done so much harm to the Church as the prohibition of clerical marriage.[6] Progress through contradiction was the scholastic method; so, though the aim of contradiction was agreement, the method kept alive all conclusions that were not self-contradictory for they alone could be finally refuted.

III The Schools, Society and the Individual

The close association between schools and government is a feature of all societies which aim at defining and enforcing an observance of doctrines which are obligatory for all. Governments with such an aim are necessarily authoritarian; but every form of authoritarian government has its own ways of making itself acceptable to the population at large, and the schools had the role of filling the gap between rulers and ruled in medieval Europe. The main way in which they did

[6] Giraldus Cambrensis, *Gemma Ecclesiastica*, *Opera*, ed. J. S. Brewer, *RS*, 1862, ii, 187–8.

this was by debates, which played a vital part in laying down rules of social and individual life which were broadly acceptable to people at every level of society. To exemplify this link between the school debates and the population of western Christendom I shall examine two subjects of vital concern to most people: legitimate marriage with its concomitant right of succession to family property, and forgiveness of sins with its consequent promise of eternal blessedness.

It may be objected that many people, then as now, had no hope of any earthly inheritance; and that many in practice paid very little attention to eternal blessedness. This situation was as clear to medieval as it is to modern observers. But there is a difference between the medieval and modern worlds in both these matters. With regard to this world, even the humblest villein's claim to succession to a pitiful area of land represented a claim to a livelihood for a lifetime and for the lives of his descendants. No doubt there were very many without even this assurance of stability; but, at least in the twelfth and thirteenth centuries, inheritance provided a firm basis of general security for most people in an agrarian society.

As for the world to come, no one could publicly proclaim, and probably very few held the opinion, that heaven and hell did not exist. Moreover – and this marks the major difference between medieval and modern attitudes to the sanction of eternal judgement – society was organized on the basis that heaven and hell did exist, and that obedience to authoritative statements about the rules for attaining eternal happiness were essential for a peaceful society in this world.

Social peace and individual acceptance of the harsh conditions depended on the supernatural end of human life being acceptably presented to people at every level. Before this could happen, there were social and theological questions which needed to be answered, and a sufficient body of officials trained in the schools had to be available as judges and advocates in the courts to give practical effect to these answers.

Broadly speaking, the northern French schools, among which Paris rapidly rose to pre-eminence, became the main source of theological answers to the problems of daily life in relation to eternal salvation. And the schools of Bologna, which emerged slightly later, were the main source of legal principles and procedures ancillary to this end. These rules and procedures affected the lives of people at every social level. Thus, during the two hundred and fifty years of sustained growth in European population and prosperity from about 1070 to about 1320, the association between the schools and government had an organizational role that was unparalleled until the next great period of comparable growth in population and technical innovation between about 1850 and the present day.

We must not be misled by the appearance of remoteness in the discussions of the twelfth and thirteenth century schools. In particular, the theological questions which were discussed and answered in the schools were all potentially significant both for government and for daily life. Since all forms of medieval government, however crudely military their outward forms may seem to be, had a role in promoting personal salvation as well as in enforcing personal rights, there could be no absolute separation between punishing crime and punishing sin, nor between defining legal rights and duties, and elaborating theological truths.

On many points, English examples in the essential transition period from the pre-scholastic to the scholastic eras are especially enlightening because the Norman Conquest made the change from traditional systems of conduct to a single and more sharply defined code of rules and rituals unusually abrupt. Consequently the transition is more abundantly documented in England than elsewhere in western Europe;[7] and this may justify my use of English examples in outlining the co-operation of schools and government in two fundamental areas of human life.

1 *Marriage and inheritance*

The most primitive of all legal rights is the right of legitimate children to succeed to their parental inheritance. Uncertainty on this subject is likely to lead to very widespread disorder and violence, and when the rules of a traditional society begin

---

[7] For detailed evidence of this abundance, see *English Lawsuits from William I to Richard I*, ed. (with translations of all the quoted texts) by R. C. van Caenegem, 2 vols, Selden Society Publications, vols cvi, cvii, 1990–91.

to dissolve, the chances of disorder become very great indeed. Especially after the Norman Conquest, there was in England an immense tangle of concurrent and conflicting jurisdictions and ill-defined codes of inheritance. The many uncertainties in the laws of marriage added a further area of confusion, and the rapidly-growing number of governmental and legal documents after 1100 reveal muddles which could only be resolved by elaborating in ever greater detail the principles and laws which would be administered at every level by officials with some degree of theological or legal training.

If we go back to the very beginning of scholastic expansion, in the late eleventh century, we find that the rules of marriage in England were a confused jumble of ancient rules of uncertain validity. On the main point, that no one could have more than one spouse, there could be no possibility of doubt. But apart from this fundamental rule there were many miscellaneous rules which were not easy to interpret, still less to obey, least of all to enforce, and impossible to harmonize. For instance, any student of Bede's *Ecclesiastical History* would know that Gregory the Great had given various instructions about marriage for the use of the English people. He had laid down that only those who were 'three or four times removed' in consanguinity might marry; that, contrary to Roman law, first cousins might not marry; that a man might not marry his widowed stepmother or his brother's widow; but that (contrary to later canon law) two brothers might marry two sisters; and that clergy might marry if, and only if, they were *extra sacros ordines*, though the precise meaning of this phrase was doubtful.[8] The question whether a Christian man might marry a pagan girl had been solved in the eighth century by the decision that it was lawful for a Christian man to marry a pagan girl, but not for a Christian girl to marry a pagan man. This was no more than an academic point by the late eleventh century, but a related, and living, issue was

---

[8] Pope Gregory's answers of 597 to the questions of Augustine, archbishop of Canterbury, were widely known from Bede, *Historia Ecclesiastica*, bk. 1, c. 27 (Plummer, i, pp. 48–62, esp. pp. 50–1). They are quoted as still being operative in about 1175 in the *Speculum Iuris Canonici*, of Peter of Blois (not the letter-writer), ed. T. A. Reiner, 1837, Berlin, p. 60, which will be discussed in the next volume of this work.

whether a free man or woman might marry a serf. On this last point there was no ruling at all, but it was a question of real practical importance.[9]

A further point that our late eleventh-century enquirer might have observed was that the main additions to marriage law in England after Gregory the Great had been made in the tenth and eleventh centuries by local councils meeting under royal authority, and that some of their rules contradicted those of Pope Gregory. Royal Councils of lay and ecclesiastical magnates meeting under King Ethelred II and King Canute had been especially active in this area, declaring that no man could marry his second cousin or the widow of his second cousin, and that no man might marry a divorced woman or a prostitute or a nun, that no woman might be sold in marriage or forced to marry a man she disliked, and that a widow had to remain unmarried for a year after the death of her husband on pain of losing all the property she held from her late husband.[10]

These kings had also supported the celibacy of priests, but only with admonitions which were widely ignored:

> We pray and enjoin all the servants of God, and priests above all, to practise celibacy . . . They know full well they have no right to marry, and if they remain celibate they will enjoy the favour of God and the status and privileges of a thegn.[11]

Such an injunction exemplifies the laws available in England in the eleventh century, and it will be seen that they raise as many questions as they answer – questions of terminology (what does it mean to be 'three or four times removed' in kinship?); of authority (what right has a king to legislate on these matters?); of contradictions between different authorities (could two brothers marry two sisters?). They also say nothing about the means of enforcing these rules. Above all they leave many questions unanswered, such as these:

[9] See Bede, *Historia Ecclesiastica*, bk. 1, c. 27, pp. 50–1. For the problem of mixed (free–serf) marriages in England after 1066, see Pollock and Maitland, i, 423–32.
[10] For the marriage laws of Ethelred II and Canute, see A. J. Robertson, *The Laws of the kings of England from Edmund to Henry I*, 1925, pp. 81–3, 92–7, 162–3, 210–13.
[11] Robertson, 1925, p. 83.

A priest 'ought not' to marry. Yet, far into the twelfth century, many did. Were their marriages invalid and their children illegitimate, or were they only illicit?

A man might not marry a nun; but could he marry a woman brought up in a nunnery who had not taken her vows or received the veil?

A valid marriage might not be dissolved; but could a formally valid marriage become invalid as a result of new information or changes of condition such as adultery, physical deformity, impotence, banishment, life imprisonment, presumed death, the carrying off of a spouse into slavery or into foreign lands, a vow of celibacy taken by one or other spouse, the discovery of fresh facts about a spouse (e.g. consanguinity) which were unknown, or if known had been concealed.

Of course, Old English rules were apt to be different from those of other peoples in Europe. But the important point is that local legislation and custom had everywhere brought into existence different codes of conduct, neither complete in themselves nor consistent with each other, and that there was no authoritative statement or agreed code for settling disputes in this large area of law. The English sample amply illustrates some of the difficulties arising from the existence of different sources of law, and from the temporary nature, incompleteness, ambiguities, and downright contradictions of the various sources. In addition, keeping the rules often required knowledge which it was almost impossible to have at the time of marriage: for example, that no godparent of either partner, or of their relatives, had been within the prohibited degrees of relationship.

No doubt these problems had arisen earlier, and we do not know how they had been solved: probably by *force majeure*. But the complicated society which was coming into existence in the early twelfth century required more refined methods of settling problems if permanent uncertainties and endless hostilities in this world were to be averted, and if the path to heaven was not to be blocked by errors. There was much work here for courts and lawyers; but neither courts nor lawyers could operate until many theological questions had been answered. For example: Was pre-marital intercourse an impediment to lawful marriage? Were children born before marriage legitimatized by marriage?

Was misinformation about the social status of one or other of the partners in marriage a sufficient ground for divorce?

Alliances and hostilities between families, the descent of property, and the status of individuals, all might depend on a satisfactory answer to one or other of these questions, and even when the principles had been established, decisions in individual cases might require the uncovering of facts of family relationships, dates of birth and marriage, and other events alleged to have taken place, sometimes in a past which was already remote. So, in all these questions, there was abundant material to exercise schools, judges, advocates and courts alike.

The clarification of doctrine was in the first place a matter for the schools. Giving doctrine the force of law was, after the Norman Conquest, a matter exclusively for ecclesiastical councils and papal decisions. Enforcement in detail was a matter for archdeacons so far as ecclesiastical sanctions were concerned, and for sheriffs' officers dealing with their secular consequences. Then, when all had been done, it sometimes needed the *fiat* of a supreme authority to settle a case which resisted settlement by judicial procedure.

For example, in one otherwise insoluble dispute, Pope Innocent III invoked the Roman law principle that in doubtful cases the *status quo* should be preserved. The case was this: a married man in the city of Perugia had gone as a mercenary in a war against Assisi and was reported to have been killed. His wife remarried and had two children. But then a man claiming to be, and recognized by some as having been, the woman's former husband, returned to Perugia declaring that he had been captured, but had escaped and had then wandered far and wide for several years. The woman declared that she did not know him; but on balance it seems likely that the man's story was true. If so, he should have regained his wife and whatever property he had in Perugia, and the two children of the woman should have been declared illegitimate.

Equally clearly he was a wholly unsatisfactory character, and no one in authority was willing to make a judgement in his favour. The case dragged on for several years, coming before a whole series of papal judges-delegate without reaching any agreed conclusion until the pope declared in favour of the wife on the principle that in cases of doubt judgement should be given in favour of the *status quo*. So, in a roundabout way, humanity prevailed against the run of the evidence.[12]

Apart from their practical importance and frequency, problems of marriage exercised a morbid fascination in the schools: there were countless debates based on the most unlikely combinations of supposed facts. It was tempting to relax in a world of fantastic sexual myths and suppositions.[13] Indeed fantasy played a part in shaping scholastic thought in the sense that extreme cases provided the best material for drawing distinctions between closely-related concepts. Much that seemed to later critics of scholasticism to be idle elaboration was a means of clarifying concepts as a first step towards creating a body of doctrines and rules covering every aspect of orthodox social and individual life.

2 *Sin and forgiveness*

Marriage was one area of life on which a substantially new body of rules needed to be provided and enforced if peace was to be maintained in the expanding society of the twelfth century. But it was only one among many. Among the others, no subject had greater universality or deeper interest for every member of society than the forgiveness of sin. Once more it must be remembered that though many acted as if there were no eternal sanctions, the existence of a future life of rewards and punishments was generally thought to be as well authenticated as any other known truth on any subject whatsoever. The consequences of this truth might be ignored, but – quite apart from the teaching of the Church which after being elaborated in the schools percolated down from the schools to the pulpit – miraculous

---

12 The very full account of the case was printed and discussed by C. R. Cheney, 'A draft decretal of Innocent III on a case of identity', *Traditio*, 15, 1959; reprinted in his collected papers, *The Papacy and England, 12th–14th Centuries*, Variorum Reprints, London, 1982.

13 There is an abundance of evidence on this point in the *Prose Salernitan Questions* of *c.* 1200, ed. Brian Lawn, *Auctores Britannici Medii Aevi*, v, London, British Academy, 1979. See esp. pp. 9–12, 247–53.

occurrences and popular stories, which were the common property of everyone, testified to the existence of this state of future rewards and punishments.

The existence of a future life of rewards and punishments was very generally accepted. Yet the rules and conditions applicable to this future life were, at the end of the eleventh century, in an even greater state of confusion and uncertainty than the rules of matrimony. Most people probably knew that remission of sins was essential for admission to a future state of blessedness, and there was a long tradition of confession of mortal sins to the parish priest in Lent. But there were many questions to which no clear or authoritative answers could be given. Here are a few of them:

Granted that there could be no forgiveness without confession, would it suffice if it were made privately to God? And, if to another person, to whom and in what circumstances? To a priest? Any priest? A deacon? A layman? How often? How explicit in detail? How complete in scope? Could some sins be confessed and others concealed?

Further, granted that there could be no forgiveness without penance, who was to determine the appropriate penance? What happened to sinners who died with their penances incomplete? Could the sinner object to unreasonable penances, and on what grounds could his objections be regarded as justified?

These were not remote and recondite questions. They were questions of everyday practicality, and they were often and early asked in the schools. But before they could be resolved, there were some even more fundamental questions which required an answer. I shall mention only two groups – the first concerning the nature and concomitants of sin; the second, the role of the confessor:

(1) In what, if any, circumstances are normally sinful acts, such as killing, lying, sexual intercourse, *not* sinful, or sinful only in some minor way?

(2) What is the purpose of confession to a person other than God? To induce shame? To provide a basis for diagnosis? To solicit aid and intercession? As the only means of obtaining absolution?

If we once more take our stand in England at the time of

the Norman Conquest, and imagine an enquirer attempting to find answers to any of these questions in any earlier legislation which was available to him, he would have found some curious facts. In the first place, as with matrimony, so with confession and penance, most of the legislation had been issued by secular rulers who in the twelfth century were held to have no standing in such matters.

Further he would have found that the richest store of legislation on this subject came from the period of disaster under Ethelred II, and that its main aim was not to promote individual salvation, but to avert communal disaster. On several occasions in the decade 1005–15, when the country was overrun by Viking armies, the King took counsel with his lay and ecclesiastical advisers and issued a varied collection of commands: first, that ships should hastily be built to attack the Viking host; and, second, that 'every Christian man shall go frequently to confession, and freely confess his sins, and readily make amends as prescribed for him'. Then, when things got still worse, the King and his councillors decreed that all adults should fast for three days before Michaelmas, go barefooted in procession to church with the priest on these days, and confess, renounce and make amends for their sins. For failure to obey this command, a number of penalties were laid down, extending from beating for a slave to a fine of 30 shillings for a thegn.[14]

Such ordinances as these show that the necessity for confession and penance had been taken seriously in the earlier period and had been the subject of legislation. Indeed, we shall never again find such precise and general commands for a whole community so clearly expressed and so carefully monitored. But in almost every way the early eleventh-century ordinances present a contrast with the legislation of the next two centuries on religious obligations. In the first place, the early eleventh-century laws covering every kind of spiritual and practical activity had been issued by the king on the advice of his combined lay and ecclesiastical magnates. Then, quite suddenly in the later years of the eleventh century – in England at the year 1066 – these two sides of human life were divided. All the rules of religious

[14] Robertson, 1925, pp. 109–10.

behaviour which King Ethelred and his advisers had thought themselves competent to lay down and enforce, including the payment of tithes and acts of confession, fell entirely into the hands of the clergy, first of all in discussions in the schools, and then in authoritative decisions taken under papal auspices in councils and in papal letters, which distributed the same message throughout the whole of western Christendom. The measures taken in this later period were not concerned with short-term survival, but with rules of life for all circumstances and for ever, and in the main their definition was the work of clerical experts in the schools and in the papal Curia. Together they formed the most powerful legislative body that has ever existed in western Europe. In their codification of the results of all earlier statements, and in their range of activity and expectation of permanence, these decisions of the twelfth and thirteenth centuries were the expression of a society that was confident of its command of the resources of the past, and consequently of a certain superiority over all previous eras of human history, and over all enemies whether internal or external.

The decisions of the earlier period up to the eleventh century were the expression of a will to survive with supernatural help in a situation of desperate danger. By contrast, the decrees of the later period outlined refined codes of behaviour designed to regulate the conduct of all individuals, immediately throughout western Christendom, and without long delay (it was hoped) throughout the whole world, for ever. Regarded simply as an attempt to regulate human life and to direct it in all its aspects towards the attainment of stability on earth and everlasting happiness thereafter, the efforts of the twelfth and thirteenth centuries – coming so soon after the most fragmented period of European invasions and resettlements – have an astonishing assurance of permanence.

Nevertheless, the earlier legislation, in its own way, also expressed a coherent view of what was thought to be a permanent state of affairs likely to exist till the end of the world. In normal circumstances, it was expected that individual conduct would be left to exhortation rather than enforced by detailed legislation. The mode of instruction of the earlier period is exemplified in such passages as this from Archbishop

Wulfstan of York during the first quarter of the eleventh century:

> I admonish all baptized Christians who have done wrong, to make a clear confession to a priest, to do penance, and to receive episcopal absolution and then communion. For it is both useful and necessary that the guilt of sin should be cleansed by episcopal supplication and absolution.[15]

This expresses the pre-scholastic hortatory and pastoral approach to the problems of individual spiritual direction in normal times. It was only in times of extreme danger that the semi-sacerdotal king with his lay and ecclesiastical counsellors gave directions that were to be followed and enforced as a public duty.

The change from this situation to the detailed regulation of conduct for everyone in all circumstances was the result of an immense change in the organization of western European society taking place under the direction of scholars drawing on what was believed to be the total deposit of earlier doctrine, refined by scholastic debate, and systematized by the continuing efforts of a constant stream of scholars. As in the past, all law had the dual aim of ensuring peace in the present and salvation in eternity. But with the new body of material, and the new hierarchy of courts, it was thought possible to lay down, and in large part enforce, rules of both corporate and individual life that would be valid in all circumstances and for ever.

The moment when the main features of the new scholastically elaborated organization of western European thought and practice begin to appear in small details over a wide range of activities is in the 1120s. It is in this decade that – without producing any single work of the highest importance – the central features of the new order can first be observed: the administrative papacy, the drive towards unity of thought and behaviour, the outlines of systematic theology and law, of comprehensive systems of knowledge, and even of the new arrangement of stresses in building which express a similar urge

[15] A. Napier, *Wulstan: Sammlung der ihm zugeschriebenen Homilien*, Berlin, 1883, p. 63.

towards the organization of a multiplicity of details in a single heaven-aspiring whole.[16]

Naturally the change did not come about without conflicts, partly intellectual and partly physical, on almost every subject and in almost every area of life. But sometimes the conflicts, though profound in their implications, left scarcely a ripple on the surface of public events. For example – to mention only one area where conflict was barely visible to the world outside the schools – on the matter of confession. Even as late as about 1130, Hugh of St-Victor wrote: 'When we tell men to confess their sins, they ask us to give our authority,' and he admitted that this was not an easy task since biblical authority was almost non-existent.[17] Even ten years later, Gratian was still struggling with a mountain of conflicting authorities. In the section of his *Decretum* dealing with confession and penance – a section of a length almost unequalled, and a confusion and inconclusiveness without parallel in his whole work – he assembled about ninety authoritative passages, and ended with the admission: 'I leave it to the reader to decide which side to favour; there are wise and religious men on both sides.'[18] But by 1215 the debate was over, and the Lateran Council of this year issued a series of directions which laid down the doctrine and practice for the whole of the western Church, which were repeated again and again during the thirteenth century in local councils throughout western Europe.[19]

---

[16] For the European-wide turning-point of the 1120s, see p. 300 for the political change associated with the death of the Emperor Henry V in 1125; p. 175 for the early stages in recruiting men from the schools for the papal curia; p. 298 for the beginnings of widespread interest in Roman law as a tool in ecclesiastical administration.

[17] For Hugh of St-Victor's very full and open-minded discussion of this problem, see his *De Sacramentis*, lib. ii, pt. 14, c. 1 (*PL*, 176, cols. 549–554).

[18] Gratian, *Decretum*, II, c. 33, q. 3, d. 1: *Si sola confessione cordis crimen possit deleri?*. Gratian's discussion is one of the longest in his whole work, covering all the main elements in the problem in ninety chapters. There are only three quotations from the Bible, all ambiguous (Pss. 31:5; 50:19; Luke, 22:55–6), but very many from Augustine, Jerome, Roman law, papal letters, etc., and Gratian concludes with the remark quoted above.

[19] Lateran Council 1215, c. 21 (*Councils*, vol. 1, p. 245; and, for later repetitions, vol. 2, especially pp. 73–5, 172–3, 188–9, 220–6, 303–4, 638–9, 1060–77. Also, for the very numerous local elaborations, see the index of Powicke and Cheney, *Councils and Synods*, ii, 1205–1313.

The root of the difficulty with regard to confession was that there was no biblical authority for any organized practice of confession, and the later authorities were full of gaps and ambiguities. There was no area of early scholastic thought where the foundation of ancient texts was so shaky. Hence, there was no subject which presented a greater challenge to those who were trying to produce clear and definitive rules for everyone – rules that would be not only clear, but capable of standing up to prolonged argument and opposition.

The road of progress towards the scholastic ideal of universal agreement among the learned, and universal compliance among the unlettered majority, lay through the refinement and codification of all previous authoritative statements on the subject, and through systematizing the result with all possible intellectual and practical rigour. It was a task which could only have been undertaken at a time of relative stability, when large and growing resources were available both for the work of clarifying principles, and for enforcing them in practice along lines which were thought to be sufficiently well established to gain general assent. These conditions broadly existed throughout the twelfth and most of the thirteenth century. So, by the end of the twelfth century, the debate about the rules of confession, which had seemed one of the most intractable subjects in practical theology, was over, and throughout the thirteenth century very considerable efforts were made to publish and enforce these rules in practice. And, broadly speaking, the same can be said of all other matters of central importance for the conduct of human life in accordance with an organized body of doctrine held to be guaranteed both by reason and Revelation.

This could not have happened without a continuing co-operation between schools and papacy. The nature of this co-operation therefore requires a brief elaboration.

IV THE SCHOOLS AND THE PAPACY

It was not an accident that the transition from what we may call the period of government based on ritual to that of government based on clearly-defined procedures and concepts coincided with the first period of bitter and prolonged conflict between popes and emperors, for these were the only two European-wide authorities with any systematic conceptual basis for their authority. In this conflict the papal claims were successful at almost every point, largely because a systematically complete set of answers to theoretical problems of belief, and of legal procedures for their enforcement in practice, had been created, and was available for circulation and for continuing refinement in the schools. Meanwhile the papacy had developed an administrative basis for giving effect to an integrated system of government throughout the whole of western Christendom; and with the death of the Emperor Henry V the empire lost any chance it might have had of establishing a secular counterpart based on Roman law.[20]

The essential development which brought this about – that is to say, the development without which the others would have been ineffective – was the growth of the schools and especially of those in Paris and Bologna. The papacy needed the schools because only they could provide the detailed elaboration of the principles on which papal sovereignty and clerical cohesion equally were based. Only the papacy could give effect to these principles, but it was only in the schools – to which the clergy alone had access – that all the learned resources of the past could be brought to bear on the task of reaching conclusions with full regard to all possible objections, and then of systematizing the results. Moreover, it was only from the body of men trained in the schools that the large administrative force of lawyers, judges, administrators and local officers necessary for giving practical effect to doctrinal elaborations could be recruited. So the schools provided both the clerical personnel and the formulation of doctrines necessary for a universally effective government, and the popes – who from 1159 onwards were almost invariably men with a distinguished scholastic record – were well aware of their debt to the schools. Equally, graduates from the schools were aware of the vast treasury of promotion for which their studies equipped them, and to

[20] See below, chapter 9, for these developments.

which they had access largely and increasingly through papal patronage.[21]

The idea of the papacy as the divinely instituted and inspired instrument for overseeing all the activities of Christendom, accessible to all litigants, first captured the minds and imaginations of the most important scholars in Europe in the late eleventh century. It was an idea which allowed the fullest scope to the creative impulses of the clergy who alone provided the scholars and administrators of Europe from the eleventh to the fourteenth centuries. By contrast, the Empire, which had expressed the most coherent political aspirations of the period from about 750 to 1050, had lost the support of the most articulate and learned part of the clergy by the late eleventh century.[22]

Quite suddenly, the fluid and ill-defined sharing of respon-·sibility between emperors and popes, kings and bishops, lay-men and priests, which had sufficed for most purposes for the last four hundred years, turned into violent and irreconcilable antagonisms.

It is hard even now, when so much has been published on the causes and background of the so-called 'Investiture' and other papal–imperial disputes – which were essentially disputes about the respective roles of the clergy and laity in a Christian society – to appreciate how deep-seated these disputes were in the social and economic developments taking place in western Europe, and how calamitous was their impact on the old rituals and mutual understandings which had been the mainstay of government in the period before the outbreak of these new conflicts of principle.

Quite apart from the well-known details of conflicting claims

---

21 For evidence of the huge flow of requests for benefices which reached the papal Curia from 1198 onwards, see *Entries in the papal registers relating to Great Britain and Ireland*, 14 volumes, H.M. Stationery Office, London, 1894–1956.

22 For evidence of the intellectual decline of the doctrine of imperial, royal and secular authority in matters of religion, see *Libelli de Lite Imperatorum et Pontificum saec. XI et XII conscripti*, in *MGH*, 3 vols, 1891, 1892, 1897; repr. 1957. The only known *systematic* defender of lay rights in ecclesiastical affairs during this vital period of change is the so-called 'Anonymous of York', *c.* 1100, in a widely ranging work preserved in a single MS (Corpus Christi College, Cambridge, MS 415) and published in facsimile by Ruth Nineham and Karl Pellens, Wiesbaden, 1977.

in the Investiture dispute, the contrasting attitudes demonstrated the need for a new clarity in defining the chain of command between God and the individual members of a Christian society. Did the chain of governmental command run from God to the people through the successors of St Peter and the Apostles as representatives of the incarnate God, or through kings and emperors as successors of those whom St Paul had recognized as the instruments of God 'not bearing the sword in vain'?

It was in the vast reorganization of thought and society in the period from about 1050 to 1150 that the conception of a day-to-day authority of the pope as the representative of Christ began to emerge as a practical possibility, and then as an assured reality. Hence the papacy came out of the religious and political crisis of the late eleventh century as the chief force capable of carrying through the reorganization of society, just at the time when the schools of Paris emerged as the main instruments for giving detailed definition to the whole system of Christian doctrine.

No two institutions in western Europe were more thoroughly grounded in barbarian Europe than the papacy and the schools. But equally, no institutions were more completely transformed in their methods of operation and in their range of influence than these two. There was indeed a natural affinity between the *magisterium* of the pope and that of the masters of the schools. In the hierarchy of the Church, the pope was the supreme *magister*, whose *sententiae* had the same status on the great stage of Christendom as the *sententiae* of individual masters on the small stage of their own schools. So there was a natural affinity between the *cathedra* of the pope and the numerous *cathedrae* of masters in their schools, and the alliance of schools and papacy was one of the binding forces in western Europe in the great period of European growth from about 1050 to 1300.

The alliance broke down when the momentum of social and economic growth throughout Europe came to an end in the early years of the fourteenth century.[23] When this happened both

[23] Note, however, a first attempt of a secular ruler to enlist scholastic support in the widely-reported willingness of King Henry II to submit his dispute with archbishop Thomas Becket to the judgement of the masters of Paris in 1169. This is widely reported in English chronicles in the *Rolls Series*: Ralph of Diceto, i, 337; M. Paris, ii, 263; *Mat. Becket*, vii, 164. And see also *C.U.Par.*, i, no. 21.

the popes and the masters began to look for new allies, and a new phase in scholastic and papal history, and in the relations between secular rulers and both schools and papacy, began.

To speak of the masters having the same role in their schools as the popes on the great stage of Christendom may seem to suggest that the popes exercised a supervisory role over the schools. But this is true only in a very remote sense. The more immediate truth is almost the opposite. The papacy certainly had a final judicial authority over all scholastic decisions, but successive popes were also active in protecting scholastic definitions from the hostile criticism of conservative thinkers when papal decisions on scholastic doctrines were called for, as they were in a very public way in 1148, 1179 and 1215.[24] Indeed, the popes were the greatest allies that the masters of the schools ever had, and the sharp diminution in papal support for the schools in the early fourteenth century was the first sign that the schools had lost the regulative force that they had enjoyed during the previous two hundred years. When this happened it announced the end of the centrality of the schools in the development of European thought and organization. And it also announced that the links which bound the papacy to the whole European community were exposed to increasing strains. But this situation lay far in the future during the period with which this volume is concerned, and before going further we must turn to trace the threads which bound western Europe and the schools together in the twelfth and thirteenth centuries.

---

[24] The great exception was the condemnation of Abelard in 1140, but for this there were special reasons which will be discussed in Volume II. For the remarkable terms of respect with which Innocent III approved Peter Lombard's statement of the doctrine of the Trinity against the essentially non-scholastic statements of Joachim of Flora, see the decrees of the Lateran Council of 1215, c. 2 (*Councils*, vol. 1, p. 232).

5

The Men and their Rewards

I Scholars in the World

The masters in their schools defined the doctrines and practices
necessary for a thoroughly organized Christian society, but there
would have been no masters without students. It was the multiplicity of students which brought into existence the multiplicity
of masters necessary for the recasting of Christian thought in
the systematic way which alone could give western Christendom
a uniformity of faith and practice. But the students of course
were responding to their need for a livelihood and to their hopes
of personal advancement without much or any regard for the
general good. Nevertheless they all depended on opportunities
being available – opportunities, that is to say, in the availability
both of schools and of employment afterwards. The questions
about the students which we should like to be able to answer
are these: How many were there? Who were they? Where did
they come from? Why did they come to the schools? Who sent
them? What did they do afterwards? These questions can be
answered only very imperfectly, but the general picture which
emerges is fairly clear.

In the first place there can be no doubt about the very great
increase in the number of students in the early years of the
twelfth century. When a writer of about 1120 tells us that
almost every city, fortified town and village in France, Germany,
Normandy and England had schools in which teachers of the
liberal Arts were, as we would say, as common as blackberries,
his intention was to deride masters who gave themselves airs of

importance, by pointing out that there were more than enough of them. Whether or not his satire was justified, there seems no doubt that there were schools in quite unimportant towns, and that their number was growing.[1]

Local schools, however, though they could provide sufficient learning for the common offices of the Church, were insufficient for the higher functions of defining and systematizing the main areas of knowledge, or for engaging in the higher functions of law and administration. It was for these purposes that the great agglomerations of schools in a few towns came into existence.

By about 1150, the main places where such agglomerations existed were already well known, and the earlier bush-telegraph among students exchanging information about masters and lodgings in various places was no longer necessary.[2] Nevertheless, even when it was no longer so necessary to have up-to-date information about the movements of masters, students were still very accident-prone. They were generally far from home, and they could not exist without funds from friends or relatives. When students became impoverished, the reason was generally an accumulation of debts due to the non-arrival of an expected remittance. The typical student was not by nature a pauper or a bohemian, though failure of funds might make him both. To be successful, he had to be ambitious, determined, tenacious, and moderately well endowed.

It would seem to have been a common practice for parents or relatives to send youths to the schools in the charge of an older man who – in addition to looking after his young pupils – was engaged in his own studies and had his own

---

[1] For the proliferation of masters during the first two decades of the twelfth century, see especially the letter published by R. Foreville and J. Leclercq, 'Un débat sur le sacerdoce des moines au XIIe siècle', in *Analecta monastica*, iv, *Studia Anselmiana*, iv sér. xli, Rome, 1957, p. 65; and, for comments, Southern, 1984, pp. 5–6.

[2] For the growing student numbers and the search for the best schools up to about 1120, the most interesting evidence is still to be found in the letters published by Lucien Merlet, 'Lettres d'Ives de Chartres et d'autres personnages de son temps, 1087–1130', *BEC*, 4th series, 1, 1855, pp. 443–71. I have discussed the significance of this evidence above in chapter 2: see especially p. 67.

ambitions. For instance, at some time between 1107 and 1112, Ranulf, the chancellor of Henry I of England, sent his two nephews to the school of Laon in the charge of William of Corbeil, who later became archbishop of Canterbury. At about the same time another scholar from England, Adelard of Bath, was at Laon, with his nephew and some others in his charge. Probably the plan was that he should teach them while he himself was studying under the widely-famous Master Anselm, but he left his pupils (perhaps in charge of another master) to pursue his own studies on the frontiers of Europe: he became a very notable scholar indeed, but he seems to have ended in a fairly undistinguished position in the royal government.[3] Fifteen years earlier, the young Peter Abelard had been going round the schools of the Loire valley in the charge of a tutor; we hear no more about the tutor, but the name of Abelard was soon ringing through the schools of northern France.[4] A little later, in about 1120, we hear of Hugh, a young man from Tournai, studying at Reims in the charge of his tutor, Walter of Mortagne. Walter was a very ambitious man seeking to make his mark in the school of the famous master Alberic, while teaching his own young pupil in private. Naturally he was more interested in the first than the second of these occupations, and he spent more of his time harassing and seeking to humiliate his own master on every possible occasion than in taking care of his pupil. He had his own way to make, and when he felt

[3]   For Adelard leaving his pupils at Laon while he went off to study the learning of the Arabs, see M. Gibson in Charles Burnett, *Adelard of Bath: an English scientist and Arabist of the early twelfth century*, p. 9. Gibson's reluctance to 'infer from this passage that Adelard was a teacher at Laon' is (I think) based on a misunderstanding: no one would suggest that Adelard taught in the school of Laon, but the system of combining studying under famous masters with teaching younger pupils was so widespread that it justifies this interpretation of the evidence, and it fits in with all that we know of Adelard's movements. For the contrast between the careers of men who (like Adelard) studied the natural sciences and those who studied theology or law, see Southern, 1992, pp. xxxiv–lv.

[4]   The evidence for Abelard's early studies is conveniently found in J. G. Sikes, *Peter Abailard*, Cambridge, 1932, pp. 2–3. For Roscelin's account of his teaching Abelard at Loches, see *PL*, 178, col. 360. For further details on Abelard's battle for academic eminence, see below, pp. 204–8.

strong enough, he set up his own school, first in Reims and later in Laon, taking, it would seem, his pupil with him.[5]

Being responsible for pupils far from home was an encumbrance, but such pupils were also an insurance, spreading the risk of the non-arrival of remittances. But pupils could also be dangerous rivals. The scholastic scene was highly competitive, and competition commonly took the form of shining in debate – best of all in defeating a well-known master in argument. This led to frequent clashes of interest in the three-sided relationship between established masters, new masters seeking to compete with them, and pupils who watched the battle with varying emotions.

We have several accounts of the way in which famous masters at the top of the tree met the challenge of competition. At the bottom of the tree, we have one pathetic story of the consequences for a pupil who did too well. The pupil was an aspiring young man from England who had been sent abroad by his parents with a tutor. He and his tutor were both studying under a 'Master T the Universal', who may plausibly be identified with Master Thierry of Chartres, who seems to have been teaching in Paris during the years when these events took place. The young English pupil became a favourite of the great master, and this partiality displeased his tutor so much that he had the young man beaten up. The

---

5 Walter of Mortagne's career (he later became bishop of Laon) is outlined in the *Life* of his pupil, Hugh, later abbot of Marchiennes (see E. Martène and V. Durand, *Thesaurus novus anecdotum*, vol. 3, 1717, cols. 1711–1713). The battle among masters for pupils in the early years of the twelfth century is well conveyed in a passage in his pupil's *Life*, which may be translated thus: *Owing to the zeal for learning at that time, Reims was so filled with students that it was hard to know whether there were more students or laymen in the town.* In particular, Walter of Mortagne was there with his young pupil Hugh, a well-born young man from Tournai. The cathedral master was Alberic, archdeacon of the town, an eloquent, expansive and well-liked man, but not expert in answering questions. Walter, who was sharp and argumentative, was one of his auditors and frequently opposed the master, who thereupon forced him to leave the city. He went first to Saint-Remi on the outskirts of Reims and set up his school there. But again the archdeacon forced him to move and he went to Laon, where pupils came to him from far and wide. After his aggressive start he became a model of respectability. For his works and later career, see Häring, 1953i, pp. 212–21, and C. Ott, 1937, pp. 126–31.

student came home with his face so bruised that his mother could not recognize him. After further persecutions from his tutor he had a nervous breakdown, and finally became a monk at St Albans.[6]

This end to a scholastic career was certainly not what his parents had intended when they sent him to study abroad. Parents generally sent their sons to foreign schools in the hope that they would equip themselves with the knowledge necessary for high positions in either secular or ecclesiastical government. We can judge their ambitions partly from the people who sent their relatives to the schools, and partly from the careers of those whom they sent. The most important men in English government were especially active in sending young relatives and protégés to the French schools (note overleaf).[7] Odo of Bayeux, half-brother of the Conqueror, was one of the earliest and greatest of the Anglo-Norman magnates to patronize the schools, and the young men whom he sent to the schools at Liège included Thomas, later archbishop of York, and Samson, later bishop of Worcester, two of the most successful ecclesiastical administrators in the last years of the eleventh century.

In the next generation, Henry I's chancellor Ranulf sent his nephews to Laon; and the greatest of all Henry I's ministers, the justiciar Roger of Salisbury, did the same for his two nephews, Alexander and Nigel, of whom the first became bishop of Lincoln, and the second became bishop of Ely and royal treasurer.

Then, if we go on to the great officials of the next generation,

---

[6] The story is told in a collection of mid-twelfth century letters in Trinity College, Dublin, MS 184, edited by Marvin L. Colker, *Analecta Dublinensia*, Cambridge, Mass., 1975, pp. 131–40. The letters record that the student later became a monk of St Albans for sixteen years and was then taken to Rome by the papal legate Alberic, bishop of Ostia, who was in England from June 1138 to January 1139. This would date the incident of his student years *c.* 1122. Colker suggests that the 'T' is a mistake, and that the master referred to was Gilbert the Universal, who became bishop of London in 1128 and died in 1134. But such evidence as we have about Gilbert's early career, apart from his connection with the school of Anselm of Laon, associates him with the cathedral of Auxerre. By contrast, Thierry, whose range of studies equally qualified him for the title *'universalis'*, certainly taught in Paris, probably already in the 1120s. See below, pp. 210–11, 216, 220, 222.

to Richard de Lucy, Roger of Salisbury's successor as justiciar, we find that the connections between the official families and the schools were still being maintained. Richard de Lucy's son, Geoffrey, studied in Paris and came back to work in the royal exchequer; thereafter he became a royal judge and ambassador, collected an armful of benefices and ended his life as bishop of Winchester. It is likely also that Geoffrey de Lucy, who also studied in Paris and became the first chancellor of the University of Oxford in 1214, was the illegitimate son of Geoffrey, bishop of Winchester; but he did not rise very high, despite all that could be done for him in the way of papal remission of his illegitimate birth. So he ended his career in the rather disappointing position of Dean of St Paul's cathedral in London.[8]

Nevertheless, all these men were model students in the sense that they did what their families expected of them: they studied in order to succeed. Such families did not send their relatives to the schools to grow long hair and indulge in the excesses for which students were already becoming notorious. They sent them to improve their position in the world and to increase the influence of their families, and this they generally did.

Of course very few students started with the advantages of the small group I have mentioned. There were many who went to the schools without adequate resources, and gradually sank under the weight of their financial embarrassments. Their situation was described by an English student in Bologna in the 1170s: although he was by no means destitute of resources, he could not leave Bologna except by stealth because of his debts and the vigilance of his creditors. If he stayed and his remittances

[7]   For the young men whom Odo of Bayeux sent to Liège and other schools, and who later became bishops and abbots of the Anglo-Norman kingdom, see Orderic Vitalis, *Ecclesiastical History*, ed. Marjorie Chibnall, vol. iv, p. 118. For William of Corbeil, who had studied under Anselm of Laon while he taught the sons of Ranulf, chancellor of King Henry I, and who later (1123–36) became archbishop of Canterbury; and for the education of Alexander, bishop of Lincoln, and Nigel, bishop of Ely, the nephews of Henry I's chief minister, Roger, bishop of Salisbury, who also had studied at the school of Anselm at Laon, see Herman, *De miraculis S. Mariae Laudunensis*, ii, cc. 6 and 13 (*PL*, 156, cols. 977, 983). Note also that Waldric, bishop of Laon 1107 to 1112, had earlier been King Henry I's chancellor.

[8]   For the family connections and career of Geoffrey de Lucy, first chancellor of Oxford University, see Southern, 1984, pp. 32–3, and Diana Greenway, *Fasti Ecclesiae Anglicanae, 1066–1300: St Paul's London*, 1968, p. 6.

from England continued to fail to arrive, his debts, and the interest on them, would grow from month to month.[9] Even if his remittances arrived and he completed his course with credit, got some pupils of his own and managed to pay his creditors, the future was still bleak until he could get a benefice and enjoy an assured position at home. Without family influence or a benevolent patron, the last step when a student had to launch himself into the world was the most difficult stage in his career. He could hover for years between success and failure, before he finally succumbed or contented himself with mediocrity, or by some stroke of good fortune attracted the attention of a bishop who could give him a benefice. There must have been very many hovering between success and failure of this kind.

The career of Peter of Blois, later to be examined in greater detail, is a good example of the difficulties and hazards encountered even by a brilliant student who had much to contribute to the household of any magnate, but who had very little family influence to help him in his career: he was in his forties before he got a steady place in the household of the archbishop of Canterbury. Even then, his troubles were not over: the death of the archbishop in 1184 left his future uncertain for nearly a year; and although the archbishop's successor retained his services, the next archbishop did not. So, although he had acquired an archdeaconry and was in no danger of starvation, he had a good deal to grumble about – constant travelling, foul food, uncomfortable lodgings, recurrent fevers, and no real prospect of eminence. He was not silent about his troubles, but there were very many scholars in a worse state. Considered simply as a tale of scholastic ambitions and setbacks, Peter of Blois's life was neither tragically unsuccessful nor glamorously great: it just happens to be exceptionally well documented because he wrote letters which made him famous but not rich.[10]

---

[9] These experiences are described by Master David of London in letters printed in *Spicilegium Liberianum*, ed. Franciscus Liverani, Florence, 1863, pp. 603–24. They are most accessibly discussed by Z. N. Brooke, in *Essays in History presented to R. L. Poole*, ed. H. W. C. Davis, Oxford 1927, pp. 227–45. The letters make it clear that Master David – like many other aspiring masters of his day – was studying Roman law. For his debts and studies, see especially the letters on pp. 603, 605. For the attraction of Roman law for budding administrators, see below pp. 283, 298–9.
[10] His career will be discussed in some detail in Volume II.

If we go back to the early decades of the twelfth century when the number of ambitious students was increasing very rapidly, we find several earlier examples of the fate of those students who had more ability than family influence. For example, there was a certain Master Lawrence, whose academic experiences will occupy us in due course. He was a man from the north of England, who went to Paris with an introduction from a monk of Durham to one of the greatest masters of his day, Hugh of St-Victor. Hugh thought sufficiently well of him to give him the task of making a record of his lectures, and this record has survived.[11] Moreover, St Bernard, who has not been given as much credit as he deserves for the trouble he took to promote masters of whom he approved, gave him a testimonial recommending him to potential employers. Yet even with these advantages promotion eluded him. The fact was that all grandees who had benefices at their disposal had many more urgent claimants than Master Lawrence, and when he returned to England from his studies in Paris he had to earn a precarious livelihood as a messenger in the lawsuits of northern monasteries.

This kind of work generally involved travelling to the papal Curia in order to obtain papal confirmations of rights claimed by monasteries. Such work was becoming widely available from the 1130s onwards. It was responsible work and needed some expert knowledge. So experienced messengers were in great demand. But their work brought no guarantee of permanence – only a distant hope of reward in the shape of a vicarage of a country church in the gift of the monastery, if one should fall vacant at an opportune moment. But all monasteries had many important claimants for these positions, and in the end Lawrence decided that his best course was to become a monk, and he took his monastic vows at St Albans. Here he was very welcome, for in the mid-twelfth century a man with Master Lawrence's experience was a boon to any monastic community which had many lawsuits on its hands. Within five years of his becoming a monk he was elected Abbot. So, from being a rootless scholar making

---

[11] See B. Bischoff, *Aus der Schule Hugos von St. Viktor*, in Grabmann *Festschrift*, 1935, repr. in Bischoff, *Mittelalterliche Studien: Ausgewählte Aufsätze zur Schriftkunde und Literaturgeschichte*, 1967, ii, 182–7.

a living in miscellaneous ecclesiastical business, he became a man of baronial rank, deeply engaged in business with the papal court on behalf of his own monastery, and in close contact with the king and his court.[12]

Men like Master Lawrence, who had studied in the schools, were drawn to the monastic life for many different reasons, but an important inducement was the difficulty of making one's way in the world without family influence. To such scholars the monasteries offered a safe haven. They were the greatest and most lavish litigants of the twelfth century, and they badly needed the services of men with a scholastic training, who would be entirely and permanently committed to their interests and capable of holding their own in international as well as local courts. By 1150, all monasteries, even the most protected and privileged, were beginning to need men in their midst with a high degree of academic training. They could not retain their privileges intact unless the experts whose services they needed were bound to them with single-minded loyalty, and this could be expected only from members of the monastic community. We can see this dilemma very clearly in the case of one of the best connected monasteries of England – that of Battle.

No English abbey seemed less in need of learned support than Battle. As the main religious monument to the success of the Norman kings, and the symbol of their victory over the English, it could rely on kings and their officials to help it in its lawsuits. But in the course of time this identity of interest between the royal court and the abbey began to crumble. The change of dynasty in 1154 meant that the royal family no longer felt closely tied to the monastery, and the glory of the famous victory nearly a hundred years earlier was growing dim. Indeed

---

[12] Like most scholastic careers Master Lawrence's has to be pieced together mainly from charters and casual mentions in chronicles. What chiefly distinguishes his case from others is the discovery referred to in the previous note. But success as a student did not ensure success in the world, as Lawrence discovered. His later life can be traced in a number of documents which show him engaged in varied business in the North of England until 1153, when (following a warning from the hermit Godric) he left a party setting out for the papal Curia and became a monk at St Albans. (See G. V. Scammell, *Hugh de Puiset, Bishop of Durham*, Cambridge, 1956, p. 15; *Libellus de Vita et miraculis Godrici heremitae de Finchale*, ed. J. Stevenson, Surtees Society, 1847, vol. 20, 1834, pp. 232–3.)

Henry II, who became king in 1154, was beginning to derive more satisfaction from seeing himself as the successor of Edward the Confessor, whose beatification he helped to promote, than from the battle of Hastings. So Battle Abbey had to seek sources of strength outside the royal court.

The day of reckoning was delayed because, for nearly twenty years after the change of dynasty, Battle Abbey had an abbot whose brother, Richard de Lucy, was the royal justiciar and the most important man in the royal administration. With such a friend at court, the monastery could continue to dispense with the learning of the schools in the management of its affairs. But in 1171 the abbot died, and his brother – the hitherto friendly justiciar – took advantage of the vacancy to procure one of the churches in the abbey's patronage for his own son, who, on the proceeds of this benefice, straightway went to study in Paris.

There was now a complete breach between the monastery and the royal administration, and the abbey was exposed to the ordinary violences of local life without any friend at court. It had already lost one of its benefices, and with it a valuable source of income. Worse still, no advocate dared to incur disfavour with the royal administration by taking up the case. The best canonists and most experienced advocates of the day, Gerard Pucelle, Bishop Bartholomew of Exeter, an unnamed lawyer in the papal legate's own retinue, even the incorruptible John of Salisbury, all alleged some more or less specious grounds of personal incapacity for refusing to take on the monastery's case.

The justiciar's son, the recipient of the purloined church and now a student in Paris, had no difficulty in commissioning an English master to appear on his behalf. The monks were in despair. They blamed their abbot for not having sent any of them to the schools to learn law so that they could have done the job themselves: 'Then [they moaned to their abbot] we could have helped you in these pressing difficulties; but now we are as brute beasts, neither able ourselves to advise you nor to get advice from anyone else for love or money.' They forgot, or never knew, that the great Council of 1139 had forbidden monks to study law, so the only legal way for monasteries to have a learned lawyer always at their service was either to hire one, which was expensive, or to recruit already trained scholars as members of the monastic community.[13]

The great lesson enforced by these complicated affairs was that men from the schools who entered monastic communities would find plenty of scope for using their scholastic knowledge. So the choice of a monastic life was a tempting solution to life's problems: it put an end to weariness, disappointment, and lack of preferment in the world, and offered the promise of a life in which their scholastic talents would be fully appreciated. What we never find in the twelfth century, so far as I know, are scholars turning from the schools to the religious life out of contempt for scholastic learning. We have to wait till the fourteenth century before we find masters rejecting the learning of the schools because they no longer thought it worth having. In the mid-twelfth century the schools stood very high in the world indeed, and even St Bernard's preaching in Paris – if it was intended as a way of drawing novices to the Cistercian Order from the schools – seems to have had very little success.[14]

In the twelfth century many people complained that the schools contained too many place-hunters and too few seekers after truth, that too many studied law and too few grammar, or too many logic and too few literature. But most students were satisfied with what they found in the schools and they would have liked to stay longer. By the time a successful master was forty, he might well begin to think that the hurly-burly of the schools could be left to a younger man. He might long for more leisure, or for making his soul in peace. For whatever reason, many masters took refuge in monasteries in later life, and mon-asteries were generally glad to have them for the contribution they could make to the community: they were likely to be better business men than most monks without a scholastic training, and

[13] For the experiences of the monks of Battle, see *The Chronicle of Battle Abbey*, ed. and translated by Eleanor Searle, Oxford, 1980, pp. 320–35.
[14] E. Vacandard, *Vie de S. Bernard*, ii, 117, says that twenty-one students abandoned their studies to make their profession at Clairvaux; but a closer study of the facts suggests that, if St Bernard hoped to recruit monks, his preaching was a failure. Indeed he was by no means hostile to scholastic studies – in the right hands – as his patronage of Robert Pullen and John of Salisbury, as well as Master Lawrence, shows.

above all better at prosecuting their obsessively pursued lawsuits in the courts.

But it would be misleading to suppose that, even in the twelfth century, the schools had achieved a position of such universal respect that a scholar at court or in a monastery had nothing to fear from the resentment of those who felt threatened by intruders from a strange and potentially hostile intellectual environment. We know that John of Salisbury, as a scholar in government in the 1150s, could not (in his own words) 'escape the teeth of my fellow civil servants'.[15] The same kind of criticism, or worse, could assail the scholar who had retired to a monastery. He might hope to retire to write his long-deferred books, but unless he chose his monastery carefully, he could find that his scholastic connections made him an object of suspicion and hostility if he chose a conservative and unintellectual community. There were some, perhaps many, such monasteries, in which distrust of the schools lingered on until the end of the twelfth century, especially when the monks felt that the new recruit brought with him a whiff of unorthodoxy. The case of Master Everard of Ypres will be discussed in a different connection in a later chapter, but it is relevant here to note that, when he retired to the Cistercian monastery of Moutier-en-Argonne, he knew what it felt like to be an intellectual outcast in a hostile community:

> When a visiting monk or abbot arrives, the monks gather round to ask him about things he has heard or seen in the world, and they listen with open mouths. But if one of their confrères raises a question about the works of God, or the writings of the Fathers, they turn on him with fury. They call him a questioner, a disputer, and they scarcely stop short of calling him a criminal.[16]

It only made things worse for Everard when he mentioned that he had once been in the household of the now aged pope, Celestine III (1191–8), for Celestine was known to have been – in the distant days of his youth – a supporter of Abelard

15 See John of Salisbury, *Metalogicon, Prol*, p. 1: *Potueram quidem scolarium et eorum qui philosophiae nomina profitentur utcumque in silentio cavere morsus, sed omnino non possum concurialium dentes evadere.*
16 For the context, see below, p. 226.

against St Bernard. The unhappy Everard describes how one of his enemies, on learning about his early connections, said with significant emphasis, 'So *now* we know.'

Schoolmen, both in the world and in conservative monasteries, had to put up with many pinpricks of this kind. But they could always find consolation in the thought that the hostility they faced had its roots in envy. It expressed the frustrations of men who had not had the advantages of scholastic training. As a body, the men from the schools could feel very satisfied with their place in the world. After 1159, when Alexander II became the first pope since Silvester II (999–1003) with a thorough scholastic training, the papal throne was filled by an almost unbroken succession of men who had made a name for themselves in the schools. This capture of the papal throne by schoolmen was the most remarkable triumph of the schools. It represented the culmination of the papal policy, which had been initiated in the 1120s, of seeking highly-trained scholastic recruits for the Curia, and it signalized the alliance between the papacy and the schools that lasted for a century and a half before it began to break down in the last years of the thirteenth century.[17]

Of course popes were not the only rulers who were aware of the contribution that schoolmen could make to the work of government. A letter of about 1125 has survived in which Henry I of England roundly denounced what, probably rightly, he regarded as an attempt of Pope Honorius II to entice the scholastically-trained abbot of his recently founded abbey of Reading to the papal Curia:

> His absence (the King wrote indignantly) would cause great damage to his monastery and its possessions, and I must tell you that if you have any plan for retaining him I would appoint no one else to succeed him, but would take back for my own use the possessions which by his persuasion I have given to that church.[18]

This was a very intemperate letter, but it showed that the king knew as well as the pope the value of having such men at

[17] The circumstances which brought about this breakdown will be dealt with in Volume III. Meanwhile see Southern, 1987.
[18] *Regesta Regum Anglo-Normannorum*, ed. Charles Johnson and H. A. Cronne, Oxford, 1956, vol. 2, 1066–1154, p. 361, no. ccvii.

his disposal. Doubtless he felt strongly about his new foundation at Reading, but what really worried him was the loss of an adviser with academic attainments; and we know this because almost at once the king moved the newly appointed abbot – or, in formal language, consented to his election – to the archbishopric of Rouen, where he continued to serve the king until he heard his last confession on his death-bed.[19] In brief, during the 1120s, and still more in the next two decades, the importance of recruiting scholastically-trained men for the work of government was becoming clear to both ecclesiastical and secular rulers. Consequently it was in these decades that the role in government of academically successful masters began to be enlarged, not least at the highest level of all, in the papal Curia.

By a strange survival of miscellaneous material, the situation can be very fully illustrated in the career of an English scholar who fell just short of the highest success both as an academic innovator and as a prince of the Church, and he deserves a somewhat lengthy excursion as a sign-post to the new age of alliance between government and the schools.

Master Robert Pullen, symbol of success

Robert Pullen belonged to a family of small land-holders near Sherborne on the frontier between the counties of Wiltshire and Dorset. At some time in the early years of the twelfth century he had studied in the school of Laon, and then – probably after teaching for some time in Exeter – he moved to Oxford where from 1133 to 1138 he was the earliest Oxford lecturer on theology. Several of his sermons of this period have survived, and he must also in these years have begun a work which is one of the earliest to deserve the title *Summa Theologiae*.[20] Oxford,

---

19 Ordericus Vitalis, bk. xiii, c. 19.
20 Robert Pullen's *Sententiae* (PL, 186, 625–1010) of c. 1135–40 are systematically divided into the following books: God (16 cc.); Creation and Fall (31 cc.); Redemption (30 cc.); Man's place in the universe (26 cc.); Baptism (42 cc.); Marriage (61 cc.); Confession and Absolution (39 cc.); Eucharist (32 cc.). For a general account, see F. Courtney, *Cardinal Robert Pullen: an English Theologian of the 12th Century*, Analecta Gregoriana, 64, 1954.

however, was not a centre of serious theological study and Pullen soon went to Paris where he would be at the centre of theological debate.

His opportunity for making this move came in a roundabout way through the offer of the archdeaconry of Rochester. This was not a very distinguished position, but it was nearer to Paris than any other English cathedral city, and – to the well-justified annoyance of his bishop – Pullen combined the office of archdeacon of Rochester with teaching theology on Mont-Ste-Geneviève. His bishop tried to insist on his giving up lecturing to concentrate on his archidiaconal duties. Pullen, somewhat surprisingly, won the support of St Bernard in urging the bishop to consider the wider needs of the Church.[21] But the bishop persisted, went to Rome, and in November 1143 procured a judgement from Pope Celestine II allowing him to appoint a new archdeacon unless Pullen had successfully appealed to Rome by 14 May (Pentecost) 1144. This action must have brought Robert Pullen to Rome, for the next we hear is that Pope Lucius II, who had succeeded Celestine II in March 1144, had revoked his predecessor's judgement, appointed Pullen as chancellor of the Roman Church, and allowed Pullen instead of the bishop to nominate his successor as archdeacon of Rochester. This left the bishop of Rochester (an old man and very weary) with very little option: he took care to record his own view of the incident for the benefit of his successors, and Pullen appointed his own nephew as his successor as archdeacon.[22]

Robert Pullen seems to have held the papal chancellorship for only about four years, and – whether through death or ill-health – he disappears from papal documents after 1148, but in his brief tenure of power he was probably responsible for a sudden increase in the number of Englishmen working in the papal Curia, who soon included Pullen's pupil John of

[21] For St Bernard's letter telling the bishop of Rochester that Pullen's teaching in Paris is necessary, see PL, 182, 372.
[22] For the documents, see Holtzmann, Papsturkunden, 1935, no. 33, pp. 177–79; no. 46, pp. 195–6. In a letter, which was preserved only at Rochester, the much harassed bishop recorded his view that Pullen had used his learning to resist episcopal authority, and (in effect) that the pope had let the bishop down – which he obviously had done. See J. Thorpe, Registrum Roffense, London, 1769, pp. 8–10.

Salisbury, Nicholas Breakspear, who later became pope Adrian IV, and Boso who became Pope Adrian's biographer.[23]

Although Pullen falls short of the highest achievement both as a scholastic innovator and as an administrator, he illustrates the growing interaction between scholastic and administrative activity during the second quarter of the twelfth century, and the way in which this interaction, while providing a powerful impetus to the development of the cosmopolitan administration of the papacy, also brought new local elements into papal government. Pullen's whole life and work – and he was surely not alone in this – are deeply embedded both in the European-wide scholastic and administrative developments of these years and in the local scene in which he had his roots. Characteristically, the local scene presented itself as a mixture of family interests and corporate loyalties, and Pullen used his new position at the centre of European affairs to promote his nephew, to increase the privileges of Sherborne Abbey where his cousin Joseph was prior, and (it would seem) to bring a quite unparalleled number of Englishmen into the papal Curia, including the only English pope.

This mixture of universal powers and local attachments is characteristic of the time. The news of Pullen's appointment as chancellor must have travelled fast, and the abbey at once dispatched its prior to Rome bearing a complaint against the bishop of Salisbury in whose diocese the abbey lay. The prior must have been in Rome by May 1145 for on June 6 he obtained papal letters appointing the archbishop of Canterbury and the bishop of Hereford as papal judges-delegate in the abbey's case against the diocesan bishop. In addition, to prevent any such diminutions of the abbey's rights in future, the pope – in a privilege drawn up 'per manum Roberti (i.e. Pullen) sacrae Romanae ecclesiae presbiteri cardinalis et cancellarii' – confirmed a tremendous list of the abbey's rights and privileges, extending from its right to elect its abbot against all wiles or acts of violence down to its right to fish in all the fish-ponds in Sherborne for the whole day

---

23   For Englishmen who joined the papal court during the years 1146–52, including Nicholas Breakspear, who became pope as Adrian IV, see R. L. Poole, *Studies in Chronology and History*, ed. A. L. Poole, Oxford, 1954 (2nd edn, 1969), pp. 250–5.

preceding every feast-day of the blessed Virgin Mary.[24]

Not content with all this, Pullen also wrote two further letters in his own name, but as papal chancellor, to the archbishop and bishop who had been appointed as judges-delegate, in which there is the following passage:

It is proper for us to be especially solicitous towards those who are joined to us in ties of consanguinity. Therefore we desire and require you in dealing with the lawsuit of the prior and his monastery to act in such a way that *he* may know that our requests have been serviceable to him, and that *we* may give you thanks.[25]

These details may be thought to belong to the *trivia*, not to say abuses, of history; but they lie at the very centre of the scene in providing evidence, first, of the new rapport between very local and very central authorities, cutting out or diminishing all intermediate agents; and, second, of the essential role of scholastically-trained masters in bringing about this new state of affairs. The letters in which these details are recorded display the scholar-administrator in all his glory; and it is worth reflecting that, though the legal and administrative refinements of the twelfth century made it possible to deal with a much greater amount of business than ever before, and although the principles governing the dispatch of business were much more rationally articulated than the appeals to force or the ordeals of an earlier age, they could only operate within the general social conventions of the time. The men who reached high positions in government as a result of their scholastic skills could reward members of their families and all who had supported or taught them during their student years, and they thought they were obeying a law of nature in doing so: it was axiomatic that whoever did not look after the interests of his own family was unlikely to look after anyone else's.

In addition to looking after their families' interests, several of the men who achieved high positions as a result of their

---

[24] For Robert Pullen's interventions at the papal court in favour of Sherborne Abbey, see Francis Wormald's full description of the liturgical manuscript (London, BL Add. 46487) in which the documents are preserved, in *Fritz Saxl: a volume of memorial lectures*, ed. D. J. Gordon, London, 1957, pp. 101–19.
[25] For the text, see W. Holtzmann, *Papsturkunden*, vol. iii, 1952, no. 48.

scholastic success left touching acknowledgements of their debt to teachers. For example, Abbot Samson of Bury St Edmunds, who had reluctantly abandoned a scholastic career and become a monk because – through lack of relatives in high positions – he had no expectation of advancement through their patronage, gave the first of the benefices which fell vacant during his abbacy to the teacher who had made it possible for him to study in Paris.[26] By the standards of the very great, Samson had only a few benefices in his gift, and for these there were many claimants. But even at the top of the ladder, the same impulse of scholastic gratitude found expression in remarkable ways. Innocent III, in one of his earliest acts as pope, gave, or attempted to give, the archdeaconry of York to his former teacher in Paris, Master Peter of Corbeil.[27] But he soon discovered that he had gone too far. Even the pope could not dispense offices in a Yorkshire cathedral against the wishes of the chapter, and he had to climb down. But he was not discouraged. Instead of the archdeaconry of York, he gave his old master the archbishopric of Sens. Evidently nothing was too good for the master of such a student.

However we look on them, whether in the offices they held or the power they exercised, or their capacity to reward their benefactors or hurt their enemies, the men who had studied in the great schools were riding very high by the end of the twelfth century. They had succeeded in establishing themselves in nearly every important position in Europe which demanded an expert knowledge of theology, law, diplomacy, or the arts of persuasion – that is to say, in every governmental activity apart from the actual use of military weapons. As a result of their command of all these spheres of activity, the men from the schools shaped the world in a scholastically defined mould, and in so doing they put the intellectual riches of the past at the service both of their families and of centralized ecclesiastical and secular government.

In brief, three symptoms of the greatness of the schools in the twelfth century were, first, the production of a systematic body

[26] See *The Chronicle of Jocelin of Brakelond*, ed. and transl. H. E. Butler, Oxford, 1949, pp. 43–4.
[27] C. R. and Mary G. Cheney, *The letters of Innocent III (1198–1216)*, Oxford, 1967, nos 67–9.

of knowledge in every important area of intellectual enquiry; second, the successful application of this knowledge, and the skills that had brought it into existence, to the work of government; and third, the combination of the greatest generality with the most copious detail both in thought and in government.

Scholars in government carried over into government the combination of vast intellectual structures with great attention to detail, which was the method they had learnt in the schools. The analysis of many divergent authorities to produce agreed bodies of knowledge was the royal road to intellectual success. This same art was also a central technique of all law and administration. The confrontation of rival testimonies, which was the basic method of progress in the schools, became also – once judgement by ritual was dispensed with – the central procedure of the law-courts. Further, the harmonizing of conflicting claims, which was the art learnt in the schools, was the central process of diplomacy; and in preserving the bonds of society generally, the maintenance of an elaborate balance between conflicting claims to service, homage, obedience and dues, became the art of government. So the mentality of the schools gradually permeated the whole western world in all its public, and in many of its private, relationships, sometimes as a substitute for violence, sometimes as a preliminary to it. This was the mark that the schools left on government in Europe.

The contribution of the losers

Yet despite all their advantages in being able to bring the power of the schools to bear on the world, individual scholars often had to struggle to survive, and many struggled in vain. As a whole, those who had gone to Laon early in the century, or to Paris or Bologna a little later, had good reason to be satisfied. The prospect of jobs for students had never been brighter. Probably they were never again so bright, for though the number of jobs in government continued to grow, the number of qualified persons seeking employment grew still faster. Hence there were many, probably an ever-growing number, of disappointed scholars of whom we know little or nothing.

Strangely enough, however, those who failed in the world have also left a mark in history almost as enduring as those who succeeded in their worldly careers. The bitterness and disappointment which they suffered brought into existence a new literature sparkling with the wit and ingenuity of the schools. The disappointed men, who had equipped themselves with all the skill and knowledge needed for the success which eluded them in the world, expressed their resentment by turning their scholastic weapons against the world. In their failure, they used their last weapon of ridicule to savage the patrons who had disappointed them, and in lines of unforgettable rancour and high-spirited despair they satirized the world which was unworthy of their learning. Thus there arose a new literature of satire and personal invective, in which those who were unsuccessful, whether by choice or by misfortune, turned their learning into poetry, and expressed their resentment in terms which were fully intelligible only to those who were familiar with the debating points and argumentative procedures of the schools.[28] In the hands of the successful, the language and substance of scholastic debate permeated the forms of government; but in the hands of the unsuccessful, the language of scholastic debate, overflowing with technical terms and distinctions of meaning, became the inspiration of a new *genre* of satirical prose and poetry mocking the successful. Such displays of wit first flourished in the twelfth century, and they lasted long.

This literature of failure has little of the practical or intellectual importance of the central works of the schools, but it contains some masterpieces. Indeed, although a vast distance separates the greater part of these productions from the greatest imaginative work of medieval European literature, Dante's *Divine Comedy* too is a work that would never have been written if its author had not himself been one of those who failed to use his learning in the service of government.

The failures of scholars were expressed in many different forms, but all of them give their own kind of testimony to the power of scholastic thought. Failures and successes alike testify

28   For an account of the two most famous of the poets who failed to get promotion, Hugh Primas and the Archpoet, see F. J. E. Raby, *A History of Secular Latin Poetry in the Middle Ages*, Cambridge, 1957, vol. 2, pp. 171–89.

to the fact that the great rewards of scholastic success were beset with many unpredictable dangers at every step. The aim of most students was to equip themselves with skills which would make them useful to patrons who could give them a benefice which would either support them for life or give them the resources for the further studies necessary for rising still higher. Men from the schools brought a diversity of offerings to their patrons. Some shone in writing well turned letters which were needed in political negotiations or legal processes. Others excelled in solving legal or ecclesiastical problems. Most no doubt were simply competent in the daily business of administrative or parochial life.

But to all, high and low alike, success could come only through having access to patrons who had benefices at their disposal. Ties of blood were by far the most generally compelling argument for such rewards. Services in the past and the prospect of more in the future came next; but the rewards might be long delayed. For men who lacked family connections, friendships made in the schools could be a useful aid. To have studied under the same master gave men a new kind of corporate identity without which an unsupported individual could easily sink in a sea of misfortunes. Life for an unsupported scholar was bound to be risky. Success required good scholastic credentials, industry, perseverance, good connections, and good luck. Each of them helped, and without the last the others might be of no avail. The 'stickit minister' of eighteenth-century Scotland had his prototypes in the twelfth century, and they were probably numerous:

> I have a pupil [wrote a Parisian master to the pope in 1167], a man of approved learning, who was my assistant and then my successor as master of my school. He toils valiantly and catholically on the Bible, but he has not yet found a bishop who will give him a benefice of any value. He lived off my table for more than twelve years, and now he lives off another's. I need not tell you how wretched it is to live off another's board.[29]

The quiet tragedies of academic life leave little record behind

[29] See J. B. Pitra, *Analecta novissima Spicilegii Solesmensis altera continuatio*, vol. 2, 1888, p. xxxix. The letter was written to Pope Alexander III by Master Odo of Soissons, no doubt in the hope of getting the pope to give his assistant a benefice.

them. Many scholars who had no talent for expressing their resentment in satire or mockery must quietly have fallen into miserable dependence as their hopes of a secure position gradually faded. But there were always enough rewards, some of them glittering, to excite the ambition or cupidity of an ever-increasing number of new aspirants. The following story comes from the late thirteenth century: it might equally have come from the twelfth, but it could not have come from the pre-scholastic centuries. It displays in a grotesque form one major driving force in the growth of the schools:

> A certain teacher of Mainz had a very serious pupil. The master asked him why he studied so hard, and the pupil replied, 'I intend to become a Master of Arts, and of Medicine and of Law. Then I can have as many churches as I like when I get home.'

Another version of the story displays a different aspect of the schools. The student is asked why he studies so hard, and he replies, 'In five years time I shall be a Master of Arts; then I shall go to Orleans, and in ten years I'll be a Doctor of Law; then I'll study Canon Law, and I'll soon become a doctor of that too; and afterwards in my old age I'll study theology.' Here speaks another creation of the schools – the perpetual student.

These moral tales were widely circulated to illustrate the vanity of human wishes. The punch-line in those I have quoted was that both students died almost as soon as their wishes were uttered. But the stories would never have circulated at all if they had not had a certain verisimilitude: they all depicted a well-known type, the would-be career-men for whom life in the schools had become the only career they could visualize. Such men were the parasites of the scholastic system, and they would not have existed if there had not been a continuing flow of masters and students with a sufficiently high success rate to encourage their ambitions. As they consolidated their positions, these scholastically-trained career-men developed some clearly marked attitudes, which included a willingness to serve the interests of any employer who could reward them. This meant that the highest technical skills were available for use on both sides of any question, and this helped to prevent the realization of one of the great aims of the schools, namely the development of a monolithic society with a single hierarchy of authority.

In their general aim and method the schools strongly supported the hierarchical principle in society. But, since the services of men with the highest scholastic skills were generally available on both sides of any dispute, the unity of western Christendom, which was the great aim and in some degree the achieved result of scholastic training and doctrine, gradually dissolved in a spate of disagreements supported by scholastic arguments.

II ANCIENTS AND MODERNS

The benefits and rewards which, from the late eleventh century onwards, induced families with an important stake in society to send their younger members to the great schools of Europe were very considerable. Nearly all of them were available only to those who had completed their studies and left the schools, but for the dedicated scholar the real rewards were in the schools themselves – in the experiences of intellectual command, of having a wide and coherent view of the world, of helping to shape a long tradition of thought, of having the esteem of colleagues and pupils, of belonging to learned communities which were changing the face of Christendom.

Moments of intellectual discovery, which had been rare in the previous five centuries, became quite common in the twelfth century. Contemporaries were aware of this, and they associated the new momentum with the idea that they were living in a time when the consummation of all knowledge, and perhaps of all history, was not far off. How did this awareness of the special role of their time in world history affect their judgements about scholastic activity in general, and individual masters in particular?

In the first place, the idea that knowledge was reaching a new and probably final peak is fairly frequently expressed or implied in their surveys of the history of knowledge. For example, the way in which the words *antiqui* and *moderni*, 'ancients' and 'moderns', were coming to be used expresses a new expectation of rapid development towards a final consummation. In traditional usage before the twelfth century, the *antiqui* were thought of as being very ancient indeed, and the *moderni* included scholars who had received and transmitted ancient learning for the last three or four hundred years. On this view of modernity, the principal characteristic of being 'modern' was simply to have served as a link in a chain of transmission stretching over several centuries preserving and conveying the learning of the ancient world to a static present.

This sense that the 'moderni' are simply 'hanging on' to the past, and that the 'antiqui' are very ancient indeed, lasted till about the end of the eleventh century. But then, in the early years of the twelfth century, there is a change: scholars even of the last generation came to be referred to as *antiqui*, not because they were very distant in time, but because their thoughts were already old-fashioned. Consequently, the word *moderni* came to be reserved for very recent scholars whose innovations were substantial. Suddenly, there is a sense of movement, and of movement towards some final goal.

The first issue which introduced this change of usage seems to have been the sharp controversy between logical nominalists (personified dramatically in Roscelin), and conservative realists who attributed objective reality to general classes of things. The change of usage focused attention on changes in modes of thought, and the individuals who were responsible for recent innovations became the *moderni*, ousting from this position the long line of simple transmitters of ancient doctrine who had previously been given this title. The new usage, which reflected a new intensity of scholarly debate, soon caught on, and the *antiqui* ceased to be genuine 'ancients' and became merely yesterday's men, contrasted with contemporary innovators, the real *moderni*.

One consequence of the new fashion was that the dividing line between *antiqui* and *moderni* now constantly moved forward from one generation to the next. This in its turn both promoted and expressed a new conception of development, which brought with it a new sense of the superiority of the present over the past. Whereas earlier usage had implied that the 'ancients' were best, and the 'moderns' were no more than transmitters, the new linguistic usage carried the suggestion that the 'moderns' were at least better than their immediate predecessors. This linguistic shift, therefore, was a symptom not only of a new time-scale, but of a new assessment of the present. The very distant past never lost its supremely authoritative position as the main source of all knowledge. But the centuries of mere transmission faded into the background. The new *moderni* were thought to be distinctly better than their immediate predecessors, and in some ways better even than their great ancient predecessors, in the sense that they could see further than the ancients. This change was accompanied by a new conception of the history of learning not simply as an age-old descent of knowledge from one generation to another, but as a process which had received a new stimulus in the very recent past, and in which it was possible to pick out the significant innovators who had imparted a new energy and aim, even a new consistency, to some area of knowledge.

An interesting feature of these new twelfth-century statements is that they always trace an intellectual descent from recent innovators, whereas earlier intellectual genealogies had envisaged simple transmission over long periods of time. The difference marks a substantial change in the conception of the present and in expectations about the future. In the earlier period, the aim was to hold on to the past in the face of threatened destruction. In the twelfth century, the aim was still not to add a really new body of knowledge – that seems scarcely to have been expected – but to improve on the past by greater refinement, arrangement and systematization, and by the rediscovery of lost texts.

To exemplify the contrast, we may compare the account given by Adémar of Chabannes, a monk of Angoulême in about 1030, with the kind of genealogies which we find in the twelfth century. Here is Adémar's account of the transmission of learning over a period of about three hundred years:

> Bede (d. 735) taught Simplicius, and Simplicius taught Rabanus, who was called from foreign parts by the Emperor Charles to become a bishop in France. Rabanus taught Alcuin, and Alcuin taught Smaragdus; Smaragdus taught Theodulf, bishop of Orleans, and Theodulf taught Elias the Scot; Elias taught Heiric, and Heiric made the monks Remigius and Hucbald the heirs of philosophy.[30]

---

[30] Adémar de Chabannes, *Chronique*, ed. Jules Chevanon, Paris, 1897, pp. 115–16.

This intellectual genealogy displays the transmission of learning from one great man to the next over a period of three hundred years, and what is recorded, with many gaps, is simply a story of *transmission*. It is like a family tree in which the greatest comes first, and the successors carry the torch of the greatness of the past.

This sense of ancient glory was never lost, but in the twelfth century even the most conservative writers found grandeur in the present. For example, two monastic writers, Sigibert of Gembloux and Honorius Augustodunensis, between about 1110 and 1125 almost simultaneously made lists of Christian writers from the first century to their own day, and one interesting feature of their lists is that they finished with contemporary writers whose works are listed with the same fullness as those of the greatest writers of the past.[31] So here two highly conservative writers detected some kind of equality between the present and the very distant past. Nevertheless, though this is a step forward in evaluating the present, there is no suggestion of progress: the great names, whether of past or present, are isolated peaks rising above the mists of an indistinct landscape.

But then, just a few years later, the picture again changes. We begin to have lists of modern writers, recorded as representing the progress of the present. The chosen names are no longer isolated peaks without past or future: they are witnesses to continuing steps forward, and writers are evaluated according to their contributions to the novelties of the age.

One example will suffice to illustrate this new phase in the evaluation of the present. Shortly after 1130 a monk of Melk in Austria, who had studied in northern France, presented a long list of learned writers of the past which he brought to an end with brief descriptions of modern authors, characterizing their particular contributions to knowledge: in canon law, Ivo of Chartres; in theology, Anselm of Canterbury and Gilbert Crispin, and Manegold 'the master of modern masters'; in politics, in opposing the claims of the Emperor, Placidius, prior

---

31 For modern authors in Sigibertus, *Liber de Scriptoribus ecclesiasticis*, see PL, 150, cols. 582–588; and in Honorius Augustodunensis, *De luminaribus ecclesiae*, PL, 172, cols. 232–234.

of Nonantela; in dialectic, Gerald of St-Blaise; for his mixture of science and theology, Gerlandus; for his amazing productivity, Rupert of Deutz.[32] Here we have an early recognition that the period from about 1080 to 1130 when these writers were active was a time of widespread innovation, of vigorous controversy, and of theological and scientific changes, which were the marks of a new age. But it will be noticed that, with the exception of Manegold, we are not yet among the men of the schools: we still have Ivo of Chartres, not Gratian, in canon law; St Anselm and Gilbert Crispin, not Abelard or Peter Lombard in theology; Gerlandus, not Thierry of Chartres or William of Conches in natural science.

The contours of this new scene in relation to the schools and the place of the masters of the schools in world history were soon drawn by the firmer hand of Otto of Freising, who was the first chronicler to make the scholastic vigour of contemporary Europe an integral part of his view of history.[33] Having described the broad historical movement which had brought the culmination of learning to western Europe, he could identify the masters who had made possible this decisive step. They were Berengar who had taught at Tours, Manegold who had taught in Paris, and Master Anselm who had taught at Laon. At last the men of the schools are beginning to be identified by their contemporaries as giving a culminating place in world history to the present.

III THE NEW AGE

Thus, by the middle years of the twelfth century, there was a growing recognition that the whole sweep of the world's intellectual and political history since the Flood had reached

---

[32] For this list, see Häring, 1966, pp. 195–211. It is generally dated later in the twelfth century, but it seems unlikely that an extremely detailed list which ends with Rupert of Deutz, who died in 1130, was compiled much later than this date.

[33] See *Ottonis episcopi Frisingensis Chronica sive Historia de duabus Civitatibus*, ed. A. Hofmeister, *MGH*, 1912, especially p. 8 with its statement of the general law: *Et notandum quod omnis humana potentia seu scientia ab oriente incepit et in occidente terminatur, ut per hoc rerum volubilitas ac defectus ostendatur. Quod in sequentibus Deo annuente plenius ostendemus.* See below, pp. 208–12.

its final stage and ultimate location in contemporary western Europe. Not all the names in these twelfth-century lists would achieve permanent fame. In Otto of Freising's list, which probably represented a Parisian view of the 1120s, Manegold – perhaps wrongly (we shall probably never know) – soon disappeared from the list of the great, and Berengar was generally remembered chiefly as a condemned heretic; but Anselm of Laon survived in the memory of several later twelfth-century accounts as the founding father of modern scholastic theology, which descended thereafter through identifiable masters, chiefly in Paris, each of whom made a significant contribution to the most important subject of contemporary learning. The result of this change of perspective was that by 1175 scholars saw themselves not simply as transmitters of ancient learning, but as active participants in the development of an integrated, many-sided body of knowledge rapidly reaching its peak.

The roll-call of twelfth-century scholars who were chiefly remembered as the authors of works that were milestones along the main road of theological development were Anselm of Laon, Hugh of St-Victor, Gilbert de la Porrée, Peter Lombard, Peter Comestor, Peter the Chanter, Peter of Poitiers, and Praepositinus. These scholars were representatives of a scene of intellectual development over a century, diversified in their contributions, but consistently developing towards a final statement of systematic truth. They were heralds of the final consummation of all knowledge within the reach of human enquiry.

Another important new feature of the names I have mentioned is that very complicated relationships of personal loyalty existed among them. One example of this loyalty became legendary. In 1148, the works of Gilbert de la Porrée were under examination for heresy at the insistence of Bernard of Clairvaux. Bernard had managed to get three of his hostile propositions agreed to, and he reached out to obtain a fourth success, when an obscure master, Robert de Bosco, who was archdeacon of Chalons and present at the Council with his bishop, rose and called for silence. He said that he had been a pupil of Master Anselm and his brother Ralph at Laon and had heard them refuse to accept the view put forward by Abbot Bernard. Moreover, he added, two other modern masters, Gilbert 'the

Universal', who had become bishop of London, and Alberic of Reims, later archbishop of Bourges, also former students of Anselm and Ralph, had supported this view. He therefore advised the assembled masters to decline to fall in with Bernard's wishes. This intervention stopped St Bernard in his tracks, and it was still being quoted in Paris nearly fifty years later as an example of scholastic fidelity thwarting an unjustified attack on a great master:

> I sat (the speaker reported Robert de Bosco as saying) at the feet of Master Anselm for seven years and heard many other learned theologians discuss the question, and I would rather have my tongue cut out than concede that God is a relationship, or that the divine nature is a quality.[34]

This kind of personal loyalty became a notable feature of scholastic history. Just thirty years after the refusal of the masters to condemn Gilbert de la Porrée at Bernard's behest, we have another even more dramatic display of scholastic loyalty. In 1177 Pope Alexander III was about to condemn a doctrine of Peter Lombard, when Master Adam Waley stood up and said: 'I was his clerk and assistant in his school, and I cannot stay to hear my master condemned.' He walked out; the pope hesitated, and the threat of condemnation was withdrawn.[35]

Of course, issues were not always so clear-cut. Scholars were often torn between loyalty to their masters and the weight of the opposing argument. But the closer we come to the central tradition of the schools, the more powerfully did the instinct of loyalty operate. Here, for example, is a complicated case. One of the most influential Parisian masters of the last half of the twelfth century, Master Peter Comestor, was discussing a familiar problem of moral theology: can faith and love revive if they have once died? The question raised issues of high concern

---

[34] For Robert de Bosco, whose intervention is reported by John of Salisbury, *Historia Pontificalis*, ed. Poole, pp. 19–20, see A. Landgraf in *Misc. G. Mercati*, vol. 2 (*Studi e Testi*, vol. 122, Vatican, 1944, p. 278. See also A. Landgraf, in *New Scholasticism*, iv, 1930, pp. 2ff. for R. de Bosco's claim to have studied with Master Anselm for seven years.

[35] For Adam Waley supporting Gilbert de la Porrée against Alexander III, see Walter of St-Victor, *Contra quatuor Labyrinthos Franciae*, ed. P. Glorieux, *AHDL*, 19, 1952, pp. 201, 234–7.

for all sinners, and it was always discussed in relation to St Peter's denial of Christ. But it got entangled also with the problem of loyalty to one's own master. This is how Master Peter Comestor dealt with it:

> The question whether Peter's love and faith utterly broke down is a great and difficult one, and there are many arguments and authorities on both sides. Master Anselm (of Laon), who glossed the Psalms, said that the love of Peter and the other disciples did not utterly fail, because they preserved their love but not its effects, the root but not its branches. Master John of Tours told me that he had heard Master Anselm give this answer in his lectures with regard to the faith of St Peter and the other disciples. But my own master (Peter Lombard) took the opposite view, and this is the view that I take.[36]

But there were limits to loyalty. Here is Peter Comestor again:

> My master conceded that the three Persons of the Trinity are three things (*tres res*), and yet one supreme thing, (*una summa res*). He conceded this because his master had said so; but it is very difficult to hold to this, for who can resist the argument, 'If they are three things, they cannot be one'?[37]

Loyalty to one's master, therefore, was not enough; but in the growing confusion of questions and answers it was an important source of stability. In the schools, as in the world, a man without ancestors was a man without roots. It was remarked on as an essential difference between Abelard and Gilbert de la Porrée that though they both held dangerous views, Gilbert had submitted himself to the authority of his masters from his earliest youth: 'He had not quickly (it was said) withdrawn himself from his master's cane', whereas Abelard had never sat under any master for long. This loyalty, breeding similar loyalty in his pupils, saved Gilbert from condemnation, whereas Abelard, though he too had stout supporters among his pupils, and though some of these

---

36 For Peter Comestor (or Manducator) and the varying opinions of Anselm of Laon, John of Tours, and himself, on the question of St Peter's loss of Faith, see I. Brady, 'Peter Manducator and oral teaching of P. Lombard' (*Antonianum*, 41, 1966, 477). For anecdotes about P. Comestor, see Giraldus Cambrensis, vol. ii, pp. 28, 30, 122, 124, 126, 187–8.
37 The danger here was a revival of the heresy of Roscelin.

were in high places in the papal Curia, lacked scholastic ancestry and was therefore more easily condemned. In the schools, a solid ancestry was a source of strength as important as good family connections in the world of politics.

This no doubt was one reason why masters liked to recall the names of their masters. They knew that individually they were very vulnerable – vulnerable to attacks on their orthodoxy, to the rivalry of other masters, to the uncertainties of life. These were common weaknesses to which all were exposed, but the bond between masters and pupils, and between pupils of the same master, lessened their dangers and added to the amenities of life.

This sense of scholarly cohesion was sharpened by the fact that scholastic thought, especially in the early days, was dependent on the spoken word. This point was made very clearly by one of the most successful teachers in Paris in the middle years of the twelfth century. At the beginning of his *Sententiae* on the Holy Scriptures, Robert of Melun says that he has based his work on two books, one by Hugh of St-Victor, the other by Abelard. Yet he felt unhappy at using books rather than spoken words as his foundation, and he excused himself in these words:

> I was a pupil of both of them, and I heard from their own lips those things which they wrote. Therefore I can more reliably and faithfully collect and combine their opinions, for a man who has seen the thing itself knows it better than one who has seen only a picture or drawing of it. For what else is writing but an obscure image of the intention of the writer?[38]

These details recall the intensity of twelfth-century debates, and the fear of isolation which made it important to have been in the presence of the great masters, and to have heard their words for oneself. Very large doctrinal issues often hung on apparently trivial arguments. But nothing was trivial that might affect the central doctrines of Christianity, and the men who took part in discussions on logic might find themselves at the centre of disputes about doctrinal definitions, and devotional practices

[38] *Oeuvres de Robert de Melun*, vol. 3, *Sententiae*, ed. R. M. Martin, (*Spicilegium Sacrum Lovaniense: études et documents*, fasc. 21, 1947) p. 47: I have abbreviated a long passage on the subject of hearing and seeing.

and disciplines arising from them, which could affect the whole of western Europe.

The parallel between the master in his school and the judge in a court must always be borne in mind in assessing the seriousness of academic debates. Masters in their individual schools were, like judges in the lowest courts, ultimately subject to the judgement of the highest court in Christendom, which consisted of the pope sitting in full panoply on his *cathedra* just like a master in his school.

Schools and law courts were the two most important institutional developments in twelfth-century Europe, and they developed for the same reason: teaching and judging formed the essential foundation for all the most important operations of governing mankind. The highest function of all rulers was judging, and judging always had in it an element of teaching. Just as the pope spoke *ex cathedra* both as teacher and judge, so too every teacher spoke *ex cathedra* in his own school, and every anointed king and every bishop also combined these two functions of teaching and judging.[39]

Moreover, the master in his school not only gave doctrinal judgements, he also had jurisdiction over the behaviour of his pupils. His school was a small kingdom, in which the three functions of teaching, judging and ruling were indissolubly linked. The world was ruled by power, judgement and doctrine, and the pope, kings, masters and judges alike combined all these functions in varying proportions. And it required no wild flight of fancy to believe that teaching was the most important function of them all, for power was misapplied, and judgement vain, without doctrine. The master seated on his *cathedra* therefore exercised within his school the three highest functions in the world.

Pictures of masters generally show them seated, cap on head, while the pupils at their feet have their heads uncovered. The master's cap was a symbol of his superiority, as also was his seated posture. In front of him, on a lectern, lies open the authoritative text of which he is imparting the substance to his

---

39 On the similarities between episcopal consecration and royal coronation services, see *Three Coronation Orders*, ed. J. Wickham Legge, Henry Bradshaw Society, London, vol. 19, 1900, pp. xxxix–xliii, 53–69, 162.

pupils. In the fully developed image there will also be a scribe recording the master's words, a recording angel in miniature. This scene was enacted in every school, and it stamped a universal image on the work of the master. Similarly in every monastery, as the *Rule* of St Benedict makes clear, the abbot is the *magister* of his monks, and the authority which this *magisterium* gave him as teacher and judge was solemnly emphasized; '*Life and death are in the power of the tongue*: it is the office of the master to speak and to teach, and of the disciple to keep silent and listen.'[40]

Unlike the monks in the *Rule*, the students of the schools were not required to keep silent: it was their duty to speak when the process of learning required them to do so. But it was also their duty to be silent and listen when the master gave his summing up and pronounced his *sententia*. So, in the end, just as it was the duty of the abbot to provide discipline and guidance to the monastery, it was the duty of the master in his school to provide discipline and guidance to his pupils and through them to the world. They were the organizing force in society, the source not only of internal cohesion but also of external glory.

IV THE GLORY AND GOSSIP OF THE SCHOOLS

That the schools were the chief glory of the West was a new idea in the twelfth century, and it was linked with another equally flattering idea, that political greatness and academic strength go together hand-in-hand throughout the whole of human history. Among secular rulers, the French kings were the first to adopt with eagerness the new estimate of the importance of the schools: Paris was the first town in northern Europe which owed a substantial part of its prestige in the world to its international body of students and teachers. Other kings took note of this and followed the example of the French kings in seeking to appropriate some share of scholastic glory and to enhance their political power by founding and endowing universities, and by enticing masters to teach, and students to study, in their cities. This was

---

[40] *S. Benedicti Regula*, c. vi.

much more than a whimsical idea. Rulers needed masters who might be expected to give what they would regard as reliable judgements on contentious points. Even the papacy experienced this need, as we shall see when we come to the remarkable story of the development of Bologna as what may almost be called the academic branch of the papal Curia. This papal example may well in its turn have been the inspiration for the Emperor Frederick II's politically motivated foundation of the University of Naples in 1224. The University of Naples could not save the Empire, but other rulers took the hint in founding universities in their territory to support their rule.[41]

At the other end of the political spectrum – in the growth of 'public curiosity' as opposed to 'public policy' – the chronicles of the late twelfth century onwards illustrate the growing interest in famous masters. The personal characteristics of the great masters of the early twelfth century, even those of Abelard, had made scarcely a ripple in the world outside the schools. But in the last years of the century, the personalities of well-known masters became the subject of anecdotes which were thought worthy of a place in universal histories. The witticisms of Simon of Tournai, and their punishment, were recorded by Matthew Paris; the chance remarks of Peter Comestor were reported by Giraldus Cambrensis; the chastity of Master Gerald Pucelle, and the sexual prowess of other grave masters, became part of the gossip of the late twelfth century, and found their way into homilies and histories; and the authors of exemplary tales reported them with relish and embellishment.

Interest in the anecdotes of the schools is only one reflection of the general awareness of their growing importance. The success of the idea that great schools made kingdoms great is another symptom of the same theme. There were also many less ambitious ways in which the new glamour of learning was expressed. When we find the abbot of Mont-St-Michel erasing entries in the monastic chronicle about forgotten public events in order to make room for significant events in the world of

---

[41] For the proliferation of universities from the foundation of the university of Naples to the late fifteenth centuries, it may suffice here to refer to the second volume of H. Rashdall's *Universities of Europe in the Middle Ages*, ed. F. M. Powicke and A. B. Emden, Oxford, 1936.

learning, such as the death of Hugh of St-Victor, the dates of Gratian's work on Canon Law, of Vacarius's work on Roman Law, and of the new translations from the Greek – all events which had been ignored by nearer contemporaries – we see an artless expression of a widespread view that the great revival of scholastic activity in western Europe had made a decisive contribution to its rise to political and cultural leadership.[42]

Viewed in this light, the proposal of Henry II of England in 1169 to refer his dispute with Archbishop Thomas Becket to the masters of Paris can be seen as something more than a diplomatic manoeuvre. It was certainly a diplomatic manoeuvre, but it was also a recognition that a new political force had come into existence in the schools.[43] Henry II's proposal came to nothing, but it has a certain importance as the first of a series of consultations and arbitrations proposed, and sometimes effected, at the behest of rulers down to the sixteenth century. Similarly Innocent III's invitation to the masters of Paris to go to Constantinople to reform the learning of the Greeks was only the first of many attempts to use the supremacy of the western schools in the interests of world-wide political and religious plans.[44]

From this general recognition, it required only one further step for rulers everywhere to want to have universities in their own territories, partly for reasons of prestige, partly to have amenable masters at their disposal. Hence the spate of new foundations of universities throughout Europe in the later Middle Ages. All these developments were continuing proofs of the authority and influence, probably in quality and range never surpassed, that the masters of the schools had gained in the course of the twelfth century.

[42] For these insertions, see *The Chronicle of Robert de Torigni*, in *Chronicles of the reigns of Stephen, Henry II and Richard I*, ed. R. Howlett, RS, 1889, iv, pp. 25–6, 114, 118, 158–9; and see below, pp. 276, 296.
[43] Archbishop Thomas Becket himself reported to the archbishop of Sens that this proposal among other possibilities had been made to him by the king when they met in November 1169 (*Materials for the History of Thomas Becket*, ed. J. C. Robertson and J. B. Sheppard, RS, 1885, vii, p. 164).
[44] C.U.Par., i, pp. 62–3. For a translation, see Southern, 1953, p. 60.

6

The Scholastic Metropolis
of Northern Europe

I OLD INSTITUTIONS: NEW NEEDS

The use of old institutions to meet needs for which they had not been created is one of the most common of all historical phenomena. It often happens in such situations that there is one among these institutions which, without having been particularly good at meeting the old needs, turns out to have some adventitious quality which makes it pre-eminently suited for the new situation. This is what happened in the early twelfth century with regard to the schools of two cities in Europe, Paris and Bologna. Both had ordinary undistinguished schools until the very end of the eleventh century, but then swept aside all other competitors in the two major fields of scholastic knowledge which had been defined by 1150 because they had qualities possessed by no other cities in western Europe.[1] Paris had room for expansion, immense amenities of life, freedom from a narrow authoritarian control,

---

[1] See the Map on p. xix for the cathedral schools of northern France, and Plates 1 and 2 for the contrast between the constricted site of Laon and the scope for expansion at Paris. For an account of the development of Paris with plans, see A. Friedmann, *Paris, ses rues, ses paroisses, du moyen âge à la Révolution*, Paris, 1959, and *Atlas de Paris et de la région parisienne*, ed. J. Beaujeau-Garnier and J. Bastié, Paris, 1967. For abundant detail about the size of French towns from the eleventh to thirteenth centuries with many city plans, see Carlrichard Brühl, *Palatium und Civitas*, vol. 1: *Gallien*, Cologne, 1975. For the contrasting social and political aspects of Bologna's rise to scholastic eminence, see the text and Map on pp. xx–xxi.

and – at least to a respectable extent – an academic foundation on which to build. Bologna, much more unexpectedly, had equally necessary requirements for a new academic discipline.

The background of their success could scarcely have been more different. Whereas Paris succeeded by the simple logic of its position, which was already beginning to assert itself by the year 1100, Bologna had very little to recommend it until success came with a rush in the 1140s as a result of some very complicated political adjustments combined with a very remarkable work of a single scholar. These two widely different influences gave each of these towns an instantaneous lead in a new subject of scholastic study, which they retained for two hundred years. But Paris was first, and must come first.

Among all the rivals of Paris there was one which, both in general situation and in possessing an old tradition, had advantages which might have marked it out as a future international centre for the new stream of masters and pupils in the liberal Arts and biblical studies. This was Laon, which was an old capital of the Carolingian kings. During the half century from about 1070 to 1120 its cathedral school under Master Anselm and his brother Ralph probably attracted more pupils from all parts of Europe than any other school, and it left a deep mark on the future of scholastic theology. Nevertheless, it had one inescapable disadvantage: the site of the town was too constricted to provide room for expansion. In some ways this smallness worked to the immediate advantage of the school, for it enabled Master Anselm to maintain his monopoly of teaching and to exclude unwelcome competitors. But, in the long run – as the whole range of studies became more complicated – the presence of many competitors was essential for the creation of a scholastic centre of continuing international influence.

Master Anselm's method of careful textual commentary interspersed with discussions on points of substance in the argument was certainly on the right lines to ensure its long-term success. On this foundation, he and his brother Ralph with their leading pupils had developed biblical studies along two main lines: first, in equipping the books of the Bible with concise and easily transportable comments; and, second, in building up a selection of comments of lasting importance on a wide range of subjects. In doing this, they had pioneered the way forward towards the systematic study of theology. Here were the makings of a great future. But even in Master Anselm's lifetime his more critical pupils discovered that his intellectual range was limited. He was strong on grammar, strong on the text of the Bible, but mediocre on logic and systematic theology. He had developed a method, built on the careful analysis of texts and proceeding to discussions on their theological meaning and bearings, which was widely admired. But with growing success, the limitations of Laon as a scholastic centre became increasingly apparent. Students needed a place of study where they could find masters with different abilities reaching differing conclusions, specializing on texts covering different areas of knowledge; and, as their numbers grew, they needed more lodgings and more schools, an abundance of food and drink, and freedom to move from one master to another. They could not find any of these amenities on the cramped hill-top site of Laon.

Then, quite suddenly, the possibility that Paris would be able to meet these new needs became obvious, and a rapid and continuing growth began which transformed the town's resources and gave it the status of a capital city in government, and a reputation for intellectual innovation unrivalled by any other northern European city. The outline maps of Laon and Paris will illustrate the cramped environment of the one and the unique scope for development of the other, and in varying degrees a comparison between Paris and all the other cathedral cities of northern France confirms the superiority of Paris.

The general thrust of Parisian growth was in two main directions. The earliest expansion was on the north bank of the river. This was the area of commercial growth, and it never became a centre either of schools or (so far as we know) of student population. But its commercial population brought to Paris a steady supply of food and drink, which could also support a large population of masters and students on the opposite side of the river. Then too the growing presence of the royal household in its permanent centre on the Île brought new life to the city, as also did the increasing clerical population of the cathedral and the growing number of parish churches.

Scholastically, above all, the growth of Paris in the twelfth century was made possible by the resettlement of the area on the south bank of the river after centuries of decay. This area had been a region of dense population during the centuries of the Roman Empire, but it had become derelict and encumbered with ruins interspersed with vineyards, partly as a result of the general decline in population from the fifth century onwards and partly through Viking devastations in the ninth century. But the whole situation was changed from the earliest years of the twelfth century onwards. While commercial growth brought development on the north bank of the river, the new pressure for scholastic growth, which began in the last years of the eleventh century, gave a new importance to the south bank. At last the development of this area became both possible and profitable. Once begun, it continued without interruption for over a hundred years, turning the whole area of the south bank as far as the top of Mont-Ste-Geneviève into the greatest conglomeration of schools and student accommodation in the whole of Europe.

The area had everything that could be desired for scholastic development: ample space for the building of new lodgings and schools; plenty of food and wine; ancient monasteries (St-Germain-des-Prés on the west, and Ste-Geneviève on the hill to the south) whose lands were exempt from the jurisdiction of the cathedral chancellor. Moreover, even where the cathedral chancellor's right of scholastic monopoly extended, successive chancellors preferred to exercise their rights, not by preventing the multiplication of independent masters, but by exacting a small annual payment for the masters' right to teach.[2]

Everything conspired to make the left bank of the Seine the greatest area of freely-ranging scholastic development in Europe from the earliest years of the twelfth century to the early thirteenth century, when individual initiatives were finally

[2] In 1170–72, Pope Alexander III issued a general prohibition against taking a fee for allowing masters to teach. A commentator says that this was especially directed against the chancellor of Notre-Dame in Paris, who exacted a fee of a mark from every master. This is perhaps confirmed by the special papal exemption of the Parisian chancellor from this prohibition, issued in 1174, on condition that the fee was moderate. See C.U.Par., i, pp. 4, 8.

superseded by the corporate power of the university and then by the arrival of the new Orders of Friars.[3]

The whole development can be summed up in a few words: growing commercial activity of the north bank, the increasing presence of royal officials and a large clerical population on the Île de Paris, and on the south bank an abundance of sites available for schools and lodgings, all combined to make the south bank of the river a perfect situation for scholastic development just at the moment when the demand for teaching in the Arts and Theology was rising to its flood.

Of course, the cathedral of Notre-Dame, like every other cathedral, also had a school going back at least to the ninth century, and although this school did not have a reputation comparable to that of Laon before 1100, it already had one notable master, William of Champeaux. He was a former pupil of Anselm of Laon, and in the 1090s he combined teaching on the Île with the office of archdeacon.

William continued in this double role until 1108–9, but in this year he unexpectedly abandoned both his archdeaconry and his school on the Île in order to settle on a desolate site on the south bank of the river. Here he offered to teach all comers free of charge. The move and his offer brought him instant fame, as can be seen from a letter written by a German student to his patron back home:

> I am now in Paris in the school of master William, who, though he was archdeacon and one of the chief advisers of the king, gave up all he possessed to retire last Easter to serve God in a poor little church. There, like Master Manegold of blessed memory, he offers his teaching to all comers free of charge, and he now directs a school of secular and sacred learning larger than any I have ever heard of or seen in my time anywhere in the world.[4]

This is a letter of extraordinary interest. In the first place it mentions another early master, Manegold, who had given up teaching to adopt a religious life and also to engage in polemical

---

[3]   This whole process is abundantly documented in the uniquely rich body of materials in C.U.Par., vols i–ii.
[4]   Jaffé, Bibl., v, 286.

writing on behalf of the papacy in its anti-imperial struggle.[5] But, more important for our present subject, the letter contains the first hint that the south bank might become an area of scholastic activity. The 'wilderness' to which master William retired soon became famous as the Augustinian abbey of St-Victor, which for the next two generations was one of the most active centres of scholastic activity in the Parisian complex, and long before 1150 the whole area of the south bank was becoming filled with students and masters.

Since no medieval historian wrote a history of Paris as an academic centre until the whole subject had become thickly encrusted with legend, it is not now possible to describe its growth in a connected sequence. But the main stages of development are reasonably clear. In addition to the cathedral school on the Île and the school of St-Victor on the south bank, there were three main areas of independent scholastic development from the earliest years of the twelfth century onwards.

The first was on the Île itself, where, from the last years of the eleventh century onwards, we hear of canons (most famously Héloïse's uncle) letting their houses or rooms in their houses to masters and pupils, and here in the early years of the twelfth century the bishop built a new hall which could accommodate two or three hundred auditors at a lecture.[6]

The second was on the Petit-Pont and in the area immediately south in the parishes of the previously abandoned churches of St-Julien-le-Pauvre and St-Séverin, which ultimately became the meeting places for the faculties of Arts and Theology respectively.

The third lay further south along the roads leading up to and within the *bourg* of Mont-Ste-Geneviève, which formed the privileged area of the monastery of this name.

All the areas south of the river were outside the geographical limits of the city of Paris, and either outside or only loosely within the jurisdiction of the chancellor of the cathedral.

---

[5] For Manegold, see O. Lottin, 'Manegold de Lautenbach, source d'Anselme de Laon', *RTAM*, xiv, 1947, 218–23; W. Hartmann, 'Manegold von Lautenbach, *Liber contra Wolfhelmum, MGH: Quellen zur Geistesgeschichte des Mittelalters*, 8, 1972.
[6] For the building of the new bishop's hall, see *Paris*, 1951, pp. 53–4. For its use as a lecture hall, see below, p. 227. For the scholastic development, see Plate 2.

Although in the early thirteenth century King Philip Augustus enclosed the whole area including Mont-Ste-Geneviève within the great wall of Paris, the tradition of its independence from Paris proper remained strong. Indeed, even as late as the nine-teenth century, its inhabitants spoke of preparing themselves for a journey into Paris with the solemnity of venturing into a hos-tile country.

The materials do not suffice to tell the story of the growth of the Parisian schools in a connected fashion, and it has to be reconstructed from the experiences of a number of unrelated individuals; but they are sufficiently numerous to establish the pattern quite clearly. Appropriately enough it begins with Abelard, who saw himself as a warrior conducting a siege of Paris with the express aim of establishing his scholastic supremacy.

II Stages in the Triumph of Paris

1 Abelard's siege of Paris

In about 1130, in writing the *History of his Calamities*, Abelard looked back thirty years to his earliest studies, and gave an account of his ambitions, aims, and enemies of that time. By way of preface, it will suffice to say that Abelard had been born in 1079, and had spent his adolescent years in the 1090s going from school to school in the Loire valley within fairly easy reach of his home at Le Pallet. Like many other young men, he probably travelled with a tutor as companion, sampling the teaching of various masters. Among these masters, he met only one with a critical mind worthy of his opposition. This was Roscelin, who was then teaching at Loches, a few miles south of the Loire. Abelard listened and differed, and they parted as life-long enemies. It was Abelard's first experience of meeting an equal.

A reliable instinct then brought him to Paris, where he arrived in about 1098. In retrospect, he saw the years which followed as a campaign to capture the academic stronghold of Paris, and the military imagery in which he describes his campaign strikingly reflects the spirit of his enterprise.[7]

The chief occupant of this stronghold at the time of his arrival was Master William of Champeaux, and Abelard's plan was quite simply to defeat William of Champeaux in argument, and to consolidate his victory by setting up his own rival school. He was one of the first, perhaps the very first, to discover that the system of teaching by questions and debate leading to the master's final *sententia*, offered every pupil a chance to supplant the master by proving him wrong. Abelard describes with relish how he hoped in this way to appropriate the fame, position and pupils of his master, and so to capture the scholastic summit of Paris itself. He planned his campaign cautiously and describes it as a series of advances towards this goal, with occasional enforced withdrawals.

When he first felt strong enough to open a school of his own, but not yet strong enough to challenge William of Champeaux in Paris itself, he withdrew to Melun, some fifty miles away just outside the bishopric of Paris. Here he set up his own first school while he gathered strength for an attack on the larger scene of Paris itself. This is how he described his strategy:

> From my school [at Melun] my fame as a logician began to spread, so that the renown of my master, William of Champeaux, not to speak of the reputation of my other contemporaries, began to wither away. As my confidence grew, I decided to transfer my school as soon as possible nearer to Paris; so I went to Corbeil, whence I could launch more frequent and strenuous dialectical assaults.[8]

At Corbeil he was only twenty miles from Paris, and he was just preparing a final attack on his master when ill-health suddenly forced him to go home to recover. This seems to have been the first symptom of that nervous instability, fluctuating between over-confidence and collapse, which was to pursue him throughout life. His recovery took about three years, probably

[7] For Abelard's 'siege of Paris' see his *Historia Calamitatum*, ed. J. Monfrin, Paris, 1959, pp. 64–7.
[8] Ibid., pp. 64–5.

from about 1106 to 1109, and when he returned to Paris he found that William had installed another master in his old school on the Île and had withdrawn to the left bank of the Seine to teach at St-Victor. In this new situation, Abelard formed a two-pronged plan of action. First, he enlisted once more as a pupil of William of Champeaux; and, as a second line of attack, he induced William's successor on the Île to hand over to himself the master's old school.

If Abelard had been able to carry out this plan, he would have reached his goal of teaching in the heart of scholastic Paris whilst harassing his old master in the suburbs. But William vetoed the transference of his old school, and Abelard had to retreat once more to Melun. Very soon, however, William of Champeaux left St-Victor, and Abelard at once moved back towards Paris – not to the city itself (where the school on the Île was still occupied by William's nominee), but to Mont-Ste-Geneviève. From this height Abelard once more began a regular siege, no longer against William himself, but against the man whom he regarded as his usurper on the Île. To quote his words:

> I pitched my scholastic camp outside the city on Mont-Ste-Geneviève in order to lay siege as it were to the man who had seized my place.[9]

This threat (as Abelard believed) brought the old master once more back to St-Victor, and the battle was resumed between the two principals supported by their rival troops of students. Abelard saw the ensuing conflict on a Homeric scale. He compared the battle to the fight between Ajax (Abelard) and Hector (William of Champeaux): 'if you ask who won, I say with modest pride, "I was not defeated".'[10]

At this point a domestic crisis arising from his father's decision to become a monk caused Abelard to break off his studies and return home. When this business was concluded he returned to his studies with the intention – perhaps stimulated

[9]   Ibid., pp. 66–7.
[10] Ibid., p. 67.

by his father's conversion – of studying *divinitas*.[11] For this purpose he went to Laon to study under Master Anselm, who had the greatest reputation as a theological teacher. With his usual over-confidence, Abelard seems to have envisaged that a sequence of arguments with the master of Laon, similar to those which he had planned against Master William in Paris, would establish his theological reputation, and he soon found grounds for contesting Anselm's explanation of a biblical text. But Laon was not Paris. Anselm's pupils at Laon were less easily persuadable than William of Champeaux's in Paris. Many of them no doubt had come from afar to hear Anselm, and they were not eager to find that they had wasted their time. Moreover, Laon was a small place and Master Anselm had no difficulty in forcing his rival to leave the town. So Abelard had to return to Paris with no more than a token victory. His scholastic career was then temporarily broken by the stormy scenes of his seduction of Héloïse, his marriage, castration and his becoming a monk at St-Denis. But even these events could not finally subdue his scholastic ambition, to which we must later return.

For the moment we are concerned only with the light that his early plans in the first decade of the twelfth century throw upon Paris as a scholastic centre at that time. Abelard's whole campaign was based on his observation that Paris could be dominated by one able and renowned master. This may have been true in the first decade of the twelfth century. But twenty years later, when Abelard returned to Paris after the failure of his monastic life, he came to a scholastic centre in which there were many masters making innovations of great importance in grammar, logic, natural science, biblical studies and systematic

---

[11] Ibid., p. 67. Abelard says that he 'returned' (from Brittany where his parents lived) 'to France' (the area of Paris and Laon) *maxime ut de divinitate addiscerem*. What does he mean by *divinitas*? After about 1140 the word was commonly used to describe the whole area of theology. But before this date it generally referred either to the nature of God, or the study of the Trinity from a logical point of view. When used in this sense it was essentially a study of the logical problems arising from the relationship between the Trinity and Unity of God, and (especially in the case of Gilbert de la Porrée) the relationship between the divine and human nature of Christ. It is extremely likely that the former of these two problems was the one with which Abelard in about 1110, as also later, was concerned. If so, he could scarcely have made a worse choice than Anselm of Laon as a teacher. But of course it is unlikely that he really expected to be *taught* by anyone.

theology. This situation no longer gave him the opportunity to aim at capturing the scholastic citadel of Paris, but it offered the possibility (which he seized) of making innovations of striking importance in the development of both systematic logic and of theology. So, in the 1130s, he had a different kind of battle on his hands, and he found a different and much more formidable enemy, no longer a single dominant master in the schools, but one, St Bernard, who dominated a wider world and was capable of administering a final *coup de grâce*. This must be left for later investigation. Here we are concerned, not with the growth of doctrine, but with the growth of the schools, and on this subject it must suffice to say that Abelard, having been the first master at the very beginning of the century to recognize that Paris had unique possibilities for making a scholastic reputation, returned in the 1130s to find a scene of diversified activity such as had not existed when he planned his first campaign.

2 *An aristocrat among students: Otto of Freising*

By 1125, the claims of Paris to scholastic pre-eminence were beginning to be widely recognized. One of the symptoms of this was the arrival of the first known student from the furthest limit of western Christendom and from a more eminent family than any earlier known student. The newcomer was Otto, son of Leopold, Margrave of Austria, grandson of the Emperor Henry IV, half-brother of the Emperor Conrad III, and uncle of Frederick Barbarossa. This glittering catalogue of relatives is concealed under the name, Otto 'of Freising', by which he is generally known. Freising was only the bishopric given him by his half-brother Conrad as one of his first acts after he became Emperor in 1138: his real distinction lay in family and in his ability.

The fact that Otto went to study in Paris at all testifies to the new role of a scholastic education in government, and to the eminence of Paris as a scholastic centre. Otto did not go to Paris to become a scholar or teacher. He went to acquire the skills necessary for assuming a position in the world worthy of the eminence of his birth. He could hope for no position of great secular eminence, for – great though the array of secular positions at the disposal of his family was – he had four older brothers who would absorb all of them. So, from his earliest days, it was envisaged that he would have a career of eminence in the Church.

He had been born in about 1110, and when he was still a child his father named him as provost of the community of secular canons which he had founded at Klosterneuburg near Vienna. A hundred years earlier no doubt he would have become a child oblate in some great Benedictine monastery: but now the clerical horizons for members of great families in government were widening, and the highest offices required a scholastic training.

So in about 1125, apparently with a considerable household, he went to Paris to study, and he spent eight years, from about the age of fifteen to twenty-three, acquiring knowledge that would be useful for his career. This was a shorter time than less distinguished students would have spent, but it was long enough for him to become thoroughly acquainted with the contribution which learning had made to empires in the past, and could be expected to make in the future.[12] He was in fact the first to articulate the theme that learning and Empire had been partners throughout history, and that, progressing from the East, they had jointly reached their ultimate goal in western Europe in his own day. He might well have written – indeed in stately prose he did argue that –

> Westward the course of Empire takes its way;
> The four first acts already past,
> A fifth shall close the drama with the day:
> Time's noblest offspring is the last.[13]

For Otto, his own family represented this final stage in world history. By descent they held the Empire; and it was his mission to bring empire and learning together in that final stage which

---

[12] For Otto of Freising's account of the transmission of learning from its earliest origins in the East to its culmination among the Franks in his own day, see the Prologue to his *Chronica sive Historia de duabus civitatibus*, ed. A Hoffmeister, *MGH*, 1912, pp. 6–9.

[13] These lines were written by George Berkeley (later bishop of Cloyne), probably in about 1725, with reference to the final extension of learning westward to America – hence the name of the Californian city.

signalized the arrival of the last age of world history. Therefore, he went to Paris.

His student years from about 1125 to 1133 were broken by one visit to his homeland, and on his final return journey, together with fifteen clerks in his entourage, he stopped at Morimund, a Cistercian monastery in the diocese of Langres with strong German connections, and they all became Cistercian monks. How far this was strictly a religious conversion and how far it was inspired by statesman-like considerations is not clear. Almost certainly it had elements of both, and it is highly unlikely that it was an impulsive decision. Otto was a man of far-sighted aims, and the Cistercian Order was an ideal instrument for the settlement of under-populated agrarian areas such as the parts of Austria dominated by his family. In fact, one of the immediate results of his home-coming was the foundation of three new Cistercian monasteries on Austrian territory: one in 1134 after his return from Paris, at Heiligenkreuz near Vienna, and then two more at Zwettl and Baumgartenberg.[14]

Otto has left no formal record of his student years. We do not know whether he attended lectures: on the whole, we may surmise, lecturers were more likely to have attended him. But there are three sources, tantalizingly meagre but worth recording in a pupil who was the first and greatest of his kind, which provide some information about his scholarly contacts during these Parisian years.

The first comes from the library of Heiligenkreuz. Among its earliest manuscripts, is one containing notes of lectures by Master Thierry on the Creation. They are very fragmentary, but they appear to be an early record of the attempt by this great master to elucidate the biblical account of Creation with the help of the scientific data provided by Plato's *Timaeus*.[15] Clearly there is need for caution in explaining how they come to be at Heiligenkreuz, but the likelihood is that they are there as a result of Otto's student years in Paris.

As for Otto himself, he wrote only two works that have been preserved, and they both bear distinct traces of his years in Paris.

[14]   For the Cistercian foundations in Austria founded under the inspiration of Otto, see L. Janauschek, *Originum Cisterciensium Tomus 1*, Vienna, 1877, pp. 36, 54, 69.
[15]   See Southern, 1979, pp. 32–4, for some details about this MS and its contents.

The first is a world history, *De duabus Civitatibus*, which may be described as a Hohenstaufen version of Augustine's *De Civitate Dei*. The second is an unfinished fragment of contemporary history describing the deeds of Otto's nephew, the Emperor Frederick Barbarossa. The aim of both works was to emphasize the co-operation of secular and ecclesiastical rulers in the triumphant rise of western Christendom, under the joint guidance of popes, emperors and scholars, culminating in those of the present day.

This co-operation was given practical expression in the commanding role played by Otto himself in the second Crusade under his half-brother, the Emperor Conrad; and it was still more strongly emphasized in his later service under his nephew, the Emperor Frederick Barbarossa, and in Otto's unfinished account of the emperor's contribution to the government of Christendom at the moment when the westward movement of learning and empire through the ages, from the Babylonians to the present day, reached its final goal.

Otto's works and career, therefore, are symptomatic of the twelfth-century realization of the close relationship between the new scholastic programme and the practical activity of government, and they have the unique distinction of associating this relationship, intellectually with the Parisian schools of his day, and politically with the Hohenstaufen Empire. As he believed, the age-long historical movement of learning and government culminated in his own day in the works of the Parisian masters, Abelard, Thierry of Chartres, Hugh of St-Victor, and Gilbert de la Porrée, and in the triumph of western Christendom under the joint guidance of popes and emperors. His two historical works contain the record of this double climax. The imperial–papal theme as a practical ideal scarcely survived his lifetime, but the intellectual theme survived and Otto was its most articulate prophet. He has left the fullest account we have of the dispute between Gilbert de la Porrée and St Bernard which reached its climax at the Council at Reims in 1148, and it is clear that his sympathies lie with the master who was attacked rather than with the great Cistercian critic.[16] Altogether, therefore, Otto's career in its various aspects is a notable landmark in the rise

[16] For Otto's account of these masters, see *Gesta Friderici Imperatoris*, i, cc. 49–62.

of the scholastically formed, and militarily dominant, western Christendom of the twelfth century.

3 The first colonial student: William of Tyre

A further stage in the development of Paris as the supreme scholastic centre of the West is announced in the career of William of Tyre, who – with a strange exception to be mentioned presently – was the earliest known student from the colonial frontier of the Latin West. His aim was similar to that of Otto of Freising in that he intended to use the new learning of the schools in the work of government in his homeland.

He had been born into the higher, but not the highest, aristocracy of the Latin kingdom of Jerusalem in about 1130. Like Otto, he was destined for a career in the Church, and as a foundation for this career he spent about twenty years, from 1146 to 1165, studying first Arts and Theology in Paris for about fourteen years, and then for a further five years, Law in the schools of Bologna, which had recently emerged as the new star in the European scholastic scene. Like Otto of Freising, and also late in life, he wrote a history of the great events of his time, in which he included – without any apparent reason – a detailed account of his student years.[17] Why did he do this? Partly perhaps because he wished to impress his own personality on his *History*; but also to express the importance he attached to organized learning as an instrument of political, and even of military, strength. So, in the middle of his account of the politics of the Latin Kingdom, he tells the world about the subjects of his studies, the length of time he spent on them, and the masters who taught him.

There were three stages in his programme of study. First, he studied grammar, rhetoric and logic, under eight masters over a period of about ten years. These masters, like those of John of Salisbury to whom we shall come presently, were divided into two categories, of regular masters, and masters whose lectures

[17] For William of Tyre's account of his studies in Paris and Bologna, see 'Guillaume de Tyr, *Chronique*, ed. R. B. C. Huygens, *Corpus Christianorum, cont. med.*, vol. lxiii, Turnhout, 1986, pp. 879–81.

or discussions he attended spasmodically. In the first category were three masters, Bernard the Breton, Petrus Helias, and Ivo of Chartres (the younger), whose lectures he attended regularly whenever their other duties left them free to teach. This reference to the interruptions caused by their other duties indicates that, though they taught in Paris, they all had ecclesiastical positions elsewhere which required their presence for some part of each year. Then, in the second category, there were five masters to whom he went 'only casually, and mainly for practice in disputation'. These masters were Alberic de Monte, Robert of Melun, Manerius, Adam de Petit-Pont and Robert Amiclas.

This habit of combining regular attendance at some lectures with casual attendance at others is as much a habit of university students now as in the twelfth century, but it can only be practised in a highly-developed scholastic centre. Indeed, the whole of William of Tyre's account provides the clearest testimony to the number and variety of the body of masters in Paris in the late 1140s, and to the existence at this time of several well-defined schools of thought among them.[18]

Then, as an afterthought but evidently in the context of his Arts lectures, he mentions that he studied ancient classical authors with an old master, Hilary of Orleans, and Geometry, especially Euclid, with William of Soissons. The last named is known to have taught in Paris; but we have no indication of the place where Hilary taught, and it is possible that he taught in Orleans and that William of Tyre had spent a preliminary year there before going to Paris.

Finally, after ten years studying the Liberal Arts in Paris in the way I have described, William spent a further six years studying Theology with two successive masters: first, with Peter Lombard from 1153 until 1159; then, when Peter Lombard gave up lecturing on becoming bishop of Paris in 1159, with Maurice of Sully, who taught theology until he succeeded Peter Lombard as bishop of Paris in 1160.

One point which emerges from this account, which we shall also find repeated in John of Salisbury, is that, although

---

[18] For a full analysis of this chapter, see R. B. C. Huygens, 'Guillaume de Tyr étudiant', *Latomus*, xxi, 1962, pp. 822-9.

attendance at the lectures of several masters on the same subject seems to have been common in the Arts, it was not practised in Theology. This may have been due, either to the comparative rarity of theological masters, or to the greater insistence of these masters on fidelity to their teaching.

Finally, in 1160, William went on to a city which was beginning to attract an international body of students and masters: Bologna. Here he studied Roman law under Masters Hugolinus, Bulgarus, Martin, and James from 1160 to 1165. The position of the schools in Bologna will concern us in a later chapter.[19]

All in all, William of Tyre gives us the most clearly depicted of all accounts of the range of subjects that could be studied in Paris from 1145 to 1160. There were only two main subjects for which it was necessary to go elsewhere: Medicine and Law. For medicine it was necessary to go to Salerno or Montpellier, and for Law to Bologna. But it may here be noted that all the students who completed their studies before 1150 had looked on theology as the final culmination of their studies, and William of Tyre is the first to have seen Law as presenting a further academic height for an ambitious student.

4 The study-years of John of Salisbury

In his *Metalogicon* – a work designed to display the related roles of grammar and logic in the general context of human knowledge – John of Salisbury gives an account of his studies in France. It is the only autobiographical account of a student's career in the schools which is comparable in fullness of detail with that of William of Tyre, and – like his – it appears at first sight to be an irrelevant intrusion in the general plan of the work in which it appears. But in both cases this first impression is mistaken. In William of Tyre's *History*, the account of his studies is rather generally related to the conduct of war and peace; in the *Metalogicon*, the autobiographical chapter exemplifies the principal thesis of the whole work – namely that logic has a very important position within the general scheme of learning

---

[19] See below, pp. 310–18 (esp. p. 316).

– provided that it is the servant, not the master. *Grammar*, of course, is fundamental in all learning, and the *Metalogicon* begins with an account of its role. Then it goes on to sketch the place of logic among the sciences, warning the reader against the danger of putting the sword of Hercules into the hands of a pygmy[20] – that is to say, of making an ignorant use of a powerful instrument, and he exemplifies from his own experience the truth that the benefits of logic can come only from a secure grounding in grammar and the other liberal arts.

He begins his account of his experiences by telling us that he went to France in the year after the death of King Henry I. Since Henry I died in December 1135, he must therefore have gone to France in the course of the year 1136; and since he says that he spent nearly twelve years as a student, this (even allowing considerable laxity in his chronology) can only mean that he continued his studies until some date in 1147 or 1148.[21]

He would have been about eighteen years old when he went to study in France, and he was already well grounded in Latin grammar. It followed naturally from this that, when he got to Paris, like many young men before and since, he plunged straight into the intricacies of dialectical disputes on Mont-Ste-Geneviève, first under Abelard, and then, when Abelard left, under masters Alberic and Robert of Melun. These studies and disputes occupied two years and John greatly enjoyed himself in the dialectical arena. But then suddenly, in his own words, he 'came to himself', took stock of his position, and perceived that he was on the wrong road. Reflection convinced him that he must first strengthen his foundation in grammar and in the whole range of Arts subjects. With this end in view he left Mont-Ste-Geneviève in 1138 and went to William of Conches,

---

[20] See *Metalogicon*, ed. C. C. J. Webb, Oxford, 1929, pp. 76–7 (ii, c. 9): *Quod inefficax est dialectica si aliarum (disciplinarum) destituatur subsidio.*

[21] For John's account of his study years, see his *Metalogicon*, ii, c. 10. He probably entered into papal service during Eugenius III's visit to Paris and Reims in 1147–48. For the evidence, see R. L. Poole, 'John of Salisbury at the papal court', in *Studies in Chronology and History*, ed. A. L. Poole, Oxford, 1934, pp. 248–58. Poole is certainly mistaken in thinking that John entered the papal service as early as 1146. He may have been recruited while the pope was in Paris (20 April – 7 June 1147), but the only certainty is that he was in papal service by March 1148 at Reims. Any date between June 1147 and March 1148 is compatible with John's own chronology of his studies.

the great grammarian whom he has already mentioned as the scholar who, with Richard Bishop, had carried on the solid – but by then generally abandoned as outdated – tradition of Master Bernard of Chartres in teaching grammar in the full and proper way.[22]

Since he says that he spent three years being taught by William of Conches, he must have studied with him from 1138 to 1141. He also says that meanwhile he 'read' many things which he never regretted,[23] and he continues: 'Afterwards I followed (the lectures of) Richard Bishop', and he goes on to give a list of the other masters whom he heard or with whom he had discussions. Besides Richard Bishop, they were: a German mathematician Hardwin, whom he says he had also earlier heard, presumably during his dialectical years from 1136 to 1138; master Thierry on rhetoric without understanding him, and Peter Helias on the same subject with better understanding. He also discussed logical problems with Adam de Petit-Pont, the central Parisian logician of the time, and with William of Soissons, who had constructed a kind of logical machine for teaching the elements of argument.

John does not specify exactly when or where he heard or consulted all these scholars, but several of them also appear among those with whom William of Tyre studied,[24] and we can be sure that all of them – with the possible exception of William of Conches himself – taught in Paris.

In outline, therefore, the course of John's studies seems fairly clear; but there is a problem. In speaking both of his studies with William of Conches and of those with the other scholars whom I have mentioned, he says that he spent three years on these studies. So the problem is this: were his three years with William of Conches preliminary to, or the same as, the three years which he spent with the other masters in Arts subjects?

Nearly all interpreters have assumed that the first of these alternatives is correct, and most recently Olga Weijers has given

22 The emphatic phrase in which John describes his abandoning the study of dialectic under Abelard and his followers in 1138 is only circumstantially related to geography: essentially it indicated a change in his philosophical outlook from a nominalist to a realist view of the nature of general concepts. On this, see *Policraticus*, vii, c. 12, *De ineptiis nugatorum qui sapientiam verba putant*.
23 See *Metalogicon*, ii, 10, p. 80.
24 See below, p. 232.

a very full and clear account of what this interpretation of John's words entails.[25] So we may begin by examining her account, first quoting John's own words when he took stock of his position in 1138 and abandoned the study of logic:

> I transferred to the grammarian (William) of Conches and heard him teaching for three years. Meanwhile I 'read' many things and I have never regretted the time that I spent. Afterwards I followed (the lectures of) Richard Bishop, and I 're-read' with him things that I had 'read' with others, including some parts of the quadrivium, which to some extent I had studied with Hardwin the German. I also 're-read' rhetoric, which – with certain other matters – I had formerly studied with Master Thierry without much understanding.[26]

Then, having mentioned the various other masters in Arts subjects with whom he studied, he goes on to mention the problem of his poverty and the advice of friends that he should earn money by teaching. Whereupon, he says, '*in fine triennii* I returned [apparently to Mont-Ste-Geneviève] and sought out Master Gilbert [de la Porrée] with whom I studied logic and divinity'.[27]

This final move was the beginning of a new phase in his studies in divinity and theology which will be outlined presently. For the moment we are concerned only with the single question: was the 'three-year period' with these other Arts masters subsequent to, or the same as, the three-year period which he spent studying with William of Conches?

Dr Weijers, who holds (like many others) that John had *two* three-year periods of Arts study after 1138, sets out the chronology which results from this interpretation. It runs as follows:

[25] Olga Weijers, 'The chronology of John of Salisbury's studies in France', in *The World of John of Salisbury*, ed. Michael Wilks, Blackwell, Oxford, 1984, pp. 109–16.

[26] *Metalogicon*, ii, 10, p. 80.

[27] *Reversus itaque in fine triennii repperi magistrum Gilebertum, ipsumque audivi in logicis et divinis; sed nimis cito subtractus est. Successit Robertus Pullus, quem vita pariter et scientia commendabant. Deinde me excepit Simon Pexiacensis, fidus lector sed obtusior disputator. Sed hos duos in solis theologicis habui preceptores.* It is clear that John makes the old distinction between *divinitas*, the study of the nature of the Trinity as a branch of logic (see above, p. 207, n. 11) as taught by Gilbert de la Porrée and Abelard, and of 'theology' as taught by his two later masters.

1. 1136–38, John studies logic on Mont-Ste-Geneviève;
2. 1138–41, he studies grammar with William of Conches;
3. 1141–44, he studies miscellaneous Arts subjects with a variety of masters mentioned above;
4. 1144–47/8, (having returned to Mont-Ste-Geneviève) he studies 'divinity' with Gilbert de la Porrée, and then – after Gilbert had left – theology with two successive masters, Robert Pullen and Simon of Poissy.

This chronology has one important consequence: it postpones his study of divinity with Gilbert de la Porrée until 1144. But this is chronologically impossible, because Gilbert de la Porrée is known to have given up teaching, and to have left Paris, in 1142 when he became bishop of Poitiers. Moreover, even if it were argued (implausibly) that he could still, as bishop of Poitiers, have continued to teach theology in Paris, this chronology would still be impossible because (as we have seen above)[28] Robert Pullen, to whom John of Salisbury went *after* Gilbert de la Porrée had left Paris, had himself left Paris at the latest by April 1144, when he had gone to Rome and become papal chancellor. So there is a double guarantee that the idea of *two* three-year periods of Arts study, first with William of Conches and then with a miscellaneous group of other masters, is chronologically impossible.

We are therefore driven back to the view that the three years which John spent studying with William of Conches were also the three years during which he went to classes and discussions with several other masters. Indeed, besides being chronologically the only possible interpretation of John's words, it is also the most satisfactory academically, for it seems to have been a general practice for students in the Arts, while having one main master, also to hear lectures and attend discussions with other masters, as William of Tyre had done. Dr Weijer's interpretation, by contrast, gives John only a single master, William of Conches, without any satellites for three years from 1138–41; and then only satellites without any main master from 1141–3. So, even if the chronological objection were not conclusive – which it is – the academic objection to Dr Weijer's reconstruction would

[28] See above, p. 177.

be strong. Consequently, the chronology I have outlined, which requires that John went to classes and discussions with the other masters whom he names at the same time as studying consistently with William of Conches from 1138 to 1141, is the only one that is consistent with John of Salisbury's account of his studies.

Nevertheless, two further objections have been raised to this chronology. The first is that it seems nonsensical for John of Salisbury to speak emphatically of moving from Mont-Ste-Geneviève if no more is intended than a move into, and later back from, the city of Paris. After all, the *Mont* is now, and has been since the early thirteenth century, an integral part of Paris within the city walls. But the answer to this objection is quite simple: in the early part of the twelfth century the *Mont* lay not only physically but also juridically outside the city. Its schools were beyond the jurisdiction of the chancellor of the cathedral, and this was important for the freedom of individual masters, as Abelard made clear when he mentions that he established his school '*extra civitatem in monte Sancte Genovefe*'.[29] Indeed this sense of separation of the left bank from the city of Paris continued long after Philip Augustus extended the city wall, and even in the nineteenth century inhabitants of the left bank would make preparations and speak of going down into the city almost as if they were going into a foreign country. So the apparent absurdity of making so much of the simple journey from the *Mont* to the city has a very long history.

Another possible objection to my account of John of Salisbury's Parisian years is that, if William of Conches was teaching in or near Paris during these years, it is strange that no one else mentioned his presence. On this point, however, John himself provides an answer. In an earlier chapter of the *Metalogicon*, while praising William of Conches together with Richard Bishop as the main continuators of Bernard of Chartres's method of teaching grammar, he adds that their method had become so unpopular on account of the great length of time it required that they 'gave up': *impetu multitudinis imperite victi, cesserunt.*[30] Richard Bishop evidently did not 'give up' completely, for John

---

[29] See above, p. 206.
[30] *Metalogicon*, i, 24, p. 58.

studied with him while he was in Paris. But William of Conches, who was much the older and more distinguished of the two, could well have been in semi-retirement by the time that John went to him.

There is, moreover, some independent evidence that he lived and died in Paris, for a remarkable epitaph has survived praising a scholar of Norman origin called William, who had died and was buried in Paris. The important lines are:

Epitaphium magistri Guillelmi

Flevit Apollonium sua Grecia, Roma Maronem,
    Gallia Guillelmum luget utrique parem:
Eius preclaret natu Normantia, victu
    Gallia, Parisius corpore, mente polus.[31]

(*Greece mourned its Apollonius, Rome its Virgil. Now Gaul mourns one born in Normandy, who lived in Gaul, whose body rests in Paris, and his soul in heaven.*)

To sum up then: in outline, John of Salisbury's studies in Paris and on Mont-Ste-Geneviève ran as follows:

1.   1136–38: He spent these two years studying logic on Mont-Ste-Geneviève, first with Abelard and then with Master Alberic and Robert of Melun, breaking off prematurely after his self-examination and determination to change direction.

2.   1138–41: He studied grammar with William of Conches as his main master, while spasmodically attending the classes and debates of various other masters: the grammarian Richard Bishop; the German mathematician Hardwin; Petrus Helias; Master Thierry; Adam de Petit-Pont; William of Soissons.

3.   1141–1147/8: For a year, 1141–2, he studied 'divinity' (that is to say, the nature of God, which was still a subject intermediate between Arts and Theology) with

---

[31] PL, 203, col. 1393. Fr. Häring 1974, p. 295, accepts the identification with William of Conches.

Gilbert de la Porrée; then for a further year, 1142–3, systematic theology with Robert Pullen; and finally, when Pullen went to Rome and became papal chancellor, he continued his study of theology with Simon of Poissy[32] until 1147/8. Then John himself – like his master Robert Pullen, supported by St Bernard – joined the papal Curia in time to be able to give an eye-witness account of the Council of Reims in March 1148.

As a student, therefore, John followed the same general plan of study as William of Tyre: in Arts, he had one special master, William of Conches, and intermittently attended the classes and discussions of several masters on a wide range of interrelated subjects; and in Theology he had three masters in succession.

It was this feature of academic life that distinguished early twelfth-century Paris from all other cities. In Paris alone we are standing at the beginnings of university life as we know it, with many masters in the Arts subjects undertaking to teach some parts of the variegated Arts curriculum and at least three or four teaching theology. It was only in theology that masters did not invite, or perhaps tolerate, competition or fluidity of attendance among students.

5 *The* Metamorphosis Goliae

The next witness to the Parisian studies of the 1140s presents evidence of a quite different nature. If William of Tyre gives the most straightforward account of a twelfth-century student's career, and John of Salisbury the most doctrinal, the anonymous *Metamorphosis Goliae* gives the most grandiose. This work may briefly be described as a twelfth-century rendering of the theme of the 'Marriage of Eloquence and Wisdom', which Martianus

---

[32] John describes Peter of Poissy as a good lecturer but weak in disputation. He was, however, a man of importance in royal government (see *La Chronique de Morigny*, ed. L. Mirot, Paris, 1912, pp. 46–7). It is also possible that he was the author of an important work on the Sacraments: see H. Weisweiler, *Maitre Simon et son groupe: De Sacramentis*, Louvain, 1937.

SCHOLASTIC METROPOLIS OF NORTHERN EUROPE

Capella had made familiar to all scholars. Following this model, the author first gives a long and colourful description of the pagan heavenly host engaged in a Bacchanalian marriage scene. Then he goes on to depict the sages of the ancient world being joined by a group of scholars who can be identified (though the author does not himself mention the geographical fact) as masters of Paris in about 1143.[33]

The poem, therefore, is one more twelfth-century assertion of fellowship – indeed still more, of equality – between the scholars of the ancient world and those of the present, and more particularly it indicates that this fellowship is to be found pre-eminently in Paris. But the theme is complicated by the fact that the greatest of the modern scholars whom it celebrates has recently been silenced, and two others have removed themselves from active participation in scholarship by leaving Paris. The greatest is Abelard, who has been removed and silenced by an iniquitous attack on him by St Bernard and his monks. The two others are Gilbert de la Porrée, who has left the schools on becoming bishop of Poitiers, and Thierry of Chartres, who has left on becoming chancellor of Chartres. However, although these three, the greatest among the scholars, have gone, there are others who are still active and they are duly celebrated by the poet: Manerius, Robert of Melun and Adam de Petit-Pont, pupils and successors of Abelard; Peter Helias, Bernard Brito and Ivo, pupils of Thierry, and (in Ivo's case) also a pupil of Gilbert; and Peter Lombard, who is the main continuator of the work both of Gilbert and of Abelard. The other two, *Reginaldus monachus* and *Bartholomeus*, have not been identified with any certainty.[34]

The poem, therefore, reaches its climax in the passage in which these masters of the Parisian schools are celebrated as being worthy to be placed in the company of the ancient scholars

---

[33] For the text of the *Metamorphosis Goliae*, see R. B. C. Huygens, 'Mitteilungen aus Handschriften' *Studi medievali*, ser. 3, vol. 3, 1962, pp. 764–72, or T. Wright, *The latin poems commonly attributed to Walter Mapes*, Camden Society, 1841. For its list of Masters at Paris, see below, p. 232.

[34] It is very likely that Bartholomaeus is the Bartholomew who later became bishop of Exeter: see Adrian Morey, *Bartholomew of Exeter, Bishop and Canonist*, Cambridge, 1937, p. 4.

mentioned earlier in the poem. The most outstanding among these Parisian scholars – Abelard, Gilbert de la Porrée, and Thierry of Chartres – have now left Paris and have given up teaching. They have been replaced by others who deserve commemoration, but no one can replace Abelard, and the poet returns to him at the end, inveighing with great bitterness against the monks who have been the cause of his removal from the scholastic scene. This bitterness needs no comment here, but it is preceded by a remarkable lament (ll. 213–216) which deserves to be quoted:

> Nupta quaerit ubi sit suus Palatinus,
> cuius totus extitit spiritus divinus;
> quaerit cur se subtrahat quasi peregrinus,
> quem ad sua ubera foverat et sinus.

(The bride asks where and why her *Palatinus* [i.e. Abelard, who is *Palatinus* because born at Le Pallet], whom she had nestled to her breast, has gone. She is told that he has been silenced by the hatred of monks, and the poem ends with a violent attack on them.)

Who then is the bride from whom Abelard is torn? It is certainly not Héloïse as we might like to think, but – as the late John F. Benton was the first to point out[35] – none other than *Philologia*, or *Learning*, whose marriage forms the central subject of the poem.

So the apparently irrelevant ending really brings the poem back to the theme with which it started: *Philologia*, the bride whose marriage was celebrated by ancient scholars at the beginning of the poem, is in modern times the bride of Abelard, who has been reft from her by the violence of monks. This is why the poem ends with its violent invective against the monks who were the cause of Abelard's expulsion from the schools. So the climax to which the poem rises is a bitter lament for the manner in which the greatest of these modern scholars had been silenced. Indeed the poet also laments the loss of Thierry and of Gilbert de la Porrée (whom he also calls a 'knight and

---

[35] See J. F. Benton, 'Philology's search for Abelard in the *Metamorphosis Goliae*', *Speculum*, 50, 1975, 199–217.

castellan' of the married pair), but he can still commemorate those who were left, and he names ten in all, who, if not as great as those who have gone, are carrying on the good work.

It may seem strange that the poet, like most of the others whose accounts we have examined, does not mention the place where all the masters whom he celebrates were teaching. This is curious, but the reason is simple. The subject of these descriptions was not places, but people; and not simply people, but the coming together of fully-formed and half-formed scholars, whose joint efforts gave these years a claim to be resuming, after a long stand-still, the rebuilding of human knowledge beyond the level reached in the greatest days of ancient learning. All who described the studies of these years emphasized the variety of effort and common purpose of the masters and students alike. That too is our theme. But we are more conscious than they could be of the intricate interaction of social and political, and therefore also of geographical and organizational forces, which combined to bring about the intellectual, religious and political changes of this period.

Unity and diversity are the marks of all great periods of intellectual discovery; and when intellectual discovery has the effect, and to some extent the aim, of bringing about large-scale changes in the organization of society, this can happen only when the close neighbourhood of many students and masters is associated with the wide dispersal of fully fledged scholars throughout the whole society. This is precisely what we have to record: close associations in study and far-flung activity in practice, leading to fundamental changes in the organization of society. These are the characteristics of the time, and the records of the writers who described their experiences as pupils show how closely the masters of the schools of Paris were inter-related in aim and general programme, and how great was the diversity of places from which they and their students had come and to which they went.

Meagre though the accounts are which describe the activity of many masters within a single general framework of knowledge, they illuminate a very great scene. The unity of effort was made possible by proximity, and the lists at the end of this chapter will show how closely these masters were related in place, as well as time and aim and programme, and they leave no room for doubt that it was in Paris and its neighbourhood that they were all active.[36]

6 *The first Greek student in Paris*

The accounts of the Parisian schools in the first half of the twelfth century which we have so far considered were written at different times and inspired by different motives, but they can all be relied on to give an account of a scene which was actually observed by the various authors who had themselves taught or studied in Paris or on the Left Bank during the period from 1098 to 1160.

The account we are now to consider was also written by a scholar who had studied and taught in Paris during these years, but its motivation is quite different from that of any of its predecessors. It presents itself as a record of a conversation which took place in the Spring of 1193 between two old acquaintances who had known each other as students in the 1140s and had then followed widely different careers.

Their conversation was dominated by the event that had taken place at Reims in 1148, when St Bernard had made a dramatic attempt to repeat his success in securing the condemnation of Abelard in 1140 by obtaining the condemnation of Gilbert de la Porrée. It is clear that St Bernard had entered the fray expecting a repetition of his earlier success, but, as contemporaries noted, Gilbert differed from Abelard in the respect with which he treated his masters: he represented the *esprit de corps* of the masters while Abelard had represented himself alone. The result was that, despite St Bernard's intense efforts to secure a conviction, his attack ended inconclusively, and Gilbert's doctrine went on being discussed and supported by a large body of masters for the next half century.

Among those who were perplexed by the points at issue between St Bernard and Gilbert de la Porrée was the writer of

[36] See below, p. 232.

the dialogue we are now to consider: Everard of Ypres. He had been a student and then a master teaching grammar in Paris in the middle years of the century, and he had also served at one time in the household of Cardinal Giacinto Bobone, who had defended Abelard against St Bernard at the Council of Sens in 1140, and had ultimately become pope in 1191. Everard himself had only a moderately successful career as a Parisian master, and had become a Cistercian monk at Moutier-en-Argonne about a hundred miles east of Paris at an unknown date, perhaps in the 1180s.[37]

Here he had been badly received by his fellow monks, who distrusted him as a man of scholastic learning, and even more as one who had been in the household of an important enemy of St Bernard. Consequently, Everard was an isolated figure in the monastic community, much occupied with his solitary thoughts. The issue that chiefly occupied his mind was the conflict between St Bernard and the great master of the Parisian schools, Gilbert de la Porrée. It was one of the most complicated and bitterly contested issues of the whole century, and Everard's perplexity was so great and long-lasting that he had gone so far as to write to Pope Urban III, who was pope between 1185 and 1187, asking him to give an authoritative ruling on the problem.[38] But the pope had done nothing, and Everard continued to be unable to make up his mind about the disputed doctrine.

According to his own account, he was still in this state of perplexity when a visitor whom he had known in his student days arrived at the monastery. Naturally they settled down to have a conversation, and it so happened that various injuries and illnesses among the visitor's servants prolonged his visit for several days. The main subject of their talk was the conflict

[37] For an account of Everard's career and the text of his conversation with Ratius, see N. M. Häring, 'The Dialogue of Ratius and Everard', *Mediaeval Studies*, 15, 1953, 243–89; and 'The Cistercian Everard of Ypres and his appraisal of the conflict between St Bernard and Gilbert of Poitiers', *Mediaeval Studies*, 17, 1955, 143–72.

[38] For Everard's letter to Pope Urban III, 1185–7, see *Mediaeval Studies*, 17, 1955, 162–68. His earlier works appear to include a translation into French of the *Disticha Catonis*: see O. Golberg, *Die Catonischen Disticha in der englischen und französischen Literatur*, Leipzig, 1883, and a *Summula decretalium questionum*, probably written in the 1180s, for which see S. Kuttner, *Repertorium der Canonistik, 1140–1234*, 187–90.

between St Bernard and Gilbert de la Porrée which had occupied Everard's mind for so many years. It happened also to be the subject on which the visitor could speak with special authority because he had been closely attached to Gilbert throughout his student years. According to the account which emerges in the course of the conversation, the visitor was a Greek from Athens who had been sent by his mother to study in the West, and (being a stranger in France) he had attached himself to Gilbert de la Porrée, who – of all western theologians – had most interest in the theology of the Greek Fathers.

Against this background, it is intelligible that the lonely Greek student in Paris in the years around 1140 should have attached himself to Gilbert's entourage. According to the account which he gave of his movements in the course of the conversation, he had followed Gilbert wherever he went, and he recalled particularly that he had heard him lecture to an audience of nearly three hundred in the bishop's palace in Paris, but to only four, including himself, in Chartres.[39] This detail has been much discussed, and the suggestion that it represented some special occasion seems to me very plausible. Gilbert would certainly not have had so many hearers at his normal lectures, which were notoriously difficult to follow and anyhow seem to have been on Mont-Ste-Geneviève. Nevertheless, this recollection explains why, while holding the office of chancellor of Chartres, Gilbert's main lecturing activity was in the Parisian area.

Everard's Greek friend also claims that, when Gilbert became bishop of Poitiers in 1142, he went with him and stayed with him, teaching the bishop Greek, while the bishop taught him Latin. Then when Gilbert died in 1154, his Greek protégé wrote one of several epitaphs composed in the bishop's honour.

All these facts emerge in the course of the conversation, but the constant subject was the dispute between Gilbert and Bernard which had perplexed Everard – like many others – for fifty years; and it was a subject on which the visitor could speak with an intimate and detailed knowledge. Almost to the end of the conversation, Everard continued to put St Bernard's case as well as he could. But gradually his doubts were resolved, and in the

[39] *Mediaeval Studies*, 15, 1953, pp. 251–2.

end he expressed his entire agreement with Gilbert's doctrine as expounded by his visitor. Whereupon the two friends parted with many expressions of mutual regard.

It would be difficult to imagine a more life-like report. In all the details of the conversation and its circumstances it is a small masterpiece of heart-felt and persuasive reporting. Moreover, if Everard's account is to be trusted, his visitor has a very special place among twelfth-century students in Paris in the 1140s. Otto of Freising had come from Vienna, William of Tyre from the Holy Land, Peter Lombard from northern Italy, John of Salisbury from England; but Everard's visitor outreached them all in having been sent from Athens by his mother at some time between about 1135 and 1140 to study in northern France. This of course is not impossible: there were many contacts between the Latin West and the Greek world in the middle years of the century, but it is nevertheless a landmark, and we must ask, is it true? or is it (as Fr. Häring believes) an invention?

To begin with the details which emerge in the course of the reported conversation. The visitor is portrayed as arriving at Moutier on his homeward journey to Athens, and as estimating that his journey across the Alps and then on to Athens will take him two hundred days. The delay caused by an injury to one of the Greek visitor's servants prolonged the visit and gave the two friends a chance to discuss fully the doctrines of Gilbert de la Porrée. Certainly, under close questioning, the visitor shows a detailed and comprehensive knowledge such as might be expected of one who had spent much time in Gilbert's company. Further, while the friends were conversing, news arrived of the capture of King Richard I of England by the Grand Duke of Austria. Since this had happened at Vienna in December 1192 and was an event of the greatest importance for the king of France, the news must have reached northern France in January, or certainly not later than February, 1193.

So the details of the visit, the close examination of Gilbert's doctrine, the recall of historical events in the past, and the many small accidents which befall the visitors during the visit, all confirm the reliability of the dialogue.

But there is one snag. The reported names of the visitor and his servants, and the members of his family who are mentioned in the course of the conversation, are clearly fictitious: the friend himself is called Ratius; the friend's mother and sister in Athens are Ratio and Sophia; and his servants are Sosius, Byrria and Davus – names borrowed from Terence's *Andria*.

Further, there is a difficulty about the Greek visitor's claim that he taught Gilbert de la Porrée Greek. A comprehensive knowledge of the Greek Fathers was certainly a central feature of Gilbert's theological standpoint, but no one has ever been able to detect a knowledge of the Greek language in his works. On the whole, however, this last detail is scarcely a serious obstacle to Ratius's claim to have taught Gilbert Greek: it is possible for an old man to learn something of the language of theologians who had profoundly influenced him without displaying his knowledge in his writings and in any case all Gilbert's writings belong to the period before he became a bishop.

So the substantial difficulty comes down to the fictitious names of the Greek visitor and his companions, and the question must be faced: are the people, the incidents, the recollections, the arguments, real or only imaginary? And, if they are imaginary, what are we to make of the contents of the work?

Fr. Häring, who edited the dialogue and commented on it, had no doubt.[40] He judged it to be purely imaginary, and he supposed that Everard himself is the source of all the knowledge of Gilbert's doctrine that is attributed in the imaginary Greek visitor. But we know that, as late as the period 1185–87 Everard was still grievously troubled with doubt about Gilbert de la Porrée's doctrines – so much so that he had written to the pope asking him for a definitive pronouncement. So something must have happened between that date and the writing of the dialogue to convince him that Gilbert's doctrine was correct. He must either have discovered reasons for himself, or have had some other source. To invent a fictitious Greek as his source would have been an implausible way of recommending a much contested doctrine which all members of his own abbey and monastic order associated with hostility to St Bernard. In the absence of any more plausible alternative, it seems to me reasonable to accept that the Greek pupil of Gilbert de la Porrée really existed,

[40] Ibid., pp. 147, 152, 153.

and that conversation actually took place and settled Everard's doubts. As for the fancy names which he gives his visitors, we may think what we like, including the possibility that he did not know how to give the Greek names a Latin form and chose an easy way round his difficulty.

III CONCLUSION

To sum up the results of this prolonged enquiry, it is abundantly clear that in the half century from 1100 to 1150, Paris had become a scene of scholastic activity of hitherto unparalleled diversity which had been built up, not by any planning body or authority, but simply by being uniquely attractive to large numbers of students from all parts of Europe and beyond, and from every class of society from the very top to far down the social scale. These students were supported chiefly by remittances from home and by the fees of such pupils as they could either bring with them or find when they arrived. They all undertook courses of study which ideally required at least seven years and often much longer to complete. As courses became more organized, it became common for students to complete their Arts course and then have a break – if possible with employment in the household of some magnate who could reward their services by presentation to a benefice – before returning to study in the higher faculty of Theology. But this degree of hierarchical organization does not seem to have existed in the first half of the twelfth century.

As for any calculation of the numbers of masters and students in Paris itself and on the south bank of the Seine, two remarks may be made.

First, it is clear that what we find in the area of Paris by 1150 is quite unlike anything in western Europe in any previous century, in the extent of territory covered by schools and scholars' lodgings, and in the number and diversity of masters and students in the area.

Second, there was no other city in northern France, or at this date anywhere else in Europe, where anything like a similar conglomeration of international masters and students could be found. There were other cities – Salerno and Montpellier particularly, with specialist masters in medicine; or Orleans and Tours, with specialists in literature and letter-writing; and after about 1150 Bologna was beginning to draw an international stream of students comparable to that at Paris. But, during the previous thirty years, no other city besides Paris could offer such facilities or such an array of masters in the subjects of central importance for the corporate life of Christendom, and in these subjects speed of development was vital.

The rapidly growing wealth and population of western Europe brought an urgent need for order, and before 1140 theology was the only body of knowledge sufficiently highly developed, and with local agents in the form of parish priests and diocesan officials sufficiently firmly established, to bring order (and the hope of eternal happiness) into the everyday life of a large part of the population. Paris alone had the resources and scholastic standing capable of creating this new order based on doctrinal certainties. Consequently those who went out from the Parisian schools had an instrument in their hands not only of great intellectual power, but also of great social importance.

But, to give practical effect to theological systematization, a new legal development was needed. As we have seen, in 1160, William of Tyre left Paris to go to Bologna. This move was symptomatic of the appearance of a new science in the scholastic firmament capable of giving this practical corporate effect both to the theological conclusions of the Parisian masters and to the stream of legislation of popes and councils. The stages in the elaboration of this science will require separate treatment in the chapters which follow. But first it may be convenient to set out the results of the enquiry into the Parisian schools in tabular form.

IV APPENDIX – *a Schedule of Masters*

A schedule of Parisian masters in the 1140s from the sources examined above. Masters appearing in all three lists of William of Tyre, John of Salisbury and the *Metamorphosis Goliae* are in bold type; those in two lists in italics.

WM. *of TYRE*	JOHN *of SALISBURY*	GOLIAS
ARTS	ARTS	ARTS AND THEOLOGY
	William of Conches	
	Abelard	*Abelard*
	Thierry	*Thierry*[41]
		Gilbert de la Porrée
Alberic de Monte	*Alberic*	
Robert of Melun	**Robert of Melun**	**Robertus theologus**[42]
Adam de Petit-Pont	**Adam de Petit-Pont**	**Adam de Petit-Pont**
Petrus Helias	**Petrus Helias**	**Petrus Helias**
Manerius		*Manerius*
Robert Amiclas	Richard Bishop	
Bernardus Brito		
Ivo of Chartres	Hardwin the German	*Robert Amiclas*[43]
	DIVINITAS	
		Bernard
	Gilbert de la Porrée	
THEOLOGY	THEOLOGY	
		Reginaldus monachus
	Robert Pullen	Bartholemew
Peter Lombard	**Peter Lombard**	**Peter Lombard**
	Simon Pexiacensis	*Ivo*
Maurice of Sully		

41 The Goliardic measure in which the *Metamorphosis* was written requires some ingenuity in listing names. Consequently Gilbert de la Porrée is described thus:

> *Et hic praesul praesulum stat Pictaviensis,*
> *Prius et nubentium miles et castrensis*

And Thierry thus:

> *Ibi doctor cernitur ille Carnotensis*

Gilbert had of course just become bishop of Poitiers, and Thierry chancellor of Chartres, and these two names could conveniently be fitted into the verse. So far as I know there is no earlier example of Thierry being called *Carnotensis*.

42 *Robertus theologus* could be either Robert Pullen or Robert of Melun.

43 Professor R. M. Thomson has pointed out to me that Dr Jennifer Shepherd has described a collection of glossal books of the Bible which belonged to Master Robert Amiclas and were later in the library of Buildwas Abbey. They are now in the library of Trinity College, Cambridge (Cambridge Bibliographical Society, ix, 1988, 281–8). Robert Amiclas has in the past been variously identified either as Robert Pullen or as Robert of Melun; but the latter is impossible because both are found in William of Tyre's list of masters; and the former is highly unlikely because Robert Pullen was closely attached to Sherborne Abbey (see above, pp. 176–9) and it is hard to see how his books could have got to Buildwas. The truth is that Robert Amiclas is just one more of the many Roberts active in the twelfth-century schools, and probably, like Robert of Melun, Robert Pullen, and Adam de Petit-Pont, of English origin.

PLATE 1 *The scholastic limitations of Laon*[1]   From the eighth to the eleventh century Laon had everything necessary for its success as a place of learning as well as of government. It had a cathedral, a highly defensible situation, an imperial tradition, and a certain amount of commercial activity. From about 1070 to 1110 its cathedral had the most widely famous school in northern France. What then was the cause of its rapid scholastic decline in the early twelfth century? In answering this question, the main clue is provided by the plan of the city reproduced above: it had no convenient area of expansion. In particular, there was no space within the town for many schools nor for lodgings for numerous masters and pupils; and outside the town, there was no area for natural or easy development. Consequently its scholastic importance shrank, while that of Paris rapidly grew.

Nevertheless, the doctrines and methods developed in the cathedral school under Master Anselm during the fifty years from about 1070 to 1120 survived and flourished elsewhere, and particularly in the schools of Paris, and these will be treated in some detail in Volume II. So, even when the school declined into unimportance, the methods developed by its most famous master, Anselm of Laon, had a lasting influence on the future.[2]

[1] For an account of all aspects of the geographical and historical development of the city, see Carlrichard Brühl, *Palatium und Civitas*, vol. 1: *Gallien*, Vienna, 1975, where city plans, including the one shown here (which comes from Johannes Jansson, *Illustriorum regni Galliae civitatum Tabulae, c.* 1680), are magnificently reproduced.
[2] See pp. 127–9, for one typical example of the doctrinal importance of the school.

PLATE 2 *The scholastic opportunities of Paris*[1] The portion of a seventeenth-century plan of Paris reproduced here covers the Île Notre Dame and the area on the south bank of the River Seine, which in the twelfth century became – and still in large part is – the university area of the city. The primitive area of scholastic activity had been the eastern half of the Île where the cathedral and canons' houses were situated. From a scholastic point of view this area reached its climax with the building of the new bishop's palace with its large hall in about 1100. But there was no room on the Île for further scholastic growth. Thereafter the main area of scholastic activity during the twelfth and thirteenth centuries was on the south bank of the river. This area had been fairly densely populated during the later centuries of the Roman Empire, but it had fallen into almost total decay culminating in the destruction caused by the Viking ravages of the ninth and tenth centuries. These ravages left the whole area largely occupied by the ruins of the Roman city interspersed with vineyards, and with two ancient monasteries. One of these, St Germain-des-Prés, was on the west near the river, and the other, Ste Geneviève, was on the *Mont* to the south.

Scholastically the whole scene began to be transformed from the early years of the twelfth century with the growing demand for schools and lodgings for students and masters. The main stages seem to have been as follows:

1. The earliest known school on the south bank was the settlement of William of Champeaux in about 1108 on a deserted site which later became the Augustinian monastery of St Victor, where a very strong scholastic tradition was kept alive throughout the twelfth century.

2. From the early years of the twelfth century, schools were beginning to appear on the Petit Pont and along the roads served by this bridge, especially in the area round the churches of St Julien-le-Pauvre (which later became the meeting place of the Faculty of Arts), and St Séverin (which later became the meeting place of the Faculty of Theology).

3. Equally, and about at the same time, the area around Ste Geneviève was seen as a convenient position for scholastic development (notably by Abelard as early as 1110), and several masters had their schools in the general area of the vicus Ste-Geneviève and the rue des écoles by the middle years of the twelfth century.

4. From these beginnings, conglomerations of schools and lodgings inhabited by masters and their pupils become conspicuous along the roads leading up to Ste Geneviève, such as those later named rue des Écoles, rue de la Sorbonne, rue des Porées, and many others. This development, which continued until well into the thirteenth century, was particularly marked by the foundation (in about 1257) by Robert de Sorbon, chaplain of King Louis IX, of the College which bears his name.

[1] The much reduced map of Paris, showing the Île Notre Dame and the university area of the city on the south bank of the River Seine is derived from the plan of Paris by Olivier Truschet and Germain Hoyau in about 1550, reproduced in the *Collection de la Societé de l'histoire de Paris et de l'Île de France*. For a full account of the topography of medieval Paris, see H. Legrand, *Paris en 1380: Plans de Restitution*, in the *Histoire Generale de Paris*, Paris, 1868.

KEY: 1 Notre Dame; 2 St-Victor; 3 Ste-Geneviève; 4 Petit-Pont; 5 St-Julien-le-Pauvre; 6 St-Séverin; 7 St-Germain de Pres; 8 rue des écoles; 9 vicus Ste-Geneviève

PLATE 3 *The Apotheosis of a Parisian Master* [1] These two closely related pictures of Gilbert de la Porrée and his pupils appear at the beginning of a late twelfth-century manuscript of his works (Valenciennes, Bibliothèque municipale, MS 197), which formerly belonged to the monastery of St Amand. They commemorate a great master who, despite the fierce opposition of St Bernard, continued to have followers for about fifty years after his death.[2] The inscription which covers both pictures says that he is shown with three of his pupils, and that a fourth (on the following page of the original manuscript–shown above) is giving a fuller exposition of the master's more difficult points. All of them are named.

Dominating the scene is the great master himself wearing a mitre. This must not be taken to mean that he is lecturing as a bishop, for two of the pupils certainly, and all of them probably, were taught by him in Paris before he left to become bishop of Poitiers in 1142. The mitre therefore simply indicates his later greatness.

The pupils at his feet are: Ivo of Chartres (not the bishop, but a theological master in the Parisian schools from the 1140s to about 1170);[3] John Beleth (also a master in Paris, but one who with conspicuous success turned his scholastic training to the task of writing a work on the liturgical year;[4] and Jordan Fantosme (who became a member of the household of Henry, bishop of Salisbury, and wrote a long poem in French on King Henry II's war against the Scots in 1173–4). [5]

Then, on the next page of the manuscript, the superior pupil Nicholas (of Amiens) is shown expounding a text of the master.

Although all these pupils left works of their own, the last is the only one who significantly developed the technique and elaborated the views of the Master, while the others branched out in different directions. So here in pictorial outline we have a glorification of a great master who inspired pupils of very diverse characters and careers.

[1] For the late twelfth century MS (Bibliothèque Municipale, Valenciennes, MS 197, from which these pictures are taken), see P. Ratkowska, '*Inluminatio a pura sapientia*: Uwagi a Miniaturze MS 197 w Bibliothèque Municipale w Valenciennes', with French translation) in *Biuletyn Historii Sztuki*, 30, 1968, 337–45. (I owe this reference to Dr Martin Kauffmann of the Bodleian Library). Warm thanks are also due to the Conservateur of the Bibliotheque Municipale of Valenciennes for allowing the photographs to be made and reproduced here.
[2] For a survey of Gilbert's influence, see Lauge N. Nielsen, 1982.
[3] For Ivo's works, see B. Smalley, *Master Ivo of Chartres, Master at Paris*, EHR, vol. 50, 1935, pp. 680–6. And, for his teaching in Paris, see below p. 232.
[4] For an account of the manuscripts of the great work of John Beleth, see the edition of his *Summa de ecclesiasticis officiis*, ed. H. Douteil, CC, xli, 1976.
[5] For Jordan Fantosme's work see M. D. Legge, *Anglo-Norman Literature and its background*, Oxford, 1963, pp. 75–81.
[6] For Nicholas of Amiens's works, see Grabmann, ii, 431; and *PL*, vol. ccx, 595–618.

PLATE 4 *Gratian and the transmission of authorized power* Although Gratian's whole aim in his *Decretum* was to articulate in greater detail than ever before the procedures for enforcing the ordering of Christian life in all its external aspects and relationships, he left a doubt at the very summit of the whole subject – namely, the delimitation of the powers of the spiritual and secular rulers of the Christian society in making and enforcing these rules. Clearly this ambiguity could, and did, raise an increasing number of problems which grew with the passage of time. Questions which had seemed rather remote in 1140, when Gratian finished his work, had become very urgent a hundred years later, when the fundamental question of the origin of all secular authority had become a matter of practical importance: in brief the question whether secular authority came to lay rulers directly from God, or by way of delegation from the spiritual authority, began to have urgent practical implications.

The two illustrations reproduced here come from two of the large number of lavishly illustrated manuscripts of Gratian's *Decretum* which began to appear in

the thirteenth century. In the first of these pictures (at the beginning of Gratian's *Decretum* in the fourteenth-century MS. clm 23552, f1, in the Bavarian Staats bibliotek, Munich), all legitimate power to rule mankind on earth is shown as coming down from God through the hierarchies of Seraphim, Cherubim, and Thrones; Dominions, Virtues and Powers; Principalities, Archangels, Angels; and then – at the point of transition from the eternal to the temporal order, where human society enters into the picture – the duty of ruling mankind is split between *spiritual* power, which is committed to the Pope, who apportions this authority to cardinals, archbishops and bishops, down to priests and the lower orders of clergy; and *secular* power, which is committed to the Emperor, and to Kings, lower nobility, and their varied officers of justice and law. So, according to this solution of the problem of power, there is a firm division made by God between the spiritual authority of the ecclesiastical hierarchy, and the secular authority of the hierarchy of lay rulers.

But the other picture (from the British Library, London, MS. Add. 15274, f.3ᵛ), at the beginning of Gratian's work, gives an entirely different answer. It leaves out the elaborate descent of power through the heavenly hierarchies, and simply shows all power of rule being committed by God to the Pope who distributes ecclesiastical power on his right hand to cardinals, bishops and lesser clergy, and secular power on his left hand to the varying grades of lay authorities from Emperor down to local secular officials.

This may seem a somewhat abstruse and remote question, but it opens up a very large practical issue indeed. On the first of these alternatives, secular rulers, though lower in dignity than the ecclesiastical hierarchy, hold their power from God, and disputes about the exact division in practice is left to be decided by mutual agreement. But, in the second picture, all authority both spiritual and secular, is placed in the hands of the Pope, and is distributed by him to the ecclesiastical hierarchy on his right hand, and to the secular hierarchy on his left hand; and this solution to the problem was being extensively supported by scholars towards the end of the thirteenth century, not least by the former lawyer Pope Boniface VIII who, in however cursory a fashion, expressed it in his bull *Clericis Laicos* of 25 February 1296. (for which see below, p. 286).

PLATE 5 *Irnerius and the Countess Matilda of Tuscany*[1] This picture occupies part of a wall in the early seventeenth-century decorations of the palace of the dukes of Tuscany at Sassuola, about forty miles west of Bologna. It shows the Countess Matilda and her husband conferring with Irnerius in surroundings which are certainly not scholastic. Justinian's Code lies on the table between them. The picture, therefore, despite its late date, recalls Irnerius's role in the lawsuits, politics and practical affairs of northern Italy to which contemporary documents also bear witness,[2] in contrast to the academic image with which he has been almost invariably associated from the mid-twelfth century onwards.

[1] I owe my knowledge of the picture in Sassuola to the book in which Enrico Spargnesi (see below, p. 278, n. 15) reproduces it together with some samples of the documents of the Emperor Henry V in which Warnerius appears as a witness. For information about the context of the picture, I am indebted to Elizabeth McGrath of the Warburg Institute, London, who refers also to A. Venturi, *Affreschi della 'delizia' estense di Sassuola* in *L'Arte*, xx, 1917, 65–98, which I have been unable to see; and to Ginny Stroud-Lewis for obtaining the reproduction with permission to print it.

[2] For the contemporary documents in which Irnerius appears, see below, pp. 278–9.

Part Two

Turning Doctrine into Law

7

The Outlook
in Northern Europe

I TRUTH AND TRUTH-ENFORCEMENT

The detailed clarification and systematization of doctrine necessary for forming and ensuring uniformity of faith in western Christendom was largely the work of the schools of northern France, and I have briefly traced the stages in assembling the forces necessary for this task. The individual efforts by which the main outlines were drawn will be the subject of chapters in the next volume of this work. But, before going further, it is necessary to recognize that there was a practical as well as a theoretical side to this enterprise. Nobody thought that it was sufficient to clarify doctrine, to organize the results in a systematic way, and then to leave these results to be accepted and given practical expression by the exercise of individual choice. Truth had to be authoritative in practice as well as in theory.

Therefore, after the schools had done their work of doctrinal clarification, it was the duty of those in authority to ensure that truths about God, redemption and damnation, and the conduct necessary for salvation, were known by all members of the western Church, and were – at least publicly – acted upon in all the appropriate ways in baptism, confirmation, the Eucharist, confession, marriage, and obedience to the laws of the Church. To fail to bring into existence, to the furthest limit of the possible, a uniformity of practice in accordance with authoritative statements of the truth would have nullified the gifts that had been bestowed upon mankind, and would have invited divine judgements of the kind that were abundantly demonstrated in the Old Testament, not to say in all that had happened to the world since then.

Consequently the task of ensuring universal observance, in practice as well as belief, of the truths which had been refined in the schools and incorporated in legislation, was imposed on all persons in positions of authority, whether ecclesiastical or lay. Apart from the alternative church of the Cathars,[1] there was little or no opposition in principle to the view that authoritative doctrines and the disciplines associated with them should be translated into practical rules to be enforced by both secular and spiritual rulers. The only real question was not whether these rules of faith and practice should be enforced or not, but what legal procedures should be followed in carrying out this duty, and how the responsibility should be divided between the ecclesiastical and secular rulers of western Christian society.

In a crude way this ideal of translating doctrine into law had been a conspicuous feature of all government since the time of the conversion of the rulers of barbarian Europe to Christianity. When the ruler was converted, those whom he ruled were baptized and came under the discipline of the received faith. Long before the new disciplines of the schools had brought more precise definition and a greater degree of system into the doctrines of the Church, conformity of faith and practice in religion was a recognized part of the life of western Europe, and this aim of general conformity was supported by a multitude of decisions of emperors and kings, popes and bishops, and of general and local councils, all of them seeking to lay down rules of behaviour in accordance with orthodox faith. Naturally decisions on these subjects were very scattered both in time and place, and by the mid-eleventh century, with the beginning of a new era of general expansion and material growth, the need was beginning to be felt for fuller, better arranged, and more clearly authoritative collections of texts. Only in this way could rulers of every kind

---

[1] The history of this very widespread heresy and way of life lies outside the scope of this study as does that of the officially tolerated but increasingly persecuted Jewish community.

have sufficiently detailed and reliable guidance in enforcing the manifold decisions of popes, kings, bishops, councils and the Fathers of the Church at many different times and occasions.

There were indeed already in existence several collections of material, which had been made for this purpose. Two of the most important of these will be examined presently, but before looking at these collections it will be well to consider the general nature of the society for which they were intended and the difficulties of enforcement. In the turbulent condition of western Europe from the sixth to the eleventh centuries, when threats of invasion and resettlements of large populations were a fairly constant feature of European life, decisions haphazardly taken and locally enforced were the best that could be hoped for, and they were generally associated with meeting immediate dangers.[2] But gradually, from about 1050 onwards, there was a possibility – and, if a possibility, then a duty – not only of systematizing the doctrinal decisions of the past, but also of producing a more detailed and universal system of oversight and enforcement than had ever been possible before.

The form that this enforcement would take, and the hierarchy of authorities under which it would be administered, still needed to be clarified. At almost every level of power, those in authority – pope, archbishops and bishops, emperor, kings, marquises, earls, counts and city communes – were claiming increased authority, and none of them thought that heresy or unbelief lay outside their areas of concern. The real problem was not whether to enforce uniformity of faith and conduct, but by whom the enforcement was to be exercised, and by what processes it was to be achieved. The boundaries of authority were at every point unclear. It was clear to most observers that, at the highest level, the pope had claims to definitive authority over doctrine and religious practice far more explicit than those of any other claimant. But a general recognition of papal primacy left room for many doubts about the extent to which it could ordinarily be exercised over archbishops and bishops, or over emperors and kings who also had claims to be 'vicars of Christ' within their own territories – claims, moreover, which

---

[2] For examples, see above, pp. 148–56.

had been formulated long before the popes claimed this title as their special prerogative.[3]

In the midst of all these difficulties, it was clearly necessary first to collect the decisions of the past, then to analyse them with a view to clarifying their scope and reconciling any apparent contradictions, and finally to arrange the reconciled texts in systematic form. These were the stages through which all doctrinal discussion had to pass, and the masters of the northern French schools had worked out very successful rules of verbal and argumentative analysis for reconciling apparent contradictions in the doctrines of authoritative texts. But, where practical enforcement was concerned, it was necessary to agree not only on the doctrine to be enforced, but also on the authority responsible for enforcing practices compatible with doctrine and for punishing dissidents.

Then, too, quite apart from the division of duties between these varied authorities, there was the further problem of providing effective procedures for communicating decisions and bringing them to bear on individual cases.

If we take our stand in the mid-eleventh century – say in the year 1059, to which on several occasions we have reverted as a pivotal moment for revealing various aspects of the quest for a new order affecting the lives of every individual in western European society – we shall better appreciate the difficulty of assembling and organizing the material, and the still greater difficulty of enforcement. In this year, a council in Rome, presided over by the recently elected Pope Nicholas II, and convoked at short notice with no advance publicity and no attempt to summon representatives from various parts of western Europe outside Italy, took four decisions of very great practical importance at widely different levels of generality.

First, it laid down a new procedure for papal elections which put all effective power into the hands of the cardinal-bishops, and effectively excluded the emperor from his traditional

---

3 For a detailed study of this change of usage, see above p. 142 and the literature cited there.

influence in future elections. Second, it definitively pronounced the nullity of marriages of clergy from the rank of deacon upwards. Third, it limited, and prepared the way for excluding, lay intervention in ecclesiastical appointments. And, finally, it was the occasion for the first condemnation of an important master of a cathedral school, Berengar of Tours, who had applied the rules of his scholastic subject to the definition of the change in the Bread and Wine in the Eucharist.[4]

These decisions touched four points of very great importance in moulding the thought and practice of all rulers and every individual in western Europe, with the single exception of the growing Jewish communities which were beginning to be established in most important towns throughout western Europe. Yet, though nearly everyone was affected by these decisions, they had virtually no circulation beyond the range of those who were present at the Council. And this essential limitation was not peculiar to the hastily summoned Council of 1059: it was a practical limitation that was first overcome in 1139, when a general council was summoned which had been carefully planned to bring representatives from many parts of western Europe, to take decisions covering a wide field of doctrine and practice, and then – in a new way to which we shall come later – to give a wide publicity to its main decisions.[5]

Until that date, when councils had been held and decisions of great importance had been taken, there was no means for conveying them to even the highest levels of either ecclesiastical or lay authorities. Indeed, not only was there no method of conveying decisions to a wider public, there was even a sense in which only those who were present felt a personal obligation to obey them.

I have remarked elsewhere on the astonishing fact that when St Anselm, having been prior, then abbot, of a distinguished monastery in Normandy for thirty years, became archbishop of Canterbury in 1093, he was unaware that the procedure

---

[4] For further details, see Southern, 1990, pp. 44–50. For the predominantly Italian participants at the Council, see D. Jasper, *Das Papstwahldekret von 1059*, Sigmaringen, 1986, pp. 110–19.
[5] See below, pp. 294–5.

by which he had been chosen and invested as archbishop was contrary to papal directives at least fifteen years old, and was in fact clearly schismatical.[6] It was only Anselm's personal presence at the Vatican Council of 1099, when Urban II unexpectedly excommunicated all who associated with clergy who had received ecclesiastical offices by lay investiture, that Anselm recognized – with an inflexibility that embarrassed Urban II's successor – his personal obligation to observe this ruling. Anselm was certainly no anti-papalist, though he was also no enthusiast for the recent claims of authority over archbishops which had been made by popes during the past twenty years. He was willing, as many other bishops were not, to obey whatever rules a pope had laid down for him personally, but he recognized no obligation to enforce them on others. Indeed the whole history of his years as archbishop draws attention to a range of obstacles to the enforcement of papal decisions: the lack of a satisfactory collection of earlier decisions, the absence of any regular mode of communicating decisions to local churches, the uncertain commitment of even a papally well-disposed archbishop to enforce decisions. In the presence of such uncertainties as these, the absence of a coherent system of courts and procedures capable of applying general decisions to individual cases scarcely mattered.

To produce a coherent, detailed and systematic body of orthodox doctrine was difficult enough, but this problem was being dealt with more or less spontaneously in the schools of northern France. To create a legal system capable of giving practical effect to an already vast and ever-growing but ill-defined body of decisions and directives was a much more complicated business than might appear on the surface. It required not only an integration of the whole mass of ancient and recent rules and procedures, but also a mechanism of enforcement which was very difficult to bring into existence, and still more difficult to operate. This last requirement could only be met by a universal system of law, and this was contrary to the whole development of northern Europe since the collapse of the Roman Empire. The

---

6 For details of this incident, see Southern, 1990, pp. 265-9; and for a further illustration of legal ignorance, see below, pp. 261-3.

technical problems of collection, refinement and integration of the material could be overcome by scholars and schools. But the wider problem of unifying divergent local traditions could be solved only by the creation and acceptance in practice of a new legal system. This situation requires some elucidation before going any further.

II Law and Society in Northern Europe

Since the fifth century, the whole area north of the Alps and Pyrenees had with few exceptions been an area of customary law modified in various particulars by interjections of imperial, royal, archiepiscopal and episcopal decisions and decrees. Except in the area of Languedoc, Roman law had left no imprint, and such unity as northern Europe possessed came from family connections and aristocratic traditions which provided more cohesion than the very frequent state of war might suggest. Although the members of the aristocracy were often in conflict with one another, they had a unity of outlook and origins which was more important than any temporary conflicts. Their wars, which occupy so great a space in the chronicles of the ninth, tenth and eleventh centuries, were chiefly symptomatic of the gradual breakdown of the unity of the Carolingian family. Below the surface of violence, the rulers, both secular and spiritual, were variously interrelated by marriages, past, present or planned. Marriages were the cement that held their society together and, as a result of their community of interests and family ties, both lay and ecclesiastical magnates were content that their affairs should be carried on within a well-established routine of custom. It was the main purpose of their councils and of the procedures of their law courts to enforce rules which were not less binding for being in the main unwritten.

An important contributory cause of the relative stability of this state of affairs was an absence of great towns which would have introduced complicated problems of commercial wealth and urban powers. There were indeed some notable towns along the Rhine and Meuse, but even they, like the countryside as a whole, were dominated by the great territorial magnates.

The only potentially universal authorities in northern Europe were the emperor and the pope: but the Empire – so far as it had ever been a source of unified government beyond the limits of the territorial possessions of successive emperors – was a spent force by the early twelfth century. As for the papacy, although recognized as the general source of ecclesiastical order, it was widely understood that this did not diminish the practical responsibility of the local hierarchies of lay and ecclesiastical authorities except in very exceptional circumstances. It followed from this that, although there were several legal compilations current in the whole area of northern Europe, these had not been made with a view to administration by a central authority: they were for the guidance of individual archbishops and bishops who looked on themselves as virtually autonomous rulers within the areas of their responsibilities.

Among these compilations, there were two which deserve a brief characterization, for they were quite widely distributed and they set out the duties, doctrines and functions of ecclesiastical – and in some degree of secular – rulers with considerable amplitude. A brief account of their contents will illustrate both their virtues and limitations as general codes of law. I shall start with the later of the two because it provides a body of rules for all persons who were not monks or nuns, and it outlines better than any other document the laws governing the Christian life as understood in northern Europe before the scholastic age.

1 The collection of Burchard, bishop of Worms, c. 1020[7]

This work is a well-ordered collection of texts from many different sources covering almost every area of non-monastic religious life. It is arranged in twenty Books, and a simple list of the

---

7   For Burchard's *Decretum*, see *PL*, 140, 537–1058. Various aspects of date, use of sources, and widespread use are summarized by F. Pelster in *Das Dekret Bischofs Burchard von Worms in Vaticanischen HSS*, in *Miscellanea G. Mercati*, Vatican City, 1946, 114–57, and in *Das Dekret Burkhards von Worms in einer Redaktion aus dem Begin der Gregorischen Reform*, in *Studi Gregoriani*, i, Rome, 1947, pp. 321–51. For an account of the organization and contents of Burchard's work, see P. Fournier and G. le Bras, *Histoire des Collections canoniques en Occident depuis les fausses Décrétales jusqu'au Décret de Gratien*, Paris, 2 vols, 1931–2.

subject-matter of the first four and last four will give a sufficient indication of the widely-ranging scope of the work.

The first four Books deal with:

1. The pope, archbishops, and bishops: their election, qualifications, and powers;
2. Holy orders in all their aspects;
3. Churches, their altars, masses, burials, powers of sanctuary, and necessary books;
4. Baptism, catechumens, confirmation; and the position of the unbaptized element (the Jews) in a baptized society.

And the last four are on:

17. Fornication;
18. Visiting the sick, with a liturgy for their use;
19. Penance (much the longest section of the whole work);
20. Contemplation.

These eight chapters comprise about a half of the whole work, and their contents will suffice to show that, although the work is broadly 'legal' in the sense that it describes the powers of those in holy orders and the duties of all Christians, several of the subjects, especially in the later books, were outside the range of any available, or even possible, legal process. Further, as to the authority of the contents, Burchard drew his material with a liberal hand from sources of every kind: from papal letters and councils; from local councils, especially those held in northern France and Germany in the presence of the Carolingian kings and emperors; and from the works of the Fathers, especially Augustine and Gregory the Great. All these are unexceptionable sources. But there are also quotations from works of indefinable status; and often, even when the names of his authorities are unexceptionable, Burchard fails to give any easily identifiable reference, and several which he gives have defied all efforts of identification by modern scholars with all the apparatus of learning available to them. Then, on top of these sources of uncertainty, Burchard sometimes altered texts in order to make them more serviceable.

These ambiguities of sources and authorities meant that, with all its merits, Burchard's work could never have been useful in a court of law; nor was it intended to be. It was essentially a handbook of rich and varied interest for bishops and archbishops to interpret as seemed to them best in the circumstances of each case. The whole work is simply a well-organized guide to a complicated mixture of ancient wisdom, patristic doctrine, and decisions of local authorities, with occasional interventions from the distant authority of popes and general councils. Only in the most general sense can it be looked on as a law book. It belongs rather to an old tradition of pastoral handbooks, of which Gregory the Great's *Pastoral Care* is the most eminent. Such books were of immense value for the guidance of prelates, perhaps of princes, but they were not intended to be, and could never have been, textbooks for systematic legal study or for use in law courts.

These few remarks may, for our present purpose, suffice as a characterization of Burchard's work. But, in addition, something must be said about another northern European compilation, also widely current in the eleventh century, which at first sight seems to have, in a way that Burchard's work did not, the stamp of precise and unchallengeable authority necessary for a legal text-book. An equally brief description of this work will suffice to indicate that it too, imposing though its claims are at first sight, also has limitations of its own, chiefly arising from its great bulk and lack of guidance as to its contents, which make it quite unsuitable as a textbook for teaching in schools or for use in law courts.

2 *The pseudo-Isidorian collection*[8]

In judging this work and its suitability as an authoritative legal textbook, we must begin by discounting the characteristic to

[8] For the text of ps-Isidore, see P. Hinschius, *Decretales Pseudo-Isidorianae*, Leipzig, 1863; and for an analysis of their sources, Fuhrmann, 1972–4, i, 167–94.

which it owes its modern epithet: 'pseudo'. It is irrelevant that, as we happen to know but as was unknown in the Middle Ages, it was neither compiled by the Isidore whose name stands on the title page, and who could plausibly be identified as the great seventh-century bishop of Seville, nor were its contents to be relied on as coming from the sources to which they are ascribed. It was the work of a group of ninth-century scholars; and many of its impressive sequence of papal letters and conciliar decrees – in particular all the documents attributed to the popes of the first four centuries of Christian history, and several of the letters attributed to later popes – are forgeries.

These are weighty facts for modern scholars, but they were unknown in the Middle Ages and must, therefore, be ignored in discussing the extent to which these texts provided authoritative rules capable of meeting the needs of the new European society which was coming into existence in the later years of the eleventh century.

Looked at from the point of view of its medieval readers, its large bulk of documents from the earliest Christian centuries gave it unshakeable force and *gravitas*. Indeed, from any point of view, its picture of the stability and elaboration of papal authority in the government of Christian society during the first seven centuries of its existence, and the very imposing bulk of texts would – forgery apart – offer as solid a foundation for the government of Christendom as could be desired. A very brief account of its contents will suffice to make clear the range of activities which it covers, while also making clear the difficulty of using the texts it contains as guidelines for the government of western Europe. It was arranged in three parts:

1. Papal letters purporting to have been written by a succession of popes from Linus, the first successor of St Peter, to Pope Miltiades in the early fourth century.
2. Decrees of councils from the Council of Nicea in 325 to the third Council of Constantinople in 680–681, together with the 'Donation of Constantine' in which the emperor was represented as giving all the imperial lands and rights in Italy to Pope Silvester I and his successors;

3. Papal letters from the early fourth century to Gregory II (714–731).

On the understanding that all these documents were genuine, no more solid testimony to the steady development of papal authority, and of the combined roles of popes, archbishops and bishops in the government of the Church could ever be found. The three parts of the pseudo-Isidorian collection presented a body of apparently unassailable papal and conciliar legislation as a basis for an authoritative system of canon law, and the schools of northern France – simply by following the methods whereby they produced a systematic body of theological doctrine during the period from about 1075 to 1150 – might surely have produced the outlines of a systematic body of ecclesiastical law from the material in the pseudo-Isidorian collection combined with Burchard's *Decretum* and a few ancillary collections.

So we must ask: why did this not happen? The question is not easy to answer. It is true that the pseudo-Isidorian collection, while being (on its own showing and in the eyes of all its readers) wonderfully well anchored in unimpeachable authority, is an immensely bulky and wholly unsystematic jungle of documents, often of great length and diffuseness, through which every individual reader had to hack his own way. Its very lengthy texts lacked any indication of subject matter, and there was no index or any other aid to following a single subject from one document to another. Although its chronological arrangement makes a great appeal to a modern historical mind, this had the drawback that it made its systematic use extremely difficult. Nevertheless, these difficulties are certainly not greater than those which faced the theological commentators on biblical texts, who – by about the year 1120 – were succeeding in producing, on the one hand, detailed glosses on the texts with comments and illustrative quotations from other sources; and, on the other hand, systematically arranged illustrative extracts from the texts, with clarifications of the problems which they raised. And they had succeeded in doing this in the face of difficulties that were certainly no less complicated than those which had to be faced in undertaking any similar enterprise in the field of canon law.

So, if the will to comment, to rearrange, to select and to

systematize had been there, results not dissimilar from those obtained by analysing biblical and theological texts could have been elicited from these collections of legal and semi-legal texts. We must therefore ask more deeply why this was not done.

The answer seems to be that, whereas there was a long tradition of making extracts and commentaries on biblical and patristic texts in the cathedrals and monasteries of northern Europe and whereas, in the eleventh century, these operations began to be conducted with increasing refinement in schools which drew masters and students from all parts of Europe, there was no similar tradition, nor any impulse to create a tradition, of glossing, analysing and finally systematizing legal texts. So far as any reason can be alleged for this state of affairs, it seems simply to be that there was no strong sense of a need for such a work. The legal processes of the whole area of northern Europe were either customary or (as in ordeals) supernatural. Neither of these called for refinements in documentary interpretation, nor did they allow for any regular system of appeal to a higher court. Moreover, bishops and archbishops felt themselves sufficiently capable of interpreting the texts to meet most requirements. If in doubt, they could on occasion refer a problem to the pope, or – more probably – to a neighbouring bishop.

The situation with regard to ecclesiastical law in northern Europe did not indeed stand still throughout the period from 1050 to 1125. But the attempts that were made to keep ecclesiastical law up to date resulted in modifications or improvements of Burchard and pseudo-Isidore rather than in an attempt to produce something much fuller or quite different. The effects of this state of affairs can be exemplified by examining the use of pseudo-Isidore and Burchard by the two scholars in northern Europe who were better equipped than any others to make the ecclesiastical law of their time effective in ways that would be approved by northern European prelates.

These two scholars were Lanfranc, who was archbishop of Canterbury from 1070 to 1089; and Ivo, Lanfranc's pupil at Bec around 1060, who in about 1078 became abbot of the community of clergy, or 'canons regular', on the outskirts of Beauvais, and then bishop of Chartres from 1090 until 1115. As northern ecclesiastical rulers, and both in different ways reformers, the compilations of ecclesiastical law which they made, used, and circulated for use by their contemporaries, are the main monuments of canon law in northern Europe between about 1050 and 1120. So their characteristics require a brief examination as representing what we may call the summits of northern European legal scholarship.

III Summits of Northern European Legal Scholarship, c. 1050–1120

1 Lanfranc at Bec and Canterbury[9]

Lanfranc was by training a lawyer in Pavia, which in his youth was the greatest legal and administrative centre in northern Italy.[10] The governmental importance of the city was rapidly collapsing in the 1020s, and Lanfranc – like many able men after him – abandoned his native land for northern France. In making this move, he abandoned law for the study of grammar and logic; and after a period of very close association with Berengar in the Loire valley, he set up his own school at Avranches. Then he experienced a religious conversion which led to his becoming a monk, and almost at once prior, at Bec in about 1042.

Despite his monastic conversion, the financial needs of the

[9]   The best general account of Lanfranc's abbreviated copy of ps-Isidore and its later circulation in England is still to be found in Z. N. Brooke, *The English Church and the Papacy from the Conquest to the reign of John*, Cambridge, 1931, pp. 57–83, 231–5. For the nature of Lanfranc's selection, see Fuhrmann, ii, 19–22. For Lanfranc in general, see Gibson, 1978.

[10]   A deeply perceptive remark made by F. Schulz, and reported in Southern, 1948, p. 29, deserves repetition here as setting to rest the doubts that continue to be raised about Lanfranc's early career as a lawyer in Pavia. Lanfranc, at Bec *c.* 1050, commenting on the word *parentibus* in 1 Tim. 5:4, explained the passage thus: '*Parentes' vocat quos superius 'filios et nepotes'. Tota enim progenies parentela dicitur, unde et in mundana lege parens parenti per gradum et parentelam succedere iubetur.* Dr Schulz – surely rightly – detected here a quotation from *c.* 153 of the Edict of Rotheri: *parens parenti per gradum et parentillam heres succedat* (*MGH, Leg.* iv, 35). Thus a single sentence illuminates Lanfranc's recollection of the laws with which he had been familiar in his youth. As for the grounds of Lanfranc's leaving Pavia, the abrupt decline in Pavia's role in northern Italy after 1020 has been brilliantly illuminated by Carlrichard Brühl, 'Das palatium von Pavia und die *Honorantiae civitatis Papiae*', reprinted in *Aus Mittelalter und Diplomatik: gesammelte Aufsätze*, 1989, i, pp. 138–69.

monastery – and no doubt his own intellectual interests – caused him to continue teaching grammar and logic in association with the study of biblical texts, and to accept pupils from many parts of Europe who had no intention of becoming monks. In addition, his immensely capacious ability also led to his becoming the Duke of Normandy's chief adviser in ecclesiastical affairs by the mid-1050s. In this capacity his main task was to get papal consent to the duke's uncanonical marriage with the daughter of the Count of Flanders. This marriage was an essential link in the chain of alliances necessary for ensuring success in the coming struggle for the kingdom of England for which Duke William of Normandy had long prepared, and it was perhaps this new range of duties which caused Lanfranc to return to the legal interests that he had abandoned in Pavia forty years earlier.

The law with which he was now concerned was not the hybrid Roman and municipal law of northern Italy, but canon law. For this he turned, not to Burchard, but to the substantial and long-continuing, more or less chronologically arranged, sequence of conciliar decrees and papal letters from the first to the eighth centuries which were to be found in pseudo-Isidore. From this huge mass of material Lanfranc made (or possibly found already made) a copious selection which served his main purpose of having at his disposal a basic body of material on ecclesiastical discipline and organization at many different levels.

Whether or not he himself made this selection of material, he was certainly responsible for the marginal symbols with which he annotated his copy and which frequently reappear in later copies. These symbols, which generally take the form of a simple '.A.' (presumably meaning something like *Attende*), clearly draw attention to important passages, but the nature of their importance is never explained. Perhaps Lanfranc kept a separate notebook in which his annotations were more fully explained; but, if so, it has not survived, and he has left not the slightest trace, either in his own copy of pseudo-Isidore or anywhere else, that he ever made critical notes or comments on these texts similar to those which he had made on the Pauline Epistles.

What is clear is that he regarded this collection of documents as a necessary – and apparently sufficient – work of reference for his administration when he became an archbishop, for he bought his original manuscript from the monks of Bec and caused copies to be very widely distributed among the English bishoprics under his jurisdiction.[11] So this was the book that he thought bishops should have to help them in their episcopal administration. Yet, lawyer though he was by origin, he showed not the slightest interest in commenting on the texts or explaining them. He simply looked on his pseudo-Isidorian collection as an administrative tool, and apparently as a sufficient legal tool, which every bishop should possess.

Lanfranc, therefore, took the same view of ecclesiastical law as other contemporary prelates in northern Europe – that is to say, he did not look on the texts preserved in pseudo-Isidore as texts for critical study; certainly not as texts for lawyers practising in ecclesiastical law courts; least of all as an instrument for promoting a centralized, papally administered, legal system. They were a source of practical guidance for prelates in dealing with problems of ecclesiastical administration. No more.

If we now ask whether this attitude was peculiar to Lanfranc or whether younger or more far-sighted prelates had a different view, the question can be answered by turning to Lanfranc's pupil Ivo, the best scholar in canon law in northern Europe before the great transformation of the subject by Gratian (of whom more presently), which – in association with the transformation of the Arts and theology in the schools of Paris – introduced a new phase in the government of Europe.

2 Ivo at Bec, Laon, and Chartres[12]

As a starting point it is important to understand Ivo's background. He was born, probably about 1040, into a modest, probably knightly, family in the area of Beauvais in northern France, and he seems always to have felt most at home in

---

11   For a list of surviving copies, see Brooke, 1931, pp. 231–5.
12   For Ivo as canonist, see R. Sprandel, *Ivo v. Chartres u. seine Stellung in den Kan. Geschichte*, Stuttgart, 1962. For the sources and influence of the canon law collections attributed to Ivo, see Martin Brett, 'Urban II and the collections attributed to Ivo of Chartres', in *Monumenta Iuris Canonici*, ser. C, subsidia, ix, 1989, pp. 27–46.

the intellectual and social environment of this society. As for his education, the mid-twelfth century chronicler and abbot of Mont-St-Michel, Robert de Torigni, asserts that he studied in the school which Lanfranc had established at Bec. Normally, it must be said, the testimony of a chronicler writing some eighty years after the event would not deserve much credence, but in this case the chronicler was an exceptionally careful historian with a special interest in noting important moments in the intellectual development of western Europe; and he had from childhood been a monk of Bec. All things considered, it is very likely that he reported a reliable tradition.[13]

Moreover, Ivo would have arrived at the school at Bec during the years between about 1055 and 1060 when Lanfranc's interests were turning from the biblical studies of his middle years to canon law and then to his controversy with Berengar. We know nothing in detail about Ivo's studies at Bec, and not much about his studies during the thirty years between his leaving the school at Bec and becoming bishop of Chartres in 1090. But the main outline of his interests and the influences to which he was exposed can be traced in three separate sources: his theological *Sententiae*, his collection of canon law texts, and his letters.

We must begin with his theological *Sententiae*, for they provide the earliest surviving records of his studies, and they make it likely that, at some stage – probably in the 1070s or later –

[13] For Ivo's studying at Bec under Lanfranc, see *The Chronicle of Robert of Torigni*, ed. R. Howlett, in *Chronicles of the reigns of Stephen, Henry II and Richard I, Rolls Series*, London, 1889, vol. 4, p. 100. For further additions to the Chronicle, on the growth of legal learning from Lanfranc to Vacarius, see below, pp. 276, and 296n. One reason for thinking that Ivo knew Lanfranc's copy of pseudo-Isidore is that Lanfranc's only substantial addition to his copy is a collection of documents connected with the Council of 1059 which includes Berengar's oath renouncing his doctrine of the Eucharist. The terms of this oath were later refined and recorded in Gregory VII's *Register*, pp. 426–7, at the time of Berengar's final condemnation in 1079. But in his *Decretum*, ii, c. 10, Ivo still quotes this oath in the earlier form preserved by Lanfranc and not in the amended form. Since Gratian (*de Consecratione* D. 2, c. 42) took his text of Berengar's oath from Ivo, it was in its 1059 form that the oath became the common property of western Christendom. I have made further comments on Lanfranc's presence at the 1059 Council, in Southern, 1990, pp. 14–29.

he was closely associated with the school at Laon where Master Anselm taught from about 1070 till his death in 1117.[14]

In order to understand these *Sententiae*, it is necessary to know, first, that the teaching at Laon appears to have consisted of detailed expositions of a text in the morning, followed by more informal discussion of miscellaneous problems arising from the text in the evening; then, second, that Master Anselm had begun his teaching career at Laon by lecturing on texts in grammar and perhaps also in logic; but by the 1080s he was mainly lecturing on various books of the Bible, and in particular on the Psalms and Epistles.[15] The informal evening discussions would then concern theological problems that had arisen from the text expounded in the morning's lecture. The subjects for discussion would often be very miscellaneous, and it is clear from the large number of surviving reports of the answers given by the master and others that the students made notes, and later circulated their records of the proposed solutions. Among these notes are found solutions proposed by other masters associated with the school at Laon: in particular, Master Anselm's brother and successor, Ralph; his most important pupil William of Champeaux; and (in order of frequency after those I have

14 For Ivo's contributions to the *Sententiae* of the school of Anselm of Laon, see F. P. Bliemetzrieder, *Zu den Schriften Ivos von Chartres*, Kaiserliche Akademie der Wissenschaften in Wien, Phil.-Hist. Kl., vol. 182, 1917, pp. 51–71; see also Bliemetzrieder, *Anselms von Laon Systematische Sentenzen*, BGPMA, vol. xviii, 2–3, 1919; also, H. Weisweiler, *Das Schrifttum der Schule Anselms von Laon und Wilhelms von Champeaux in deutschen Bibliotheken*, BGPMA, xxxiii, 1936; and O. Lottin, *Psychologie et Morale aux XIIe et XIIIe Siècles*, vol. 5, 1959, pp. 10–12, 136, 250, 392. Margaret Gibson, *Lanfranc of Bec*, Oxford, 1978, p. 36 also draws attention to Ivo's notes on Exod. 29, 2–3, in Oxford, Bodleian Library, MS Laud misc. 216, f. 2v. The extent of Ivo's involvement in the theological collections of the school of Laon may be judged from the following statistics. Two of the main composite collections of *Sententiae* of the school of Laon are MSS Troyes MS 425 and Avranches MS 19. Of the attributed quotations in the Troyes MS, 71 are from Master Anselm, 42 from his main pupil William of Champeaux, 29 from Ivo of Chartres, 3 from Ralph, Anselm's brother and successor as master of the school, and 1 from Lanfranc. In Avranches MS 19, 52 *Sententiae* are attributed to Master Anselm, 50 to William of Champeaux, 17 to Ivo, 3 to Ralph, and 1 to Lanfranc. In brief, although Ivo was not a central contributor to the theological *Sententiae* of the school at Laon, his contributions are more numerous than any except those of Master Anselm himself and William of Champeaux.
15 The work and influence of Anselm of Laon will be dealt with in greater detail in Volume II.

named) Ivo of Chartres. Just where Ivo fits into the school of
Laon, it is impossible to say, but one of the notable features
of Ivo's contributions is that they show a marked emphasis on
those areas where religion impinges on practical life – and in
particular the buying and selling of benefices.

Then a final element in Ivo's life during these pre-episcopal
years is that in 1078 the bishop of Beauvais made him abbot
of a new kind of religious community following the Rule of St
Augustine, in the suburbs of his episcopal town, which was also
the town or neighbourhood from which Ivo came. Such communities, leading a corporate life much simpler in their liturgical
obligations, with meagre endowments compared with the earlier
great Benedictine monasteries, and generally closely connected
with growing urban centres, were one of the great innovations
of the later years of the eleventh century in their emphasis on
modesty of life, close contact with urban centres, and religious
life in its most ordinary circumstances.[16]

So what, we may ask, do these scattered fragments of information about Ivo's background contribute towards understanding his view of the task of turning doctrine into law?

In the first place, they help to explain why he was more
concerned with the strictly local scene than Lanfranc. Lanfranc,
in becoming a monk, had thoroughly abandoned the world, but
as a member of a Benedictine monastery, and still more as
the archiepiscopal head of the ancient monastic community at
Canterbury, he belonged to a grander world than Ivo either as
abbot of a semi-urban Augustinian community at Beauvais or as
bishop of Chartres. Humble though Lanfranc seems to have been
in his personal life, there was nothing humble in his conception
of the ecclesiastical organization to which he belonged or of his
own position in it. Lanfranc saw every issue in its grandest
dimensions, whether in taking on the task of defending the
Eucharistic formula reached at the Roman Council of 1059, or in
his root-and-branch reorganization of the monastic community

[16] A good general account of the nature of this new monastic order is J. C.
Dickinson, *The origins of the Austin Canons and their introduction into England*,
London, 1950; at a deeper level, see Horst Fuhrmann, *Papst Urban II und der Stand
der Regularkanoniker*, *Sitzungsberichte der Bayerischen Akademie*, Munich, 1984.

at Canterbury, or in his very grandiose view of the powers of his archbishopric of Canterbury. The central features of his world-view consisted of great kingdoms, great archbishoprics, great conciliar pronouncements guaranteeing doctrinal certainty. He saw everything, except the role of the papacy, on a grand scale.

By contrast, Ivo viewed the ruling bodies of the Christian world as an interlocking system of bishops and archbishops, with secular magnates and kings as aids, and the pope as a distant and revered authority. No doubt, as he himself declared, his view was coloured by his own modest social origin and his surprise that the pope, Urban II, should so unexpectedly have chosen him to replace a deposed simoniac as bishop of Chartres. Ivo was above all modest. He was never, what Lanfranc always was, a grandee. He looked on his bishopric as a burden that he would gladly renounce, but while he held it he would carry out his episcopal duties to the full in association with other bishops and with reasonable regard to the rights of the king of France. He looked on every issue from the point of view of local order, and he was the upholder of all the clearly defined virtues of regular Christian life. These concerns had been the basis of his contributions to the theological problems of the school of Laon, and they were the basis of his life as bishop, and of his studies in canon law.

No one could have written more respectfully than Ivo to the pope or even to the over-mighty papal legate, whose interference in local affairs he deplored: but his suavity of manner and his genuine devotion to Urban II and to the papacy generally, only served to emphasize his commitment to the rights and roles of local bishops and of lay rulers within the proper scope of their authority. Whereas Lanfranc saw everything on a grand scale, with the pope as first among the great metropolitans, Ivo saw all government on a local scale under the paternal oversight of the pope.

Consequently, like Lanfranc but without his grandiose archiepiscopal claims, Ivo viewed the practical application of canon law as a matter, not for the papal Curia, nor for officials, courts, and lawyers, but for bishops. Like Lanfranc, he was prepared to allow lay rulers an active part in ecclesiastical affairs, and neither of them thought that frequent, still less permanent, papal legates should have any role in exercising a superior authority over local bishops and archbishops. Neither Lanfranc nor Ivo belonged in outlook or aspiration to the scene of highly developed law and administration which came into existence during the century after their death.

As for Lanfranc, he thought that, in so far as any intermediate authority was needed between pope and bishops and archbishops, the proper mode lay in superior permanent metropolitan archbishops like those of Hamburg-Bremen and (as he envisaged the case) Canterbury. Lanfranc was primarily an archiepiscopal system-builder. By contrast, Ivo's outlook was essentially pastoral, like that of Burchard of Worms. It is not surprising therefore that, whereas Lanfranc chose Isidore's compilation of canon law as his *vade mecum* as archbishop, Ivo chose Burchard's as his model for episcopal government. The work that Ivo compiled was wider in scope, more fully and more accurately documented than Burchard's, but it was made in the same mould.[17]

A good many years after he had begun collecting his material, and probably when he thought it had achieved its final shape, Ivo wrote an introduction to his compilation in which he explained his method and the uses he expected his material to serve. He clearly envisaged a growing demand for copies. But, in this regard, he must have been disappointed, for very few copies have survived. It seems clear that later generations of bishops and episcopal administrators, who faced a much more complicated situation than Ivo had envisaged, demanded more readily accessible information about the law, more legal expertise, and anticipated more appeals to higher courts. They lived in a world of administration, whereas Ivo's compilation was essentially a pastoral work, and an extract from the Introduction

---

[17] Nevertheless, Ivo had clearly studied ps-Isidore, as is shown in the quotations in his letters: *Yves de Chartres, Correspondance*, ed. J. Leclercq, vol. i (all published), 1949, esp. 8, 16, 27, 35, 47. Although, therefore, Burchard provided his model, Ivo also had an extensive knowledge of ps-Isidore. Paul Fournier's calculation that, out of 3760 extracts cited in Ivo's *Decretum*, 1600 came from Burchard, while no doubt correctly identifying the main source of Ivo's inspiration, gives an exaggerated impression of the degree of Ivo's dependence.

which he wrote for it will convey better than any words of mine
the spirit in which he approached his task:

> With no little labour I have brought together in a single body
> extracts of ecclesiastical rules, partly from the letters of Roman
> pontiffs, partly from the conciliar decrees of catholic bishops, partly
> from the treatises of orthodox Fathers, partly from the regulations
> of catholic kings, in order that those who cannot have ready access
> to the writings from which these extracts have been taken may
> here find what is suitable for their purpose. Beginning with the
> statements of the Faith which are the foundation of the Chris-
> tian religion, I go on to the sacraments of the Church, then to
> instruction on conduct and its correction. I have so arranged these
> materials that those things which it is necessary to know in vari-
> ous situations are brought together under general headings. Thus
> it will be unnecessary for the reader to go through the whole
> volume to find what he wants: he needs only to seek the gen-
> eral heading bearing on the particular business in hand, and then
> to run through the detailed chapters without irrelevant distrac-
> tions.
>
>   It is, however, necessary to warn the prudent reader that, if
> he does not at once fully understand what he reads, or if he
> finds apparent contradictions, he should not immediately censure
> the author, but consider that there are some things that are to
> be understood rigorously and others with flexibility. The reason
> for this is that some extracts represent judgements and others are
> counsels that are to be interpreted mercifully. The guiding principle
> of the whole building is charity: that is to say, a concern for
> the salvation of our neighbours, which requires us to do unto
> others as we would be done unto. If every ecclesiastical teacher
> so interprets the rules to ensure that his teaching is based on
> this rule of charity, he will neither err nor sin. Let him there-
> fore, in giving thought only for the salvation of his neighbours,
> so shape the holy institutes to their due ends by following the
> dictum of St Augustine, who says in his treatment of ecclesiastical
> discipline, *Have charity and do whatsoever you will: in reproving,
> reprove with charity; in remitting, remit with charity.*[18] In what-
> soever you do, therefore, take care so to purify your mind's eye
> that – whether in punishing or in remitting – you follow sincere
> charity and ensure that you do not follow your own good, for if
> you do that, you will incur the condemnation of having *sought to*

[18] Ivo repeats this quotation with an attribution to Augustine *in tractatu 'De Disci-
plina Ecclesiastica'* in *Ep.* 231 (PL, 162, 235B).

slay souls that should not die and to save souls that should not live.[19]

These sentences are no more than a brief extract from Ivo's long Preface, but they will suffice to show how far he was from writing as a lawyer. They are the words of a pastor, and they establish the pastoral intention of the whole work. In brief, they show that Ivo's *Decretum* moves, not in the ambit of a law court, but in the ancient tradition of Pastoral Care. On a smaller scale, and with more limited objectives, Ivo's work belongs to the tradition of Gregory the Great's *Regula Pastoralis* instructing those in authority in the discharge of their pastoral duties. These duties indeed included judgements, but they are the judgements of a confessor rather than a lawyer.

Ivo's *Decretum* is clearly the work of a man learned in all aspects of the Christian life, widely read both in the original sources and in the compilations of these sources made by earlier scholars. Besides his borrowings from Burchard, Ivo also took texts from more recent compilations. For instance, he quotes from a nearly contemporary compilation that includes recent papal letters which could have been found only in the papal archives. It has sometimes been supposed that Ivo may himself have made these extracts, and this is not impossible for he was in Rome in 1090 when he was nominated as bishop of Chartres by the pope on the deposition of a simoniacal bishop. But, whatever his sources – and however he came by them – it is likely that he made his collection for his own use in the first place, and that it had been taking shape for a good many years before he became a bishop and decided to make his collection available for others.

It was this decision, taken during the early years of his episcopate, which caused him to write the Preface from which I

---

[19] *Prologus in Decretum Ivonis, PL,* 161, cols. 47–48. It should be noted that the Prologue circulated in many different contexts: as an Introduction to the *Decretum,* which seems to have been its original place; as an insertion at various points among Ivo's letters, e.g. after Ep. 103 with the title *Exceptiones ciii*; as a Prologue to the *Panormia*; also on its own. A broad idea of the various contexts in which it appears can be gained from the two volumes of Dom A. Wilmart's catalogue of the Vatican *Reginenses Codices.* It should also be noted that, although the Prologue gives a broadly correct account of the organization of the *Decretum,* the account it gives bears no relation to the organization of the *Panormia.*

have quoted, explaining its arrangement and purpose. As for its arrangement, Ivo claims that anyone can easily find the subject of his special interest by remembering the sequence of subjects in which the contents are arranged: first, Faith; then, the Sacraments; then, virtues and vices; then various types of *negotia*. The whole work, Ivo declares, is so divided under general titles that it is only necessary for the user to look for the general title bearing on the business of his enquiry to find what he wants. A little experience will soon convince any reader that this is an optimistic assessment, and the small number of copies that have been preserved seems to show that twelfth-century readers had the same experience of frustration.[20]

Ivo's collection, like Lanfranc's, was a book for those who wanted general guidance rather than precise definitions or rules of procedure. In particular it was for bishops who had to take decisions, not for lawyers who had to present arguments or for diocesan officials who needed rapid access to clear-cut rules. But it was precisely with these that the future lay. Hence also Ivo's compilation – too deep for ordinary parochial and diocesan clergy, who might need to look up such things as the prohibited degrees of consanguinity, and too general for lawyers, who needed precise rules and precedents on which to base their case – was a failure in a scene of rapidly increasing complexity. For general purposes, a much smaller and simpler manual was needed, and this was provided by someone – almost certainly not, in my opinion, Ivo himself – who greatly reduced the bulk of Ivo's *Decretum*, and gave it the grandiose title of *Panormia*, whatever that might mean.[21] For humble officials, it might do very well: they would at least get the scent of the great work. But real experts needed a work that was much fuller and more concerned with legal procedures.

The main interest of Ivo's *Decretum*, therefore, lies not in its future influence, which is negligible, but in its testimony to the state of thought about canon law in northern Europe in the last decade of the eleventh century. It portrays the mind of a very serious and learned bishop in this area, only a few years

---

20 For the MSS of Ivo's *Decretum*, see P. Landau, *Das Decret des Ivo von Chartres*, *ZRG Kan. Abt.* 70, 1984, 1–44. I owe this reference to Dr M. Brett.
21 For the *Panormia*, see *PL*, 161, 1041–1344.

before the great revolution that was to change the whole face of ecclesiastical administration and the whole relationship between bishops in their dioceses and the papacy. Ivo's *Decretum* was the last great medieval lawbook of an episcopally-centred Church and a locally-based ecclesiastical administration.

IV FEDERALISM *v.* CENTRALIZATION

Widely different, therefore, though Lanfranc's pseudo-Isidorian and Ivo's Burchardian collections were, they were both directed to the task of bringing order into the government of a broadly federal Church under the direction of archbishops and bishops working in collaboration with secular rulers, with only occasional reference to the pope. Neither Lanfranc nor Ivo saw ecclesiastical government as a hierarchy of ruridecanal, archidiaconal, episcopal, archiepiscopal and legatine courts leading up to the papal Curia; with lectures in the schools providing an essential training for those whose work would be in courts either as administrators or as lawyers; and with the hiring of lawyers for actions in the courts as a necessary step in safeguarding rights and enforcing duties.

Such was to be the shape of the future, but it was not a future that either Lanfranc or Ivo envisaged or worked for. In their numerous letters, both of them showed an intense and detailed concern for order in the Church as an organization of divine origin mediated through the various authorities sacramentally commissioned for their task at every level in the ecclesiastical hierarchy. Clearly they expected that the pope would be consulted on important issues, but essentially they looked on bishops and archbishops as normally independent sources of order within their own areas of authority. The men in authority were more important than the books which they used.

On this point, as on many others, the well documented career of Anselm as archbishop of Canterbury is illuminating. His work as archbishop was beset with many difficult problems of canon law, but he shows no sign of having studied either Lanfranc's abbreviated pseudo-Isidore, or Ivo's *Decretum*, though he paid close attention to the local privileges of the archbishopric of

Canterbury. Consequently, when the abbot of Fécamp wrote to ask his advice on a small problem of canon law, he went about the task in a way that would have seemed very odd, not to say blameable, forty years later.

The problem was this: in the course of various repairs in the abbey church at Fécamp, an altar had been moved, and the abbot was uncertain about its continued use: could it simply be brought back into use, or did it need reconsecrating, or some form of blessing, or was it henceforward unuseable? He wrote to Anselm to ask his advice. Anselm pondered the question and made some enquiries among his episcopal colleagues. He did not himself, he wrote, remember having read anything about this *in decretis vel canonibus*, but one of the bishops whom he consulted said that he thought he had read somewhere that Pope Eugenius had decreed that, in such a case, an altar could be re-used after re-blessing. Having got this far with his enquiries, Anselm left England in 1097 to consult the pope about his never-ending difficulties with the king of England, and while he was in Rome he raised the problem of the abbot of Fécamp with Pope Urban II and a group of bishops who were present. The pope said that he thought that an altar which had been moved should not be used again as an altar. But some of the bishops who were present took the view that in such a case an altar could be used either after reconsecration or after a simple ceremony of reconciliation. At this point Anselm thought he had got as far as he could and he sent an account of these opinions to the abbot of Fécamp, expressing his own view that the last of these solutions was the best.[22]

So this was how he went about solving a small question of canon law, and it is surely strange that he never consulted the works of either Burchard or Ivo of Chartres, and that neither the pope nor the bishops who were present with him at Rome thought of mentioning either of these works or any other. It may of course be pure accident that neither the pope nor any of the

---

22 Anselm's letter is III, 159, in *PL*, 159, 194–5. For its omission from F. S. Schmitt's edition of Anselm's Works, see Southern, 1990, p. 257n. Although Anselm did not think of consulting Ivo of Chartres, the abbot of Fécamp seems to have done so, for Ivo wrote him a long letter (no. 80; *PL*, 162, 101–3) with a complete solution of the problem.

bishops who discussed the question referred to Burchard or Ivo or any other compilation. But no one immediately thought of the question as having a place in a great body of legal decisions that had been accumulating over the last thousand years and had been collected in a succession of works which should be consulted before saying anything more. They all, like Anselm himself, looked on it as a problem to be discussed on grounds of general principles of theological propriety. Moreover, it did not occur to Anselm that Ivo of Chartres, with whom he was in correspondence on other matters, was the most learned scholar on canon law in northern Europe and the obvious person to ask. In fact, the unknown bishop who thought he had somewhere read a decree of Pope Eugenius came nearest to quoting a canonical source, for it is clear that he simply misremembered a decree attributed to the first-century Pope Hyginus (not, as he thought, Eugenius), which he must have seen either in Burchard's or in Ivo's *Decretum*. Apart from him, everyone discussed the problem on grounds of general theological propriety. So the enquiry illustrates the ambiguous status of canon law as a systematic body of knowledge at the end of the eleventh century – and this not only in northern Europe.

Curiously enough, in Bologna of all places, some twenty years later we shall find a comparably simple question being asked without an answer being found; but then, on application to the papal Curia, a ready answer to the problem that baffled the local authorities was provided.[23]

So, in retrospect we can say that, at the moment when the study of the Bible in northern Europe was already showing the first signs of turning into the systematic study of doctrine, canon law was not yet recognized as a systematic subject with an easily consultable textbook. The question, therefore, now is: how, and by what steps, did this situation change in the first forty years of the twelfth century?

The main instrument of change was the appearance of a work that took the world by storm: Gratian's *Decretum*. This will require a chapter to itself. But first something must be said about the environment in which it was produced.

[23] See below, p. 271.

8

The Outlook in Northern Italy

I CULTURAL POTENTIALITIES AND LIMITATIONS

Northern Italy was the one area in western Europe where a tradition of complicated administration based on codes of written law going back into a distant past still existed in the early twelfth century. Indeed, if there had been a question in the early *eleventh* century of providing expert knowledge and practical experience for a unified legal system throughout western Europe, an easy answer could have been given. At that time, northern Italy had everything necessary for this task. Besides possessing the remains of an ancient imperial administrative and legal system, it was also the leading area of economic activity and of potential intellectual growth in western Europe. All the trade between Europe and the then flourishing Byzantine Empire passed through its towns, and several of these towns had large populations and expectations of future growth far beyond those of any other area in western Christendom.

This combination of intellectual skills and growing resources was precisely what finally gave a lasting stimulus to general European development in the late eleventh and throughout the twelfth and thirteenth centuries. But much had happened to northern Italy in the eleventh century to diminish both the intellectual and the commercial importance of this whole area. In particular, the break-up of its political unity, the abrupt disintegration of imperial power, the declining trade with Byzantium, the growing internal conflicts in the cities, had all combined by the early twelfth century to diminish the potential influence of northern Italy on European development.

The result of these changes was that, though in the early

twelfth century the towns of northern Italy still had larger schools, more written law, more complicated legal procedures, and a more widely dispersed general literacy than could be found anywhere in northern Europe, its towns were all deeply torn by the strains and divisions of their own intense political rivalries. This inner turbulence made it unlikely that they either would or could produce large-scale plans for intellectual or institutional growth – more unlikely still that these plans would envisage a European-wide body of law, and least of all a body of systematic ecclesiastical law under papal supervision.

That this happened, and happened quite suddenly with Bologna as its centre, during the decades after 1140 was the result of an extremely complicated series of occurrences which could not have been predicted even as late as 1125. Whereas in northern France the steady growth of Paris had, even by 1100 and most conspicuously by 1120, made the city and its environs the centre of a European-wide intellectual development, in northern Italy the comparable development of Bologna was brought about by a unique individual effort linked with a quite unexpected combination of political circumstances.

In many ways the Bolognese achievement was even more remarkable than that of Paris. The schools of Paris simply concentrated in a single locality and gave a sharper definition to intellectual efforts which already had a long history of preparation, and which were to have an equally long history in bringing the results to bear on practical religious life.

But the schools of Bologna, which emerged in the 1150s with students from all parts of Europe, offered a programme of academic study which – though unheard of fifty years earlier – had immediate consequences for the detailed organization of the whole of western European society. Moreover, this Bolognese programme owed its intellectual cohesion very largely to the efforts of a single scholar who probably never taught the subject which he created, but whose work was the main instrument in bringing into existence a single body of law and a single system of courts such as Europe had never had since the fourth century.

These statements may seem surprising, and the aim of this and the following chapter is to explain them and provide their historical justification. What in outline we are to observe was the most remarkable revolution in European affairs, and to understand the immensity of the individual achievement we must first understand the environment which made it possible, the practical obstacles that lay in the way of its achievement, and the ingredients which had to be combined to produce the final result. The subject is so large that it can be dealt with here in only an episodic fashion, but this will suffice for our purpose, beginning with two exemplary towns which will illustrate the nature and extent of the opportunities and constraints which brought into existence a new science and a new scholastic metropolis.

We have already seen that the emergence of a systematic body of *doctrine* capable of shaping in detail the lives and beliefs of the whole population of western Europe was the culmination of a slow process of preservation and systematization, to which the growth of wealth, population and relative stability gave a final impetus in the early twelfth century. We are now to observe the very different process in northern Italy, which had the effect of providing the legal framework for this development.

Just as the elaboration of systematic grammatical, logical and theological doctrine, and the training of experts in these areas of knowledge, required a suitable urban base, so too the elaboration of systematic legal doctrine, and the training of men who could give effect to the legal consequences of the doctrinal system, also required the resources of a stable urban community. But the process of legal development was quite different from that of doctrinal development. Already by the year 1120 it was clear that Paris was becoming the *doctrinal* scholastic centre of western Europe, and in the next forty years its pre-eminent position was fully established. By contrast, the need for a comparable legal centre had scarcely arisen by 1120. Yet by 1160 Bologna was as fully established as the legal centre of western Christendom as Paris was as its doctrinal centre. The course of this development in Paris has been traced above. How the legal development came about is the subject of our present enquiry, and we may begin by examining the credentials and the shortcomings of Milan, which scholastically was the best equipped city in northern Italy. Its failure to develop as a European legal centre will provide a model for the failure of other great towns which in varying degrees had the same weaknesses. We shall then briefly look at Bologna to see whether it promised to do better than Milan.

Two north Italian cities: Milan and Bologna

Milan was the greatest town and the most distinguished ecclesiastical centre in Lombardy in the early twelfth century, and its immensely impressive resources for scholastic growth were already apparent by the mid-eleventh century. We have an account of the resources of the cathedral in about 1050 which lists a staff of thirty-six priests, seven deacons, seven subdeacons, and eighteen lectors, not to speak of many scribes and notaries. The singing masters alone had two schools in the forecourt of the church for training the choirboys; and there were two further schools in the north transept of the cathedral for advanced classes in the liberal arts, to which clergy from the town were admitted.[1] It is safe to say that no cathedral in northern Europe could show anything like this wealth of resources.

This splendid array of scholastic equipment was certainly appropriate for a cathedral which boasted of its ancient and unique liturgical rites, and its assets showed no sign of diminution in the early twelfth century. Yet, from a European point of view, there was one fatal weakness. The writer who tells us of the city's splendid provision for learning took it as a matter of course that any Milanese clerk who looked for higher learning in the Arts or theology would go to the schools of Germany, Burgundy or France to find what he sought. He would not find it in Milan.

The only boast of the Milanese writer was that, wherever students from his native town were congregated, they could be recognized by the sobriety and decorum of behaviour which they had learnt in the Ambrosian choir. Pride and localism, therefore, went hand-in-hand, concentrating on the task of

---

[1] For these details, see Landulf of Milan's *Historia Mediolanensis, MGH, Scriptores in folio*, vol. 8, pp. 70–4.

maintaining existing standards and discouraging innovation. In a town with such a past and present there was no place for an expansive view of the world's problems, or for any exploration of new intellectual disciplines. All that could be aimed at was the survival of what had been already achieved.

Even this was not easy, as appears from another vivid account of this basically unchanging but increasingly complicated state of affairs half a century later. We owe this account to Landulf of St Paul, a Milanese writer who belonged to one of the best clerical families in the city, and whose uncle was the hero of one of the popular religious movements of his time. Landulf was in the thick of Milanese politics from 1095 to 1135, and his pride in Milan was intense. But this did not prevent him making three journeys to France for higher studies. In 1103, he went to Orleans. Then, in 1106–7, he went to Tours and on to Paris to study under William of Champeaux. Finally, two or three years later, he went to Laon to study under Master Anselm and his brother Ralph.[2] So, surrounded though he was with all the resources of Milan in which he took so much pride, he chose the northern French schools for his higher studies as any student from France, Germany or England might have done. Landulf's career, therefore, while illustrating the intensity of corporate life in one of the great north Italian towns, confirms a cheerful acquiescence in the scholastic superiority of northern France.

This contrast is symptomatic of the strength and weaknesses of the great Italian cities generally. Their strength lay in the vigour and widespread literacy of local life; their weakness in their localized outlook. This combination was not accidental: it was inherent in their situation. There was so much going on in these large municipal conglomerations that there was no room for dealing with the broader problems of Christendom. Indeed this combination of intense activity and intense localism became a permanent feature of the Italian role in European history, and during the vital half century from about 1070 to 1120, when western Europe was emerging with a new intellectual, economic

2 Landulf of St Paul, *Historia Mediolanensis*, MGH, *Scriptores in folio*, vol. 20, p. 29.

and governmental identity, the great complexity of local problems in the north Italian towns severely limited the contribution
that they could make to this larger scene.

A few further details about the later life of Landulf of St
Paul will illustrate this point.

When he got back to Milan after his final visit to the northern French schools in about 1110, he found that his enemies
had taken advantage of his absence to seize his goods and the
sources of his income. But he was less worried by this misfortune than one might have expected, for Milan offered plenty of
opportunities for making a living, which he describes in the following terms:

> I bought a house in the area where my friends and relatives lived,
> and set myself up as a lector, scribe, and teacher of the young,
> taking part in public life and composing letters for the rulers of
> the city.[3]

Here we see at a glance both the scope and the limitations
of a learned career in a north Italian town, and we note particularly the nature of his main contribution to government: letter-
writing. The divisions in the town produced problems full of
complexities which offered scholarly men ample opportunities
for local employment and made it unnecessary – indeed impossible – for them to look beyond the problems of the urban community in which they lived.

In particular, the peculiar mixture of partly conflicting, partly
complementary, systems of Roman, Salian, customary and ecclesiastical law, under which the inhabitants of the city lived,
provided plenty of employment for a large number of highly
educated men – clerks and laymen alike – who took part in local
government, taught pupils the art of writing the letters necessary
for every situation, and themselves wrote official documents and
letters of special importance (footnote overleaf).[4]

So it came about that the complicated legal and political tan-
gles of Milan and of other north Italian towns, together with the
elaborations of the divine offices in grand cathedrals, formed the
mental horizons of even the brightest spirits. Those who were

[3] Ibid., p. 30.

not satisfied with these horizons emigrated, as Lanfranc (among the first) had done when he left Pavia in about 1030 to seek his fortune in northern France. Others continued to follow the same route, most famously Peter Lombard, who – almost exactly a century later than Lanfranc – after exploring the possibilities of a succession of north Italian towns, crossed the Alps first to Reims and then to Paris in about 1130 and never returned. During the next thirty years, he lectured, wrote the fundamental theological textbook of the Middle Ages, and died as bishop – all in Paris. In every important respect his life and learning belonged to northern France, and all he retained of his north Italian origin was the by-name, 'the Lombard', by which he was known as one of the brightest stars of the Parisian schools till the end of the Middle Ages.

This then was the problem of northern Italy as a possible source of the legal learning necessary for the reorganization of western Christendom. It had everything except the impulse to undertake the work. It had great cathedral schools, a multitude of independent schools set up by individual masters, an abundance of legal learning, an unbroken tradition of written law, a continuing contact with Justinian's great legal code of the ancient world, many learned men. But all this learned capital was entirely devoted to the tasks of dealing with the all-consuming tensions and complexities of local town life. There was more literacy than anywhere else in Europe. But the energies of the literate were consumed in immensely complicated legal issues, and in struggles between semi-rural aristocracies and urban oligarchies, between ecclesiastical hierarchies and town-based heretical groups, between imperial, papal and municipal political pretensions.

Add to all these conflicts the complexities of popular move-

---

4 Lucca is the Italian town which has preserved the most abundant collection of pre-twelfth century documents illustrating the mixture of laws, mainly the vernacular forms of Roman or Salian law, under which the inhabitants lived. See *Regesto del Capitolo di Lucca*, ed. G. E. Parenti, *Istituto storico italiano*, i, 1910, e.g. nos 614 (1101, a father and son living under Roman law); 682 (1108, a widow and her former husband under Roman law); 696 (1109, a widow and daughter living under Salian law); 700 (1110) and 706 (1111): two deaconesses under Roman law.

ments, which did not appear elsewhere in Europe on a large scale until the fourteenth century, and we have an explanation of the general failure of the northern Italian cities to take an early lead in providing the new sciences on which the government of western Christendom during the twelfth and thirteenth centuries was based.

Indeed, nothing is more striking than the contrast between the apparatus of learning, which could be brought to bear on the minutiae of secular rights, and the primitive expedients which had to be resorted to in matters of more general importance. For example, in Milan in 1095, when the leader of a popular religious party accused the archbishop of simony, he had to prove his case not by adducing any evidence of the kind so abundantly available in small disputes about property, but by submitting himself to an ordeal by fire.[5]

This contrast between the wealth of learning available for local disputes and the poverty of information about matters of ecclesiastical law can also be confirmed – rather strangely in view of future developments – in Bologna. In about 1125, some English pilgrims passing through the town, which was on the normal route from England to Rome and southern Italy, had left behind them an abandoned child. No one knew whether the child had been baptized, and – despite all the legal learning in the city – no one knew the correct procedure in such a case. In the end, the bishop had to write to the pope, Honorius II, and he got the simple reply that the child should be conditionally baptized.[6]

The pope did not say, but may have thought, that very little research would have answered this not very recondite question: it had long ago been dealt with in papal letters, which were quoted in the collections both of Burchard and of Ivo of Chartres.[7]

The date of this exchange of letters was almost certainly

---

[5] Landulf of St Paul, *Historia Mediolanensis, MGH, folio*, vol. 20, pp. 27–8.
[6] The letter to the pope and his reply on the subject of re-baptism are found in the collection of letters in the work of Adalbertus Samaritanus described below (see n. 8), where grounds are given for dating the letters 1125.
[7] The solution to the problem is in Burchard, bk. 3, c. 44; in Ivo's *Decretum*, i, 166; and in the *Panormia*, i, 92.

1125.[8] In view of the central position that Bologna was going to have in the study of canon law by the 1140s, it is very remarkable that there should have been no easily available information on so simple a point only fifteen years earlier. Clearly too much should not be read into this single incident, but it illustrates the secularity, and no doubt also localism, of the great body of legal and administrative knowledge that undoubtedly existed in Bologna as in other north Italian cities in the first quarter of the twelfth century. And, further, it is significant that the evidence for this small tell-tale detail comes from a school-book – a work on the art of letter-writing – intended to provide the knowledge necessary for the conduct of business in a busy urban community. The letters were preserved as examples of epistolary formulae, but also as part of a general education in doctrines, historical facts and legal procedures.

In Bologna, as in Milan, there were several schools: the cathedral school for clergy, and several independent secular schools for both clergy and laity. The letters I have just quoted come from a treatise on letter-writing compiled for one of the latter in which the master taught this essential skill for the conduct of every kind of business. We must not be misled by the very humble place which books on letter-writing, answering the age-old question 'How Shall I Phrase It?', now have. Today their use is looked on as a sign of illiteracy; but in the twelfth century they were vehicles for imparting knowledge essential for every kind of legal, administrative and personal business.

---

[8] The letter to the pope and his reply on the subject of re-baptism are found in the collection of letters attached to the *Rationes dictandi prosaice* of Hugh canon of Bologna, in L. Rockinger, *Briefsteller und Formelbücher des XI bis XIV Jahrhunderts*, in *Quellen u. Erörterungen zu bayerisch. und deutschen Geschichte*, Munich, ix, 1863–4, pp. 53–94. All the letters in this collection in which a pope is mentioned indicate that Calixtus II (1110–1124) was pope, except the two on baptism, which are to or from Calixtus II (Dec. 1124–1130). This strongly suggests a date c. 1125 for these two letters. We may further note the evidence provided in this collection for the prevalence of instruction in letter-writing as a central feature of teaching: in the course of his work the author refers disparagingly to the doctrines of two contemporary rivals, Aginulf and Adalbertus Samaritanus. For the latter, see the edition by F. S. Schmale, *MGH, Quellen zu Geistesgeschichte des Mittelalters*, iii, 1961. For the general scene, see C. H. Haskins, 'An Italian master Bernard', in *Essays in History, presented to R. L. Poole*, Oxford, 1927, pp. 211–26, which will be discussed in Volume II of this work.

Letter-writing was an art which the secular schools of Bologna in the early years of the twelfth century seem to have been especially well equipped to teach, and two important Bolognese treatises on the subject have survived from the period about 1115–25. The range of learning which they sought to promote may be judged from the very wide range of authors quoted in their texts, who included Cicero, Horace, Juvenal, Priscian, and Ambrose, Augustine, Jerome. So they were introductions to doctrine and authors of many different kinds.

It has often been alleged that there were also law schools in Bologna from an early date, and that such schools were increasingly active in the early twelfth century. The existence of such schools has been largely inferred from the frequent appellations *magister* or *doctor* attached to lawyers practising in the courts. But on this subject caution is necessary: in themselves these appellations, which were used to describe men who were judges or advocates in courts of law, no more justify the inference that the person so described taught in a school than the existence of *magistri militum* would justify the comparable inference that there were schools of war. Only evidence of textbooks, or of lectures, class-rooms, courses of study, groups of students and teachers, and discussions can justify the inference that there were schools of law.

Of course lawyers have always had pupils following them from their chambers to the law courts, listening to their pleading and employed in subordinate tasks, to whom they may have given private instruction. The neighbourhood of Bologna was – as we shall see – notable for lawsuits in the courts of the Emperor Henry V and of the Countess Matilda. But this is a very different matter from being a centre of schools with courses in civil law. Pupils following a famous lawyer from his chambers to courts of law were preparing themselves for practising in similar courts, they were not cosmopolitan students expecting to return to all parts of Europe. So far as we know, nothing of this kind existed in Bologna during the first third of the twelfth century when Paris was rising to a position of genuine scholastic leadership in northern Europe (footnote overleaf).[9]

Thus, despite the very great body of legal learning in Bologna as in other towns of northern Italy, we must refrain from speaking of the law schools of Bologna until there is evidence of the existence of students and lecture-courses, and (we may hope) of notes taken at lectures. All these forms of evidence, despite the fragmentary state in which they have been preserved, are quite abundant from Laon and Paris from the first quarter of the twelfth century onwards. Whether, and in what subjects and in what form, such evidence is to be found in Bologna or any other north Italian town in the first quarter of the twelfth century, is a question to which we must return.

Meanwhile it must suffice to say that, although the idea of a universal body of internationally applicable ecclesiastical law was making a strong appeal in the papal Curia, the way forward towards achieving this aim was obscure except on one point: it was generally agreed that one of the dangers most to be feared was the revival of Roman law.[10] Roman law had long been thought of as a sleeping lion in the path of the papacy, relatively harmless so long as it was only one ingredient in the municipal laws of the north Italian towns, but capable – if revived in its ancient splendour – of doing immense damage to the growth of papal jurisdiction. The grounds for thinking that this fear was well justified, and that the danger was growing, needs some investigation before we go further.

II IRNERIUS AND THE MENACE OF ROMAN LAW

Besides the complexities of local town and community life,

[9] It has been pointed out by H. Kantorowicz and B. Smalley, 'An English theologian's view of Roman law', MARS, 1943, i, 2, p. 241, that the phrase *legis doctor* is the usual designation of a doomsman (i.e. one who pronounces what the law is), and that a *causidicus* is likewise called *legis doctus*: these phrases designate a practical, not a teaching function, and have a very long history in this sense before the twelfth century. It is no doubt in this sense that the lawyer Pepo, who was the permanent advocate of the monastery of S. Salvatore di Montamiata in the territory of Siena, in various cases between 1072 and 1078, is called *legis doctor* when he appears as a doomsman. See further, G. Santini, 'Legis doctores et sapientes civitatis', *Archivio giuridico*, 6th ser., vol. 38, 1965, pp. 114–71, and C. Manaresi, *I placiti de Regno Italiae*, 3 vols, Rome, 1955–60, for descriptions of lawyers during the eleventh century as *scholasticissimus* (1032), *grammatici, legum doctores, docti, sapientes*, etc. None of these phrases can be used as evidence for the existence of law schools.

[10] For Peter Damian's criticism of Roman law as detrimental to canon law and to papal authority, see his *De parentillae gradibus* (Opusculum 8), PL, 145, 191–204.

which absorbed all the energies and expertise of the many lawyers of the area, another obstacle to the creation of a European
ecclesiastical jurisprudence in northern Italy was the ambiva-
lent role of Roman law. On the one hand it had been preserved through the centuries and adapted to the needs of towns
with great diversities of people subject to different legal systems
according to their family origins and occupations. This legal
diversity certainly helped to keep Roman law alive as one of
the varieties of law in an extremely complicated situation. But
it consigned the original texts and their systematic interpretation
to near oblivion.

Despite this neglect, a diligent search at any time would
probably have brought to light most of the original *Corpus
Iuris Civilis* as constructed by the legal advisers of the Emperor
Justinian in the sixth century, and there is evidence that lawyers
engaged in the ordinary lawsuits of the north Italian courts sometimes found maxims and even procedures in Justinian which they
could use with good effect. Nevertheless, the first strong impetus
to the renewed study of Roman law was associated with attempts
to use Justinian's texts either to assert imperial rights over the
Church in opposition to the claims of the Hildebrandine party
in the Church, or (on the Hildebrandine side) to answer these
attempts, either by finding heresy in the imperial laws, or by
discovering that they contained passages consistent with papal
claims to sovereignty in all matters of faith and ecclesiastical
organization.[11]

In addition, the existence of a scholarly interest in legal texts
on the part of practising lawyers must not be overlooked.
At all times there have probably been practising lawyers with an
interest in the fundamental texts of their subject quite independent of the existence of courses of study or pupils to be taught.
The names of John Selden and F. W. Maitland at once spring
to mind in this connection, and it is likely that the founder
of the study of Roman law in the Middle Ages, whose name
had been smoothed from Guarnerius to Irnerius by being passed

---

[11] For the remarkable number of references to Roman law in the imperial–papal
dispute, already in the eleventh century, see the indexes to *Libelli de Lite Imperatorum
et Pontificum saec. XI et XII conscripti*, MGH, 3 vols, 1891–97 (repr. 1957).

around among men of many nations, should be added to this list.[12]

From the mid-twelfth century onwards, it was believed that the initiator of the serious study of Roman law, which was by then firmly established as providing legal principles for canon law, was a certain Irnerius. Nothing was known about him, but it was assumed that he was a teacher with pupils, like his successors. The earliest reporter of this myth was Robert of Torigni-sur-Vire, abbot of Mont-St-Michel in the third quarter of the twelfth century, who (as I have already mentioned with regard to Ivo of Chartres and Lanfranc, and shall mention again with regard to Gratian) was very alert to the scholarly movements of his time. He believed them to be so important that he disfigured his monastery's Chronicle by scratching out various entries about petty political events in order to insert entries recording, not always accurately, but with much perspicuity, the intellectual innovations of his lifetime. The earliest of these insertions, under the year 1033, runs as follows:[13]

> Lanfranc of Pavia and his colleague Garnerius, having found at Bologna the Roman Laws which the Emperor Justinian had abbreviated and corrected in the year 530, turned their attention to lecturing on them and taught them to others. Garnerius persevered in this work, but Lanfranc went to France and taught the liberal Arts and Holy Scripture, and finally went to Bec and became a monk.

The abbot, who made this insertion in about 1170, calls this earliest expert on Roman law 'Garnerius', which is in fact much

---

12 For the comments on the *Corpus Iuris Civilis* attributed to Irnerius, see Gustav Pescatore, *Glossen des Irnerius*, 1888, and in *ZRG, rom. Abt.*, xxxiii, 1912; E. Besta, *L'Opere d'Irnerio*, 2 vols., Turin, 1896; Hermann Fitting, *Summa Codicis des Irnerius*, and *Questiones de Iuris Subtilitatibus des Irnerius*, Berlin, 1894. In support of the view of the environment of these early students of Roman law put forward here, Heinrich Denifle, in his *Die Entstehung der Universitäten des Mittelalters*, 1885, p. 144, had already remarked that the proliferation of jurists in Pisa, Florence, Parma, Reggio, Bologna, Padua, etc. in the eleventh century, did not prove the existence of law schools. Irnerius was also the author of a collection of theological extracts from the Augustine, Gregory and Ambrose (see below, p. 279, n. 17), but it has never been suggested that he taught theology.
13 For Robert of Torigni on Garnerius, see *Chronicle of the reigns of Stephen, Henry II and Richard I*, ed. R. Howlett, RS, 1889, iv, pp. 25–6.

nearer to the form 'Warnerius' in which his name appears in contemporary records than the 'Irnerius' of all later references. But the chronicler shows his assimilating instincts in two ways. First, as himself a former monk of Bec, he associates him with the other great lawyer, who was vividly present in his mind, Lanfranc, formerly prior of the monastery in which he had been brought up. In doing this he antedates what is now known to have been the period of Garnerius's activity by about seventy years. And, further, he supposes that these two great lawyers were engaged principally in teaching law in schools rather than in practising it in courts.

I shall come presently to the reasons for thinking that this supposition was false. But first another, even later, but better informed, chronicler, Burchard, Provost of Ursberg in South Germany, needs to be noticed, for he gives a different twist, somewhat nearer to the actuality, to this great historical event.

Although he was writing in the early thirteenth century, he had some good early sources, and the following surprising assertion arrests our attention:

> About this time [he is writing of the period around about 1110], dominus Wernerius, urged by the Countess Matilda, renewed the study of the books of the Laws compiled by the Emperor Justinian, which had hitherto been neglected.[14]

So here again, in the new and surprising context of having been urged by the Countess Matilda of Tuscany, we have the story of 'Irnerius's' great innovation, and scholars have long attempted to elaborate these tantalizing glimpses of an intellectual revival which plays a conspicuous part in the creation

---

[14] *Die Chronik des Propstes Burchard von Ursberg*, ed. O. Holder-Egger and B. von Simson, *Scriptores rerum Germanicarum in usum scholarum*, vol. 50, 1916, pp. 15–16. His words are remarkably precise: *Eisdem temporibus dominus Wernerius libros legum qui dudum neglecti fuerant, nec quisquam in eis studuerat, ad petitionem Matilde comitisse renovavit et, secundum quod olim a divo recordationis imperatore Iustiniano compilati fuerant, paucis forte verbis alicubi interpositis eos distinxit.* For the evidence that Matilda became much less strongly attached to the papal cause in her later years, see below, pp. 281–2. I have not been able to see G. G. Mor, 'I giudici della contessa Matilde e la rinascita del diritto romano', in *Studi in memoria di Benevenuto Donati*, Bologna, 1954, pp. 43–59.

of a European-wide system of law. Like the two chroniclers, they have generally concentrated on seeing Irnerius as a teacher and as the forerunner of the whole army of teachers who made the schools of Roman law at Bologna famous from the mid-twelfth century onwards, and established Roman law as one of the major influences in the developments of European legal thought.

It is only fairly recently that material has been investigated which shifts the emphasis away from legal study to law courts, and to the clashes of mighty litigants attempting to strengthen their political hold on the northern Italian cities. Documents have come to light – and they are the only strictly contemporary documents about Irnerius/Warnerius that we have – which show him engaged, not as a teacher, but as a practising lawyer in the courts: first, in cases before the bishop of Ferrara and Countess Matilda of Tuscany in 1112 and 1113; then very active in the service of the Emperor Henry V and in cases before his court during his Italian expedition from 1116 to 1118; then politically active from 1118 to 1122; and finally once more active as an advocate in the courts on behalf of the monastery of S. Bendetto di Polizone in 1125.[15]

In these documents, we have a body of historical material of the highest importance, showing Irnerius deeply involved in the emperor's struggle to reassert his political rule in northern Italy in defiance of the Donation of Constantine and of the recent papal claim to the lands of the Countess Matilda. The extent of Irnerius's political involvement is illustrated by the important part he took in the election of the imperial anti-pope Gregory VIII in March 1118, and by his subsequent excommunication in the company of other supporters of Henry V at the Council

---

15   The first collection of documents illustrating the activity of Warnerius and other *iudices* in the courts of the Emperor Henry V and the Countess Matilda in the general area of Bologna was published by Conrado Ricci in *I primordi dello studio di Bologna*, 2nd edn, 1882, in which he printed thirty-five documents testifying to the wide variety of lawsuits in courts often summoned either by the Emperor or by the Countess Matilda, in which Warnerius and other *iudices* took part. More recently Enrico Spargnesi, *Wernerius Bononiensis iudex*, Academia toscana di sc. e lettere, *Studi*, xvi, 1970, has discussed these documents with special regard to the legal and political role of the man whom I shall henceforward refer to as Irnerius.

of Reims in 1119.[16] It is clear, therefore, that the fear of Roman law expressed by those who supported the extension of papal authority could find much justification in the part that Irnerius played in supporting the anti-papal policy of the Emperor Henry V between 1112 and 1125.

The surviving documents show Irnerius in two roles. First, judicial records show him as an advocate, judge, and politician; and it was as *iudex Boloniensis* that he was excommunicated in 1119. And second, the manuscripts of the *Corpus Iuris Civilis* show him as the the writer of very numerous glosses on the original texts. Even if (as is probable) many of them are incorrectly attributed to him, it is overwhelmingly likely that a large proportion are his.[17] What then are we to think of his later fame as the founder of the teaching of Roman law in the schools of Bologna? I think it is reasonable to say that, long after his political activities had been consigned to the rubbish bin of history, his memory lived in his glosses on Justinian. The later users of these glosses were associated with the schools, and so they naturally thought that the writer of such glosses must also have been active in the schools, and that his glosses were the record of his lectures. Indeed, it is very likely that, like all successful practitioners, Irnerius had pupils, and that at least two of the four great masters of Roman law in Bologna in the 1150s had been among them. But this does not mean that they were students listening to their master lecturing in a class-room: they had a much better way of learning by hearing him discuss his cases in his chambers, by helping him to prepare his briefs and going

---

[16] For Irnerius's political role and his deployment of legal learning in the imperial cause, the account in Landulf's *Historia Mediolanensis* of Irnerius's part in the election of an imperial anti-pope after the death of Paschal II on 21 January 1118 is exceptionally important. (See *MGH, Scriptores in folio*, xx, pp. 40–1.) It was as a consequence of this that *Guarnerius Bononiensis legis peritus*, together with the emperor and others, was excommunicated at the Council of Reims in 1119. For a list of those excommunicated with him see R. Holtzmann, *Zur Geschichte des Investitursstreites* (Englische Analecta, ii), *Neues Archiv*, 50, 1935, 318–19. But his documented connection with the imperial court goes back to 25 May 1100, when he was a *missus imperialis*.

[17] In addition to the glosses on Justinian ascribed to Irnerius, the Ambrosian Library, Milan, MS Y43 sup. ff. 7–85, contains a *Liber Sententiarum quas Garnerius iuris peritissimus ex Dictis Augustini aliorumque doctorum excerpsit*. The contents are briefly described by Grabmann, vol. 2, pp. 131–3.

with him and hearing him in court, and by reading his learned notes in his copy of the *Corpus Iuris Civilis*. Just as an aspiring artist will find the studio of a great master the best place to learn his art, so for a lawyer the chambers and pleadings of a great practitioner are the best places for learning to emulate him. The important point is, not that Roman law had already in the time of Irnerius become a subject for academic study, but that it had come to life again in the practical world of law courts and high politics, which are the only areas of Irnerius's activity for which contemporary evidence exists.

But if this is the real message of Irnerius's career, why is he invariably, from the mid-twelfth century onwards, depicted as a teacher of law? Why was his work in the courts on behalf of both the Countess Matilda and the Emperor Henry V forgotten, as also was his involvement in the emperor's political anti-papal activities?

The simple answer to these questions is that later reporters were not interested in Irnerius's legal career or even in his political activity. They were interested only in identifying the source of the great stream of Roman law studies, which had spread the name and influence of the Bolognese schools throughout Europe. They knew many glosses on Roman law with Irnerius's name attached to them, and these glosses encouraged the scholars and teachers of the next generation to think of the writer of them as one of themselves. No class of people have ever more avidly sought a respectable pedigree for their studies than university lecturers, and no more successful forebear has ever been found than Irnerius. No one bothered to enquire whether he had ever actually given a lecture in the schools.

Of course, even if he never himself gave a lecture Irnerius was ideally the master of all later masters of Justinian's texts. He was a pioneer in the close study of the original texts of Roman law, and he showed that this was the way forward. Distinguished practising lawyers at all times have been interested in digging deeply into the great texts of their profession, in studying their doctrines and in applying them in politics. And it would seem that Irnerius, the founder of medieval Roman law studies, should be added to their number: first making his appearance in courts on behalf of such distinguished clients as Countess

Matilda of Tuscany and the Emperor Henry V; then, in a political role, as one of the emperor's main agents in attempting to re-establish imperial power in northern Italy and to reassert the emperor's position as 'protector' and main elector of the pope; and then, on the death of his imperial patron, reverting once more to his practice in the courts on behalf of wealthy litigants. In all these roles he was sustained by his knowledge of Roman law. This was his legacy to future lawyers who were not interested in his law-suits.

But there is one remaining difficulty. To anyone familiar with the bitterly anti-papal policy of the Emperor Henry V and with the reputation of the Countess Matilda as a main supporter of the Hildebrandine popes throughout her whole life, the most surprising feature of Irnerius's career as it is now disclosed is his close association with *both* of them. Here, however, there are two points to remember.

First, it is in the nature of lawyers to work for clients with divergent interests, and of litigants to employ the most formidable advocates whatever their political opinions might be. And, second, although the Countess Matilda is well known as the most notable of all lay supporters of the Hildebrandine papacy, there are strong indications that her devotion to Gregory VII was not extended in anything like equal measure to his successors. Urban II had, for political reasons, been responsible for her hateful marriage to Welf V, Duke of Bavaria, and in her later years – having got rid of her husband – she thought that imperial rights were being unduly diminished by papal policy. This caused her to make provision to ensure that some of her famous heritage should come under imperial control after her death (footnote overleaf).[18] It would lead too far from the main line of our present enquiry to go deeply into this question. So it must suffice to say that even those who were, in general, supporters of Hildebrandine aims did not always support the political measures of Gregory VII's successors. And this seems particularly true of the Countess Matilda in her later years.

In general, moreover, it is as true of the twelfth century as of the twentieth that those interested in tracing the rise of great academic institutions were apt to give little attention to the political and social environment which made these studies possible and determined the speed, the location and the practical aims of their development. In particular, it is as sure as anything can be that Irnerius's legal studies were the foundation of his work for clients who included – among others – both the Countess Matilda and the Emperor.

It is against this background that the revival of the study of Roman law must be understood: not as a contribution to an academic subject, but in the context of a legal and political career. It is not after all so very uncommon for active lawyers also to have a deep interest in the theoretical background of their life's work, and what we must now ask is whether an early background of practical life in the courts may not also help to put into its correct context the most influential for the future of Europe of all the legal, and arguably quite simply of *all*, the scholastic compilations of the Middle Ages: the *Concordia Discordantium Canonum*, and of the author to whose aim and circumstances we must now turn.

[18]   In May 1111, Matilda had a three-day meeting with the recently crowned Emperor Henry V at her castle at Pujanello (arr. Canossa). At this meeting Henry made Matilda his representative in Tuscany and Matilda made Henry the heir to some part of her Italian titles and rights. On the meeting, see *Vita Mathildis*, ii, 18, by Donizo, ed. Luigo Simeoni, *Rerum Italicarum scriptores*, v, ii, 1931; and G. Meyer von Kronau, *Jahrbücher der deutschen Geschichte: Heinrich IV und V*, vi. 132–3, 179. One purpose of Henry V's return to Italy in 1116, when he made his great effort to gain control of Bologna (see p. 314 below), was to take possession of that part of Matilda's lands which he inherited as a result of the agreement of 1111. (See G. Meyer von Kronau, *Jahrbücher des deutschen Reiches unter Heinrich IV und V*, 1909, vol. 7, p. 3.) It should be noted moreover that the only contemporary 'document' recording the gift of her lands to the papacy, with the date 1102, is a fragmentary marble slab in the Grotte Vaticane, of which various copies remain, but of which there is no authenticated copy. I know of no discussion about the genuineness of this gift, which played a central role in the papal claim to Matilda's inheritance. But the possibility of forgery is obvious.

9

The Integration of Doctrine and Law: Gratian

I DEMAND AND RESPONSE

We have seen that when Ivo of Chartres died in 1115, despite the careful labour and thought which shaped his work on canon law, he had not produced – and had not intended to produce – a scholastic textbook, nor a body of precedents or procedures capable of serving as a basis for a unified and European-wide system of law. Nor was there any likelihood that any scholar or school in northern Europe would fill this gap in the spectrum of scholastic studies.

Nevertheless, from about 1130 onwards though not earlier, there is evidence of a continuing succession of independent scholars and administrators in northern Europe who were searching for a more comprehensive body of legal principles and procedures than had so far been produced. Even at the diocesan level of government, bishops and archdeacons who had no interest in promoting the growth either of scholastic studies or of papal authority, felt the need for a body of legal doctrine which would give a greater unity and compulsory force to the ecclesiastical legislation of the past. These stirrings of a new interest in legal doctrine and procedures were not necessarily attached to any particular doctrine of papal or royal authority. They could arise simply from the perception among active bishops and archdeacons that everywhere around them growing wealth and increasing population were creating more disputes and conflicting claims, ecclesiastical as well as lay, and consequently a need for clearer procedural rules in courts of law, and for a hierarchy of courts to which dissatisfied litigants could appeal.

It is against this general background that we must attempt to understand the astonishing success of a work in which for the first time a very comprehensive body of doctrines, principles and procedures for regulating every aspect of religious behaviour was displayed, not indeed in perfect order, but in sufficient order and with enough suggestions of points that needed clarification, to make it a suitable book both for teaching and for making ecclesiastical law an effective instrument of government.

The author of this work was a scholar called Gratian, about whom almost nothing is known except his name and the date of the completion of his work. As for his work, it was a vast, unwieldy, curiously organized compilation, which is generally known simply as his *Decretum*, but to which he himself gave a name – *Concordantia discordantium Canonum* – which suggests that the author had some knowledge of the teaching methods of the northern French schools, and particularly perhaps of the teaching of Abelard.[1] But even this suggestion takes us beyond the scope of the knowable.

The main, indeed the only substantial, evidence we have about the mind, the aims, and the stimulus behind this work, which did more than any other to reshape the organized religious life of western Christendom in the twelfth and thirteenth centuries, is to be found in the work itself. It is a work, as Bishop Stubbs said of constitutional history, that 'cannot be mastered – can scarcely be approached – without an effort . . . but has a deep value and abiding interest to those who have courage to work upon it'.[2]

Here, where others have ploughed, sown and harvested, I can do no more than scratch the surface in attempting to place the man, his work and his influence in the general context of the social, political and intellectual developments of the early twelfth century.

To this end I shall consider first the man and some major

---

1 See below, n. 6.
2 W. Stubbs, Preface to *The Constitutional History of England in its origin and development*, vol. 1, Oxford, 1874.

characteristics of his work, then the circumstances of the time of its composition, and finally the future of his work and the place where this future was made.

Although Gratian's work was produced without any public notice or recorded preparation, it conveys the strange impression that no other author and no other place could have produced the instrument that the time required. Dante, writing two hundred years later, seems to have experienced a sense of a strange unearthly achievement when he described Gratian, in the circle of the greatest scholars of the Middle Ages, as 'smiling at having given such aid to ecclesiastical and civil law as is acceptable in Paradise'.[3] Dante rightly paired Gratian with Peter Lombard, who nearly twenty years later (in 1159 to be precise) completed his comparable scholastic outline of theology. But, in doing this, Peter Lombard had a more straightforward task than Gratian: he was completing and systematizing a body of knowledge along lines that had been explored and already tentatively laid down by a large group of near contemporaries with whom he had worked in close proximity.

By contrast, Gratian seems to have had no associates and strictly no predecessors who laid down the main lines along which he could work. He had of course many general predecessors, some of whom have been briefly surveyed above. But none of them had produced anything at all resembling what he called his *Concordantia discordantium Canonum*. As for the future, others were to abbreviate or attempt to reorganize his work; and very many others were to comment on it and make it accessible throughout western Europe. But no other scholar can claim a place beside him in giving canon law a textbook which at once won a place in the schools not only for itself, but for a whole subject which had not previously been recognized as having an academic content. So Gratian is rightly the only lawyer in the circle of those great scholars of medieval Christendom – indeed the only lawyer in Paradise – whom Dante depicts as being introduced to him by Thomas Aquinas, the greatest master of them all.

Gratian had, I think, been a lawyer in early life. But he was

---

[3] Dante, *Paradiso*, x, ll. 104–105. Dante's description of Gratian's work, *che l'uno e l'altro foro aiuto*, probably refers to his support for Roman as well as canon law.

more than a lawyer. When all allowance has been made for his own probable legal background and for his having then, in retirement from the courts, completed the legal work of a long succession of earlier compilers, it must finally be added that Gratian's great work is essentially a theological and political document, preparing the way – and intended to prepare the way – for the practical asserting of the supreme authority of the papacy as the lawgiver of Christendom. It may be noted that he leaves an ambiguity about the extent of papal authority in secular matters, which Boniface VIII – himself a canon lawyer trained in Bologna – resolved in favour of the papacy.[4] But even allowing for this ambiguity, his work formed the basis of the most centralized legal system that Europe has ever known.

With this in mind we may now turn to more personal matters.

II THE MAN AND HIS WORK

Reliable writers after his death affirmed that Gratian was a Benedictine monk of the Camaldolesian Order, a small Italian branch of the Benedictines, which combined austerity of life with considerable freedom to contribute to the work of the Church in a wide variety of ways. Although there is no contemporary evidence for his monastic vocation, one earlier convert to this Order, Peter Damian, well illustrates the freedom which it gave its members to contribute to the Church's needs at a particular moment.[5] This is what Gratian did. He engaged

---

[4] See the general terms of Boniface VIII's *Clericis laicos* of 25 February 1296 in *Les Registres de Boniface VIII*, vol. 1, iv, no. 1567, p. 584 (*Bibliothèque des écoles françaises d'Athènes et de Rome*, 1907). See also Plate 4.

[5] If – as seems highly likely – they were both members of the same branch of the Benedictine Order, they complement each other in their services to the Hildebrandine phase of papal history, and Gratian's initial distrust of Roman law entirely agrees with the view of Peter Damian. As for later statements that Gratian was a Camaldolesian monk, a monastery of S. Felice of this order is mentioned in a bull of Paschal II of 1113; and a MS of Gratian at Geneva, Bibliothèque publique et universitaire, MS Lat. 60, with the inscription: *Anno domini MCL a Gratiano S. Feliciani Bononiensis monacho editum.*

in a very un-monastic branch of study, and produced a law book which became the most widely distributed and probably the most generally used of all the masterpieces of twelfth-century learning.

Beyond this, we know no single fact about Gratian's career with certainty, but the work on which he spent the last years of his life shows that he was very familiar with the detailed procedures of law courts and had a tendency to see every part of life as amenable to proceedings in a court of law. In addition, his choice of title for his work, *Concordantia discordantium Canonum*, suggests that he was familiar with the dialectical procedures of the schools of northern France as illustrated, for instance, in Abelard's *Sic et Non*.[6] And his references to the Benedictine *Rule* and to incidents in the life of St Benedict as reported in the *Dialogues* of Gregory the Great, support the tradition that he spent his last years as a monk. In short, if we imagine a lawyer who had spent his early and middle years working in north Italian law courts, and who at some stage during this period had visited the schools of northern France, and later retired with the idea of turning his legal expertise to the service of the Church and papacy, we shall probably get as close as we can to forming a view of the man, his earlier career, and his intentions.

Later writers also asserted of him, as of Irnerius, that he was a *teacher* of canon law, and to this point we shall return. But we have already learnt, from the case of Irnerius, to treat with reserve the tendency of later observers to suppose, in the absence of any evidence, that the founding fathers of a great scholastic discipline had been lecturers in the schools like themselves. Meanwhile it can be said that none of the earliest users of his work claims to have been taught by him, and that his intense interest in the minutiae of legal processes suggests that he had once been more familiar with law courts than with schools.

---

[6] For similarities with *Sic et Non*, see the incomplete new edition by Blanche Boyer and Richard McKeon, 1976. Appendix III has a table of parallel passages in Abelard, Ivo, Gratian, and Lombard. For Gratian's familiarity with works of the northern schools, see also G. le Bras, 'Algar de Liège et Gratian', *Revue des sciences Philosophiques et théologiques*, xx, 1931, 5–26.

So, provisionally at least, we may think of Gratian before he became a monk as having had a legal career. If we add to this a very extensive knowledge of the Bible, which is apparent in all parts of his work, and some acquaintance at least with the method of discussing texts as practised in the schools of northern France, we have said about as much as can be said about his background, and we may now approach the work itself.

III THE ORIGINALITY OF HIS WORK

Gratian's work stands resolutely on its own, summing up all the efforts of previous collectors of decrees and ecclesiastical regulations, yet dealing with them all in his own way.

There are three main characteristics which distinguish his work from all earlier collections. First, it is far more complete and clearly aimed at bringing together in a single volume everything capable of being given legal definition in pseudo-Isidore, Burchard and Ivo of Chartres, as well as more recent collections of texts and the decrees of the two Councils of 1123 and 1139, held during the years when he was either contemplating or engaged on his great work.

Second, he shows a persistent interest in the processes of courts of law and the steps necessary for authenticating or authorizing even such humble enterprises as going on pilgrimage.[7] This procedural interest provides one of our best clues to the author's mind, for no earlier compiler of legislative and semi-legislative texts had shown such familiarity with or concern for legal niceties.

Third, following from this, he shows a strong tendency to see every area of life as a possible subject for litigation in an ecclesiastical court. Nearly two-thirds of the whole work – its whole central core – takes the form of generally imaginary, but

---

[7] This small point provides an example of Gratian's persistent interest in the precise forms of authorization of various activities: see *Decretum*, Part III, *De Consecratione, Dist.* V, c. xxxvii: a cleric may not go on pilgrimage *praeter iussionem episcopi*; and a layman may not go *sine canonicis litteris, id est formata*. For further remarks on this aspect of Gratian's work, see below, p. 291, n. 10.

sometimes evidently real, situations at every level of magnitude, which give rise to astonishingly complicated disputes in a hierarchy of ecclesiastical courts of law.

This great central core of lawsuits is sandwiched between an introductory section dealing rather slightly with general legal principles, and a concluding section dealing essentially with the sacraments of baptism, confirmation, the Eucharist, marriage and holy orders, but also with miscellaneous subjects, great and small, such as churches and church furnishings, feast-days and fast-days.

This final section comes closest to the later books of Burchard and Ivo of Chartres. Here he lays down the necessary conditions for individuals seeking full citizenship of the Church on earth, and therefore full rights in the Christian community. Any falling short in meeting these requirements may lead to legal processes with a view to either rectifying behaviour, or transferring rights, or punishing deviations. Here Gratian is least the lawyer and most nearly the theologian; but in the end, the two roles are equally necessary for the conduct of life in a thoroughly organized orthodox, Christian community. Consequently, when a few years later Peter Lombard in Paris compiled the definitive theological textbook of the schools, he made extensive use of two parts of Gratian's work: first, of Gratian's personal *dicta*, which are scattered throughout the whole work and were little regarded by lawyers; and, second, of the two final sections of the *Decretum*, *De Penitentia* and *De Consecratione*. It is in these sections that Gratian writes least as a lawyer and most as a widely read observer of the necessary requirements for a full orthodox Christian life.[8] It may also be observed that, in his personal *Dicta*, Gratian shows a full knowledge of every part of the Bible.[9]

---

[8] Peter Lombard's references to Gratian are fully listed in the edition of his *Sentences*, 3rd edition, *Spicilegium Bonaventurianum*, 1981, vol. 2, pp. 578–80, where the large number of references to Gratian's *Dicta* and the author's high opinion of Gratian are clearly apparent.

[9] For an index of biblical quotations in Gratian's comments on the texts in the *Decretum*, see Franciscus Germovnik, *Index biblicus ad Decretum Gratiani*, 1971, De Andreis Seminary, Lemont, Illinois, in which it is possible to distinguish between Gratian's own quotations and those of his sources.

Nevertheless, similar though Gratian and Peter Lombard are in their general aim and outlook, there are two great differences between them. First, whereas Gratian concentrates on the rules of behaviour, whether individual or corporate, which must be observed in a fully integrated, fully orthodox, Christian community, Peter Lombard is concerned primarily with doctrine and only secondarily with the consequences of theoretical deviation. And, second, whereas Peter Lombard in Paris was able to build on the works of a whole series of recent predecessors in whose footsteps he was following, and from whom he had inherited an already mature basis of argument, organization, and theological definition, Gratian had to pioneer the way towards imposing a strictly juridical order on his widely-scattered materials. No one before him had tried to do this on anything like the scale of Gratian's work. In this respect as in the others mentioned in the previous chapter, Ivo of Chartres, though he was Gratian's nearest and most frequently quoted predecessor, had lived in a different world.

Moreover, Gratian had a further difficulty. To organize a body of knowledge according to subject matter, and to organize it in the form of possible legal actions arising from conflicts between theory and practice, are two quite different things. Marriage, baptism, absolution and the Eucharist are theologically all sacraments, and all have some common theological features arising from this fact; but the legal problems to which they may give rise demand different forms of action, different kinds of evidence, different sanctions. It was with these problems that the main central part of Gratian's work was occupied. Peter Lombard, in working out the theological system of the sacraments, had only to consider doctrine and its sources, and he had many predecessors. Gratian, in working out the legal implications of breaches in sacramental requirements, had to consider both doctrine and a wide variety of misdoings, as well as the appropriate procedures for dealing with them, and he was often treading where no one had been before. This difference between Theology and Law reflects the famous remark of Tolstoy that all happy families are happy in the same way, but all unhappy ones have their own ways of being unhappy. So with Theology and Law: everything in the former hangs together on a few uniting principles, but everything in the latter reflects the chaos of an unruly world.

Inevitably, therefore, in making a way through the jungle of fact and doctrine, of legal procedures and different levels of judicial authority, Gratian's work is much less systematic than Peter Lombard's; less even than Burchard's or Ivo of Chartres's; less no doubt than it might have been. But what Gratian's work lacks in systematic presentation, it makes up for by his knowledge of the procedural differences between one case and another, and especially by his detailed knowledge of the whole system of appeals to a higher court.[10] Indeed, Gratian's work has the singular eminence, at one and the same time, of outlining a new system of practical ecclesiastical law, and of creating a whole new scholastic discipline with a new set of technical terms grounded in the new processes of the ecclesiastical law courts.[11]

Then there is one final characteristic of great interest for understanding the author and his work: it has been shown that the greater part of his many quotations from Roman law

[10] The evidence of this interest in legal procedure is to be found everywhere in Gratian except in the final section, *De Consecratione* (cols. 1293–1424) – in effect on the Sacraments – where Gratian's personal interventions are very few. For his distinguishing between various kinds of letters and discussing their significance with regard to the legal procedures which they require or the actions which they authorize, see c. 2, q. 6, c. xxxi (col. 478) *Forma apostolorum haec est . . .* ; *litteris apostolicis vel formatis pleniter instructus . . .* ; Similarly on *litterae commendatoriae*, see cols. 259, 16; 839, 43; and on *litterae dimissoriae*, see cols. 839, l. 43, and 854, ll. 9, 12, 20. Further, with regard to the administrative arrangements of the Church, the differing roles of *episcopi*, and *corepiscopi* (the former only in cities, the latter in villages), and the different kinds of letters appropriate to their office *(Episcopi tribuunt epistolas formatas, corepiscopi non 'nisi commendaticias et pacificas valent)*, are all indications of Gratian's concern for the practical organization of the Church. Individually they are trifles, but they disclose a mind familiar with such minutiae and concerned with the day-to-day work of legal administration. They also indicate – as one might expect from Gratian's situation in Bologna – a strong local emphasis on the archdiocese of Ravenna. I may say that, in tracing these minutiae, I owe much to the recently published and invaluable *Wortkoncordance zum Decretum Gratiani*, ed. Timothy Reuter and Gabriel Silagi, *MGH Hilfsmittel*, no. 10, 5 vols, 1990.
[11] In addition to Gratian's knowledge of the special forms of letter required for an appeal to the papal Curia at different stages in a case, the number of his *dicta* on the subject of appeals to Rome is specially notable (see for example, C. II, q. vi. after cc. 10, 12, 14, 19, 21, 27 (cols. 468–483); also his knowledge of Roman law in its bearing on this subject, especially in cc. 28, 29, 30, 31.

represent a change of mind which took place while he was actually engaged on his work.[12] This is a change of such importance for understanding both the environment in which he worked and the success of the work as a textbook for the schools, that it requires special consideration. But first of all we must take account of the method by which, and – so far as they can be reconstructed – the circumstances in which, the work was compiled.

IV METHOD OF WORK AND DATE OF COMPILATION

There can be no doubt that the work was nearing completion between the years 1140 and 1142.[13] In any precise sense it was probably never completed, but it seems certain that Gratian himself added nothing to the text after the second of these two dates. The only chronological problem is: when did he start? Apart from the size of the work and the labour involved in its composition, we have no evidence. So we must consider the extent of the labour involved and the circumstances in which it was compiled.

In its main substance Gratian's *Concordia Discordantium Canonum* consists of about four thousand extracts from papal letters, conciliar decrees, and works of the Fathers, especially Augustine, Jerome and Gregory the Great. Most, indeed perhaps all, of his material up to the time of Gregory VII was taken

---

12 The discovery that Gratian had changed his mind about the use of Roman law in the course of compiling his *Decretum* was made by A. Vetulani towards the end of a series of articles in *Revue historique de droit français et étranger*, xvi, 1937, 461–79, 674–92; xxiv, 1946–7, pp. 11–48; and 'Encore un mot sur le droit roman dans le Decret de Gratien', in *Graziano: testi e studi Camaldolese*, 5, Rome, 1949, p. 130. See also, S. Kuttner, in *Seminar: an annual extraordinary number of the Jurist*, xi, 1953, pp. 12–50, for an account of the discovery; and 'New studies on the Roman law in Gratian's *Decretum*', *Seminar*, 11, 1953, 12–50, for an analysis (pp. 42–7) showing 'an amateur's insecure grasp of the technicalities involved in his source materials'; and 'Additional notes on the Roman law in Gratian', *Seminar*, 12, 1954, 68–74; and 'On the place of canon law in a general history of Roman law during the Middle Ages', *Seminar*, 13, 1955–6, pp. 51–5.
13 See A. M. Stickler, *Historia Iuris Canonici Latini*, i, *Historia Fontium*, 2nd edn, 1974, pp. 202–4.

from earlier compilations – pre-eminently from pseudo-Isidore, Burchard and (most extensively of all) Ivo of Chartres, as well as several smaller collections, notably the strongly Hildebrandine work of Anselm of Lucca. Substantially, therefore, Gratian's task consisted in picking out 'law-worthy' passages from the vast body of material already collected by earlier compilers. The important work he had to do was selection and arrangement, fitting the chosen passages into his very complex pattern of imaginary cases and doctrinal expositions, which itself shows signs of changes of mind in the course of compilation.

To understand the labour and judgement required for doing this we may imagine Gratian studying his assortment of previous compilations, marking passages suitable for his design, having scribes at hand to copy them on separate pieces of parchment, and then himself arranging these hundreds of *fiches* under their appropriate subjects according to a predetermined scheme of subjects and imaginary cases, meanwhile adding his own doctrinal and procedural comments.

As a rough analogy, we may compare Gratian's work with that of Dr Johnson compiling the first seriously documented dictionary of the English language. First he had to mark the passages to be extracted from a large number of authors, then he had copyists at hand to write the marked passages on slips, then these slips had to be arranged by Johnson under the appropriate section of the word they had been selected to illustrate, and lastly he had to add his definitions and comments.[14]

Gratian's work required a similar process of selection and copying of thousands of passages, arranging them and explaining their significance within a highly intricate array of sub-sections. We may suppose that he had a group of copyists similar to those of Dr Johnson, but Gratian's task of arrangement was vastly more complicated than Johnson's. Whereas for Johnson the alphabet provided a settled framework for each word that required elucidation, Gratian had to decide, at every step, into which section and sub-section of his work every particular

---

[14] For Johnson's plan of work in compiling his dictionary with the help of six amanuenses, see J. H. Sledd and G. J. Kolb, *The Composition of Dr Johnson's Dictionary*, Chicago, 1955. The subject is also illuminated in several pages in Boswell's *Life of Dr. Johnson* and in Johnson's Letters.

extract should be fitted. Presumably he had decided on a main framework of principal subjects and cases at a fairly early stage in his work, but – even without changes of mind, which there certainly were – it must have been extraordinarily difficult to decide the appropriate place for each quotation. A further complication was that he had to take account of new decisions, and especially of the texts of the most recent Lateran Councils of 1123 and 1139.

His use of the decrees of these two councils provides a crucial test of his contemporaneity, for – like Gratian's work itself – they publicly announced a new phase in the practical extension of papal authority. But the nature of this conciliar 'announcement' presents some delicate problems. Modern observers have been struck by the fact that, in the long series of councils commonly known as 'general' or 'ecumenical', these two councils are the first which were attended by no representatives of the Greek Church, and this fact marks a significant milestone in the development of a purely western Catholic church. But this consideration appears to have had no significance for Gregory VII, or for Calixtus II or Innocent II after him – or for Gratian. How do we know this? We know it, first, because Gregory VII had already more than once described councils held in his presence, and even councils held by legates authorized by him, as 'General Councils'.[15] In other words, it was the pope's presence, or even his delegating of full power on legates, which conferred generality on the councils. This 'generality' had nothing to do with the participants or lack of participants. On this view, therefore, the pronouncements at the Councils of 1123 and 1139 had no more generality than any other papal pronouncements. And Gratian clearly held this view, as we can see from a single fact: although he quotes parts of the texts of fifteen out of the twenty-two decrees of the 1123 Council, and of eighteen out of the thirty decrees of the 1139 Council, he quotes all except one without even mentioning the Council – he only mentions the pope. And since more than a thousand columns of texts in Friedberg's edition separate the first from the last of Gratian's

15 For Gregory VII's use of the phrase 'General Councils', see E. Caspar, *Das Register Gregors VII (MGH Epistolae Selectae*, 1920, repr. 1968), pp. 60, 392, 549.

excerpts from the Council of 1139, no reader would suspect that they all came from this single Council.[16]

These details may seem too trivial to deserve mention, but they are the rare footprints in the sand which reveal Gratian's mental processes. His treatment of these conciliar decrees makes it evident that, in his view, the attendance of some hundreds of bishops simply added to the number of witnesses of the papal pronouncements: they added nothing to their authority. Moreover, Gratian has left another testimony to this point of view: four of the decrees of the Council of 1123, and one of 1139, were repetitions of earlier decisions of Urban II, and Gratian attributed all of them to Urban without even mentioning that they were reiterated by the Councils. How Gratian knew of their earlier issue we do not know, but it is clear that he thought the papal initiative more important than the Conciliar publication.

Further, Gratian's numerous quotations of decrees of recent popes show that he was thoroughly up to date in his knowledge of events as seen from the papal Curia, and this is a conspicuous symptom of his commitment to a thoroughly papally directed Church in which both theological decisions and legal procedures throughout the whole of western Europe were in papal hands. His whole work was designed to assist the process of making this a reality as well as an ideal.

As for his inclusions from the distant past, of course he had earlier compilations from which he got most of his material. It was largely from Ivo that he took about four hundred and sixty passages from pseudo-Isidore's papal letters from the first century to 590, and another two hundred and forty-five passages from the letters of Gregory the Great. But he always made an independent decision about his selections and their place in his own compilation. He made no attempt at all, as Ivo had done, to follow the arrangement of material as he found it in

---

[16] Friedberg, in his Introduction to Gratian's *Corpus Iuris Canonici*, vol. i, col. xxv, lists fourteen quotations from the 1123 Council in Gratian and seventeen from the 1139 Council, but the actual numbers are slightly larger: fifteen out of twenty-two from the Council of 1123, and eighteen out of thirty from the Council of 1139. (For the texts of these Councils and details of their appearance in Gratian, see *Councils*, 1990, vol. i, pp. 190–4, 197–203.)

any of his predecessors. Similarly, his nearly five hundred passages from Augustine, his hundred and fifty from Ambrose, and his eighty-four from Gregory the Great's pastoral works, were largely taken from Ivo, but he found new homes for all of them in his own complicated plan of cases and problems.

It becomes clear as we watch him at work that he was not a scholar remote from the events of his own time just sitting in solitude in a monastery in Bologna. He includes at least one contemporary case in which he had some involvement,[17] and he shows detailed knowledge of the sources from which recent decrees of the Lateran Council of 1139 were drawn, which suggest an awareness of recent litigation and contact with experts in the papal Curia who knew whence these decrees had been drawn.[18] So, in addition to his work of selecting and arranging his material, and generally directing the work of copyists, he must be thought of as being in contact with contemporary bishops, and – at least during the later stages of his work – with some members of the papal Curia.

Then, too, he sometimes changed his mind. Most of these changes were concerned only with the arrangement of his material, and the changes must have been time-consuming. But

[17] See below, p. 302, for the extremely complicated and prolonged case of the contemporary bishop of Bologna in the court of the archbishop of Ravenna.
[18] In addition to the evidence that, in 1139, Gratian probably had an informant in the papal Curia, there is one other piece of evidence of an even earlier connection with the Curia that should be noted. Stephen of Rouen, monk of Bec, in his *Draco Normannicus* (*Chronicles of the Reigns of Stephen, Henry II and Richard I*, vol. II, 1885, *Rolls Series*, ed. R. Howlett, p. 650) gives an account of Innocent II's visit to northern France in 1131. One of the details of this visit which he reports in some detail is the sermon which was preached by Gratian, who is described as the great expert on Roman and canon law. Moreover, this account of Gratian must also be linked with the additions to the *Chronicle* of Mont-St-Michel (see above, p. 276), which give the year 1130 as the date of the compilation of Gratian's *Decretum*. The connection between these two witnesses is that the writer of the *Draco* was the nephew of the writer of the *Chronicle*, and both had been monks of Bec, and later they both were members of the community at Mont-St-Michel, one as abbot and the other a monk. So they clearly had a single common source of information about Gratian, which may have been that of an eyewitness. The weakness of their evidence is that they both wrote their account at least fifty years after the event, and in any case we can be sure that Gratian was not then a great Roman lawyer, and probably not yet a great canonist. So the evidence must simply be reported without further comment until some satisfactory explanation can be given.

there was one change of quite fundamental importance for the whole work: at some stage in mid-career he changed his mind about the role of Roman law in the whole system of canon law. This caused a considerable intellectual and practical disturbance to the whole work, and it must be examined presently. But, for the moment, it will suffice to say that a change of this magnitude must have lengthened the time taken to complete the work.

In the light of all these complications, we must ask: how long was the whole work likely to have taken him? If he ended in 1142, when did he start? To revert once more to a comparison with Dr Johnson's *Dictionary*: with the help of his copyists, Johnson's work of selection, copying, arranging, commenting, required eight years' work. Gratian's work, with all its additional complications, may well have taken twice as long.

In all the circumstances, we shall probably not be far wrong if we imagine him starting in the middle or late 1120s and bringing his work as near to a conclusion as it ever reached by 1142. As for his change of mind about Roman law, it appears to have been taking full effect by about 1135, perhaps somewhat earlier, and something more must now be said about its significance.

V GRATIAN'S CHANGE OF MIND ABOUT ROMAN LAW

In the earlier stages of its development, Gratian allowed Roman law a very small place in the contents of his book: apart from defining (not always correctly) the various branches of law in a way that shows some knowledge of Roman law, he seems deliberately to have kept it at arm's length. The strong tradition of ecclesiastical distrust, the long hostility between papal and imperial interests, and the recent example of Irnerius's exploitation of his legal expertise in aid of the Emperor Henry V, provide good reasons for this caution. But at some stage he changed his mind, and began to introduce a quite large number of references both to the doctrines and to the procedures of Roman law. It is unclear when the change took place, but Roman law was certainly well established in his work both in the discussion of principles and in procedures during the second half of the 1130s.[19]

Why did he change his mind? Since he has left no indication either of the fact of his change or the reason for it, it might be thought that speculation is useless. But in several ways the status of Roman law was changing during the period from 1125 to 1142, and it is likely that he was well aware of the significance of the changing scene.

In the first place it was becoming clear to active men in different parts of Europe that – in order to cope with the growing number of disputes about marriages, the descent of property and ecclesiastical appointments – more refined and accessible procedures and concepts were needed than had hitherto existed, and that Roman law (certainly not canon law) contained both the answers to many procedural problems and the concepts which could lead to further refinements. Hence, from the 1130s onwards, we find scholars and administrators – quite independent of each other and without any pro- or anti-imperial leanings – going from northern Europe to northern Italy to find out about Roman law.

For example, in 1133, Arnulf of Lisieux, a young, able and ambitious man with strong Norman connections, reports that he is in northern Italy studying – it is noticeable that he does not say where or how – Roman law.[20] And a little later, Gilbert Foliot, a Cluniac monk who became successively bishop of Hereford and London, recommends the study of Roman law as an aid to episcopal government.[21] Moreover, in his very elaborate defence of female (i.e. of the Empress Matilda's) right

19 The case quoted below (see n. 27) as reaching its climax in 1141 is very fully documented with references to Roman law. By this date, therefore, Gratian's work was thoroughly imbued with Roman law principles and procedures.
20 Arnulf, later archdeacon and then bishop of Lisieux, in his *Invectiva in Giraldum Engolismensem episcopum*, written in 1133, says that he is in Italy studying Roman law (*MGH: Libelli de Lite Imperatorum et Pontificum*, iii, p. 85). Where in Italy or how he was studying are quite unknown, but it is clear that he was not studying with a polemical, but only a practical, purpose.
21 See Adrian Morey and C. N. L. Brooke, *Gilbert Foliot and his Letters*, Cambridge, 1965, pp. 59–69, and *The Letters and Charters of Gilbert Foliot*, Cambridge, 1967, esp. pp. 53, 65, 129, 151–2, 176, 259.

of succession to the Crown of England, he made very extensive use of Roman law. This case was certainly argued in Rome, and it was a matter to which canon law made no contribution.[22]

Then, a few years later, in about 1143, Theobald, Archbishop of Canterbury, found that although he had collected an impressive body of scholars to help in the government of his archbishopric, he had no one with the expert legal knowledge necessary for dealing with the rapidly growing number of disputes. This lack was a serious threat to his own primatial position, which was not an issue on which he could expect much help from canon law, and after an unsuccessful visit to the papal Curia in 1144 – his homeward route taking him through Bologna – he seems to have recruited for his household an expert on Roman law, Vacarius. Not unnaturally, since Roman law had been one of the main supports on which the case of the rival claimant to the throne had been built, King Stephen did his best to exclude the lawyer from his kingdom, and for several years Vacarius seems to have been the only scholar in England with an expert knowledge of Roman law. He was evidently a valuable acquisition for he was rapidly snatched from Canterbury by the archbishop of York, whom he served for more than forty years.[23] These prelates were not motivated by any special degree of enthusiasm for or against papal jurisdiction. What they sought was legal expertise for use in their own business, and this could best be found in men who had studied Roman law. Curiously enough, these important ecclesiastical administrators seem not to have been much concerned by their inadequate knowledge of canon law: they probably thought that they already had sufficient aids in this field with Burchard's

[22] See *Letters and Charters*, pp. 60–6. For a very full review of the evidence for discussion of the issue at the Lateran Council of 1139, see Giles Constable, *The Letters of Peter the Venerable*, vol. 2, pp. 252–6, Harvard, 1967. Later, in 1153, Gilbert wrote to Robert de Chesney, bishop of Lincoln, about a copy and gloss of the *Digest* which was being made for the bishop (ibid., p. 144). So by this date Roman law, with or without any special training, was recognized as a necessary tool of ecclesiastical administration.

[23] I have discussed the case of the recruitment of Vacarius, first by the archbishop of Canterbury, and then by the archbishop of York, in Southern, 1976, pp. 257–86, and shall return to him in Volume II.

Decretum, and Lanfranc's abbreviated pseudo-Isidore and one or other form of Ivo of Chartres's work. But Roman law promised something new in helping to give law a systematic existence in an increasingly complicated society, and for this knowledge they had to go to Italy.

As for Gratian's original reluctance to allow Roman law any substantial place in his *Decretum*, this is easily explained by the general threat to papal jurisdiction that it continued to offer until the death of the Emperor Henry V in 1125. Until this date imperial claims to authority in Italy were closely related to the position of the emperor as the source of law. But, after this date, the imperial position in northern Italy and in Europe generally was in terminal decline, and – despite the attempt of Frederick Barbarossa to revive the Empire by recalling the ancient alliance with Roman law in the 1150s – the traditional association between imperial authority and Roman law was dead. The position had been undermined by Henry V's two imperial successors, Lothair III from 1125 to 1137, and Conrad III from 1138 to 1152: both of them were elected emperors with papal support in the well-grounded expectation that they would play no part in opposing papal influence in north Italian politics, and nearly all their energies were spent either in Germany or on Crusade. Consequently, at any time between 1125 and 1152, but not earlier than 1125, the doctrines and procedures of Roman law could be appropriated by canon law without any danger of promoting imperial ambitions.[24]

It follows from this that, whatever may have been the precise cause or date of Gratian's change of mind, at any time during the years when he was compiling his *Decretum*, Roman law could be safely appropriated in the service of canon law. As to the value of this appropriation, any lawyer could see – as administrators all over western Europe were also seeing – that Roman law, and Roman law alone, could provide the theoretical

---

24 Innocent II felt so confident that the Emperor Lothair presented no threat to papal power in Italy that he granted the Matildine lands to him for an annual payment. See A. Theiner, *Codex diplomaticus dominii temporalis Sanctae Sedis*, Rome, 1861, i, p. 12. The removal of the imperial threat in northern Italy left the papacy in unchallenged control of Bologna. The ultimate extent of this control may be judged by the extremely detailed survey drawn up for Gregory XI in 1371. See Theiner, *Codex diplomaticus*, ii, 516–27.

and procedural resources which canon law hitherto had conspicuously lacked. It could be appropriated for canon law not only safely but as an essential aid to the future government of western Christendom.

VI THE PERSONALITY BEHIND THE WORK

Unlike all earlier compilations of canon law, Gratian's work, formidably technical though it is, exhibits many personal traits. In particular, there are two areas where his personality shows through the forest of quotations which make up the greater part of its contents. First, each section of his work is prefaced by a series of introductions – Dicta as he calls them – which express his own views on many problems. They are not strictly authoritative, but they contain many indications of Gratian's personal religious interests.[25] On some practical subjects, such as trade and war, Gratian was notably uninterested; on others, such as simony, as befitted a member of the Camaldolesian Order, he was notably severe.[26] But on those sacraments which

[25] The Dicta abound in observations such as these from Part 1, which may be paraphrased thus: Dist. 8: 'The law of nature differs both from custom and from positive law, for by the law of nature all things are held in common, and this is found only in the Acts of the Apostles or in Plato. Dist. 11: 'custom must be held inviolable unless it is contradicted by canons or laws'. Dist. 13: 'there is no dispensation against natural law, except when it is necessary to choose between two evils'. Dist. 85: 'hospitality is so necessary in bishops that, if anyone is judged incapable of this virtue, consecration may properly be refused'. Dist. 86, c. 4: 'a bishop should display the authority of Holy Scripture; it is no part of his duties to teach grammar or to sing the praises of Jupiter'. Dist. 99, c. iv: 'not even the Roman Pontiff himself is to be called "universal"'. For very valuable details about Gratian's quotations from the Fathers, see C. Munier, Les sources patristiques du droit de l'église du viii au xii siècle, 1957; and A propos des textes patristiques du Decret de Gratien, Monumenta Iuris canonici, vol. iv, Proc. of the third Congress of Medieval Canon Law, 1971.
[26] Simony occupies by far the longest section in Gratian's whole work and introduces the first of the thirty-six Causae with a case of characteristic complexity: a man pays for the privilege of his son being accepted to become a monk in a monastery; the boy reaches maturity, becomes a priest, and then, by his father's influence, a bishop. The father, unbeknown to the son, has paid the archbishop's officials for the son's consecration. Thereafter the son consecrates others, sometimes for a payment, sometimes without payment. From this sequence of events there arise seven main questions, beginning with 'Is it a sin to buy spiritual gifts?', which occupy eighty columns (cols. 357–438) of the Decretum.

have the most direct bearing on practical matters he expressed the consensus of his day. His greatest achievement was that his work made continuing recourse to the decisions of the past unnecessary, and future popes could go on from where he left off, relying on the foundations which he had laid.

As for his special interests, he seems to have seen general issues most clearly when they were presented as concrete problems in a court of law. The result of this is that, despite the vast bulk of quotations largely borrowed from previous compilers, Gratian's personality, his principal interests, even his own intellectual development while writing his great book, have gradually emerged from the close study of his comments and the emphasis he gives to various areas of possible dissension.

Forbidding though it is in size and subject-matter, the *Decretum* is clearly the work of an individual mind of considerable sensitivity to the needs of its time. And yet it leaves one great subject of enquiry virtually unilluminated: namely the immediate environment and human scene within which it came into existence. Whereas all the great contemporary theological works of northern France are quite closely associated with a busy scholastic scene and with the relationships between different masters and their pupils, Gratian's compilation is almost devoid of personal or local references. Nevertheless, the procedures he describes can very occasionally be given a local and even personal setting which can be used for elucidating them.

I have already mentioned one case which is treated in extraordinary detail. It concerns a protracted action in the court of Walter, Archbishop of Ravenna, against Henry, Bishop of Bologna, who (if I understand the matter aright) was accused of fornication by a layman supported by two monks, one subdeacon, and one deacon. Gratian elaborates the various stages of this action, describing the appropriate form of action compatible with the dignity of the accused and the status of the accusers, providing hints on the movements of the case from episcopal to archiepiscopal, and thence to the papal court itself.

In addition, there is one feature that separates this case from all the others in his book: Gratian not only provides (which is rare) the names of the archbishop of Ravenna (Walter, 1119–44) and of the bishop of Bologna (Henry,

1129–45), but also (which is unique) provides one precise date consisting of the year and the day of the week *pridie Kal. Maii feria quarta* (Wednesday, 30 April). The year is variously corrupted in the manuscripts, but there is one year – and one only – which fits all the indications of day and month: it is 1141. And there appears to be only one manuscript, used in an eighteenth-century edition, which gives this date correctly together with the names of the archbishop of Ravenna and the bishop of Bologna. So here at least we have a precise insight into a particular case associated with the time and circumstances in which Gratian lived and worked. The details are so carefully described and the stages and correct procedures so exactly analysed as to leave a distinct impression that Gratian must have had some part in the proceedings.[27]

We can be virtually certain that, as a monk, he would never himself appear in court, but it seems extremely likely that in this case and probably in others, he had been asked to give advice to the bishop or archbishop or to someone in the papal Curia, or to all three. His work, therefore, can in this case be given a local and chronological setting. Despite the ambiguity in which he veils his own past and present, he emerges as a man who has spent a large part of his life in law courts and in thinking about procedures, and in reading the Bible.

VII DID GRATIAN TEACH CANON LAW?

We can say with almost complete assurance that before Gratian there was no such thing as the academic study of canon law. So we must ask: was he himself the first to teach the subject which

[27] Unlike the first *Causa* on simony, which had a central role in the Hildebrandine reform programme, the interest of the second *causa* (cols. 438–502) is largely procedural, and Gratian's *Dicta*, especially that on q. 6, c. 31 (Friedberg, col. 478), testify to his interest in the intricacies of legal processes, and particularly in the correct forms to be observed in appealing from a lower court, in this case the court of the archbishop of Ravenna, to the papal Curia on the ground of an alleged breach of correct procedure by the archbishop. It appears that the only edition in which the year is correct is that of Iustus Henningius Böhmer, 1747, appreciatively described by Friedberg on p. xci of his edition, but not followed in his text.

academically he created? There is certainly nothing in the layout of his work to suggest that it, any more than the Bible itself, represented a course of lectures. Nevertheless, they both influenced the practical life of Europe very largely through their use in the schools. Consequently, later generations looked back to Gratian, as they looked back to Irnerius, primarily as a teacher: 'Magister Gratianus' was his frequent appellation among later writers. But, as one of his earliest commentators remarked, this title was to be understood as an example of 'antonomasia'.[28] That is to say, it meant, not that he actually taught as a master, but that he was the Master of all Masters who came after him. The title, therefore, tells us nothing about his having actually taught pupils canon law, any more than Dante's calling Aristotle il maestro mio means that he had sat in Aristotle's classroom.

There are moreover two reasons for thinking that Gratian did not himself teach law – at least not in a class-room. The first is that, although other scholars made some very early alterations and additions to the text of the Decretum, none of them claimed to have been taught by him – and this was a claim that early commentators on a great scholar's works were very ready to make. The other reason for doubting whether he ever taught the subject is that the General Council of 1139, in a decree which Gratian includes in his work, forbade monks to study law in the schools.[29] It is possible of course to say that this would not be applicable to Gratian, but it increases the likelihood that he never had regular pupils: the book, and not the teaching of pupils, was the offering that Gratian's monastic life brought to the Church, and – whether for good or ill – it was an offering of unique importance. Everything that was later designed to facilitate the study of canon law was either a commentary on, or an addition to, or a simplification of, Gratian's work, and the only later medieval collections of authoritative canon law texts were issued by popes. So in a curious way he was both the first and the last of his kind.

[28] See 'The *Summa Parisiensis* of the *Decretum Gratiani*', ed. T. P. McLaughlin, Toronto, 1952, p. 1: *Magister Gratianus in hoc opere antonomasice dictus 'Magister'*. The editor dates the work 1154–9.
[29] 1139, c. 9 (*Councils*, vol. 1, p. 198) gives references to earlier prohibitions.

VIII The First Masterpiece of Scholastic Humanism

Before Gratian, canon law did not exist as an academic subject, and there was no European-wide demand for scholastic expertise in canon law. When decisions had to be taken, they were taken by bishops, who could consult one or other of the collections of canon law discussed in chapter 7, or the pope in cases of special difficulty. This state of affairs seems to have satisfied most rulers, both lay and ecclesiastical, until the early twelfth century. But the growing complexity of society was bringing about a change, which took the form of an increasing pressure to take issues to some supreme court from whose decisions there could be no appeal. This pressure came as much from litigants as from the papal reformers who had inspired the increasing volume of papal legislation since 1059. And this new legislation, while itself being an indication of the growth of this complexity, stimulated the growth of legal business, and by about 1150 the flow of directives from above and of appeals from below were beginning to change the organizational map of western Europe.

It was at this point that Gratian's book emerged with a vital role to play. It came just at the right moment to meet the need for a basic textbook covering a whole new branch of ordinary litigation. This need continued to increase, and the flow of summaries of, and glosses on, his book began very early and long continued. By the end of the century, more than a hundred different abbreviations, glosses or commentaries had appeared. No other work of the twelfth century so rapidly became a school textbook indispensable for an area of essential knowledge.[30]

It was quickly recognized that it had many faults. For one thing, since the arrangement of the long central section depended on intricacies of imaginary lawsuits, the layout of subject-matter was necessarily highly erratic. The earliest users at once spotted

[30] It must suffice here simply to say that the foundation of all modern discussion about the place of Gratian's *Decretum* in twelfth-century scholastic thought is the epoch-making work of Stephan Kuttner, *Repertorium der Kanonistik (1140–1234)*, (*Studi e Testi*, 71), Vatican, 1937. For a survey of twelfth-century glossators of Gratian's work, see R. Weigard, *Die Glossen zum Dekret Gratians, Studia Gratiana*, xxvi, Rome, 1991.

this weakness, and several attempts were made by scholars to improve its arrangement.[31] But its success was so immediate, and its dissemination in all parts of Europe so rapid, that it soon became clear that it would be better to live with its faults than to introduce new confusions by attempting any widespread reorganization. Besides, the disadvantages of its arrangement were largely and quickly overcome, first by the growth of law schools in which the contents of the work were expounded systematically, and second by the appearance of indexes and guides to the huge body of material. It was easier to adjust the student to the book than to alter a text which had become the foundation of a new science.

Above all, its mentality was that of the new age, and it was so much fuller than any earlier collection that it could be accepted as an essentially complete summary of all earlier ecclesiastical law. It was a great convenience that popes after Gratian could add to the law simply by adding supplements to his work without the need for further research into the past. Despite every idiosyncrasy, it could be taken that his work expressed the consensus of the past and that there was no need to go behind it.

Apart from its comprehensiveness, the most valuable feature of Gratian's work was that it bridged the gap between principle and practice in a way that no earlier compilation had even attempted. If we compare his work with those of pseudo-Isidore or Burchard, or with Lanfranc's abridgement of the former or Ivo of Chartres's extension of the latter, or with any other earlier work, Gratian's greater emphasis on practical application is at once apparent. Lanfranc had required those who used his abridgement of pseudo-Isidore to make their own notes on its contents. And though Ivo of Chartres had made the use of his compilation easier by arranging his materials systematically, he provided no aids for its use in lawsuits. Like other northern compilers, he had been chiefly concerned to present the sources and leave their application to the discretion of bishops and other users of his collection of materials.

By contrast, Gratian met the needs of legal experts, whether

---

31 Interesting examples of such attempts are Bodleian MSS, Hatton 16 (12 C.) with parts of Gratian and glosses referring to a complete copy, and Bodl. 291 in 101 *distinctiones* with a long introduction.

operating in schools or in ecclesiastical courts, by his steady unremitting attention to the implications of law in every part of life. On many aspects of personal religious life he was inadequate, but in the great middle area of ecclesiastical organization, from ministers and religious corporations of the Church to problems connected with property, married life, sexual behaviour and the treatment of heretics, he had something to say. And on every subject, he saw deviations from orthodox behaviour as a possible subject for legal action. More than any other work of the Middle Ages, therefore, Gratian's *Decretum* provided a juridical basis for the social and religious reorganization of western society within the framework of papally-directed orthodoxy. It would be wrong to say that Gratian reduced Christianity to a legal system, but he certainly saw every situation which involved a *breach* of orthodox Christian doctrine, whether in word or in deed, as a possible subject of legal action.

One essential consequence of this manner of treating the decisions of the past was that there had to be law courts to deal with all aberrations from the norm. Consequently, since every complete and self-sufficient legal system needs a supreme court, and since the pope was the supreme source of orthodox doctrine, Gratian's work gave to the papal court a more systematically directing role than it had been given by any earlier writer. Moreover, in the areas in which he left ambiguities, he prepared the way for further papal definitions and enactments. In fact, in large measure, he put the papacy where Justinian's *Codex iuris civilis* had put the emperor. Consequently Gratian's book influenced the whole governmental scene of western Europe by showing how the new surge of legal disputes about ecclesiastical lands and appointments, sacred offices and sacraments, human rights and relationships, especially in matters of marriage and holy orders, could be dealt with, first in local ecclesiastical courts, and thereafter channelled along routes which led from all parts of Europe to the papal Curia. In doing this, his work had a more immediate and lasting influence on the future of European government than any other work of the century.

Naturally not everyone who saw this process taking place looked on it with favour. In particular, of course, lay rulers –

especially the Hohenstaufen emperors and the Angevin kings – have a well-known role in resisting the increase of papal jurisdiction. More surprisingly, St Bernard observed with apprehension the consequences of the growing activity of the papacy as a court of appeal. In his *De Consideratione*, written to Pope Eugenius III in 1152, he protested that the flow of appeals to the papal court threatened to engulf the whole role of papal oversight of the Church, and to make the papacy primarily a court of appeal at the apex of a legal structure.[32]

St Bernard gives examples of this process within his immediate knowledge: first, a wedding in Paris being interrupted by someone declaring that he had himself been married to the bride, and everything being held up to await a judgement from Rome; second, another wedding, also in Paris, being interrupted by someone alleging consanguinity between bride and bridegroom, refusing to accept a local judgement and appealing to Rome; third, the election of a bishop of Auxerre in 1152, which might have taken place quickly and successfully, being held up by a vexatious appeal to the papal Curia. In all these cases St Bernard was angered and dismayed by the use of appeals to the papal Curia for personal ends, but much more by the deflection of papal energies from spiritual inspiration to legal business. Strong papalist though he was, he feared the debasement of the highest office in Christendom by its immersion in the worries of the moment.

This was the most perceptive criticism ever made of the extension of scholastic humanism to the practical work of government: what St Bernard said about the debasement of the papacy by its submersion in details is equally applicable to the debasement of scholastic humanism generally by the grubbing processes of ever greater minuteness of enquiry. St Bernard's protest came just ten years after the completion of

---

32 See *De Consideratione*, bk. 3, in which Bernard considers the nature and method of universal papal authority. In the chapter *De abusione appellationum* Bernard relates the incidents which I have outlined below. (See *Sancti Bernardi Opera*, ed. J. Leclercq and H. M. Rochais, Rome, 1963, vol. 3, pp. 437–9.) St Bernard concludes his account of these incidents by remarking that he could add many others, *sed memor propositi mei, contentus interim occasionem dedisse, ad alia transeo*, and he goes on to urge the pope to withdraw from the pressure of daily business and to engage in contemplation.

Gratian's textbook, when the rising tide of students in Bologna was just beginning to become conspicuous. And it was just at this moment too that the growing number of exact observations in the natural sciences was beginning to turn astronomy – not indeed yet into a thoroughly observational science – but into a science demanding increasingly accurate data for its progress.[33] Both of these processes were ultimately to have the direst consequences for scholastic humanism, but it was already too late to stem the flood either of litigation or of observation. The force of conflicting interests which drew litigants to Rome, like the desire to predict the future, which was the driving force in the growth of astronomy, was irresistible. We are not at present concerned with the second of the processes. But so far as litigation was concerned, Gratian's work did more than any other single instrument to make the papal court the ordinary court of appeal for the whole of western Europe.

At a less exalted level of activity, Gratian's work had all the necessary qualities of a successful scholastic textbook. It is full of complicated matter which requires an expert to elucidate, and this matter was of essential importance for organized life at every level. It provides opinions, but also the material for arriving at different conclusions. Although itself unsystematic, it has the materials for a system and presents a challenge to systematizers. And, to crown all, there is an ambiguity at its centre: while leaving no doubt about papal supremacy in all ecclesiastical, religious and moral aspects of life, and being equally clear about the freedom of all members of the clerical hierarchy from secular jurisdiction, it leaves a doubt at the very heart of its message about the extent to which the laws and rules of secular life also are subject to papal authority.[34]

[33] A vivid picture of the concurrent scientific development during these years is given in the *Catalogue of the writings of Adelard of Bath and closely associated works*, in *Adelard of Bath: an English scientist and Arabist of the early twelfth century*, ed. Charles Burnett, London, Warburg Institute, 1987, pp. 163–96.

[34] This ambiguity is well brought out by the two illustrations to Gratian's work (see Plate 4) in which the second shows all authority, spiritual and temporal, mediated from God through the Pope; whereas the first shows spiritual power being mediated through the Pope and temporal through the Emperor. Either view is compatible with everything in Gratian. But see above, p. 286, n. 4, for Pope Boniface VIII's definition which points towards total papal sovereignty.

This stretching out to embrace all aspects of life is emphasized by another unexpected characteristic. To a quite surprising extent Gratian's *Decretum* attracted the attention of pictorial artists. Of course, we might expect that a work of which very many copies were made would sometimes have decorative initial letters marking the beginnings of its many separate sections. But the urge to illustrate the work went much deeper than this. There are at least a hundred copies still in existence which have numerous pictorial representations of the subject-matter of different sections of the work.[35] In this it differs from the other two scholastic works of comparable generality, Peter Lombard's *Sentences* and Thomas Aquinas's *Summa Theologiae*. So far as I know, there are no pictures in any copy of these great works.

The grounds for this surprising contrast are that Gratian's work has its foundation in the events of ordinary life whereas the theological works I have mentioned have their foundation in spiritual realities and general formulations which cannot easily be translated into images. Gratian's work is full of human situations from which contradictory possibilities emerge. Artists and jurists alike interpreted these situations in their own ways.

It would have surprised Gratian to learn that his work would attract artists, but the artistic interest is a sign that it touches human life at every point. And so, more than any other work of this period, it deserves the 'humanistic' epithet.

IX TIME AND PLACE REVIEWED

As a starting point, in reviewing the rise of Bologna as a scholastic centre of European-wide importance, a distinction may be drawn between two types of large-scale historical change: the first is a cumulative process resulting from a slow build-up of detailed adjustments over a long period of time; the second may be called 'catastrophic' in that the injection of some new element

---

[35] For a survey of illustrated copies of Gratian with many reproductions, see A. Melnikas, *The Corpus of the miniatures in MSS of the Decretum Gratiani*, 3 vols, Rome, 1975.

in a general situation brings about a large-scale transformation for which there had been no long period of local preparation. Broadly speaking, the emergence of the schools of Paris from a group of comparable cathedral schools of northern France to a position of unchallenged supremacy and of decisive and European-wide influence provides an example of the cumulative process: the advantages of the geographical situation of Paris and its unequalled physical opportunities for growth caused it to draw ahead of all rivals when the demand for systematic biblical and theological teaching, which had been pioneered in the northern French cathedral schools throughout the eleventh century, reached a level that could be satisfied only by the larger resources that were available in Paris and its adjacent countryside.

It has often been thought that the growing success of the schools of Bologna very shortly after the rise of the Parisian schools was the result of a comparable and parallel development during the period from about 1090 to 1150, with Irnerius in Bologna playing the initiating role which Master Anselm played at Laon, and being followed by a comparable succession of systematizing pupils and developers. On this view, the sequence of Parisian masters – William of Champeaux, Gilbert de la Porrée, Hugh of St-Victor, Peter Lombard, with Abelard as the disturbing influence in the scene – has its contemporary parallel in Bologna in the sequence: Irnerius, Bulgarus, Martin, James and Hugh in Roman law, with Gratian crowning the development by the intercalation of a vast new area of activity in canon law. This broad similarity is built on the assumption that Bologna was a centre with law schools in which Roman law was taught from the later years of the eleventh century and to which systematic canon law was added by Gratian and his successors.[36]

The difficulty with this doctrine is that the development

---

[36] The founder of the generally received view of the growth of legal schools in Bologna from the late eleventh century onwards was H. Fitting in his *Die Anfänge der Rechtsschule zu Bologna*, Berlin and Leipzig, 1888; see also his *Pepo zu Bologna* in *Zeitschrift der Savigny-Stiftung für Rechtsgeschichte, Romanistische Abteilung*, xxiii, 1902. For an up-to-date statement of the case, see Giorgio Cencetti, 'Studium fuit Bononie: note sulla storia dell'università di Bologna nel primo mezzo secolo della sua esistenza', *Studi Medievali*, 3rd ser., 1966, vol. 7, pp. 781–833.

which is very extensively documented in Paris, is not supported by any solid historical evidence in Bologna. That there were lawyers active in Bologna, as in other north Italian cities, during this whole period, cannot be doubted. Nor can it be doubted that Irnerius among his legal colleagues was an innovative scholar in his close study of the *Corpus Iuris Romani* of Justinian. But there is not the slightest evidence of any regular system of Roman law teaching, attended by students whose aim was to gain a systematic knowledge of ancient Roman law, until the steady flow of students in both Roman and canon law began in the 1140s. The first evidence of distinct class-room lecturing in law does not appear until about 1150 in Stephen of Tournai's recollection of sitting with a friend *in auditorio Bulgari*. And we know from another source that Bulgar's lecture room was a room in his house, where he also pronounced judgement as a papal judge-delegate.[37] No doubt Parisian masters also lectured in their own homes; but Bulgar's house was a palace.

In this scene the teaching element in Bulgar's life would seem still to be fairly new, still under the wing of his private practice. The route by which Bulgar had arrived at this mingling of formal teaching with his legal practice was systematically different from the route travelled by the Parisian masters who are found in positions of fame and security at about the same date. Broadly the difference was that Bulgarus and his Bolognese contemporaries had first made their fortunes as practitioners in the courts, and turned to be teachers on a grand scale when the European-wide re-shaping of government brought a flood of those who were willing to pay to share the knowledge, and ultimately the prosperity, of the master. And it may be remarked that even when the lawyers became university teachers they never lost their independence as individual practitioners, laying down the terms on which they would consent to stay in Bologna town and add to its prosperity by attracting students to it. Hence, in

---

37 For Stephen of Tournai studying under Bulgarus, see his letters, 38 and 63, in *PL*, 211. For William of Tyre studying under Bulgarus, 1160–65, see above, p. 214. Bulgarus also acted as papal judge-delegate on 8 July 1151 when he gave judgement in his own house. It is notable that he uses a Roman law term to describe his position (*cognitor ex concessione domini papae Eugenii*). See J. Ficker, *Forschungen zur Reichs- und Rechtsgeschichte Italiens*, 1874, iv, p. 163, doc. nos 119, 602.

Bologna, it was the *pupils* who needed to organize themselves as a *universitas* to enforce their rights, while the professors were great men who dealt individually with the town, and corporately only with the papacy.[38]

After 1150 the stream of students became a flood, and there is no difficulty in adding names to the numbers of students and masters. The demand for legal teaching was growing to European proportions at the moment when Gratian was coming to the end of his *Decretum*. Probably if Gratian had not provided the impetus for the European-wide use of Roman law in the ecclesiastical courts, someone else would have done so. But the place, the manner and the time of its happening would have been different, with consequences that are beyond discovery. It was he who provided the necessary tool, combining the two great forms of law that had previously been thought by their nature and sources of authority to be antipathetic. It was in Gratian's work that their compatibility was first demonstrated and they were first discovered to be complementary, and thereafter they were forever and at a single stroke inseparably combined.

There were several north Italian towns which had the necessary resources of plentiful lodgings and food supplies, freedom for masters to set up schools without the constricting control of a cathedral, and lawyers who had some knowledge of Roman law. But it is clear that no town would be a suitable location for the development of canon law unless it was firmly pro-papal in its political orientation. In this regard, Bologna began with one great advantage: it was included among the papal territories in the *Donation* of Constantine, which had been confirmed by the Emperor Louis the Pious in 817 and by the Emperor Henry III in the mid-eleventh century. Nevertheless the city was in a very exposed position as the western bastion of the former exarchate of Ravenna, and the two emperors Henry IV and V made great efforts to strengthen their hold on the city.

---

[38] For a sketch of the contrast between the constitutions of the universities of masters at Paris and Oxford, and the universities of students at Bologna, see H. Rashdall, *The Universities of Europe in the Middle Ages*, ed. F. M. Powicke and A. B. Emden, vol. 1, pp. 148–52 and 298–304.

By 1093 they had succeeded to the extent of having had two successive bishops who were adherents of the anti-pope Clement III.[39] But in that same year the imperial party in the city suffered some kind of undocumented reverse, and thereafter Pope Urban II and his successors assumed complete control of episcopal appointments in Bologna, cutting out the rights both of the local clergy and of the archbishop of Ravenna.[40] The main imperial riposte to this papal initiative was a privilege issued by the Emperor Henry V on 16 May 1116, on his second expedition into Italy, in which he took all the inhabitants of Bologna and their possessions under imperial protection, and gave them freedom of movement without the payment of tolls on all public ways by land or water to Venice or into Lombardy. This, combined with his new power-base in Italy as successor to the Countess Matilda, who had died in 1115, represented a most serious challenge to papal power in northern Italy. But, after Henry's death in 1125, with two successive emperors appointed under papal influence, imperial ambitions in northern Italy collapsed and there was never again – despite the grandiose ambitions of Frederick Barbarossa – the slightest chance that Bologna would become an imperial city. From this date, Bologna was well placed to become the scholastic capital of canon law studies closely dependant on papal support.

Unlike Paris in the Arts and Theology, Bologna had no overwhelming natural advantages that made it the obvious centre for the study of law. But it had some political advantages

---

39   For a convenient text of the *Constitutum Constantini* and the confirmation by Louis the Pious, see Pietro Fedele, *Fonti per la storia delle origini del dominio temporale della chiesa di Roma*, Rome, 1939, pp. 91–119. This grant, which included the whole exarchate of Ravenna with its cities (including Bologna) had also – unluckily for the imperial cause under Henry IV and V – been confirmed by the Emperor Henry III in the time of Pope Benedict IX (1032–45) JL, 4847.

40   For the defeat of the imperial element in the city in 1093, see Urban II's letter of 19 September 1096 to the clergy and people of Bologna (JL, 5670); and for Paschal II's removal of Bologna from the archdiocese of Bologna and putting it under the immediate jurisdiction of the pope in 1114, see JL, 6387. For the texts of these letters see *PL*, 151, col. 483, and *PL*, 163, col. 351. For the Emperor Henry V's privilege to Bologna on 15 May 1116, by which he hoped to attract the loyalty of the citizens of Bologna back to the Empire, see Paolo Silvani, 'Bologna e la politica italiana di Enrico V', in *Atti e memorie della r. Deputazione di storia patria per l'Emilia e la Romagna*, 1936–7, ii, 145–72.

which no other city possessed: size without factions, and the closest association with the papacy of all the ancient lands of the Roman church in northern Italy.[41] It was also the place where Gratian's work, his materials and some at least of his helpers would have been available from the moment when he finished it, and when many people were finding that the combination of canon and Roman law, which he had succeeded in bringing into harmonious union, was what they needed.

It was not until Gratian's book had been launched on the world in the 1150s that we begin to find the beginnings of a cosmopolitan flow of students in Bologna comparable to that which had begun to appear in Paris thirty years earlier. It may be argued that once Gratian's work was completed, it could be studied anywhere. But the existence of his original manuscript and his first helpers in Bologna, combined with the presence of well-known lawyers such as Bulgarus, Martin, James and Hugo, with whom William of Tyre studied in the 1160s, all helped to give Bologna a European-wide attraction, which, under the patronage of successive popes, it did not lose for two hundred years.

That there had long been many lawyers in the town, as in other north Italian towns, is certain. It is also clear that by 1130 Bologna had a reputation as a place where good practical legal advice was to be had.[42] Equally, there were schools in Bologna – the best of them specializing in the art of letter-writing.[43] But these too existed in several other north Italian towns and could never alone have made Bologna a place of European-wide fame as a scholastic centre. Of the features of its situation which

[41] The text and Map on pp. xx–xxi give some indication of the combination of advantages of Bologna as a centre for the combined study of Roman and canon law.
[42] This emerges from a poem written in about 1130 describing a war between Como and Milan which lasted intermittently from 1118 to 1127. Various towns are represented as bringing contributions to help Milan. What Bologna brought was legal knowledge: *Docta suas secum duxit Bononia leges* (l. 211), and *Docta Bononia et huc venit cum legibus suis*. Clearly this was not referring to its law schools, but to the wealth of practical legal knowledge and advice it could provide. See *De bello Mediolanensium adversus Comenses*, vv. 211 and 1848, in Muratori, *Rerum Italicarum Scriptores*, 1723–51, vol. 5, pp. 418, 453. For John of Salisbury's account of the logician who left Paris to study logic at Bologna and then returned to Paris, see his *Metalogicon*, ii, c. 10.
[43] For letter-writing as a main subject of the schools of Bologna, see above, pp. 272–3.

THE INTEGRATION OF DOCTRINE AND LAW

gave Bologna a commanding position both in canon law and in Roman law as its auxiliary science, the most important in the long run was the close association of the town with the papacy, the heir to the ancient emperors as the source of a European-wide body of law.

In brief, therefore, whereas Paris rose to scholastic pre-eminence in the Arts and Theology among the cathedral towns of northern France because, among several rivals, it alone had the physical resources necessary for a town with many masters and large numbers of students, Bologna rose much more suddenly to its unique scholastic eminence because, in the decades on either side of 1150 when the new European-wide demand for a systematic knowledge of Roman and canon law suddenly erupted, Bologna had everything that the moment required. A striking indication of this switch of emphasis is to be found in a letter of Otto of Freising. In the 1120s he had been a pioneer in going to Paris from a distant part of Europe to study. But in 1157–8 we find him advising a young protégé that it would be more advantageous for his future to study in Bologna than Paris. This letter reflects the quite sudden growth of a European-wide demand for expert knowledge of the combined subjects of Roman and canon law, to which Gratian's work provided the key and for which Bologna, and Bologna alone, had all the necessary resources.[44]

It is true that many (probably the brighter) students who went to Bologna to study from 1150 onwards concentrated on Roman, rather than on canon law. Roman law after all was, then as later, the most intellectually stimulating branch of legal study. But students of Roman law – such as the two Peters of Blois, to whom we shall come in due course – knew very well

[44] Otto of Freising's letter is quoted by Peter Classen, 'Zur Geschichte der Frühscholastik in Oesterreich und Bayern' in *Mitteilungen des österreichischen Institut für Geschichtsforschung*, 67, 1959, 249–77, from S. Tengnagel, *Monumenta vetera contra schismaticos*, 1611, 385–7. The growing popularity of legal studies soon began to attract criticism and attempts to limit its development. On this subject, see S. Kuttner, 'Papst Honorius III und das Studium des Zivilrechts', *Festschrift Martin Wolff*, 1952, 79–101, and C.U.Par., i, no. 32 (Pope Honorius III's letter to the university of Paris 16 November 1219, elucidated by Kuttner) and no. 235, an apocryphal letter of Innocent IV to the prelates of France, England, Scotland, Wales, Spain and Hungary, denouncing clergy who deserted *philosophicas disciplinas* and still more *divina scientia* for *saeculares leges*. The letter, despite its apocryphal status, is indicative of popular perceptions.

that, in their daily work, Roman law would be no more than a tool providing procedures and principles which were applicable in ecclesiastical courts all over western Europe. The vast growth in the number of students and masters after this date is essentially a reflection of the European-wide growth of canon law as the effective instrument of government over a very wide area of contention, for Roman law only became an international commodity attracting large numbers of students from all parts of Europe when it became the servant of canon law.

It is a remarkable testimony to the alertness of St Bernard's European-wide vision that in 1153 he was the first to recognize that this new growth, while giving the papacy an unprecedented influence in the daily affairs of western Europe, threatened one of the ancient sources of papal strength: its remoteness from the day-to-day work of the world. Henceforward the papacy was a business centre, often itinerant like every other medieval government, but with Bologna firmly established on papal territory as its stable and permanent academic arm.

Even with all its advantages, however, Bologna could not in the long run keep so vast and so widely sought-after a subject to itself. By 1170 there were masters teaching both Roman and canon law in Paris, and before 1200 also in Oxford.[45] But by then Bologna already had a lead which it never lost so long as the combination of Roman and canon law formed the central core of all European legal study. The study of law was forbidden for members of religious orders. So the combination of Roman and canon law remained the preserve of active secular students while theology from the late thirteenth century onwards became an increasingly remote subject, rent by dissensions and increasingly dominated by the friars or by teachers with special axes to grind. Meanwhile the success of Bologna as a scholastic centre drawing students from all parts of western Christendom was assured at least until the mid-fourteenth century. It was a future that would have seemed very unlikely even as late as 1130, and nothing did more to bring it about than Gratian's

[45] For the teaching of Roman law in Paris in the 1170s, see Gerald of Wales, *De Gestis Giraldi*, in *Giraldi Cambrensis, Opera*, ed. J. S. Brewer, RS, 1861, i, 45–8; and for Roman and canon law in Oxford, *The History of the University of Oxford*, vol. 1, ed. J. L. Catto, Oxford, 1984, pp. 9–21, 519–64.

change of mind about Roman law, which ensured that canon law from the very beginning of its academic career would be linked with a science capable of the highest refinement.

Index

letter-writing taught in, 272–3,
315
Otto of Freising's advice to a
nephew on, 316
papal influence in, 313–15
schools of: development of, 3,
59, 76–7, 198–9, 231, 265–6,
273–4, 311–13, 317; masters
named, 311–12; preferred
to Paris, 316; students at,
168–9, 212, 316
see also Bulgarus
Boniface VIII, pope, 286, 309n
Bulgarus, Roman lawyer in
Bologna, 311–12
papal-judge delegate, 312
taught Stephen of Tournai,
c. 1150, 311–12
and William of Tyre, 1160–65,
214
Burchard of Ursberg, 277
Burchard of Worms:
his *Decretum*, 244–6
compared with Gratian, 293,
306
compared with Ivo, 257, 263,
271, 293

Calvin, 124–5
canon law before Gratian, 242–63
in Bologna, 271–2
and Roman law, 316–18
see also Anselm (St); Burchard;
Gratian; Ivo of Chartres;
Lanfranc
Cathars, 238
Celestine II, pope, 177
Celestine III, pope, 174–4, 226
celibacy of clergy, 136–7, 145,
149–50
chancellors of cathedrals, duties of,
64, 67–8, 91–2, 227
Chartres, school of, 59–100, 227
Clerval, A., 69–72, 87–90
confession, development of
doctrine of, 153–8
Corbeil, Abelard's school at, 205

COUNCILS:
Carolingian, 135
Papal:
1059, 136
1078, 143
1099 Vatican, 242
1119 Reims, 278–9
1123 Lateran, 294
1139 Lateran, 294–5
1148 Reims, 190–1
1215 Lateran, 162

Damian, Peter, 274n, 286
Dante:
the *Divine Comedy* a monument
to political failure, 182
on Gratian, 285
a summit of scholastic
humanism, 43–4
Denys the Carthusian, 123
doctor: various meanings of the
word, 274n
see also lawyers, *schola*
divinitas and *theologia*, 207, 217n,
220–1
Donation of Constantine, 247,
313, 314n
Dronke, P., 89, 95, 100–1

England, its position in Europe:
interpretation of ancient laws,
147–50, 154
role of Papacy in, 148–9, 176–9
Roman law in, 298–9
students in French schools,
165–71, 177–8
see also John of Salisbury
Ethelred II, King, laws of, 149,
154–5
Eugenius III, pope, 308
Everard of Ypres, 100, 174–5,
226–30
Exeter, school at, 176

fear: physical symptoms, 130–1

unlikely that he himself taught
 canon law, 303-4
His future
antonomastically the Master
 of all later teachers of the
 subject, 304n
his attraction for illustrators,
 310
created canon law as an
 academic subject, 286
his place in Dante's *Paradiso*,
 285
his place in Peter Lombard's
 Quatuor Libri Sententiarum,
 289
rapid success responsible
 for failure of attempts to
 improve structure of
 Gratian's work, 306
Greek science, its transmission to
 western Europe, 37-9
Greek student in Paris, 227-30 (*see
 also* Everard of Ypres; Gilbert
 de la Porrée)
Gregory the Great, pope:
 his *Dialogues* largely quoted in
  Gratian's work, 287
 his letters extensively quoted by
  Ivo, 298
 on marriage, 148-9
 the tradition of his *Pastoral Care*
  in Ivo of Chartres, 259
Gregory VII, pope,
 and Countess Matilda, 281-2
 and 'General Councils', 294
Grosseteste, Robert:
 on the Bible, 103-4
 on the Incarnation, 41-3
 relations with Oxford university,
  103
Guido, nephew and deputy of
 Gilbert de la Porrée as
 chancellor of Chartres, 91

Hardwin the German, teaching in
 Paris, 216, 217, 220, 232
Häring, N. M., 89-91, 228-9

Hauréau, B., 62
Henry I, King of England:
 scholastic training of his officials,
  167, 168n, 175
 his death, 175, 215
Henry II, King of England
 interest in natural science, 132
 Peter of Blois's writings for,
  132-3
 seeks scholastic arbitration,
  161n, 197
Henry V, Emperor:
 his ambitions in northern Italy,
  273
 his employment of Irnerius,
  278-82
 his death and its importance,
  159, 300
Hermann of Carinthia, 85n, 92n
Honorius II, pope, 271
Honorius Augustodunensis, 188
Hugh of St Victor:
 on Confession, 157
 a reporter of his lectures, 170
 see also Lawrence; Robert of
  Melun
Hugolinus, taught William of Tyre
 Roman law at Bologna, 214
Humanism:
 is there a Chartrian humanism?,
  93-101
 cultivation of sensibility
  (literary), 18, 20
 extension of rational understanding (scientific), 20,
  22-35, and *passim*
 scholastic, 20-5, 52-5, 305, 308,
  310

Innocent II, pope, 294-5, 300n
Innocent III, pope:
 bases a decision on a Roman law
  principle, 151-2
 his respect for: Parisian masters,
  197; Peter of Corbeil; 180
  Peter Lombard, 162n
insolubilia, 12

INDEX

IRNERIUS (corruption of Warnerius
    or Garnerius)
  his collection of Patristic
    excerpts, 279n
  urged by Countess Matilda to
    renew the study of Roman
    law, 277, Plate 5
  his glosses on *Corpus iuris civilis*,
    276n, 279
  in imperial service, 278–9
  in lawsuits, 278
  the master of all later masters in
    Roman law, 287
  in twelfth-century legend, 276
  see also Plate 5
Isidore *see* pseudo-Isidore
Islamic scientific learning, 37
Italy, northern cultural
  characteristics of, 264–74
IVO, Bishop of Chartres, 1090–
  1115:
  appointed abbot of Augustinian
    monastery of Beauvais, 255
  appointed bishop of Chartres by
    Urban II, 256
  assessment of, 259–61
  b. near Beauvais, *c.* 1040, 252–3
  his collection of canon law
    (*Decretum*), 257–61
  compared with Burchard
    of Worms, 257n
  compared with Gratian, 189,
    283, 288–9, 290–1, 293,
    295
  contributed to theological *dicta*
    of the school of Laon, 253–5
  his general outlook in contrast to
    that of Lanfranc, 255–8
  intention of: 259, 283, and its
    lack of success, 260
  papal letters and, 271
  probably not responsible for the
    revised edition (*Panormia*),
    260
  the significance of St Anselm's
    failure to consult him, 262–3
  studied under Lanfranc at school
    of Bec, 253

James, taught William of Tyre
  Roman law at Bologna, 214
Jeauneau, E., 32n, 101
Jews, 115, 238n
John XXII, pope, on poverty of
  Christ, 47
JOHN OF SALISBURY:
  attitude to logic, 19, 215
  his study-years in Paris and
    Ste-Geneviève, 1136–47/8,
    214–21
  his change from logic to a
    broader arts course, 215–16
  his move from Mont-Ste-
    Geneviève to Paris, 1138,
    215–21
  the intellectual importance of the
    move, 215–16
  his return to Mont-Ste-
    Geneviève, 1141–47/8,
    217–20
  his masters, 220–1
  answers to critics of Parisian
    chronology, 218–21
John of Tours, master, 192
'just price', 48–9
'just war', 50

Klibansky, R. 92, 95, 97

Landulf of Milan, 267n
Landulf of St Paul, 268–9
Lanfranc, archbishop of
  Canterbury, 250–2
  his abbreviated copy of
    ps-Isidore, 253n: its
    circulation and importance,
    252
  early legal studies, 250n
  his school at Bec, 250–1
  his ideal of large patriarchates,
    255–6
  revival of his legal interests, 251
  his world-view, 255
LAON:
  importance of school, 199–200

INDEX

Melk abbey, 188
Melun:
  Abelard's school at, 205
  Robert of Melun, named after his
    earlier school at, 232–3
Merlet, L., 62, 67, 69, 72, 164n
Metamorphosis Goliae, 100,
  221–4, 232
Milan, city and schools, 266–9,
  271, 272, 315n
Milton on scholasticism, 18n, 21
miracles and relics, 138–9
monastic life:
  its attraction for retirement of
    schoolmen, 171–3, 250–1
  its early social function, 138–9
  see also Abelard; Baldwin;
    Everard; Lawrence; Thierry
Montpellier, 231
Mont-St-Michel, 196, 376
Moutier-en-Argonne, Cistercian
  abbey, 226–30
  see also Everard of Ypres

Naples, university, 196
Newman, Cardinal, on
  scholasticism, 131
Nicholas II, pope, 240
Nicholas of Lyre, on the Bible,
  110

Odo, bishop of Bayeux, as a patron
  of schools, 167, 168n
Orleans, school at, 184, 213, 231,
  268
OTTO OF FREISING:
  his student years in Paris,
    209–10
  on the alliance of schools
    and empire, 21n, 189–90,
    209–10
  his becoming a Cistercian monk,
    210
  his career in service of Frederick
    Barbarossa, 211
  in 1157–8 recommends study at

Bologna rather than Paris,
  316
on Bernard of Chartres and
  Thierry, 70
on Gilbert de la Porée and St
  Bernard, 211
Oxford:
  schools at, 176
  Roman law taught by 1200, 317
  see also Geoffrey de Lucy;
    Grosseteste, Robert; Robert
    Pullen; Vacarius

Panormia, see Ivo of Chartres
PAPACY:
  curia of, 177–9, 196, 261, 263,
    274, 296, 307
  'Investiture' dispute, 160–1
  letters of popes, 247–8, 258, 259,
    271–2
  primacy of, 159–62, 239–40,
    261, 308–9
  recruitment of schoolmen for the
    curia 177–9
  Roman law and, 274, 279, 300
  scholastically-trained popes,
    175
  territorial conflict with Empire
    in northern Italy, 278–9:
    remitted, 1125–1152, 300;
    see also Map, xx–xxi;
    during this period curia
    becomes an active legal
    centre, 317
  see also Bernard (St); Gratian;
    Gregory VII; Urban II;
    Innocent II and III; Emperor
    Henry V
Parent, J. M., 65–6
PARIS:
  association of Arts and Theology,
    207–8
  the attraction of
    Mont-Ste-Geneviève, 205
  canons of, 203
  canon law taught at by 1170,
    317

326

INDEX

Reims:
  Council of 1119, 278–9
  Council of 1148, 211, 221, 225
  school at, 165–6
Richard I, King of England, 228
Richard Bishop, 63, 216, 217,
  219–20, 232
Richard de Lucy, 168, 172
Richard of St Victor, 27–8
Robert Amiclas, 213, 232–3
Robert de Bosco, 190–1
Robert Grosseteste, see Grosseteste
Robert of Melun (see also Melun)
  pupil of Abelard and Hugh of St
    Victor, 193
  on the supremacy of the spoken
    word, 193
  teaching in Paris, c. 1135–45,
    213, 215, 220, 232–3
ROBERT PULLEN, 176–9, 218, 221,
  232–3
  his family background, 176,
    178
  taught theology in Oxford,
    c. 1133–8, 176
  archdeacon of Rochester,
    c. 1138–43, 177
  taught theology in Paris,
    c. 1138–44, 177
  papal chancellor and cardinal,
    1144–8, 178
  used his power to promote family
    and local interests, 178–9
  his Summa Theologiae, 176
  supported by St Bernard against
    his bishop's protests, 177
Robert of Torigni, responsible for
  scholastic insertions in Mont-
  St-Michel Chronicle, 197, 253,
  276–7
Roger, royal justiciar and bishop of
  Salisbury:
  sent his nephews to French
    schools, 167–9
  see also Geoffrey and Richard de
    Lucy
ROMAN LAW:
  cited by Innocent III, 151 (see

also Bulgarus; Hugolinus;
  Martin, James)
diluted in local Italian codes,
  250n, 270n: undiluted in
  Libelli de Lite, 275n
Gratian, 292, 279–80, 313
Irnerius and later practitioners
  and teachers, 276–82
its use as an instrument of canon
  law, 297–299, 311–17
Roscelin, 165n, 186, 204
Rupert of Deutz, 189

St Albans Abbey, 167, 170
St-Victor, school of, 203, 206
  see also William of Champeaux;
    Hugh, and Richard of St
    Victor
Salerno, medical school at, 231
Salernitan Questions, 152
Samson, abbot of Bury
  St Edmunds, 180
satire and the schools, 182–4
Schaarschmitt, B., 62, 73–4
schola, various meanings of
  the word, 135
  see also Map, xix; Avranches;
    Bec; Bologna; Chartres;
    Corbeil; Exeter; Laon;
    Liège; Melun; Milan;
    Montpellier; Naples;
    Orleans; Oxford; Paris;
    Salerno; Tours
scholastic aims and method, 2, 11,
  121–2, 125–31, 145, 248–9
scholastic knowledge as an
  instrument of government,
  139–42, 144, 184–5, 261–7,
  305–9, 316–18: and of lay education, 120–1, 131–3, 145–7
scholastic pedigrees, 187–9, 190–3
Sherborne Abbey, 178–9
Sigibert of Gembloux, 188
Silvester II, pope, 175
Simon of Poissy, 218, 221
Simon of Tournai, 196
sin, definition of, 152–3,

Index